Narratives of the
New England
Witchcraft Cases

Narratives of the
New England
Witchcraft Cases

Edited by
George Lincoln Burr

DOVER PUBLICATIONS, INC.
Mineola, New York

Published in Canada by General Publishing Company, Ltd., 895 Don Mills Road, 400-2 Park Centre, Toronto, Ontario M3C 1W3.

Published in the United Kingdom by David & Charles, Brunel House, Forde Close, Newton Abbot, Devon TQ12 4PU.

Bibliographical Note

This Dover edition, first published in 2002, is an unabridged, unaltered republication of the work originally published in 1914 by Charles Scribner's Sons, New York, under the title *Narratives of the Witchcraft Cases 1648–1706,* in the series Original Narratives of Early American History, under the auspices of the American Historical Association.

Library of Congress Cataloging-in-Publication Data

Narratives of the Witchcraft Cases 1648–1706
    Narratives of the New England witchcraft cases / edited by George Lincoln Burr.
      p. cm.
    Unaltered republication of: Narratives of the witchcraft cases 1648–1706. New York : Scribner, 1914, in series: Original narratives of early American history.
    Includes index.
    ISBN 0-486-42055-8 (pbk.)
    1. Witchcraft—United States. I. Burr, George Lincoln, 1857–1938. II. Title.

BF1573 .N37 2002
133.4'3'0973—dc21

2001047770

Manufactured in the United States of America
Dover Publications, Inc., 31 East 2nd Street, Mineola, N.Y. 11501

CONTENTS

CONTENTS

FACSIMILE REPRODUCTIONS

NOTE

THE first of the illustrations is a facsimile of the first page of the original manuscript of Cotton Mather's narrative of the case of Mercy Short, *A Brand pluck'd out of the Burning*. For the privilege of printing both the facsimile and the text we are indebted to the American Antiquarian Society, in whose library at Worcester the manuscript is preserved, and to Mr. Clarence S. Brigham, librarian of the society. The facsimile is slightly reduced.

The second plate is intended to elucidate the question whether *More Wonders of the Invisible World* was written by Robert Calef the elder or by his son Robert Calef the younger. Most writers hitherto have attributed it to the younger Calef; Professor Burr may be regarded as having settled the question (pp. 291–295) in favor of the elder. The plate shows facsimiles of the following: (1) from the Mather-Calef paper of 1694–1695 (see p. 306, note 1), the last three or four lines of Mather's text, with the marginalia of Robert Calef at the side, and the first three or four lines of Calef's marginalia beneath—lines unquestionably penned by the author of *More Wonders*; (2) from the letter written to Lord Bellomont by that author, accompanying a copy of the book (see p. 292, note 1, below), the first three lines and the last, with signature; (3) from the appraisers' report of 1693 (*ibid.*), the signature; (4) from the coroner's verdict of 1696, the signature; (5) from the arbitrators' report of 1697, the first three or four lines and the signature—all these of the elder Robert; (6) from the selectman's report of 1717 (?), the lines showing it the elder Robert's as a selectman of Roxbury, with the lines at the end and the signature; (7) signature of Robert Calef the younger, 1708; (8) signature of Robert the younger, 1719, with the words adjoining it in the receipt. For the second of these we are indebted to Mr. Wilberforce Eames of the New York Public Library, for the others to Mr. Worthington C. Ford of the Massachusetts Historical Society and to the official custodians of the various documents, in Boston.

The third illustration is a facsimile, slightly reduced, of the petition of Mary Esty, preserved at Salem, Massachusetts, in the files of the Superior Court for Essex County. By the kindness of the clerk, and of Mr. George Francis Dow, secretary of the Essex Institute, it is here reproduced in such a manner as to show both pages of the original.

J. Franklin Jameson,
General Editor
Original Narratives of Early American History
1914

PREFACE

THESE narratives of witchcraft are no fairy tales. Weird though they seem to us, they were to thousands of men and women in seventeenth-century America the intensest of realities. They were the bulletins of a war more actual, more cruel, more momentous, than any fray of flesh and blood. Nor were they bulletins alone, these messages of each latest skirmish in that age-long war of Heaven with Hell. To those enlisted in that war they were instruction, encouragement, appeal, as well; and as, in our day, to men once fascinated by world-politics, so in that to those awakened to these vaster interests of a universe, all pettier concerns seemed trivial and provincial. To count the matter a panic local to New England, or even a passing madness of the Christian world, is to take a narrow view of history.

But to the modern student there is danger of a graver error. For to count that witch-panic a something incident to human nature, and common to all lands and times, is to repudiate history altogether. Whatever in universal human experience anthropology or folk-lore may find akin to it, the witchcraft our fathers feared and fought was never universal, in place or time. It belonged alone to Christian thought and modern centuries; and clear as day to the historian of ideas is its rise, its progress, its decline.

It was not till the later thirteenth century that the theologians worked out their theory of human relations with Satan. Not till the fourteenth did the Holy Inquisition draw witchcraft fully into its own jurisdiction and, by confusing it with heresy, first make the witches a diabolic sect and give rise to the notion of the witch-sabbath. It was in the fifteenth that the theory and the procedure spread to the secular courts, and that in these, as in the ecclesiastical, the torture began to prove an inexhaustible source of fresh accusations, fresh delusions. In the sixteenth the Reformation for a little distracted attention to heresy; but soon Protestant was vying with Catholic in the quest of the minions of Satan, and it was in the later

sixteenth century and the earlier seventeenth that panic and persecution reached their height. Italy, Spain, France, which earliest
had suffered, were earliest to listen to reason. Germany, long hesitant to begin, passed all other lands in thoroughness and in persis-
tence. How many were the victims is even here a matter for guess-
work; but they counted by many, many thousands. At Osnabrück
121 were burned in 1583, 133 in 1589; at Ellwangen 167 in 1612; at
Würzburg a careful list in February, 1629, names 158 burned since
1627, and the burnings were still going briskly on. Not even Scotland could rival this German zeal; and Scotland was later to begin.

England, lacking both the Inquisition and the torture, long escaped; but the religious exiles who flocked back from the Continent
at the accession of Elizabeth brought the epidemic with them, and
protest was hushed when in 1603 there mounted the English throne
the king, a Scot and a Calvinist, whose own royal hand had plied
against the witches both torture and the pen. The advent of James
was followed, in 1604, by the enactment of a sterner statute, which,
like those of Scotland and the Continent, embodied the teaching of
the theologians and subordinated the crime to the sin. But, though
for a time English zeal against witches was quickened, it was not
till the Civil Wars threw the courts into the hands of men more
prone to religious excitement that England knew a witch-panic like
those of neighbor lands. Then, in 1645–1647, her Puritan Eastern
counties, having found in enforced sleeplessness a substitute for the
torture, sent witches to death by the score; and then it was, in 1647
and 1648, that in her New England colonies witch-trials first appear. Of their story there our narratives will tell us. In the home
land the superstition slowly waned, and, despite the able protests of
its advocates and the occasional zeal of a pious judge, England saw
her last witch-execution in 1682. Trials, indeed, there were till 1717,
and in Scotland till the very eve of the act of Parliament which in
1736 ended the matter in British lands. On the Continent the trials
dribbled on till the eighties.

But let it not be thought that there were ever wanting those who
doubted and protested. We shall find them in seventeenth-century
America; and, happily, they too have left us narratives.

Though, all told, the number of America's contributions to this eerie literature is not great, not all could find a place in the present volume. The general editor of the series has, however, included all that can be counted classical—those most quoted in their day or in ours. Narratives, not documents, have of course been preferred for the volume; but, for those regions where no narrative of witchcraft exists (*i. e.*, outside New England), court records have had to take their place. And since, even in New England, the narratives rest often on such records and by the critical student must be compared with these, the notes attempt to point out where these records, if printed, may be found.

Not a few of the narratives here reprinted have now grown costly or even unprocurable; but only one is here for the first time published—Cotton Mather's *A Brand pluck'd out of the Burning* (1693). A full account of its source and history will be found in the prefixed introduction (pp. 247 *ff*.). As in the other volumes of this series, the order of the narratives is chronological—though often with much overlapping. Where there is a connection between their themes, and especially where (as with the Salem witchcraft) the narratives deal with the same events, the introductions and notes aim to make the connection clear and to invite a parallel study. Of course, however, the present volume is not a history, and must pass in silence much that should interest the student of witchcraft in America.

Besides aiding the narratives to explain each other and guiding the student to the further materials for their critical study, it has been the editor's aim to clear up whatever is obscure; but he has nowhere attempted to set forth the theory underlying the belief in witchcraft or to discuss the questions which still divide scholars.[1] His effort has been only to put before the reader, with fairness and exactness, what can throw light on these American episodes.

It remains but to add a word of gratitude to those into whose

[1] To those who need such help the editor may venture to name an older study of his own on *The Literature of Witchcraft* (in the *Papers of the American Historical Association*, IV.), which undertakes a survey of the development of that theory. Further light may be had from the familiar chapters of Lecky and of Lea, and from Dr. Wallace Notestein's *History of Witchcraft in England*, now an indispensable guide to the English background of American dealings with witchcraft. And, for a discussion of certain fundamental issues, he may add two papers (by Professor G. L. Kittredge and himself) in the *Proceedings* (n. s., XVIII., XXI.) of the American Antiquarian Society.

labors he has entered. Most of these are adequately cited in the introductions or the notes; but certain whose help has been more general should find mention here. Samuel G. Drake's *Annals of Witchcraft in New England and elsewhere in the United States* (Boston, 1869) is still the best clew to American witch-episodes as a whole. Justin Winsor's chatty paper on *The Literature of Witchcraft in New England* (American Antiquarian Society, *Proceedings*, n. s., X.) is a convenient introduction to that literature, and George H. Moore's *Notes on the Bibliography of Witchcraft in Massachusetts* (in the same society's *Proceedings*, n. s., V.) is, like every word written on this subject by that acute scholar, a precious aid in its study. Quite indispensable as a conspectus of the literature as a whole is now the *List of Works in the New York Public Library relating to Witchcraft in the United States*, prepared in 1908 for that library by Mr. George F. Black, a scholar from whose studies in the history of witchcraft other fruit is to be hoped.

The thanks of the reader as well as the editor's are due to the American Antiquarian Society, at Worcester, for the generous courtesy with which it has permitted the printing here of the unpublished narrative of Cotton Mather—a courtesy enhanced by help received from its librarians. Warm gratitude, too, is due to the Massachusetts Historical Society, to the Boston Public Library, to the New York Public Library, and to the custodians of the public records at Boston, for the use of the autographs which figure in our plate devoted to the identification of Robert Calef. But, should mention be made of all those to whom this volume is in debt for personal help, the list would be too long. Yet the editor cannot lay down his pen without a word of gratitude to his old teacher and lifelong friend, ex-President Andrew D. White, of Cornell, who first inspired him with an interest in this subject and a sense of its importance, and whose unflagging generosity has made possible the gathering of that library on witchcraft, now perhaps unequalled, which has been a chief source of the present volume.

GEORGE L. BURR.

CORNELL UNIVERSITY, March, 1914.

FROM "AN ESSAY FOR THE RECORDING OF IL-
LUSTRIOUS PROVIDENCES," BY INCREASE
MATHER, 1684

INTRODUCTION

INCREASE MATHER (1639–1723), divine, historian, college president, colonial statesman and diplomat, is a familiar figure to the student of American history. Born the youngest son of a religious leader known in Old England as well as New, and graduated from Harvard in 1656, while Puritanism was still dominant in the mother land, he had choice of two worlds for his career, and at first elected for the old, where two of his brothers were already prospering. First a student for his master's degree at Dublin, then a preacher in England and in the Channel Islands, he would gladly have remained beyond sea, but for the religious restrictions of the Restoration, which drove him home in 1661—though not until he had come into a permanent closeness of touch with British thought and feeling. In Boston he speedily became the minister of the new North Church, and he retained this pastorate throughout his life, though from 1685 to 1701 he added to its duties those of the presidency of Harvard.[1]

But not his diligence as a student nor his devotion to his influential pulpit could blind him to the larger affairs of New England and of the Christian world. It was he who in 1679 stirred up his colleagues and the General Court to the convening of a synod of the clergy, which should consider what evils had "provoked the Lord to bring His Judgments on

[1] As to his career see especially the careful study of Sibley, in his *Biographical Sketches of the Graduates of Harvard University* (henceforward to be cited as *Harvard Graduates*), I. 410–470, and the authorities there named.

3

New-England" and what was to be done "that so these Evils may be Reformed"; and it was he who put into form the result of their deliberations. Some of the "judgments"—King Philip's war, the small-pox, the two great fires—he felt to call for lay activity as well as clerical; but the others complained of, the decay of piety and the departure from the fathers' ways, were ills for pastoral healing, and in 1681, the year that followed the final session of that "reforming synod," another general meeting of the ministers took, at his instance, that action for "the recording of illustrious providences" which is recounted in the following pages.

Such a method of arousing men to religion was nothing new in Christian history. So, a thousand years before, Pope Gregory, culling (precisely as did now the New England leader) the experiences of his fellow clerics, had compiled those *Dialogues* whose tales of vision and apparition served for centuries to make the invisible world as real as that of sight and touch; and from his day onward such "providences" had been to clerical historians the tissue of their story. In the later Middle Ages there multiplied collections of these *exempla*. Nor did the Reformation interrupt their use. Luther's own sermons and table talk were for Protestants a mine of "modern instances"; and out of such materials a Hondorff, a Lonicer, a Philip Camerarius, compiled their treasuries for the Lutheran pulpit, while their Zwinglian and Calvinistic neighbors were yet better equipped by the industry of Theodor Zwinger and Simon Goulart. Puritan England had found such purveyors in Beard and Taylor and Samuel Clarke. But it was of the nature of these attempts to keep abreast of the warnings of Heaven that they speedily went out of date. Only an enterprise like that devised by Matthew Poole for their continual registry could meet the needs of callous and forgetful man.

But the suggestion of Poole was twenty years old, and

even the draft found in John Davenport's papers must for
some years have been in Mather's hands: what new impulse
stirred him now to action? It is not hard to guess. The
group of Platonists who at Cambridge, the mother of New
England Puritanism, had now inherited the spokesmanship
of positive religion, laid the emphasis of their teaching on
what they called "the spiritual world"; and since the Restoration they had found a notable ally. Joseph Glanvill, a
young Oxford theologian, one of the keenest of English phil-
osophic minds, and withal one of the most rational, had taken
a brief for the defence, and in a brilliant essay on "the vanity of dogmatizing" had in 1661 turned the guns of the ra-
tionalists upon themselves. It was not the dogmatizing of
theology, but that of the audacious rising science of things
natural and human, whose premises he attacked and seemed
to sweep away; and great was the applause of all committed
to the "eternal verities." But he speedily discerned that the
strength of his skeptical adversaries lay in their denial and
ridicule of what they counted the "old wives' tales" of
religion. "Atheism is begun in Sadducism. And those that
dare not bluntly say, There is no God, content themselves
(for a fair step, and Introduction) to deny there are Spirits,
or Witches." Wherefore, with astounding boldness, he came
in 1666 to the defence of ghosts and witches in an essay, oft
reprinted, whose most telling title was *A Blow at Modern Sadducism*. He had now adopted to the full the tenets of the Cambridge Platonists, whose leader, Henry More, became his correspondent, almost his colleague, and like them he championed
all old tales; but his keen sight discerned that "things remote, or long past, are either not believed, or forgotten,"
whereas "Modern Relations," "being fresh, and near, and attended with all the circumstances of credibility, it may be
expected they should have more success upon the obstinacy
of Unbelievers." To his essay he therefore now appended,

and swelled with each successive edition, a "collection of modern relations," which should demonstrate from present experience "the real existence of apparitions, spirits and witches." This was indeed to carry the war into Africa, and the Africans rallied to their guns. John Wagstaffe in 1669 and 1671, the anonymous author of *The Doctrine of Devils* in 1676, John Webster in 1677, came to the defence of challenged incredulity. Glanvill died in 1680, leaving unfinished that enlarged edition which should be his reply; but in 1681 it was published by his friend Henry More (with additions of his own, including a mass of new "relations") under the aggressive title of *Sadducismus Triumphatus*.[1]

It was for a share in this battle royal, to which his book makes many allusions, that Increase Mather now marshalled the hosts of New England orthodoxy. Their broadside, delivered in 1684, was this *Essay for the Recording of Illustrious Providences*.[2] Almost at the same time (1685) George Sinclar, professor at Glasgow, brought out in Scotland the "choice collection of modern relations" which he called *Satan's Invisible World Discovered*. How English Puritanism echoed we shall see betimes.

Mather's book was forthwith welcome. It went through two or three impressions in 1684—at least the title-page was thus often reprinted—and a part of the copies went to the London market, equipped with the imprint of an English bookseller. The book is best known, not by the long title of its title-page, but by its running caption of "Remarkable Providences"—already his son quotes it by this name—and it was under this title, *Remarkable Providences illustrative of the Earlier Days of American Colonisation*, that a convenient

---

[1] "Sadducism Triumphed Over." More spells it *Saducismus*; but this was not Glanvill's usage, and the later editions have a double *d*.

[2] It is true the book of Mather is not wholly on "the world of spirits": other "providences" fill half the volume. But it is more largely so than any earlier collection of its sort, and in this the author's interest clearly centres.

little reprint, "with introductory preface by George Offor," was published at London in 1856 (as a volume in John Russell Smith's "Library of Old Authors"), and again in 1890.

AN ESSAY FOR THE RECORDING OF ILLUSTRIOUS PROVIDENCES

An Essay For the Recording of Illustrious Providences, Wherein an Account is given of many Remarkable and very Memorable Events, which have happened in this last Age; Especially in New-England.

By Increase Mather, Teacher of a Church at Boston in New-England. Psal. 107. 5. Oh that men would praise the Lord for his goodness, and for his wonderful works to the Children of Men. Psal. 145. 4. One Generation shall praise thy works to another, and shall declare thy mighty acts.

Boston in New-England, Printed by Samuel Green for Joseph Browning, And are to be sold at his Shop at the corner of the Prison Lane. 1684.[1]

The Preface.

ABOUT six and twenty years ago, a Design for the Recording of illustrious Providences was under serious consideration among some eminent Ministers in England and in Ireland.[2] That motion was principally set on foot by the Learned Mr. Matthew Pool, whose *Synopsis Criticorum*, and other Books by him emitted, have made him famous in the World.[3] But before any thing was brought to effect, the

---

[1] This is the wording of what is believed the earliest impression of the title-page. It has a misprint in the first citation of Scripture: "Psal. 107. 5" should be Psal. 107. 8.

[2] As the author signs his preface on January 1, 1684 (and he used our present calendar), the design of twenty-six years before must belong to 1658 or thereabouts. At that time he was himself in the British Isles and in close touch with their leading Puritan divines: it is highly probable that he speaks of the project from personal knowledge.

[3] Matthew Poole (1624–1679) was one of the ablest scholars among the English Presbyterians. Educated at Emmanuel College, Cambridge, like so

Persons to have been imployed, had their thoughts diverted another way. Nevertheless, there was a MSS. (the Composer whereof is to me unknown) then written, wherein the Subjects proper for this Record, and some Rules for the better managing a design of this nature, are described. In that MSS. I find notable Stories related and attested, which elsewhere I never met with. Particularly, the Story of Mr. Earl of Colchester, and another mentioned in our subsequent Essay.[1] And besides those, there are some very memorable Passages written, which have not as yet been published, so far as I understand. There are in that MSS. several Remarkables about Apparitions, e. g. It is there said, that Dr. Frith, (who was one of the Prebends belonging to Windsor) lying on his Bed, the Chamber Doors were thrown open, and a Corps with attending Torches brought to his Bed-side upon a Bier; The Corps representing one of his own Family: After some pause, there was such another shew, till he, the said Dr., his Wife and all his Family were brought in on the Bier in such order as they all soon after died. The Dr. was not then sick, but quickly grew Melancholly, and would rising at Midnight repair to the Graves and monuments at Eaton[2] Colledge; saying, that he and his must shortly take up their habitation among the Dead. The Relater of this Story (a Person of great integrity) had it from Dr. Frith's Son, who also added, My Fathers Vision is already Executed upon all the Family but my self, my time is next, and near at hand.

In the mentioned MSS. there is also a marvelous Relation concerning a young Scholar in France: For, it is there affirmed, that this prophane Student, having by extravagant courses outrun his means, in his discontent walking solitarily, a Man came to him, and enquired the cause of his sadness. Which he owning to be want of Money, had presently a supply given him by the other. That being quickly consumed upon

many of the religious leaders of New England, he was at first a pastor in London, but, ejected in 1662 by the Act of Uniformity, devoted himself to scholarship, and is best known by the *Synopsis Criticorum*, into whose five huge folios (1669–1676) he condensed the substance of earlier commentators on the Scriptures. Of his scheme for the recording of illustrious providences we know only what is here told us.

[1] These stories are told in the chapter on "Apparitions," not here reprinted.
[2] Eton.

his Lusts, as soon as his Money was gone his Discontent returned; and in his former Walk, he met with his former Re-
liever, who again offered to supply him; but askt him to contract with him to be his, and to sign the contract with his
Blood. The woful wretch consented: but not long after,
considering that this contract was made with the Devil, the
terrors of his Conscience became insupportable; so as that he
endeavoured to kill himself to get out of them. Some Ministers, and other Christians, being informed how matters were
circumstanced, kept dayes of Prayer for him and with him:
and he was carefully watched that so he might be kept from
Self-Murder. Still he continued under Terror, and said he
should do so, as long as the Covenant which he had signed,
remained in the hands of the Devil. Hereupon, the Ministers
resolve to keep a day of Fasting and Prayer in that very
place of the Field where the distressed creature had made
the woful Bargain, setting him in the midst of them. Thus
they did, and being with special actings of Faith much enlarged to pray earnestly to the Lord to make known his power
over Satan, in constraining him to give up that contract, after
some hours continuance in Prayer, a Cloud was seen to spread
it self over them, and out of it the very contract signed with
the poor creatures Blood was dropped down amongst them;
which being taken up and viewed, the party concerned took
it, and tore it in pieces. The Relator had this from the mouth
of Mr. Beaumond,[1] a Minister of Note at Caon[2] in Nor-
mandy, who assured him that he had it from one of the Ministers that did assist in carrying on the Day of prayer when
this memorable providence hapned. Nor is the Relation impossible to be true, for Luther speaks of a providence not
unlike unto this, which hapned in his Congregation.[3]

This MSS. doth also mention some most Remarkable
Judgments of God upon Sinners, as worthy to be Recorded

---

[1] Jean de Baillehache, seigneur de Beaumont. Two of the name, father
and son, held in succession the Huguenot pastorate at Caen, and were of like
eminence.

[2] Caen.

[3] The "providence" he means is that related by Samuel Clarke (*Mirrour
. . . of Examples*, fourth ed., London, 1671—the edition used by Mather—I. 34)
of a young man at Wittenberg whose contract the Devil threw in at the church
window.

for Posterity to take notice of. It is there said, that when
Mr. Richard Juxon was a Fellow of Kings Colledge in Cambridge, he led a most vicious life: and whereas such of the
Students as were serious in matters of Religion, did endeavour
by solemn Fasting and Prayer to prepare themselves for the
Communion which was then (this was about the year 1636)
on Easter-Day, This Juxon spent all the time of preparation in Drunken wild Meetings, and was up late and Drunk
on the Saturday night.   Nevertheless, on the Lords day, he
came with others to the Communion, and sat next to the
Relator, who knowing his Disorder the night before, was
much troubled: but had no remedy; Church-Discipline not
being then so practised as ought to have been.   The Communion being ended, such of the Scholars as had the fear of
God in their hearts, repaired to their Closets.   But this Juxon
went immediately to a Drunken-meeting, and there to a Cock-
fight, where he fell to his accustomed madness, and pouring
out a volley of Oaths and Curses; while these were between
his Lips, God smote him dead in the twinkle of an eye.   And
though Juxon were but young, and of a comely person, his
Carcase was immediately so corrupted as that the stench of
it was insufferable, insomuch that no house would receive it;
and his Friends were forced to hire some base Fellows to
watch the Carcase till night; and then with Pitch and such
like Gums covered him in a Coffin, and so made a shift to endure his Interment.   There stood by a Scholar, whose name
was George Hall, and who acted his part with Juxon in his
prophaneness: but he was so astonished with this amazing
Providence of God, as that he fell down upon his knees, begging pardoning mercy from Heaven, and vowing a Reformation; which vow the Lord enabled him to keep, so as that
afterwards he became an able and famous Minister of the
Gospel.
      One strange passage more I shall here relate out of the
MSS. which we have thus far made mention of.   Therein I
find part of a Letter transcribed; which is as followeth:

      Lismore, Octob. 2. 1658.   In another part of this Countrey, a
poor man being suspected to have stollen a Sheep was questioned
for it; he forswore the thing, and wished that if he had stollen it,

God would cause the Horns of the Sheep to grow upon him. This
man was seen within these few dayes by a Minister of great repute
for Piety, who saith, that the Man has an Horn growing out of one
corner of his Mouth, just like that of a sheep: from which he hath
cut seventeen Inches, and is forced to keep it tyed by a string to
his Ear, to prevent its growing up to his eye: This Minister not
only saw but felt this Horn, and reported it in this Family this week,
as also a Gentleman formerly did, who was himself an eye-witness
thereof. Surely such passages are a Demonstrative evidence that
there is a God, who judgeth in the Earth, and who though he stay
long, will not be mocked alwayes.

I shall say no more concerning the MSS. only that it was
sent over to Reverend Mr. Davenport,[1] by (as I suppose)
Mr. Hartlib.[2] How it came to lie dormient in his hands I
know not: though I had the happiness of special Intimacy
with that worthy Man, I do not remember that ever I heard
him speak any thing of it. But since his Death, looking over
his MSS's I met with this, and communicated it to other
Ministers, who highly approved of the noble design aimed at
therein. Soon after which, some Proposals in order to the
reviving of this work were drawn up, and presented at a general Meeting of the Ministers in this Colony, May 12, 1681,
which it may not be unsuitable here to recite.

Some Proposals concerning the Recording of Illustrious Providences.

I. In Order to the promoving[3] of a design of this Nature, so
as shall be indeed for Gods Glory, and the good of Posterity, it is

---

[1] John Davenport (1597–1670), one of the most eminent of the Puritan divines, who, after a career as preacher in London and in Amsterdam, came in 1637
to New England and became the founder and leader of the New Haven theocracy.
When at last that colony was merged in that of Connecticut he accepted (1668)
the call of the conservative First Church in Boston, and there died.

[2] Samuel Hartlib (c. 1600–c. 1670), son of a Polish merchant of German
extraction and of an English mother, was born in Prussia, but spent most of his
life in England. He is perhaps best known as the friend of Milton; but "every-
body knew Hartlib." By business a merchant, he was deeply interested in religious affairs, and had a wide correspondence with Protestant scholars throughout Christendom, laboring for their union and incidentally carrying on at London
a sort of general news agency. Writing September 3, 1661, to Governor Winthrop of Connecticut, Hartlib sends therewith "a small packet" for Mr. Davenport, to whom he "cannot write for the present." (Mass. Hist. Soc., *Proceedings*,
1878, p. 212.)   [3] Promoting.

necessary that utmost care shall be taken that All, and Only Remarkable Providences be Recorded and Published.

II.   Such Divine Judgements, Tempests, Floods, Earth-quakes, Thunders as are unusual, strange Apparitions, or what ever else shall happen that is Prodigious, Witchcrafts, Diabolical Possessions, Remarkable Judgements upon noted Sinners, eminent Deliverances, and Answers of Prayer, are to be reckoned among Illustrious Providences.

III.   Inasmuch as we find in Scripture, as well as in Ecclesiastical History, that the Ministers of God have been improved[1] in the Recording and Declaring the works of the Lord; and since they are in divers respects under peculiar Advantages thereunto: It is proposed, that each one in that capacity may diligently enquire into, and Record such Illustrious Providences as have hapned, or from time to time shall happen, in the places whereunto they do belong: and that the Witnesses of such notable Occurrents[2] be likewise set down in Writing.

IV.   Although it be true, that this Design cannot be brought unto Perfection in one or two years, yet it is much to be desired that something may be done therein out of hand, as a Specimen of a more large Volumn, that so this work may be set on foot, and Posterity may be encouraged to go on therewith.

V.   It is therefore Proposed that the Elders may concurre in desiring some one that hath Leisure and Ability for the management of such an undertaking, with all convenient speed to begin therewith.

VI.   And that therefore other Elders do without delay make Enquiry concerning the Remarkable Occurrents that have formerly fallen out, or may fall out hereafter, where they are concerned, and transmit them unto the aforesaid person, according to the Directions above specified, in order to a speedy Publication.

VII.   That Notice be given of these Proposals unto our Brethren, the Elders of the Neighbour Colonies, that so we may enjoy their Concurrence, and Assistance herein.

VIII.   When any thing of this Nature shall be ready for the Presse, it appears on sundry Grounds very expedient, that it should be read, and approved of at some Meeting of the Elders, before Publication.

These things being Read and Considered, the Author of this Essay was desired to begin the work which is here done;

---

[1] Made good use of: the usual meaning of "improve" in these narratives.
[2] Occurrences.

and I am Engaged[1] to many for the Materials and Informations which the following Collections do consist of. It is not easie to give an Account of things, and yet no circumstantial mistakes attend what shall be related. Nor dare I averr, that there are none such in what follows. Only I have been careful to prevent them; and as to the substance of each passage, I am well assured it is according to Truth. That rare accident about the Lightning which caused a wonderful change in the Compasses of a Vessel then at Sea, was as is in the Book expressed, Page 91, 92. Only it is uncertain whether they were then exactly in the Latitude of 38. For they had not taken an Observation for several dayes, but the Master of the Vessel affirms that to be the Latitude so near as they could conjecture. Since the Needle was changed by the Lightning, if a lesser Compass be set over it, the Needle therein (or any other touched with the Load-stone) will alter its polarity and turn about to the South, as I have divers times to my great admiration experimented. There is near the Northpoint a dark spot, like as if it were burnt with a drop of Brimstone, supposed to be caused by the Lightning. Whether the Magnetic impressions on that part of the Needle being dissipated by the heat of the Lightning, and the effluvia on the South end of the Needle only remaining untouched thereby, be the true natural reason of the marvelous alteration; or whither it ought to be ascribed to some other cause, the Ingenious may consider.

There is another Remarkable Passage about Lightning which hapned at Duxborough[2] in New-England, concerning which I have lately received this following Account.

September 11, 1653, (being the Lords Day) There were small drizling Showers, attended with some seldome and scarce perceivable rumbling Thunders until towards the Evening; at what time Mr. Constant Southworth of Duxbury returning home after evening Exercise, in company with some Neighbours, Discoursing of some extraordinary Thunder-claps with Lightning, and the awful effects and consequents thereof, (being come into his own House) there were present in one room himself, his Wife, two Children, *viz.* Thomas (he was afterwards drowned) and Benjamin, (he was long after this

---

[1] Indebted.   [2] Duxbury, Massachusetts.

killed by the Indians) with Philip Delano (a Servant,) there broke perpendicularly over the said House and Room a most awful and amazing clap of Thunder, attended with a violent flash, or rather flame of Lightning; which brake and shivered one of the Needles of the Katted or Wooden Chimney, carrying divers Splinters seven or eight Rods distance from the House: it filled the Room with Smoke and Flame. Set fire in the Thatch of a Leanto which was on the backside of a Room adjoyning to the former, in which the five persons abovementioned were. It melted some Pewter, so that it ran into drops on the out-side, as is often seen on Tin ware; melted round holes in the top of a Fire-shovel proportionable in quantity to a small Goose-shot; struck Mrs. Southworths Arm so that it was for a time benummed; smote the young Child Benjamin in his Mothers Arms, deprived it of Breath for a space, and to the Mothers apprehension squeased it as flat as a Planck; smote a Dog stone-dead which lay within two foot of Philip Delano, the Dog never moved out of his place or posture, in which he was when smitten, but giving a small yelp, and quivering with his toes, lay still, blood issuing from his Nose or Mouth. It smote the said Philip, made his right Arm senseless for a time, together with the middle finger in special (of his right hand) which was benummed, and turned as white as Chalk or Lime, yet attended with little pain. After some few hours that finger began to recover its proper colour at the Knuckle, and so did gradually whiten unto its extremity; And although the said Delano felt a most violent heat upon his body, as if he had been scorched in the midst of a violent burning fire, yet his Clothes were not singed, neither had the smell of fire passed thereon.

I could not insert this story in its proper place, because I received it after that Chapter about Thunder and Lightning was Printed. Some credible persons who have been Eye-witnesses of it, inform me, that the Lightning in that House at Duxborough did with the vehemency of its flame, cause the Bricks in the Chimney to melt like molten lead: which particular was as Remarkable as any of the other mentioned in the Narrative, and therefore I thought good here to add it.

In this *Essay*, I design no more than a Specimen; And having (by the good hand of God upon me) set this Wheel a going, I shall leave it unto others, whom God has fitted, and shall incline thereto, to go on with the undertaking.[1]

[1] We shall see how this suggestion fruited in the *Memorable Providences* and the *Wonders* of his son Cotton; and in 1694 the President and Fellows of

Some Digressions I have made in distinct Chapters, handling several considerable Cases of Conscience, supposing it not unprofitable, or improper so to do; since the things related gave the occasion: both Leisure and Exercise of Judgement are required in the due performance of a Service of this Nature: There are some that have more leisure, and many that have greater Abilities than I have: I expect not that they should make my Method their Standard; but they may follow a better of their own, as they shall see cause. The Addition of Parallel Stories is both pleasing and edifying: Had my reading and remembrance of things been greater, I might have done more that way, as I hope others will in the next Essay.   .

I could have mentioned some very memorable Passages of Divine Providence, wherein the Countrey in general hath been concerned. Some Remarkables of that kind are to be seen in my former Relations of the Troubles occasioned by the Indians in New-England.[1] There are other particulars no less worthy to be Recorded, but in my judgement, this is not so proper a season for us to divulge them. It has been in my thoughts to publish a Discourse of Miscellaneous observations, concerning things rare and wonderful, both as to the works of Creation and Providence, which in my small Readings I have met with in many Authors:[2] But this must suffice for the present. I have often wished, that the Natural History of New-England might be written and published to the World; the Rules and method described by that Learned and excellent person Robert Boyle Esq.[3] being duely observed

Harvard College (Increase Mather being himself the President, and Cotton one of the eight fellows) addressed once more to the ministers of New England an appeal for the recording and reporting of "remarkables." It may be found in bk. VI. of Cotton Mather's *Magnalia* (1702), at the head of his collection of such providences, into which he incorporated many of those already related by his father.

[1] He doubtless means both his *A Brief History of the War with the Indians in New-England* (Boston, 1676) and his *A Relation of the Troubles which have hapned in New-England* (Boston, 1677).

[2] This project was never carried out.

[3] Robert Boyle (1627–1691) was then the glory of English science. But he was also governor of the Corporation for the Spread of the Gospel in New England. His "Heads for the Natural History of a Country" may be found in vol. III. (pp. 5–14) of his *Philosophical Works* (London, 1725).

therein. It would best become some Scholar that has been
born in this Land, to do such a service for his Countrey.
Nor would I my self decline to put my hand (so far as my
small capacity will reach) to so noble an undertaking, did
not manifold diversions and employments prevent me from
attending that which I should account a profitable Recreation.
I have other work upon me, which I would gladly finish before I leave the World, and but a very little time to do it in:
Moreover, not many years ago, I lost (and that's an afflictive
loss indeed!) several Moneths from study by sickness. Let
every God-fearing Reader joyn with me in Prayer, that I
may be enabled to redeem the time, and (in all wayes wherein
I am capable) to serve my Generation.

INCREASE MATHER.

Boston in New-England,
January 1, 168¾.

.   .   .   .

CHAP. V.

Concerning things preternatural which have hapned in New-
England. A Remarkable Relation about Ann Cole of
Hartford. Concerning several Witches in that Colony. Of
the Possessed Maid at Groton. An account of the House in
Newberry lately troubled with a Dæmon. A parallel Story
of an House at Tedworth in England. Concerning another
in Hartford. And of one in Portsmouth in New-England
lately disquieted by Evil Spirits. The Relation of a Woman
at Barwick in New-England molested with Apparitions, and
sometimes tormented by invisible Agents.

INASMUCH as things which are præternatural, and not accomplished without diabolical operation, do more rarely happen,[1] it is pitty but that they should be observed. Several

---

[1] More rarely, that is, than those *super*natural wonders that proceed from
God. It is of these—of "remarkable sea-deliverances," of "other remarkable
preservations," of "remarkables about thunder and lightning"—that earlier
chapters have told. In chapter IV., however, the author argues that thunder-
storms are sometimes the work of Satan, and he is now ready to take up Satanic
marvels.

Accidents of that kind have hapned in New-England; which I shall here faithfully Relate so far as I have been able to come unto the knowledge of them.

Very Remarkable was that Providence wherein Ann Cole of Hartford in New-England was concerned.[1] She was and is accounted a person of real Piety and Integrity. Neverthe-less, in the Year 1662, then living in her Fathers House (who has likewise been esteemed a godly Man) She was taken with very strange Fits, wherein her Tongue was improved by a Dæmon to express things which she her self knew nothing of. Sometimes the Discourse would hold for a considerable time. The general purpose of which was, that such and such persons (who were named in the Discourse which passed from her) were consulting how they might carry on mischievous designs against her and several others, mentioning sundry wayes they should take for that end, particularly that they would afflict her Body, spoil her Name, etc. The general answer made amongst the Dæmons, was, She runs to the Rock. This having been continued some hours, the Dæmons said, Let us confound her Language, that she may tell no more tales. She uttered matters unintelligible. And then the Discourse passed into a Dutch-tone (a Dutch Family[2] then

---

[1] This story was reported by the Rev. John Whiting, from 1660 a pastor at Hartford, the home of his family, in a letter of December 4, 1682, now in the keeping of the Boston Public Library and published (1868) in the *Mather Papers* (Mass. Hist. Soc., *Collections*, fourth series, VIII.) at pp. 466–469. The incidents occurred in 1662. This was by no means the earliest of Connecticut's witch cases. On these in general see the sane and lucid study of C. H. Levermore, in the *New Englander*, XLIV. (1885), 788–817, and, condensed, in the *New England Magazine*, new series, VI. (1892), 636–644; also F. Morgan's in *Connecticut as a Colony and as a State* (Hartford, 1904), I. 205–229, and in the *American Historical Magazine*, I. (1906), 216–238; and J. M. Taylor's little monograph, *The Witchcraft Delusion in Colonial Connecticut* (New York, 1908). On this episode in particular and the surviving records see also C. J. Hoadly, "A Case of Witchcraft in Hartford," in the *Connecticut Magazine*, V. (1899), 557–560.

[2] The name of this Dutch family, as appears from a letter of Governor Stuy-vesant of New Amsterdam addressed October 13, 1662, to the authorities at Hartford, was Varleth, or Varlet. Stuyvesant accredits his brother-in-law (Capt. Nicholas Varleth), now "necessitated to make a second voyage" to aid "his distressed sister Judith Varleth," imprisoned on the charge of witchcraft, and urges on her behalf "her well known education, life, conversation and pro-fession of faith"—and with success, for this Judith, becoming at her father's death his heiress, repaired to New Netherland and there (1666) marrying Stuy-

lived in the Town) and therein an account was given of some afflictions that had befallen divers; amongst others, what had befallen a Woman that lived next Neighbour to the Dutch Family, whose Arms had been strangely pinched in the night, declaring by whom and for what cause that course had been taken with her.[1]   The Reverend Mr. Stone (then Teacher of the Church in Hartford)[2] being by, when the Discourse hapned, declared, that he thought it impossible for one not familiarly acquainted with the Dutch (which Ann Cole had not in the least been) should so exactly imitate the Dutch-tone in the pronunciation of English.   Several Worthy Persons, (*viz.* Mr. John Whiting, Mr. Samuel Hooker, and Mr. Joseph Hains)[3] wrote the intelligible sayings expressed by Ann Cole, whilest she was thus amazingly handled.   The event was that one of the persons (whose Name was Greensmith) being a lewd and ignorant Woman,[4] and then in Prison on suspicion for Witch-craft, mentioned in the Discourse as active in the mischiefs done and designed, was by the Magistrate sent for; Mr. Whiting and Mr. Haines read what they had written; and the Woman being astonished

vesant's able nephew, Nicholas Bayard, shared with him his notable rôle in the life of that colony. See Walker, *History of the First Church in Hartford* (Hartford, 1884), p. 177, note; Taylor (as above), pp. 151-152; *Connecticut Colonial Records*, 1636-1665, p. 387; *Documents relating to the Colonial History of New York*, XIV. 518; *Records of New Amsterdam* (New York, 1897), V. 130, 137; *New York Genealogical and Biographical Record*, X. (1879), 35-36.

[1] She was, says Mr. Whiting, a sister of one of the ministers in Hartford. Of Mr. Whiting himself?

[2] Samuel Stone (1602-1663), educated at Cambridge, came to Massachusetts in 1633 with Cotton and Hooker, became the latter's associate in the pastorate, and took part with him in 1636 in the founding of Hartford, where he remained a minister till his death.   As to both Stone and Whiting (and as to this episode) see especially Walker, *History of the First Church in Hartford* (Hartford, 1884).

[3] By "Mr. John Whiting" (see preceding notes) is of course meant Mather's informant himself; but in his letter he says that he "came into the house some time after the discourse began."   Hooker, a son of the founder of the Connecticut colony and, like Whiting, of the Harvard class of 1653, had in 1662 just become pastor at the neighboring Farmington.   Haynes (1641-1679), son of the governor, was an incipient divine, destined in 1664 to succeed Stone as Whiting's fellow-pastor at Hartford.

[4] "Considerably aged," adds Whiting.   She had twice been married before she became the wife of Nathaniel Greensmith, and by her first husband, Abraham Elson, had two daughters, who were now aged about seventeen and fifteen.

thereat, confessed those things to be true, and that she and
other persons named in this preternatural Discourse, had had
familiarity with the Devil: Being asked whether she had made
an express Covenant with him, she answered, she had not,
only as she promised to go with him when he called, which
accordingly she had sundry times done; and that the Devil
told her that at Christmass they would have a merry Meeting, and then the Covenant between them should be subscribed. The next day she was more particularly enquired
of concerning her Guilt respecting the Crime she was accused
with. She then acknowledged, that though when Mr. Hains
began to read what he had taken down in Writing, her rage
was such that she could have torn him in pieces, and was as
resolved as might be to deny her guilt (as she had done before),
yet after he had read awhile, she was (to use her own expression) as if her flesh had been pulled from her bones, and so
could not deny any longer: She likewise declared, that the
Devil first appeared to her in the form of a Deer or Fawn,
skipping about her, wherewith she was not much affrighted,
and that by degrees he became very familiar, and at last
would talk with her. Moreover, she said that the Devil
had frequently the carnal knowledge of her Body. And that
the Witches had Meetings at a place not far from her House;
and that some appeared in one shape, and others in another;
and one came flying amongst them in the shape of a Crow.
Upon this Confession, with other concurrent Evidence, the
Woman was Executed; so likewise was her husband, though
he did not acknowledge himself guilty.[1] Other persons accused in the Discourse made their escape.[2] Thus doth the

---

[1] Nathaniel Greensmith and Rebecca his wife were hanged at Hartford in
January, 1663. They seem to have been well-to-do, but not over-reputable,
people. The Greensmiths, Whiting tells us, lived next door to the Coles. "The
instance of the witch executed at Hartford," says Mather in his next chapter,
"considering the circumstances of that confession, is as convictive a proof as
most single examples that I have met with." And of Ann Cole he elsewhere
adds (*Providences*, ch. IV.): "I am informed, that when Matthew Cole was
killed with the lightning at North-Hampton, the dæmons which disturbed his
sister, Ann Cole (forty miles distant), in Hartford, spoke of it, intimating their
concurrence in that terrible accident."

[2] Beside the Greensmiths and perhaps Judith Varlet there was implicated
by Ann Cole a "Goodwife Seager," and Goodwife Greensmith is known to have

Devil use to serve his Clients. After the suspected Witches
were either executed or fled, Ann Cole was restored to health,
and has continued well for many years, approving her self a
serious Christian.

There were some that had a mind to try whither[1] the
Stories of Witches not being able to sink under water, were
true; and accordingly a Man and Woman mentioned in Ann
Cole's Dutch-toned discourse, had their hands and feet tyed,
and so were cast into the water, and they both apparently
swam after the manner of a Buoy, part under, part above
the Water. A by-stander imagining that any person bound
in that posture would be so born up, offered himself for trial,
but being in the like matter gently laid on the Water, he
immediately sunk right down. This was no legal Evidence
against the suspected persons; nor were they proceeded
against on any such account; However doubting that an
Halter would choak them, though the Water would not, they
very fairly took their flight, not having been seen in that
part of the World since. Whether this experiment were law-
ful, or rather Superstitious and Magical, we shall ($\sigma\upsilon\nu$ $\theta\epsilon\omega$)[2]
enquire afterwards.[3]

Another thing which caused a noise in the Countrey, and
wherein Satan had undoubtedly a great influence, was that
which hapned at Groton.[4] There was a Maid in that Town

mentioned several as accomplices, among them Judith Varlet and Goodwife
Ayres. The latter and her husband are believed to be the "Man and Woman"
told of in the next paragraph.

[1] Whether.   [2] " With God," *i. e.*, God willing.

[3] This was, of course, the well known "water test" for witches. Its origin
in witch procedure is obscure; but it gained vogue in the later sixteenth century,
finding its chief spokesman in the German schoolmaster Scribonius. As admin-
istered on the Continent, the witch was "cross-bound," *i. e.*, with right thumb
made fast to left great-toe and left thumb to right great-toe, and then flung, or
let down, supine into the water (usually thrice in succession), and was counted
guilty on failure to sink wholly under the water. The theory was that the pure
element refused to receive a witch into its bosom or that dealing with Satan made
the witch too light to sink—reputed phenomena which found many explanations.
Rejected by the majority, both of jurists and theologians, the practice eventually
lived on only as an illegal procedure of the mob. In pages not here reprinted
Increase Mather discusses it and sharply condemns it as superstitious.

[4] This case was reported by the Rev. Samuel Willard (1640-1707), who had
witnessed it as pastor at Groton, but who from 1678 to his death was the eminent

(one Elizabeth Knap)[1] who in the Moneth of October, Anno 1671, was taken after a very strange manner, sometimes weeping, sometimes laughing, sometimes roaring hideously, with violent motions and agitations of her body, crying out Money, Money, etc. In November following, her Tongue for many hours together was drawn like a semicircle up to the roof of her Mouth, not to be removed, though some tried with their fingers to do it. Six Men were scarce able to hold her in some of her fits, but she would skip about the House yelling and looking with a most frightful Aspect. *December* 17, Her Tongue was drawn out of her mouth to an extraordinary length; and now a Dæmon began manifestly to speak in her. Many words were uttered wherein are the Labial Letters, without any motion of her Lips, which was a clear demonstration that the voice was not her own. Sometimes Words were spoken seeming to proceed out of her throat, when her Mouth was shut. Sometimes with her Mouth wide open, without the use of any of the Organs of speech. The things then uttered by the Devil were chiefly Railings and Revilings of Mr. Willard (who was at that time a Worthy and Faithful Pastor to the Church in Groton.) Also the Dæmon belched forth most horrid and nefandous Blasphemies, exalting himself above the most High. After this she was taken speechless for some time. One thing more is worthy of Remark concerning this miserable creature. She cried out in some of her Fits, that a Woman, (one of her Neighbours) appeared to her, and was the cause of her Affliction. The Person thus accused was a very sincere, holy Woman, who did hereupon with the Advice of Friends visit the poor Wretch; and though she was in one of her Fits, having her Eyes shut,

minister of the Old South Church in Boston. The exceedingly minute and exact account is not a letter to Mather, but an inclosure in one, and is clearly a contemporary journal completed in January, 1672, when the episode was barely at an end. It is printed in full in the *Mather Papers* (Mass. Hist. Soc., *Collections*, fourth series, VIII.) at pp. 555–570, and with yet greater care by Dr. S. A. Green, in his *Groton in the Witchcraft Times* (Groton, 1883), pp. 7–21. No document is more fundamental to the study of New England witchcraft. Mather's brief summary is but a hint of its contents; but he must have used other sources as well (perhaps a lost letter of inclosure and doubtless Willard's sermon on the subject, printed in 1673 with others in his *Useful Instructions*).

[1] A girl of sixteen—born April 21, 1655 (Green, *Groton*, p. 6).

when the innocent person impeached by her came in; yet could she (so powerful were Satans Operations upon her) declare who was there, and could tell the touch of that Woman from any ones else.   But the gracious Party thus accused and abused by a malicious Devil, Prayed earnestly with and for the Possessed creature; after which she confessed that Satan had deluded her, making her believe evil of her good Neighbour without any cause.   Nor did she after that complain of any Apparition or Disturbance from such an one.[1]   Yea, she said, that the Devil had himself in the likeness and shape of divers tormented her, and then told her it was not he but they that did it.

As there have been several Persons vexed with evil Spirits, so divers Houses have been wofully Haunted by them.   In the Year 1679, the House of William Morse in Newberry[2] in New-England, was strangely disquieted by a Dæmon.   After those troubles began, he did by the Advice of Friends write down the particulars of those unusual Accidents.   And the Account which he giveth thereof is as followeth;

On *December* 3, in the night time, he and his Wife heard a noise upon the roof of their House, as if Sticks and Stones had been thrown against it with great violence; whereupon he rose out of his Bed, but could see nothing.   Locking the Doors fast, he returned to Bed again.   About midnight they heard an Hog making a great noise in the House, so that the Man rose again, and found a great Hog in the house, the door being shut, but upon the opening of the door it ran out.

On *December* 8, in the Morning, there were five great Stones and Bricks by an invisible hand thrown in at the west

---

[1] Very different as to this kernel of the story is Willard's MS.: "She declared that if the party were apprehended shee should forthwith bee well, but never till then; whereupon her father went, and procured the coming of the woman impeached by her, who came downe to her on Thursday night, where (being desired to be present) I observed that she was violently handled, and lamentably tormented by the adversarye, and uttered unusual shriekes at the instant of the persons coming in, though her eyes were fast closed: but having experience of such former actings, wee made nothing of it, but waited the issue: God therefore was sought to, to signifye something whereby the innocent might bee acquitted, or the guilty discovered, and hee answered our prayers, for by 2 evident and cleere mistakes she was cleered, and then all prejudices ceased, and she never more to this day hath impeached her of any apparition."

[2] Newbury.

end of the house while the Mans Wife was making the Bed,
the Bedstead was lifted up from the floor, and the Bedstaff [1]
flung out of the Window, and a Cat was hurled at her; a
long Staff danced up and down in the Chimney; a burnt
Brick, and a piece of a weatherboard were thrown in at the
Window: The Man at his going to Bed put out his Lamp,
but in the Morning found that the Saveall of it was taken
away, and yet it was unaccountably brought into its former
place.[2]   On the same day, the long Staff but now spoken
of, was hang'd up by a line, and swung to and fro, the Man's
Wife laid it in the fire, but she could not hold it there, inasmuch as it would forcibly fly out; yet after much ado with
joynt strength they made it to burn.   A shingle flew from the
Window, though no body near it, many sticks came in at the
same place, only one of these was so scragged that it could
enter the hole but a little way, whereupon the Man pusht it
out, a great Rail likewise was thrust in at the Window, so as
to break the Glass.

At another time an Iron Crook that was hanged on a
Nail violently flew up and down, also a Chair flew about, and
at last lighted on the Table where Victuals stood ready for
them to eat, and was likely to spoil all, only by a nimble
catching they saved some of their Meal with the loss of the
rest, and the overturning of their Table.

People were sometimes Barricado'd out of doors, when
as yet there was no body to do it: and a Chest was removed
from place to place, no hand touching it.   Their Keys being
tied together, one was taken from the rest, and the remaining two would fly about making a loud noise by knocking
against each other.   But the greatest part of this Devils feats
were his mischievous ones, wherein indeed he was sometimes
Antick enough too, and therein the chief sufferers were, the
Man and his Wife, and his Grand-Son.   The Man especially
had his share in these Diabolical Molestations.   For one while

---

[1] A "bedstaff" was a stick used to help in making a bed which stood in a
recess, and the same name was given to the stick then fixed to the side of a bed
to keep the bed-clothes from falling off: doubtless the same staff served both
purposes.   Later in this account we shall find it called a "bed-board": at least
Cotton Mather, repeating the tale in his *Magnalia*, identifies the two.

[2] The "lamp" was of course a candle, and the "saveall" was a contrivance
at the base enabling the wick to burn to the very bottom without waste.

they could not eat their Suppers quietly, but had the Ashes on the Hearth before their eyes thrown into their Victuals; yea, and upon their heads and Clothes, insomuch that they were forced up into their Chamber, and yet they had no rest there; for one of the Man's Shoes being left below, 'twas filled with Ashes and Coals, and thrown up after them. Their Light was beaten out, and they being laid in their Bed with their little Boy between them, a great stone (from the Floor of the Loft) weighing above three pounds was thrown upon the mans stomach, and he turning it down upon the floor, it was once more thrown upon him. A Box and a Board were likewise thrown upon them all. And a Bag of Hops was taken out of their Chest, wherewith they were beaten, till some of the Hops were scattered on the floor, where the Bag was then laid, and left.

In another Evening, when they sat by the fire, the Ashes were so whirled at them, that they could neither eat their Meat, nor endure the House. A Peel[1] struck the Man in the face. An Apron hanging by the fire was flung upon it, and singed before they could snatch it off. The Man being at Prayer with his Family, a Beesom[2] gave him a blow on his head behind, and fell down before his face.

On another day, when they were Winnowing of Barley, some hard dirt was thrown in, hitting the Man on the Head, and both the Man and his Wife on the back; and when they had made themselves clean, they essayed to fill their half Bushel but the foul Corn was in spite of them often cast in amongst the clean, and the Man being divers times thus abused was forced to give over what he was about.

On *January* 23 (in particular) the Man had an iron Pin twice thrown at him, and his Inkhorn was taken away from him while he was writing, and when by all his seeking it he could not find it, at last he saw it drop out of the Air, down by the fire: a piece of Leather was twice thrown at him; and a shoe was laid upon his shoulder, which he catching at, was suddenly rapt from him. An handful of Ashes was thrown at his face, and upon his clothes: and the shoe was

[1] A fire-shovel; or a similar implement for getting things into an oven or out of it.
[2] A broom.

then clapt upon his head, and upon it he clapt his hand, holding it so fast, that somewhat unseen pulled him with it backward on the floor.

On the next day at night, as they were going to Bed, a lost Ladder was thrown against the Door, and their Light put out; and when the Man was a bed, he was beaten with an heavy pair of Leather Breeches, and pull'd by the Hair of his Head and Beard, Pinched and Scratched, and his Bed-board[1] was taken away from him; yet more in the next night, when the Man was likewise a Bed; his Bed-board did rise out of its place, notwithstanding his putting forth all his strength to keep it in; one of his Awls[2] was brought out of the next room into his Bed, and did prick him; the clothes wherewith he hoped to save his head from blows were violently pluckt from thence. Within a night or two after, the Man and his Wife received both of them a blow upon their heads, but it was so dark that they could not see the stone which gave it; the Man had his Cap pulled off from his head while he sat by the fire.

The night following, they went to bed undressed, because of their late disturbances, and the Man, Wife, Boy, presently felt themselves pricked, and upon search found in the Bed a Bodkin, a knitting Needle, and two sticks picked[3] at both ends. He received also a great blow, as on his Thigh, so on his Face, which fetched blood: and while he was writing a Candlestick was twice thrown at him, and a great piece of Bark fiercely smote him, and a pail of Water turned up without hands. On the 28 of the mentioned Moneth, frozen clods of Cow-dung were divers times thrown at the man out of the house in which they were; his Wife went to milk the Cow, and received a blow on her head, and sitting down at her Milking-work had Cow-dung divers times thrown into her Pail, the Man tried to save the Milk, by holding a Piggin[4] side-wayes under the Cowes belly, but the Dung would in for all, and the Milk was only made fit for Hogs. On that night ashes were thrown into the porridge which they had made ready for their Supper, so as that they could not eat

---

[1] See p. 24, note 1.   [2] Morse was a shoemaker.
[3] Pointed, sharpened.
[4] A small wooden pail, with one stave long, to serve as a handle.

it; Ashes were likewise often thrown into the Man's Eyes, as he sat by the fire. And an iron Hammer flying at him, gave him a great blow on his back; the Man's Wife going into the Cellar for Beer, a great iron Peel[1] flew and fell after her through the trap-door of the Cellar; and going afterwards on the same Errand to the same place, the door shut down upon her, and the Table came and lay upon the door, and the man was forced to remove it e're his Wife could be released from where she was; on the following day while he was Writing, a dish went out of its place, leapt into the pale, and cast Water upon the•Man, his Paper, his Table, and disappointed his procedure in what he was about; his Cap jumpt off from his head, and on again, and the Pot-lid leapt off from the Pot into the Kettle on the fire.

February 2.   While he and his Boy were eating of Cheese, the pieces which he cut were wrested from them, but they were afterwards found upon the Table under an Apron, and a pair of Breeches: And also from the fire arose little sticks and Ashes, which flying upon the Man and his Boy, brought them into an uncomfortable pickle; But as for the Boy, which the last passage spoke of, there remains much to be said concerning him, and a principal sufferer in these afflictions: For on the 18 of December, he sitting by his Grandfather, was hurried into great motions and the Man thereupon took him, and made him stand between his Legs, but the Chair danced up and down, and had like to have cast both Man and Boy into the fire: and the Child was afterwards flung about in such a manner, as that they feared that his Brains would have been beaten out; and in the evening he was tossed as afore, and the Man tried the project of holding him, but ineffectually.   The Lad was soon put to Bed, and they presently heard an huge noise, and demanded what was the matter? and he answered that his Bed-stead leaped up and down: and they (*i. e.* the Man and his Wife) went up, and at first found all quiet, but before they had been there long, they saw the Board[2] by his Bed trembling by him, and the Bed-clothes flying off him, the latter they laid on immediately, but they were no sooner on than off; so they took him out of his Bed for quietness.

[1] See p. 25, note 1.   [2] See p. 24, note 1.

December 29. The Boy was violently thrown to and fro, only they carried him to the house of a Doctor in the Town, and there he was free from disturbances, but returning home at night, his former trouble began, and the Man taking him by the hand, they were both of them almost tript into the fire. They put him to bed, and he was attended with the same iterated loss of his clothes, shaking off his Bed-board, and Noises, that he had in his last conflict; they took him up, designing to sit by the fire, but the doors clattered, and the Chair was thrown at him, wherefore they carried him to the Doctors house, and so for that night all was well. The next morning he came home quiet, but as they were doing somewhat, he cried out that he was prickt on the back, they looked, and found a three-tin'd Fork sticking strangely there; which being carried to the Doctors house, not only the Doctor himself said that it was his, but also the Doctors Servant affirmed it was seen at home after the Boy was gone. The Boys vexations continuing, they left him at the Doctors, where he remained well till awhile after, and then he complained he was pricked, they looked and found an iron Spindle sticking below his back; he complained he was pricked still, they looked, and found Pins in a Paper sticking to his skin; he once more complained of his Back, they looked, and found there a long Iron, a bowl of a Spoon, and a piece of a Pansheard. They lay down by him on the Bed, with the Light burning, but he was twice thrown from them, and the second time thrown quite under the Bed; in the Morning the Bed was tossed about with such a creaking noise, as was heard to the Neighbours; in the afternoon their knives were one after another brought, and put into his back, but pulled out by the Spectators; only one knife which was missing seemed to the standers by to come out of his Mouth: he was bidden to read his Book, was taken and thrown about several times, at last hitting the Boys Grandmother on the head. Another time he was thrust out of his Chair and rolled up and down with out cries, that all things were on fire; yea, he was three times very dangerously thrown into the fire, and preserved by his Friends with much ado. The Boy also made for a long time together a noise like a Dog, and like an Hen with her Chickens, and could not speak rationally.

Particularly, on *December* 26. He barked like a Dog, and clock't like an Hen, and after long distraining to speak, said, there's Powel, I am pinched; his Tongue likewise hung out of his mouth, so as that it could by no means be forced in till his Fit was over, and then he said 'twas forced out by Powel.[1] He and the house also after this had rest till the ninth of January: at which time because of his intolerable ravings, and because the Child lying between the Man and his Wife, was pulled out of Bed, and knockt so vehemently against the Bedstead Boards,[2] in a manner very perillous and amazing. In the Day time he was carried away beyond all possibility of their finding him. His Grandmother at last saw him creeping on one side, and drag'd him in, where he lay miserable lame, but recovering his speech, he said, that he was carried above the Doctors house, and that Powel carried him, and that the said Powel had him into the Barn, throwing him against the Cart-wheel there, and then thrusting him out at an hole; and accordingly they found some of the Remainders of the Threshed Barley which was on the Barn-floor hanging to his Clothes.

At another time he fell into a Swoon, they forced somewhat Refreshing into his mouth, and it was turned out as fast as they put it in; e're long he came to himself, and expressed some willingness to eat, but the Meat would forcibly fly out of his mouth; and when he was able to speak, he said Powel would not let him eat: Having found the Boy to be best at a Neighbours house, the Man carried him to his Daughters, three miles from his own. The Boy was growing antick as he was on the Journey, but before the end of it he made a grievous hollowing, and when he lighted, he threw a great stone at a Maid in the house, and fell on eating of Ashes. Being at home afterwards, they had rest awhile, but on the 19 of January in the Morning he swooned, and coming to himself, he roared terribly, and did eat Ashes, Sticks, Rug-yarn. The Morning following, there was such a racket with

---

[1] This sentence is clearly of the nature of an interpolation; for the "rest" mentioned in the following clause must date from the events narrated in the preceding paragraph. The "Powel" meant was of course Caleb Powell—see p. 31, note 1.

[2] See p. 24, note 1; yet head-board and foot-board may here be meant.

the Boy, that the Man and his Wife took him to Bed to them.
A Bed-staff was thereupon thrown at them, and a Chamber
pot with its Contents was thrown upon them, and they were
severely pinched. The Man being about to rise, his Clothes
were divers times pulled from them, himself thrust out of his
Bed, and his Pillow thrown after him. The Lad also would
have his clothes plucked off from him in these Winter Nights,
and was wofully dogg'd with such fruits of Devilish spite,
till it pleased God to shorten the Chain of the wicked Dæmon.

All this while the Devil did not use to appear in any visible
shape, only they would think they had hold of the Hand that
sometimes scratched them; but it would give them the slip.
And once the Man was discernably beaten by a Fist, and an
Hand got hold of his Wrist which he saw, but could not catch;
and the likeness of a Blackmore[1] Child did appear from under
the Rugg and Blanket, where the Man lay, and it would rise
up, fall down, nod and slip under the clothes when they endeavoured to clasp it, never speaking any thing.

Neither were there many Words spoken by Satan all this
time, only once having put out their Light, they heard a
scraping on the Boards, and then a Piping and Drumming
on them, which was followed with a Voice, singing, Revenge!
Revenge! Sweet is Revenge! And they being well terrified
with it, called upon God; the issue of which was, that suddenly
with a mournful Note, there were six times over uttered such
expressions as, Alas! Alas! me knock no more! me knock no
more! and now all ceased.

The Man does moreover affirm, that a Seaman (being a
Mate of a Ship) coming often to visit him, told him that they
wronged his Wife who suspected her to be guilty of Witchcraft; and that the Boy (his Grandchild) was the cause of
this trouble; and that if he would let him have the Boy one
day, he would warrant him his house should be no more
troubled as it had been; to which motion he consented. The
Mate came the next day betimes, and the Boy was with him
until night; after which his house he saith was not for some
time molested with evil Spirits.

Thus far is the Relation concerning the Dæmon at William

[1] Blackamoor, negro.

Morse his House in Newbery.[1] The true Reason of these strange disturbances is as yet not certainly known: some (as has been hinted) did suspect Morse's Wife to be guilty of Witchcraft.

One of the Neighbours took Apples which were brought out of that house and put them into the fire; upon which they say, their houses were much disturbed. Another of the Neighbours, caused an Horse-shoe to be nailed before the doors, and as long as it remained so, they could not perswade the suspected person to go into the house; but when the Horse-shoe was gone, she presently visited them. I shall not here inlarge upon the vanity and superstition of those Experiments,

[1] This "relation" was undoubtedly received from the Rev. Joshua Moodey, then minister at Portsmouth, in a letter of August 23, 1683 (*Mather Papers*, pp. 361–362); for a postscript speaks of its enclosure and says that he had it from William Morse himself. That Morse was its author we know only from Mather. Happily, there exist also many documents of the two witch-trials arising from the affair—those of Caleb Powell and Mrs. Morse. Some of these, preserved in the court records at Salem, were printed by Joshua Coffin in his *History of Newbury* (Boston, 1845), at pp. 122–134; and again, more carefully, with others, by W. E. Woodward in his *Records of Salem Witchcraft* (Boston, 1864), II. 251–261. Others, which had strayed from public keeping, were published by S. G. Drake, then their owner, in an appendix (pp. 258–296) to his *Annals of Witchcraft* (Boston, 1869), in which he summarizes the story (pp. 141–150). Two (her conviction at Boston and her release) have been printed in the *Records of the Court of Assistants*, I. (Boston, 1901), pp. 159, 189–190. Others still are in the Massachusetts archives (vol. CXXXV., fol. 11–19), where they have been used by Mr. W. F. Poole (see, in the *N. E. Hist. and Gen. Register*, XXIV., his note, p. 386, to an unpublished draft of Governor Hutchinson's account). These documents supplement, and sometimes correct, the relation of Morse. Thus, from sworn statements of December, 1679 (Coffin, *Newbury*, pp. 124, 131–133), it is clear that the events above ascribed to December 3 belong to November 27, that the grandson's name was John Stiles, that the "seaman" who charged him with the mischief was Caleb Powell, that the day the boy was in his keeping was December 2, 1679, and that on the very next day Morse instituted proceedings against Powell, who was indicted for witchcraft on December 8 (the day on which the disturbances were resumed) and was tried at Ipswich in March. He succeeded in clearing himself, but at the cost of Goodwife Morse. She was a midwife, and had long been suspected of witchcraft by some of her neighbors. Indicted in March, she was tried at Boston in May before the magistrates of the colony, was found guilty and sentenced to death, but was reprieved by the magistrates, and in June, 1681, after more than a year's imprisonment, permitted, though without acquittal, to return to her home, "provided she goe not above sixteen rods from hir oune house and land at any time except to the meeting house." For the end of her pitiful story see p. 412, below.

reserving that for another place: All that I shall say at present is, that the Dæmons whom the blind Gentiles of old worshipped, told their Servants, that such things as these would very much affect them; yea, and that certain Characters, Signs and Charms would render their power ineffectual; and accordingly they would become subject, when their own directions were obeyed. It is sport to the Devils when they see silly Men thus deluded and made fools of by them. Others were apt to think that a Seaman[1] by some suspected to be a Conjurer, set the Devil on work thus to disquiet Morse's Family. Or it may be some other thing as yet kept hid in the secrets of providence might be the true original of all this Trouble.

A Disturbance not much unlike to this hapned above twenty years ago, at an house in Tedworth, in the County of Wilts in England, which was by wise men judged to proceed from Conjuration.

Mr. Mompesson of Tedworth being in March 1661, at Lungershall,[2] and hearing a Drum beat there, he demanded of the Bailiff of the Town what it meant, who told him, they had for some dayes been troubled with an idle Drummer, pretending Authority, and a Pass under the hands of some Gentlemen. Mr. Mompesson reading his Pass, and knowing the hands of those Gentlemen, whose Names were pretended to be subscribed, discovered the Cheat, and commanded the Vagrant to put off his Drum, and ordered a Constable to secure him: but not long after he got clear of the Constable. In April following, Mr Momposson's house was much disturbed with Knockings, and with Drummings; for an hour together a Dæmon would beat *Round-heads and Cuckolds*, the *Tattoo* and several other points of War as well as any Drummer. On November 5, The Dæmon made a great noise in the House, and caused some Boards therein to move to and fro in the day time when there was an whole room full of People present. At his departure, he left behind him a Sulphurous smell, which was very offensive. The next night, Chairs walked up and down the Room; the Childrens Shoes were hurled over their heads. The Minister of the Town being there, a Bed-staff was thrown at him, and hit him on the Leg, but without the least hurt. In the latter end of December, 1662, They heard a noise like the jingling of Money, the occasion of which was thought to be, some words spoken the night before, by one in the Family;

---

[1] Caleb Powell.   [2] Ludgershall.

who said that Fairies used to leave money behind them, and they
wished it might be so now. In January Lights were seen in the
House, which seemed blue and glimmering, and caused a great stiffness in the eyes of them that saw them. One in the room (by what
Authority I cannot tell) said, "Satan, if the Drummer set thee a work
give three knocks and no more", which was done accordingly. Once
when it was very sharp severe Weather, the room was suddenly filled
with a Noisome smell, and was very hot though without fire. This
Dæmon would play some nasty and many ludicrous foolish tricks.
It would empty Chamber-pots into the Beds; and fill Porringers
with Ashes. Sometimes it would not suffer any light to be in the
room, but would carry them away up the Chimney. Mr. Mompesson coming one morning into his Stable, found his Horse on the
ground, having one of his hinder legs in his mouth, and so fastened
there, that it was difficult for several men with a Leaver to get it
out. A Smith lodging in the House, heard a noise in the room, as
if one had been shoeing an Horse, and somewhat come as it were
with a Pincers snipping at the Smith's Nose, most part of the night.
The Drummer was under vehement suspicion for a Conjurer. He
was condemned to Transportation. All the time of his restraint and
absence, the House was quiet. See Mr. Glanvil's *Collection of Modern Relations*, P. 71, etc.[1]

But I proceed to give an account of some other things
lately hapning in New-England, which were undoubtedly præternatural, and not without Diabolical operation. The last
year did afford several Instances, not unlike unto those
which have been mentioned. For then Nicholas Desborough
of Hartford in New-England was strangely molested by stones,
pieces of earth, cobs of Indian Corn, etc., falling upon and
about him, which sometimes came in through the door, sometimes through the Window, sometimes down the Chimney,
at other times they seemed to fall from the floor of the Chamber, which yet was very close; sometimes he met with them
in his Shop, the Yard, the Barn, and in the Field at work.
In the House, such things hapned frequently, not only in the
night but in the day time, if the Man himself was at home,
but never when his Wife was at home alone. There was no

---

[1] This famous relation was first printed in 1668 as an appendix to the third
edition of Glanvill's essay on witchcraft (see above, pp. 5–6), and was much
enlarged in the edition of 1681. What is here printed is not the briefer original
form but an abridgment of Mather's own.

great violence in the motion, though several persons of the
Family and others also were struck with the things that were
thrown by an invisible hand, yet they were not hurt thereby.
Only the Man himself had once his Arm somewhat pained by
a blow given him; and at another time, blood was drawn from
one of his Legs by a scratch given it.   This molestation began
soon after a Controversie arose between Desborough and another person, about a Chest of Clothes which the other said
that Desberough did unrighteously retain: and so it continued for some Moneths (though with several intermissions).
In the latter end of the last year, when also the Man's Barn
was burned with the Corn in it; but by what means it came
to pass is not known.   Not long after, some to whom the
matter was referred, ordered Desberough to restore the Clothes
to the Person who complained of wrong; since which he hath
not been troubled as before.   Some of the stones hurled were
of considerable bigness; one of them weighed four pounds,
but generally the stones were not great, but very small ones.
One time a piece of Clay came down the Chimney, falling on
the Table which stood at some distance from the Chimney.
The People of the House threw it on the Hearth, where it
lay a considerable time: they went to their Supper, and
whilest at their Supper, the piece of Clay was lifted up by an
invisible hand, and fell upon the Table; taking it up, they
found it hot, having lain so long before the fire, as to cause
it to be hot.[1]

Another Providence no less Remarkable than this last
mentioned, hapned at Portsmouth in New-England, about
the same time: concerning which I have received the following account from a Worthy hand.[2]

---

[1] These experiences of Nicholas Desborough were reported by the Rev.
John Russell, of Hadley, in a letter of August 2, 1683, which may be found in the
Mather Papers (pp. 86–88). Russell says he received the account from "Capt.
Allyn, a neer neighbour to Disborough."   John Allyn, long secretary of the
colony, was one of the foremost men in Connecticut.

[2] The "worthy hand" was again that of the Rev. Joshua Moodey, of Portsmouth. His earliest letter about the matter does not appear in the *Mather
Papers*; but in a later one (July 14, 1683—*Mather Papers*, pp. 359–360) he writes
thus: "About that at G. Walton's; because my Interest runs low with the Secretary, I have desired Mr. Woodbridge to endeavour the obtaining it, and if I can
get it shall send it per the first; Though if there should bee any difficulty there-

On June 11, 1682, Being the Lords Day, at night showers of stones were thrown both against the sides and roof of the house of George Walton:[1] some of the People went abroad, found the Gate at some distance from the house, wrung off the Hinges, and stones came thick about them: sometimes falling down by them, sometimes touching them without any hurt done to them, though they seemed to come with great force, yet did no more but softly touch them; Stones flying about the room the Doors being shut. The Glass-Windows shattered to pieces by stones that seemed to come not from without but within; the Lead of the Glass Casements, Window-Bars, etc. being driven forcibly outwards, and so standing bent. While the Secretary[2] was walking in the room a great Hammer came brushing along against the Chamber floor that was over his head, and fell down by him. A Candlestick beaten off the Table. They took up nine of the stones and marked them, and laid them on the Table, some of them being as hot as if they came out of the fire; but some of those mark't stones were found flying about again. In this manner, about four hours space that night: The Secretary then went to bed, but a stone came and broke up his Chamber-door, being put to (not lockt), a Brick was sent upon the like Errand. The abovesaid Stone the Secretary lockt up in his Chamber, but it was

about, you may doe pretty well with what you have already." And writing again on August 23 (*Mather Papers*, pp. 360–361), he says his endeavors have not been wanting to obtain it, but he finds it difficult. "If more may bee gotten, you may expect when I come, or else must take up with what you had from mee at first, which was the summe of what was then worthy of notice, only many other particular actings of like nature had been then and since. It began of a Lord's day, June 11th, 1682, and so continued for a long time, only there was some respite now and then. The last sight I have heard of was the carrying away of severall Axes in the night, notwithstanding they were laied up, yea, lockt up very safe, as the owner thought at least, which was done this spring." The "Secretary" (*i. e.*, of the province) was that Richard Chamberlain from whose own pen we have the fuller account of the episode printed later in this volume (pp. 58–77); and there can be little doubt that what Mather gave to the press rests on the basis of his journal. As to "Mr. Woodbridge" see p. 65, note 1.

[1] Walton (1615–1686) was a prosperous Quaker. "George Walton, and his wife Alice, and Daughter, Abishag . . . lived on the great Island in Piscataqua, and this Alice was one of the most accounted of the Women, for Profession in the Island, whom it troubled them to lose; but Truth took her, and overturned the Priest." (Bishop, *New-England Judged*, pp. 466–467.) Great Island (now Newcastle), then a part of the township of Portsmouth, was often the seat of the provincial government, and the secretary lodged at Walton's house. As to Walton's family and estate see his will (*Probate Records of the Province of New Hampshire*, I. 299, and *N. E. Hist. and Gen. Register*, IX. 57).

[2] Richard Chamberlain, secretary of the province. See preceding notes.

fetched out, and carried with great noise into the next Chamber. The Spit was carried up Chimney, and came down with the point forward, and stuck in the Back-log, and being removed by one of the Company to one side of the Chimney, was by an unseen hand thrown out at Window. This trade was driven on the next day, and so from Day to Day, now and then there would be some inter-mission, and then to it again. The stones were most frequent where the Master of the house was, whether in the Field or Barn, etc. A black Cat was seen once while the Stones came and was shot at, but she was too nimble for them. Some of the Family say, that they once saw the appearance of an hand put forth at the Hall Window, throwing stones towards the Entry, though there was no body in the Hall the while: sometimes a dismal hollow whistling would be heard; sometimes the noise of the trotting of an horse, and snorting but nothing seen. The Man went up the great Bay in his Boat to a Farm he had there, and while haling Wood or Timber to the Boat he was disturbed by the Stones as before at home. He carried a stirrup iron from the house down to the Boat, and there left it; but while he was going up to the house, the iron came jingling after him through the Woods, and returned to the house, and so again, and at last went away, and was heard of no more. Their Anchor leapt over-board several times as they were going home and stopt the boat. A Cheese hath been taken out of the Press and crumbled all over the floor. A piece of Iron with which they weighed up the Cheese-press stuck into the Wall, and a Kittle hung up thereon. Several Cocks of English-hay[1] mowed near the house were taken and hung upon Trees; and some made into small whisps, and put all up and down the Kitchin, *Cum multis aliis*,[2] etc. After this manner, have they been treated ever since at times; it were endless to particularize. Of late they thought the bitterness of Death had been past, being quiet for sundry dayes and nights: but last week were some Return-ings again; and this week (Aug. 2, 1682) as bad or worse than ever. The Man is sorely hurt with some of the Stones that came on him, and like to feel the effects of them for many dayes.

Thus far is that Relation.

I am moreover informed, that the Dæmon was quiet all the last Winter, but in the Spring he began to play some ludi-crous tricks, carrying away some Axes that were locked up

---

[1] Doubtless what is now known as "timothy." In 1807 Kendall found this still called "English grass" in Connecticut.

[2] "With many other things."

safe.   This last Summer he has not made such disturbances as
formerly.   But of this no more at present.[1]

There have been strange and true Reports concerning a
Woman now living near the Salmon Falls in Barwick[2] (formerly called Kittery) unto whom Evil Spirits have sometimes
visibly appeared;   and she has sometimes been sorely tormented by invisible hands: Concerning all which, an Intelligent Person has sent me the following Narrative.[3]

*A Brief Narrative of sundry Apparitions of Satan unto and Assaults
at sundry times and places upon the Person of Mary the Wife of
Antonio Hortado, dwelling near the Salmon Falls: Taken from
her own mouth, Aug. 13, 1683.*

In June 1682 (the day forgotten) at Evening, the said Mary
heard a voice at the door of her Dwelling, saying, What do you here?
about an hour after, standing at the Door of her House, she had a
blow on her Eye that settled her head near to the Door post, and
two or three dayes after, a Stone, as she judged about half a pound
or a pound weight, was thrown along the house within into the Chimney, and going to take it up it was gone; all the Family was in the
house, and no hand appearing which might be instrumental in throwing the stone.   About two hours after, a Frying-pan then hanging
in the Chimney was heard to ring so loud, that not only those in
the house heard it, but others also that lived on the other side of
the River near an hundred Rods distant or more.   Whereupon the
said Mary and her Husband going in a Cannoo over the River, they

---

[1] "As for Walton, the Quaker of Portsmouth, whose house has been so
strangely troubled," adds Mather in the following chapter, "he suspects that one
of his neighbours has caused it by witchcraft; she (being a widow-woman) chargeth
him with injustice in detaining some land from her.   It is none of my work to re-
flect upon the man, nor will I do it; only, if there be any late or old guilt upon his
conscience, it concerns him by confession and repentance to give glory to that God
who is able in strange wayes to discover the sins of men"—and see also p. 214.

[2] Berwick, on the Maine side of the river.

[3] This narrative too came from the Rev. Joshua Moodey (see his letters of
July 14 and August 23, 1683—*Mather Papers*, pp. 359–361), but at Mather's
instance.   "I was very earnest with Mr. Emerson," writes Moodey, "and at
length obtained the enclosed, which I transcribed from Mr. Tho. Broughton, who
read to mee what he took from the mouth of the woman and her husband, and
judge it credible, though it bee not the half of what is to be gotten.   I expect
from him a fuller and farther account before I come down to the Commence-
ment."   John Emerson, the schoolmaster, we shall meet again at Salem (see p.
377, note).   Thomas Broughton was a well known Boston merchant, then sojourning in New Hampshire.

saw like the head of a man new-shorn, and the tail of a white Cat about two or three foot distance from each other, swimming over before the Cannoo, but no body appeared to joyn head and tail together; and they returning over the River in less than an hours time, the said Apparition followed their Cannoo back again, but disappeared at Landing. A day or two after, the said Mary was stricken on her head (as she judged) with a stone, which caused a Swelling and much soreness on her head, being then in the yard by her house, and she presently entring into her house was bitten on both Arms black and blue, and one of her Breasts scratched; the impressions of the Teeth being like Mans Teeth, were plainly seen by many : Whereupon deserting their House to sojourn at a Neighbours on the other side of the River, there appeared to said Mary in the house of her sojourning, a Woman clothed with a green Safeguard, a short blue Cloak, and a white Cap, making a profer to strike her with a Firebrand, but struck her not. The Day following the same shape appeared again to her, but now arrayed with a gray Gown, white Apron, and white Head-clothes, in appearance laughing several times, but no voice heard. Since when said Mary has been freed from those Satanical Molestations.

But the said Antonio being returned in March last with his Family, to dwell again in his own house, and on his entrance there, hearing the noise of a Man walking in his Chamber, and seeing the boards buckle under his feet as he walked, though no man to be seen in the Chamber (for they went on purpose to look) he returned with his Family to dwell on the other side of the River; yet planting his Ground though he forsook his House, he hath had five Rods of good Log-fence thrown down at once, the feeting of Neat Cattle plainly to be seen almost between every Row of Corn in the Field yet no Cattle seen there, nor any damage done to his Corn, not so much as any of the Leaves of the Corn cropt.

Thus far is that Narrative.

I am further informed, that some (who should have been wiser) advised the poor Woman to stick the House round with Bayes, as an effectual preservative against the power of Evil Spirits. This Counsel was followed. And as long as the Bayes continued green, she had quiet; but when they began to wither, they were all by an unseen hand carried away, and the Woman again tormented.

It is observable, that at the same time three Houses in three several Towns should be molested by Dæmons, as has now been related.

THE NEW YORK CASES OF HALL AND HARRISON, 1665, 1670

INTRODUCTION

It is not strange that in the Dutch colony of New Netherland we hear nothing of witches. The home land of the Dutch had, beyond all others, outgrown the panic. It was a physician of Netherlandish birth, Johann Weyer, who in the later sixteenth century first wrote effectively against its cruelties. When his English pupil, Reginald Scot, protested yet more boldly, it was in Holland alone his book found reimpression. So far as is known, the seventeenth century saw there no executions for witchcraft, and after 1610 no trials. If the leaders of Dutch Calvinism were content with silence, the most eloquent spokesman of their Arminian rivals, Episcopius, was a frank disbeliever in the witch-pact and the witch-confessions. It was his fellow Arminian, Grevius, who first demonstrated the iniquity of torture, the fruitful source of such confessions throughout Christendom; and that other Dutchman, Balthasar Bekker, who in 1691 struck at the root of the terror by doubting the Devil himself, was but the last of a long line of such bold thinkers. These were of course in advance of their fellows; but that Holland was throughout the century a refuge for the victims and the foes of witch-persecution in neighbor lands would seem to point to a general skepticism, and how cautious, with all their credulity, even Calvinist divines had grown in such an atmosphere, New England learned in 1692 when she asked an opinion from her New York neighbors.[1]

No wonder, then, that (as Mrs. Van Rensselaer tells us) "the one and only sign of the delusion . . . to be found in the

[1] Mass. Hist. Soc., *Proceedings*, second ser., I. 348–358. See p. 195, below.

annals of the Dutch province is a fear expressed by Governor
Kieft that the Indian medicine-men were directing their in-
cantations against himself." [1]   Accusations of witchcraft the
New York jurisdiction did not wholly escape; but they followed the English occupation and were, in differing ways, a
legacy from New England.   Even the Dutch dominion had
included towns peopled from New England; and it was to
these that in 1662 (the same year in which, as we have seen,
he was interceding with the Connecticut government for his
young kinswoman Judith Varlet) [2] Governor Stuyvesant
found it wise, while granting them their own magistrates and
their own courts, to prescribe that "in dark and dubious
matters, especially in witchcrafts, the party aggrieved might
appeal to the Governor and Council." [3]   But when in 1664
the English king bestowed upon his brother, the Duke of
York, the territory occupied by the Dutch colony and equipped
him with the means to take it by force, he added to the gift
that greater eastern half of Long Island which had not only
been settled, but till now had been governed, by the New
Englanders.   There, from the first, witchcraft was in thought;
for the earliest settlement, at Southampton, had adopted for
its code the law of Moses as codified by the Rev. John Cotton, with the death penalty both for witchcraft and for consulting a witch. [4]   Already in 1658 Elizabeth Garlick, of
Easthampton, had been indicted for witchcraft and sent to
Connecticut for trial. [5]   It is intelligible, therefore, that in

---

[1] *History of the City of New York in the Seventeenth Century*, I. 203.

[2] See p. 18, note 2.

[3] Bolton, *History of the County of Westchester* (revised ed., New York, 1881),
II. 280, quoting vol. XXI. 233–238 of the "Albany Records."

[4] Howell, *Southampton*, pp. 47, 465; *The First Book of Records of the Town
of Southampton* (Sag Harbor, 1874), p. 18 ff.

[5] The evidence against her may be found in the *Records of the Town of East-
Hampton* (Sag Harbor, 1887 ff.), I. 128–140, 152–155, the record of the Connecti-
cut court (she was acquitted) in the *Historical Magazine*, VI. 53, and a letter of
Governor Winthrop to the Easthamptonians in the *Public Records of Connecticut*,

1665, the very first year of English control at New York, there came up from Seatalcott, or Setauket, the later Brookhaven, whose settlers had been drawn from the region of Boston, a case of witchcraft for trial by the supreme court of the colony, the "Court of Assizes." [1]

The two documents which make up the extant record of this case, with those relating to a woman who crossed the border after trial for witchcraft in Connecticut, form, so far as is known, the entire witch-annals of the New York province. They must serve us here in lieu of a narrative.

The documents of the Hall case, first printed perhaps in the New York *National Advocate* (August 2, 1821) and thence borrowed by Niles's *Weekly Register* (August 11), were included by Yates (with a part of the Harrison papers) in the appendix to his edition of Smith's *History of New York* (Albany, 1814), and more fully printed by O'Callaghan in his *Documentary History of New York* (quarto ed., IV. 85–88; octavo ed., IV. 133–138). Those of the Harrison case, more fully ferreted out by Mr. Paltsits, are printed by him with especial care and with valuable notes, in the *Minutes of the Executive Council of New York* (Albany, 1910), I. 390–395, II. 52–55. The originals of the Hall documents perished in the fire which befell the State Capitol at Albany on March 29, 1911; the Harrison documents were but slightly damaged.

I. 572–573. That Mary Wright, of Oyster Bay, who in 1660 was punished for Quakerism in Boston, was sent thither on a charge of witchcraft, as has been stated, seems contradicted by what we know of her case (see Hutchinson, *History of Massachusetts*, I., ch. I., *sub anno* 1660; Bishop, *New-England Judged*, ed. of 1703, pp. 220, 340, 461; *N. Y. Gen. and Biog. Record*, III. 37 ff.)

[1] This colonial "Court of Assizes" was made up of the governor and his council, with the sheriff of the colony and the justices of the three "ridings." It was a new creation, and, having come together on September 28 for its first annual session, it found this among its earliest cases. It was, however, with the aid of members of this court that in the preceding winter Governor Nicolls had drawn the code—"the Duke's Laws," as they were to be called—which now governed the colony.

THE CASES OF HALL AND HARRISON

At the Court of Assizes held in New Yorke
the 2d day of October 1665 etc.
*The Tryall of Ralph Hall and Mary his wife, upon suspicion
of Witchcraft.*[1]

The names of the Persons who served on the Grand Jury.[2]

Thomas Baker, Foreman of the Jury,
of East Hampton.
Capt John Symonds of Hempsteed.
Mr Hallet
Anthony Waters } Jamaica

[1] Their troubles antedated the change in government, and it would seem
that at first their neighbors were on their side; for, under date of June 9, 1664,
the town records recite that "The magistrates haveing Considdered the Com-
plaintes of Hall and his wife against mr. Smith, doo judge the sayde mr. Smith
hath not suffitienly made good what he hath sd. of her, and therefore mr. Smith
is orderred to pay the woman five markes." (*Records, Town of Brookhaven, up
to* 1800, Patchogue, 1880, p. 38.) But they had made a dangerous foe, for at
Setauket "Mr." Smith could then hardly have meant any other than that well-
known Long Island character, Richard Smith, the founder of Smithtown, who
had himself at Boston and at Southampton experienced imprisonment and
banishment for Quakerism or Quakerly behavior, but was now a man of note in
his region—the "Bull" Smith of local legend. (Bishop, *New England Judged*,
ed. of 1703, p. 11; Howell, *Early History of Southampton, L. I.*, second ed.,
Albany, 1887, p. 438; *Early Long Island Wills*, New York, 1897, p. 78 ff.)

[2] Of this jury only the foreman was from the part of Long Island just
gained from New England. The four next named, though English, were from
those western townships which under Dutch rule had been a place of refuge for
sectaries of every sort. "Mr. Hallet" was probably William Hallett, the sheriff
who in 1656 had lost his place by opening his house to Baptist preaching. Most
puzzling is "Mr. Nicolls of Stamford"—for Stamford was not even claimed by
the New York province. Can it be that William Nicolls (son of Matthias Nicolls,
now secretary of the province and a member of the court), who was later to have
so large a place in New York history, had temporarily established himself at
Stamford, on the border? Notable among the six New Yorkers is the name of
Jacob Leisler, later to play so strange a rôle.

Thomas Wandall of Marshpath[1] Kills.

Mr Nicolls of Stamford

Balthazer de Haart

John Garland

Jacob Leisler

Anthonio de Mill   } of New Yorke.

Alexander Munro

Thomas Searle

The Prisoners being brought to the Barr by Allard Anthony, Sheriffe of New Yorke, This following Indictmt was read, first against Ralph Hall and then agst Mary his wife, vizt.

The Constable and Overseers of the Towne of Seatallcott, in the East Riding of Yorkshire[2] upon Long Island, Do Present for our Soveraigne Lord the King, That Ralph Hall of Seatallcott aforesaid, upon the 25th day of December, being Christmas day last was Twelve Monthes,[3] in the 15th yeare of the Raigne of our Soveraigne Lord, Charles the Second, by the Grace of God, King of England, Scotland, France and Ireland, Defender of the Faith etc, and severall other dayes and times since that day, by some detestable and wicked Arts, commonly called Witchcraft and Sorcery, did (as is suspected) maliciously and feloniously, practice and Exercise at the said towne of Seatalcott in the East Riding of Yorkshire on Long Island aforesaid, on the Person of George Wood, late of the same place, by wch wicked and detestable Arts, the said George Wood (as is suspected) most dangerously and mortally sickned and languished, And not long after by the aforesaid wicked and detestable Arts, the said George Wood (as is likewise suspected) dyed.

Moreover, The Constable and overseers of the said Towne of Seatalcott, in the East Riding of Yorkshire upon Long Island aforesaid, do further Present for our Soveraigne Lord the King, That some while after the death of the aforesaid

---

[1] Maspeth.

[2] When, in honor of its new proprietor, New Amsterdam became New York, Long Island was for the same reason named "Yorkshire." Its "East Riding" was the portion, now Suffolk county, which had hitherto been New England's.

[3] *I. e.*, a year ago last Christmas—December 25, 1663: the years of Charles II.'s reign were reckoned from the death of his father.

George Wood, The said Ralph Hall did (as is suspected) divers times by the like wicked and detestable Arts, commonly called Witchcraft and Sorcery, Maliciously and feloniously practise and Exercise at the said Towne of Seatalcott, in the East Riding of Yorkshire upon Long Island aforesaid, on the Person of an Infant Childe of Ann Rogers, widdow of the aforesaid George Wood deceased, by wh wicked and detestable Arts, the said Infant Childe (as is suspected) most dangerously and mortally sickned and languished, and not long after by the said Wicked and detestable Arts (as is likewise suspected) dyed, And so the said Constable and Overseers do Present, That the said George Wood, and the sd Infante sd[1] Childe by the wayes and meanes aforesaid, most wickedly maliciously and feloniously were (as is suspected) murdered by the said Ralph Hall at the times and places aforesaid, agst the Peace of Our Soveraigne Lord the King and against the Laws of this Government in such Cases Provided.[2]

The like Indictmt was read, against Mary the wife of Ralph Hall.

There upon, severall Depositions, accusing the Prisonrs of the fact for which they were endicted were read, but no witnesse appeared to give Testimony in Court *viva voce*.

Then the Clarke[3] calling upon Ralph Hall, bad him hold up his hand, and read as followes.

Ralph Hall thou standest here indicted, for that having not the feare of God before thine eyes, Thou did'st upon the 25th day of December, being Christmas day last was 12 Moneths, and at sev'all other times since, as is suspected, by some wicked and detestable Arts, commonly called witchcraft and Sorcery, maliciously and feloniously practice and Exer-

---

[1] This repetition of "s^d" is clearly accidental.

[2] "The Laws of this Government"—"the Duke's laws," as they were later called—had been drawn up in the preceding winter by Governor Nicolls himself, with the aid of other members of this court; and, though based on those of the New England colonies, they omitted all mention of witchcraft. That was significant; but it meant only that there was no provision for its punishment *per se*, as insult to the majesty of Heaven: harm wrought by witchcraft, whether to person or property, was covered by the general statutes, and where, as in this case, the harm charged was death, the offense (as the indictment shows) was accounted murder.

[3] The clerk.

cise, upon the Bodyes of George Wood, and an Infant Childe
of Ann Rogers, by which said Arts, the said George Wood and
the Infant Childe (as is suspected) most dangerously and mortally fell sick, and languisht unto death. Ralph Hall, what
dost thou say for thyselfe, art thou guilty, or not guilty?

Mary the wife of Ralph Hall was called upon in like manner.

They both Pleaded not guilty and threw themselves to
bee Tryed by God and the Country.

Where upon, their Case was referr'd to the Jury, who
brought in to the Court, this following verdict *vizt.*[1]

Wee having seriously considered the Case committed to
our Charge, against the Prisonrs at the Barr, and having well
weighed the Evidence, wee finde that there are some suspi-
tions by the Evidence, of what the woman is Charged with,
but nothing considerable of value to take away her life. But
in reference to the man wee finde nothing considerable to
charge him with.

The Court there upon, gave this sentence, That the man
should bee bound Body and Goods for his wives Apperance,
at the next Sessions, and so on from Sessions to Sessions as
long as they stay wthin this Government, In the meane while,
to bee of their good Behavior. So they were return'd into
the Sheriffs Custody, and upon Entring into a Recognizance,
according to the Sentence of the Court, they were released.

A Release to Ralph Hall and Mary his wife from the Recognizance they entred into at the Assizes.

These Are to Certify all whom it may Concerne That
Ralph Hall and Mary his wife (at present living upon Great
Minifords Island)[2] are hereby released and acquitted from
any and all Recognizances, bonds of appearance or othr obligations—entred into by them or either of them for the peace
or good behavior upon account of any accusation or Indic-
temt upon suspition of Witch Craft brought into the Cort
of Assizes against them in the year 1665. There haveving
beene no direct proofes nor furthr prosecucion of them or

---

[1] *Videlicet*, "to wit": we now abbreviate it by "viz."
[2] Now "City Island"—in Long Island Sound, at its western end.

eithr of them since.—Given undr my hand at Fort James in New Yorke this 21th day of August 1668.

R. Nicolls.

At the Fort July 7th 1670.
Before the Governor.

Upon the Complaint of Thomas Hunt Sen'r and Edward Waters on behalfe of the Towne of West Chester against a Woman suspected for a Witch who they desire may not live in their Towne; The Woman appeares with Capt. Ponton[1] to justify her selfe; her Name is Katharine Harryson.[2]

Their Peticion, as also another from Jamaica against her settling there were read.

Shee saith shee hath lived at Wethersfield 19 yeares, and came from England thither; Shee was in Prison 12 Months.

Shee was tryed for Witchcraft at Hartford in May last, found guilty by the Jury, but acquitted by the Bench, and released out of Prison, putting her in minde of her Promise to remove.[3]

---

[1] Captain Richard Panton, of West Chester, in whose home she had found shelter.

[2] Katharine Harrison was the widow of John Harrison, of Wethersfield, who died in 1666, leaving her an ample estate and three daughters. Rebecca, the eldest (born February 10, 1654), became at some time before June 28, 1671, the wife of Josiah Hunt of West Chester, or Westchester, son of that Thomas Hunt who now (July 7) is named as a complainant against her on behalf of that town, but in a following document (August 24) appears on her behalf. It is possible that this marriage antedated her coming to West Chester and explains it, but more likely that it was a result of it and explains the changing attitude of Thomas Hunt. (See Adams and Stiles, *History of Ancient Wethersfield*, New York, 1904, I. 682, II. 416; *N. E. Hist. and Gen. Register*, XVIII. 58; *N. Y. Gen. and Biog. Record*, XLIII. 117; *N. Y. Executive Council Minutes*, I. 53, note.)

[3] There then follows a transcript, from the records of the Connecticut Court of Assistants, of this action in her case—in its session of May 20, 1670. The documents of her trial, still extant at Hartford in the records of the county court and in those of the Court of Assistants (I. 1–7), and in part printed in the *Connecticut Colonial Records* (II. 118, 132), in Adams and Stiles, *Ancient Wethersfield* (I. 682–684), and in Taylor, *The Witchcraft Delusion in Colonial Connecticut* (New York, 1908), pp. 47–61, show that she was imprisoned and indicted in May, 1669, tried in October and found guilty by a jury, but by a special Court of Assistants, to which the General Assembly had referred the matter with power, was in May, 1670, dismissed, as stated above, with a reminder of her promise to leave Wethersfield.

An Ordr for Katherine Harrison to Remove from Westchestr.

Whereas Complaint hath beene made unto me by the Inhabitants of Westchestr agt Katherine Harrison late of Wethersfeild in his Ma'ties Colony of Conecticott widdow. That contrary to the consent and good liking of the Towne she would settle amongst them and she being reputed to be a person lyeing undr the Supposicion of Witchcraft hath given some cause of apprehension to the Inhabitants there, To the end their Jealousyes and feares as to this perticuler may be removed, I have thought fitt to ordr and appoint that the Constable and Overseers of the Towne of Westchestr do give warning to the said Katherine Harrison to remove out of their precincts in some short tyme after notice given, and they are likewise to admonish her to retorne to the place of her former abode, that they nor their neighbours may receive no furthr disturbance by her. Given undr my hand at Fort James in New Yorke this 7th day of July 1670.

[Francis Lovelace].

An Ordr for Katherine Harrison and Captn Richard Panton to appeare at the Fort before the Governor.

Whereas Complaint hath beene made unto me by the Inhabitants of Westchestr agt Katherine Harrison widdow That she doth neglect or refuse to obey my late Ordr concerning her removall out of the said Towne, These are to require you that you give notice unto the said Katherine Harrison as also unto Captn Richard Panton at whose house she resydeth, That they make their personall appearance before me in this place on Wednesday next being the 24th of this Instant month, when those of the Towne that have ought to object agt them doe likewise attend, where I shall endeavor a Composure of this difference betweene them. Given undr my hand at Fort James in New Yorke this 20th day of August 1670.

[Francis Lovelace.]

To the Constable of Westchestr.

Pres't   At the Fort. Aug: 24th 1670.

    The Governour
    Mr. Delavall
    The Secretary

The Matt'r to bee considered of is the Complaint of the Towne of West-chester against Katharine Harryson Widdow suspected of Witch-craft etc:

They being all appointed to appeare before the Governour this day;

There appeared for the Towne Edward Waters Constable and John Quinby;

For the Woman Capt. Ponton, Thomas Hunt Senr, and Junr, Roger Townsend, and one More.[1]

Capt. Ponton produced a Lett'r from Capt. Talcott[2] to him in Justification of the Womans Innocency, and another Letter from John Allen Secretary of Connecticott Governm't, in excuse of not sending the Womans Papers.

Josiah Willard[3] being desired to say what hee knew concerning the Woman, making Relation of what is certifyed by Mr. Allen, hee is one of that Governm't that knew of her Arraignment, and was spoken to (that hee would bee present) by the Constable, but hath nothing to say further.

It being taken into Consideracion, It is Ordered that the Discussion of this Matter bee referrd to the next Gen[er]al Court of Assizes; In the meane time that shee give Security for her good Behaviour, during the time of her Abode amongst them at West-Chester.

A warrant to the Constable of Westchestr to take an Account of the Goods of Katherine Harrison.

These are to require you to take an Account of such Goods as have lately beene brought from out of his Ma'ties Colony of Conecticott unto Katherine Harrison, and having taken a

---

[1] *I. e.*, one more appeared.

[2] Captain John Talcott, then treasurer of the Connecticut colony, was one of its foremost men. He was a member of the Court of Assistants, and was doubtless largely responsible for its action. He was well known at West Chester, for in 1663 at the head of a troop from Connecticut he had taken the place from the Dutch.

[3] Of Wethersfield—a trader, and doubtless here on some mercantile errand. He was a brother of the Rev. Samuel Willard, whom we have met (pp. 21–22) and shall meet again.

Note of the perticulers that you retorne the Same unto me for
the doeing whereof this shall be yor warrant. Given undr my
hand at Fort James in New Yorke this 25th day of August 1670.

[FRANCIS LOVELACE.]

To the present Constable of Westchester.

An Ordr concerning Katherine Harrison.

Whereas severall Adresses have beene made unto me by
some of the Inhabitants of Westchestr on behalfe of the rest
desiring that Katherine Harrison late of Wethersfeild in his
Ma'ties Colony of Connecticott widdow at present residing
in their Towne may be ordered to remove from thence and not
permitted to stay wthin their Jurisdiction upon an apprehension they have of her grounded upon some troubles she hath
layne undr at Wethersfeild upon suspition of Witchcraft, the
reasons whereof do not so clearly appeare unto me, Yett not-
wthstanding to give as much satisfaction as may be to the
Complts[1] who pretend their feares to be of a publique Concerne, I have not thought fitt absolutely to determyne the
mattr at present, but do suspend it untill the next Genrll
Cort of Assizes, when there will be a full meeting of the Coun-
cell and Justices of the peace to debate and conclude the
same. In the meane tyme the said Katherine Harrison wth
her Children may remaine in the Towne of Westchestr where
she now is wthout disturbance or molestation, she having
given sufficient security for her Civill carriage and good behaviour. Given undr my hand at Fort James in New York
this 25th day of August in the 22th yeare of his Ma'ties
Raigne Annoq.[2] Domini 1670.

[FRANCIS LOVELACE.]

Anno 1670.

*Appeals, Actions, Presentmts etc. Entred for Hearing and Tryall
    at the Gen[er]all Cort of Assizes to bee held in New Yorke be-
    ginning on the first Wednesday of Octobr 1670.*

Katherine Harryson bound over to appeare upon the
Complt of the Inhabitants of Westchester upon suspicion of
Witch-craft.

---

[1] Complainants.

[2] *I. e.*, "*and* in the year of Our Lord": the *q* stands for the enclitic *que*, and.

In the case of Katherine Harryson Widdow, who was bound to the good Behaviour upon Complt of some of the Inhabitants of Westchester untill the holding of this Court, It is Ordered, that in regard there is nothing appears against her deserving the continuance of that obligacion shee is to bee releast from it, and hath Liberty to remaine in the Towne of Westchester where shee now resides, or any where else in the Governmt during her pleasure.[1]

[FRANCIS LOVELACE.]

---

[1] Alas, it is to be feared that her neighbors did not make her life happy. Certain documents as to her property (printed in the *N. Y. Executive Council Minutes*, II. 393–395) make it probable that she left Westchester in May; and an entry of May 9, 1672, in the records (yet unpublished) of the Connecticut Court of Assistants—"The court upon acc't of work done by Katherin Harrison for Daniel Gerrad doe see cause to remit of the five pounds Katherin Harrison is to pay Dan'll Gerrad Twenty Shillings"—may mean that she was permitted to return to Hartford, though perhaps it refers to work done while she was in custody. In any case, she was in New York later, for, "during the temporary occupation of New York by the Dutch in 1673, an accusation was brought against her before Governor Colve, but was promptly and contemptuously dismissed" (Drake, *Annals of Witchcraft*, Boston, 1869, pp. 133–134; Levermore, "Witchcraft in Connecticut," in the *New Englander*, XLIV. 812).

LITHOBOLIA, BY RICHARD CHAMBERLAIN,
1698

INTRODUCTION

THAT the "R. C. Esq." who in 1698 published at London the following narrative was Richard Chamberlain, sometime secretary of the province of New Hampshire, is beyond all doubt. His own statement that he was in that province in His Majesty's service, and lodged at George Walton's, in a year easily recognized by internal evidence as 1682, would suffice to identify him; for not only was there no other "R. C." in that well-known circle, but the Puritan pastor at Portsmouth, writing at that very time of this very episode (see p. 35, above), makes the secretary a lodger at George Walton's and a source of information as to these happenings. Nor can this story be any bookseller's expansion of the narrative then published; for its mass of added detail squares not less perfectly with every local tradition. If "the Contents hereof" are not now to be found in the records of His Majesty's "Council-Court held for that province," where Chamberlain himself doubtless inscribed them, it is amply explained by the mutilation and scattering of those records; and enough remains (see p. 31, note) to show the affair matter of record.

There was reason, too, why precisely Richard Chamberlain should have been one of the objects of such wrath, human or infernal, as found utterance in this "stonery." It was the very crisis of a dispute that for half a century had disturbed the peace of New Hampshire. John Mason, to whom in 1629 that region had been granted and who in 1631 had undertaken its settlement, had died in 1635 without making adequate provision for its administration. The multiplying col-

onists, who even before and during his personal control had
occupied lands by other title than his grant, now ignored his
claims; and the widow and infant grandchildren who were
his heirs soon left them wholly to their own devices. The
growing Puritan element leaned on the neighboring Massachusetts, and that colony discovered that its own charter
could be interpreted to include the territory now settled in
New Hampshire. Lands were thenceforward often granted by
the Boston government, and oftener by the town authorities
set up by it in New Hampshire; and the feeble protests of
the Mason heirs found little hearing, the political changes in
England making it impossible to enforce them. But with the
Restoration, in 1660, matters changed, and by 1680 Robert
Mason had not only won from a venal court the rejection of
the Massachusetts claim and full recognition of his proprietor-
ship in New Hampshire, but was given a seat in the Council
of the royal province into which the colony was now recon-
stituted and was permitted to nominate its governor and secretary. A governor was not at once found; but as its secretary he named Richard Chamberlain.

Of Chamberlain's history we know little. The Lords of
Trade had stipulated that the new secretary should be "well
versed in the law," and there can be little doubt that he was
that "Richard Chamberlayne, son and heir of William C., of
London, gent.," who in May, 1651, was admitted to Gray's
Inn (not six months after Mason's all-powerful kinsman and
adviser, Edward Randolph), who was "called to the bar 11 Nov.
1659, ancient 17 April 1676," and whose daughter Elizabeth
was in 1695 wedded to that "much Honoured Mart. Lumley,
Esq.," to whom he dedicates this booklet. If so he was of a
good family, whose pedigree can be traced for several generations in the visitations of the heralds. Perhaps already an
acquaintance of Mason, he soon became his intimate friend.
They crossed the sea together, arriving in New Hampshire

in December, 1680, and at once entering on their functions in the government. Though outvoted in the Council, Mason proceeded to the enforcement of his territorial claims, and soon by his demands, however legal, earned fear and hate not only for himself but for Chamberlain, who was believed to have instigated them. The colonists were left their improved lands, on payment of a moderate quit-rent; but all wild lands, including their pastures and their woodlands, Mason counted his, to grant at will. But the colonists, except a few Quakers, stoutly held out, and Mason returned to England to urge his case, leaving Chamberlain to bear the brunt. The latter had his abode on Great Island, under the guns of the fort, at the house of the Quaker George Walton; and it is there, in the summer of 1682, that the following narrative has its scene.

The booklet is now very rare, and this is probably the first complete reimpression of it. With the exception of the prefatory matter it was, however, reprinted in 1861 in the *Historical Magazine*, V. 321–327.

LITHOBOLIA

Lithobolia: or, the Stone-Throwing Devil. Being an Exact and True Account (by way of Journal) of the various Actions of Infernal Spirits, or (Devils Incarnate) Witches, or both; and the great Disturbance and Amazement they gave to George Waltons Family, at a place call'd Great Island in the Province of New-Hantshire in New-England, chiefly in Throwing about (by an Invisible hand) Stone, Bricks, and Brick-bats of all Sizes, with several other things, as Hammers, Mauls, Iron-Crows, Spits, and other Domestick Utensils, as came into their Hellish Minds, and this for the space of a Quarter of a Year.

By R. C. Esq; who was a Sojourner in the same Family the whole time, and an Ocular Witness of these Diabolick Inventions.

The Contents hereof being manifestly known to the Inhabitants of that Province, and Persons of other Provinces, and is upon Record in his Majesties Council-Court held for that Province.

London, Printed, and are to be Sold by E. Whitlook near Stationers-Hall, 1698.[1]

To The much Honoured Mart. Lumley, Esq;[2]

Sir,

As the subsequent Script deserves not to be called a Book, so these precedent Lines presume not to a Dedication: But, Sir, it is an occasion that I am ambitious to lay hold on, to discover to You by this Epitome (as it were) the propension

---

[1] Title-page of the original.

[2] Martin Lumley, Esq. (1662–1710), son of Sir Martin Lumley, of Great Bardfield, Essex, himself succeeded to that baronetcy in 1702. When *Lithobolia* was written he had probably just become a kinsman of the author; for in 1695 he married for his second wife "Elizabeth, daughter of Richard Chamberlayn of Gray's Inn." (See article of J. W. Dean, in *N. E. Hist. and Gen. Register*, XLIII. 183–185.)

and inclination I have to give a more full and perfect demonstration of the Honour, Love, and Service, I own (as I think my self oblig'd) to have for You. To a Sober, Judicious, and well Principled Person, such as your Self, plain Truths are much more agreeable than the most charming and surprising Romance or Novel, with all the strange turns and events. That this is of the first sort, (as I have formerly upon Record attested) I do now aver and protest; yet neither is it less strange than true, and so may be capable of giving you some Diversion for an hour: For this interruption of your more serious ones, I cannot doubt your candor and clemency, in pardoning it, that so well know (and do most sensibly acknowledg) your high Worth and Goodness; and that the Relation I am Dignified with, infers a mutual Patronization.

Sir, I am

Your most Humble Servant,

R. C.

To the much Honoured R. F. Esq;[1]

To tell strange feats of Dæmons, here I am;
Strange, but most true they are, ev'n to a Dram,
Tho' Sadduceans cry, 'tis all a Sham.

Here's Stony Arg'uments of persuasive Dint,
They'l not believe it, told, nor yet in Print:
What should the Reason be?   The Devil's in't.

And yet they wish to be convinc'd by Sight,
Assur'd by Apparition of a Sprite;
But Learned Brown[2] doth state the matter right:

Satan will never Instrumental be
Of so much Good, to' Appear to them; for he
Hath them sure by their Infidelity.

But you, my Noble Friend, know better things;
Your Faith, mounted on Religions Wings,
Sets you above the Clouds whence Error springs.

---

[1] "R. F., Esq.," has not been identified.
[2] Sir Thomas Browne. See his *Religio Medici*, pt. I., § 30.

Your Soul reflecting on this lower Sphear,
Of froth and vanity, joys oft to hear
The Sacred Ora'₤les, where all Truths appear,

Which will Conduct out of this Labyrinth of Night,
And lead you to the source of Intellect'ual Light.

Which is the Hearty Prayer of
Your most faithful Humble Servant,
R. C.

Lithobolia: or, the Stone-throwing Devil, etc.

SUCH is the Sceptical Humour of this Age for Incredulity, (not to say Infidelity,) That I wonder they do not take up and profess, in terms, the Pyrrhonian Doctrine of disbelieving their very Senses. For that which I am going to relate happening to cease in the Province of New-Hampshire in America, just upon that Governour's Arrival and Appearance at the Council there, who was informed by my self, and several other Gentlemen of the Council, and other considerable Persons, of the true and certain Reality hereof, yet he continued tenacious in the Opinion that we were all imposed upon by the waggery of some unlucky Boys;[1] which, considering the Circumstances and Passages hereafter mentioned, was altogether impossible.

I have a Wonder to relate; for such (I take it) is so to be termed whatsoever is Præternatural, and not assignable to, or the effect of, Natural Causes: It is a *Lithobolia*,[2] or Stone-throwing, which happened by Witchcraft (as was supposed) and maliciously perpetrated by an Elderly Woman, a Neighbour suspected, and (I think) formerly detected for such kind of Diabolical Tricks and Practises;[3] and the wicked Instiga-

---

[1] Edward Cranfield, first royal governor of New Hampshire. He arrived in October, 1682, and left in June, 1685. Though Mason's nominee, he for some time leaned to the side of the colonists against the methods of Mason and Chamberlain.

[2] "*Lithobolia*" is, of course, only Greek for "stone-throwing."

[3] Who she was it is not hard to guess. On July 4, 1682, Hannah Jones begged the "advice and relief" of the President and Council "in regard of George Walton's dealing with her, who falsely accuseth her of what she is clear of, and hath so far prevailed that upon that account your humble petitioner is bound in a bond of the peace; since which said Walton's horse breaks into her pasture and

tion did arise upon the account of some small quantity of Land in her Field, which she pretended was unjustly taken into the Land of the Person where the Scene of this Matter lay, and was her Right; she having been often very clamorous about that Affair, and heard to say, with much Bitterness, that her Neighbour (*innuendo*[1] the fore-mentioned Person, his Name George Walton)[2] should never quietly injoy that

doth her damage." (Provincial Records, in New Hampshire Hist. Soc., *Collections*, VIII. 99.) Of her being "formerly detected" in witchcraft there is no record; but she was a daughter of Thomas Walford, and her mother, Jane Walford, had in 1656 been tried for witchcraft, and, though cleared, found it necessary in 1669 to bring an action for slander against a physician who again accused her. (N. H. Hist. Soc., *Collections*, I. 255–257; *Documents and Records relating to the Province of New Hampshire*, I. 217–219; *Probate Records of the Province of New Hampshire*, I. 87–92, 222–224.) Jane Walford was now dead (*Probate Records*, I. 92); but there was reason enough for George Walton to fear the malice of her daughter. For Thomas Walford, a blacksmith who in 1623 had come with Gorges to Weymouth, who had later become the earliest settler in Charlestown, and who in 1631, expelled from the Bay for his Anglican tenets, had found a refuge at Portsmouth, had prospered at last, and at his death in 1666 left to his heirs broad acres. But these lands were among those forfeit to the Mason claim, and Walton was a buyer. (*Probate Records*, I. 299, and *cf.* p. 37, above, note 1.) Now that the government was passing into the hands of the Mason party, what hope was there except from Heaven or Hell? "Your petitioner," prayed Hannah Jones, "being under bond, knows not what to do to help herself." It was doubtless Secretary Chamberlain who as a justice had put her under bond; but the planters still had a majority in the Council, and Goodwife Jones was ordered to complain to Captain Stileman "if she be at any time, during her being bound to the good behavior, injured by the said Geo. Walton." Her complaint came: on August 31 Elizabeth Clark, aged forty-two, made affidavit to Deputy-President Stileman "that she heard George Walton say that he believed in his heart and conscience that Grandma Jones was a witch, and would say so to his dying day." But Walton, too, had evidence to offer: on September 4 Samuel Clark testified "that he was present when Goody Jones and Geo. Walton were talking together, and he heard the said Goody Jones call the said Walton a wizzard, and that she said, if he told her of her mother, she would throw stones at his head, and this was on Friday, the 25th of August, 1682." And other witnesses testified that on that day "they saw several stones to fly," though they "saw no hand or person to throw them," and that "the said George Walton was hit several times." (Provincial Records, in N. H. Hist Soc., *Collections*, VIII. 99–100.) But this is to anticipate the relation.

[1] "Hinting at."

[2] As to Walton see introduction and p. 35, note 1, above. A letter from the Rev. Lucius Alden, of Newcastle, printed in 1862 in the *Historical Magazine*, VI. 159, describes his house and its site and identifies other people and places mentioned in this narrative.

piece of Ground. Which, as it has confirm'd my self and others in the Opinion that there are such things as Witches, and the Effects of Witchcraft, or at least of the mischievous Actions of Evil Spirits; which some do as little give Credit to, as in the Case of Witches, utterly rejecting both their Operations and their Beings, we having been Eye-Witnesses of this Matter almost every Day for a quarter of a Year together; so it may be a means to rectifie the depraved Judgment and Sentiments of other disbelieving Persons, and absolutely convince them of their Error, if they please to hear, without prejudice, the plain, but most true Narration of it; which was thus.

Some time ago being in America (in His then Majesty's Service) I was lodg'd in the said George Walton's House, a Planter there, and on a Sunday Night,[1] about Ten a Clock, many Stones were heard by my self, and the rest of the Family, to be thrown, and (with Noise) hit against the top and all sides of the House, after he the said Walton had been at his Fence-Gate, which was between him and his Neighbour one John Amazeen an Italian,[2] to view it; for it was again, as formerly it had been (the manner how being unknown) wrung off the Hinges, and cast upon the Ground; and in his being there, and return home with several Persons of (and frequenting) his family and House, about a flight shot distant from the Gate, they were all assaulted with a peal of Stones, (taken, we conceive, from the Rocks hard by the House) and this by unseen Hands or Agents. For by this time I was come down to them, having risen out of my Bed at this strange Alarm of all that were in the House, and do know that they all look'd out as narrowly as I did, or any Person could (it being a bright Moon-light Night), but cou'd make no Discovery. Thereupon, and because there came many Stones, and those pretty great ones, some as big as my Fist, into the Entry or Porch of the House, we withdrew into the next Room to the Porch,

---

[1] June 11, 1682. See p. 35, above, and *Mather Papers*, p. 361.

[2] "John the Greek," as he was called, the illiterate constable of Great Island, was one of the most stubborn in refusing to pay dues to Mason. He had married the widow of Jeremiah Walford (Hannah Jones's brother) and was the guardian of his son and estate. (*Probate Records*, I. 222–224; Provincial Records, in N. H. Hist. Soc., *Collections*, I. 71, 118.)

no Person having receiv'd any Hurt, (praised be Almighty
Providence, for certainly the infernal Agent, constant Enemy
to Mankind, had he not been over-ruled, intended no less than
Death or Maim) save only that two Youths were lightly hit,
one on the Leg, the other on the Thigh, notwithstanding the
Stones came so thick, and so forcibly against the sides of so
narrow a Room. Whilst we stood amazed at this Accident,
one of the Maidens imagined she saw them come from the
Hall, next to that we were in, where searching, (and in the
Cellar, down out of the Hall,) and finding no Body, another
and my self observed two little Stones in a short space successively to fall on the Floor, coming as from the Ceiling close
by us, and we concluded it must necessarily be done by means
extraordinary and præternatural. Coming again into the
Room where we first were (next the Porch), we had many of
these lapidary Salutations, but unfriendly ones; for, shutting
the Door, it was no small Surprise to me to have a good big
Stone come with great force and noise (just by my Head)
against the Door on the inside; and then shutting the other
Door, next the Hall, to have the like Accident; so going out
again, upon a necessary Occasion, to have another very near
my Body, clattering against the Board-wall of the House;
but it was a much greater, to be so near the danger of having
my Head broke with a Mall, or great Hammer brushing along
the top or roof of the Room from the other end, as I was walking in it, and lighting down by me; but it fell so, that my
Landlord had the greatest damage, his Windows (especially
those of the first mention'd Room) being with many Stones
miserably and strangely batter'd, most of the Stones giving
the Blow on the inside, and forcing the Bars, Lead, and hasps
of the Casements outwards, and yet falling back (sometimes
a Yard or two) into the Room; only one little Stone we took
out of the glass of the Window, where it lodg'd its self in the
breaking it, in a Hole exactly fit for the Stone. The Pewter
and Brass were frequently pelted, and sometimes thrown down
upon the Ground; for the Evil Spirit seemed then to affect
variety of Mischief, and diverted himself at this end after he
had done so much Execution at the other. So were two Candlesticks, after many hittings, at last struck off the Table where
they stood, and likewise a large Pewter Pot, with the force of

these Stones. Some of them were taken up hot, and (it seems) immediately coming out of the Fire; and some (which is not unremarkable) having been laid by me upon the Table along by couples, and numbred, were found missing; that is, two of them, as we return'd immediately to the Table, having turn'd our backs only to visit and view some new Stone-charge or Window-breach; and this Experiment was four or five times repeated, and I still found one or two missing of the Number, which we all mark'd, when I did but just remove the Light from off the Table, and step to the Door, and back again.

After this had continued in all the parts and sides of the first Room (and down the Chimney) for above four hours, I, weary of the Noise, and sleepy, went to Bed, and was no sooner fallen asleep, but was awakened with the unwelcome disturbance of another Battery of a different sort, it issuing with so prodigious a Noise against the thin Board-wall of my Chamber (which was within another) that I could not imagin it less than the fracture and downfall of great part of the Chamber, or at least of the Shelves, Books, Pictures, and other things, placed on that side, and on the Partition-Wall between the Anti-Chamber and the Door of mine. But the Noise immediately bringing up the Company below, they assured me no Mischief of that nature was done, and shewed me the biggest Stone that had as yet been made use of in this unaccountable Accident, weighing eight pound and an half, that had burst open my Chamber Door with a rebound from the Floor, as by the Dent and Bruise in it near the Door I found next Morning, done, probably, to make the greater Noise, and give the more Astonishment, which would sooner be effected by three Motions, and consequently three several Sounds, *viz.* one on the Ground, the next to and on the Door, and the last from it again to the Floor, then if it had been one single Blow upon the Door only; which ('tis probable) wou'd have split the Door, which was not permitted, nor so much as a square of the Glass-Window broken or crack'd (at that time) in all the Chamber. Glad thereof, and desiring them to leave me, and the Door shut, as it was before, I endeavoured once more to take my Rest, and was once more prevented by the like passage, with another like offensive Weapon, it being a whole Brick that lay in the anti-Chamber Chimney, and used again to the same malicious purpose as before, and in the same manner too, as by the mark in the Floor, whereon was some of the dust of the Brick, broken a little at the end, apparant next Morning, the Brick it self lying just at the Door. However, after I had lain a while, harkning to their Adventures below, I drop'd asleep again, and receiv'd no further Molestation that Night.

In the Morning (*Monday* Morning) I was inform'd by several of the Domesticks of more of the same kind of Trouble; among which the most signal was, the Vanishing of the Spit which stood in the Chimney Corner, and the sudden coming of it again down the same Chimney, sticking of it in a Log that lay in the Fireplace or Hearth; and then being by one of the Family set by on the other side of the Chimney, presently cast out of the Window into the Back-side. Also a pressing-Iron lying on the ledge of the Chimney back, was convey'd invisibly into the Yard. I should think it (too) not unworthy the Relation, that, discoursing then with some of the Family, and others, about what had past, I said, I thought it necessary to take and keep the great Stone, as a Proof and Evidence, for they had taken it down from my Chambers; and so I carried it up, laid it on my Table in my Chamber, and lock'd my Door, and going out upon occasions, and soon returning, I was told by my Landlady that it was, a little while after my going forth, removed again, with a Noise, which they all below heard, and was thrown into the anti-Chamber, and there I found it lying in the middle of it; thereupon I the second time carried it up, and laid it on the Table, and had it in my Custody a long time to show, for the Satisfaction of the Curious.

There were many more Stones thrown about in the House that Morning, and more in the Fields that Day, where the Master of the House was, and the Men at Work. Some more Mr. Woodbridge,[1] a Minister, and my self, in the Afternoon

[1] The Rev. Benjamin Woodbridge, who had begun in 1680 at Bristol, Rhode Island, his career as a preacher, but had dissatisfied a part of his flock (*Mather Papers*, pp. 695–696), and seems to have been seeking a fresh one in the north. It was through him that Pastor Moodey of Portsmouth sought, for Increase Mather's *Providences*, an account of the happenings on Great Island. (See above, p. 34, note 2, and *Mather Papers*, p. 360.)

did see (but could not any Hand throwing them) lighting near, and jumping and tumbling on the Grass: So did one Mrs. Clark, and her Son, and several others; and some of them felt them too.   One Person would not be perswaded but that the Boys at Work might throw them, and strait her little Boy standing by her was struck with a Stone on the Back, which caused him to fall a crying, and her (being convinc'd) to carry him away forth-with.

In the Evening, as soon as I had sup'd in the outer Room before mine, I took a little Musical-Instrument, and began to touch it (the Door indeed was then set open for Air), and a good big Stone came rumbling in, and as it were to lead the Dance, but upon a much different account than in the days of Old, and of old fabulous Inchantments, my Musick being none of the best.   The Noise of this brought up the Deputy-President's Wife,[1] and many others of the Neighbourhood that were below, who wonder'd to see this Stone followed (as it were) by many others, and a Pewter Spoon among the rest, all which fell strangely into the Room in their Presence, and were taken up by the Company.   And beside all this, there was seen by two Youths in the Orchard and Fields, as they said, a black Cat, at the time the Stones were toss'd about, and it was shot at, but missed, by its changing Places, and being immediately at some distance, and then out of sight, as they related: Agreeable to which, it may not be improper to insert, what was observed by two Maids, Grand-Children of Mr. Walton, on the Sunday Night, the beginning of this *Lithoboly.*   They did affirm, that as they were standing in the Porch-Chamber Window, they saw, as it were, a Person putting out a Hand out of the Hall Window, as throwing Stones toward the Porch or Entry; and we all know no Person was in the Hall except, at that instant, my self and another, having search'd diligently there, and wondring whence those should come that were about the same time drop'd near us; so far we were from doing it our selves, or seeing any other there to do it.

On *Monday* Night, about the Hour it first began, there were more Stones thrown in the Kitchin, and down the Chim-

---

[1] Mrs. Elias Stileman. Till the arrival of Governor Cranfield President Waldron and Deputy-President Stileman remained in power.

ney, one Captain Barefoot,[1] of the Council for that Province, being present, with others; and also (as I was going up to Bed) in an upper Chamber, and down those Stairs.

Upon *Tuesday* Night, about Ten, some five or six Stones were severally thrown into the Maid's Chamber near the Kitchin, and the Glass-Windows broke in three new places, and one of the Maids hit as she lay. At the same time was heard by them, and two young Men in the House, an odd, dismal sort of Whistling, and thereupon the Youths ran out, with intent to take the suppos'd Thrower of Stones, if possible; and on the back-side near the Window they heard the Noise (as they said) of something stepping a little way before them, as it were the trampling of a young Colt, as they fancied, but saw nothing; and going on, could discover nothing but that the Noise of the stepping or trampling was ceas'd, and then gone on a little before.

On *Saturday* Morning I found two Stones more on the Stairs; and so some were on Sunday Night convey'd into the Room next the Kitchin.

Upon *Monday* following Mr. Walton going (with his Men) by Water to some other Land, in a place called the Great Bay, and to a House where his Son was placed, they lay there that Night, and the next Morning had this Adventure. As the Men were all at work in the Woods, felling Wood, they were visited with another set of Stones, and they gathered up near upon a Hat-full, and put them between two Trees near adjoining, and returning from carrying Wood, to the Boat, the Hat and its contents (the Stones) were gone, and the Stones were presently after thrown about again, as before; and after search, found the Hat press'd together, and lying under a square piece of Timber at some distance from thence. They had them again at young Walton's House, and half a Brick thrown into a Cradle, out of which his young Child was newly taken up.

Here it may seem most proper to inform the Reader of a parallel passage, (*viz.*) what happened another time to my Landlord in his Boat; wherein going up to the same place

---

[1] The bluff and jovial Walter Barefoot, physician, politician, speculator, rescuer of Quakers and horror of Puritans, soon to be commandant, judge, acting governor, and at this moment as deputy collector especially obnoxious to the Massachusetts party, is well known to all students of New Hampshire history.

(the Great Bay) and loading it with Hay for his use at his own House, about the mid-way in the River (Pascataqua)[1] he found his Boat began to be in a sinking Condition, at which being much surpriz'd, upon search, he discover'd the cause to be the pulling out a Plug or Stopple in the bottom of the Boat, being fixed there for the more convenient letting out of the Rain-Water that might fall into it; a Contrivance and Combination of the old Serpent and the old Woman, or some other Witch or Wizard (in Revenge or innate Enmity) to have drown'd both my good Landlord and his Company.

On *Wednesday*, as they were at work again in the Woods, on a sudden they heard something gingle like Glass, or Metal, among the Trees, as it was falling, and being fallen to the Ground, they knew it to be a Stirrup which Mr. Walton had carried to the Boat, and laid under some Wood; and this being again laid by him in that very Boat, it was again thrown after him. The third time, he having put it upon his Girdle or Belt he wore about his Waste, buckled together before, but at that instant taken off because of the Heat of the Weather, and laid there again buckled, it was fetch'd away, and no more seen. Likewise the Graper, or little Anchor of the Boat, cast over-board, which caus'd the Boat to wind up; so staying and obstructing their Passage. Then the setting-Pole was divers times cast into the River, as they were coming back from the Great Bay, which put them to the trouble of Padling, that is, rowing about for it as often to retrieve it.

Being come to his own House, this Mr. Walton was charg'd again with a fresh Assault in the out-Houses; but we heard of none within doors until Friday after, when, in the Kitchin, were 4 or 5 Stones (one of them hot) taken out of the Fire, as I conceive, and so thrown about. I was then present, being newly come in with Mr. Walton from his middle Field (as he call'd it), where his Servants had been Mowing, and had six or seven of his old troublesome Companions, and I had one fall'n down by me there, and another thin flat Stone hit me on the Thigh with the flat side of it, so as to make me just feel, and to smart a little. In the same Day's Evening, as I was walking out in the Lane by the Field before-mentioned, a great Stone made a rusling Noise in the Stone-Fence between

---

[1] The Piscataqua.

the Field and the Lane, which seem'd to me (as it caus'd me
to cast my Eye that way by the Noise) to come out of the
Fence, as it were pull'd out from among those Stones loose,
but orderly laid close together, as the manner of such Fences
in that Country is, and so fell down upon the Ground. Some
Persons of Note being then in the Field (whose Names are
here under-written) to visit Mr. Walton there, are substantial Witnesses of this same Stonery, both in the Field, and
afterward in the House that Night, *viz.* one Mr. Hussey, Son
of a Counsellour there.[1] He took up one that having first
alighted on the Ground, with rebound from thence hit him on
the Heel; and he keeps it to show. And Captain Barefoot,
mentioned above, has that which (among other Stones) flew
into the Hall a little before Supper; which my self also saw as
it first came in at the upper part of the Door into the middle
of the Room; and then (tho' a good flat Stone, yet) was seen
to rowl over and over, as if trundled, under a Bed in the same
Room. In short, these Persons, being wonderously affected
with the Strangeness of these Passages, offer'd themselves
(desiring me to take them) as Testimonies; I did so, and
made a Memorandum, by way of Record, thereof, to this
effect. *Viz.*

These Persons under-written do hereby Attest the Truth of
    their being Eye-Witnesses of at least half a score Stones
    that Evening thrown invisibly into the Field, and in the
    Entry of the House, Hall, and one of the Chambers of
    George Walton's. *Viz.*

SAMUEL JENNINGS, Esq; Governour of West-Jarsey.
WALTER CLARK, Esq; Deputy-Governour of Road-Island.
Mr. ARTHUR COOK.
Mr. MATT. BORDEN of Road-Island.
Mr. OLIVER HOOTON of Barbados, Merchant.
Mr. T. MAUL of Salem in New-England, Merchant.
Captain WALTER BAREFOOT.
Mr. JOHN HUSSEY.
And the Wife of the said Mr. Hussey.[2]

[1] Of Christopher Hussey, of Hampton.
[2] The governors of West Jersey and Rhode Island are sufficiently identified by
their titles. Both were Quakers, as were all the others excepting Barefoot. Cook

On *Saturday, July*[1] 24, One of the Family, at the usual
hour at Night, observ'd some few (not above half a dozen)
of these natural (or rather unnatural) Weapons to fly into the
Kitchin, as formerly; but some of them in an unusual manner
lighting gently on him, or coming toward him so easily, as
that he took them before they fell to the Ground. I think
there was not any thing more that Night remarkable. But
as if the malicious Dæmon had laid up for Sunday and Monday,
then it was that he began (more furiously than formerly)
with a great Stone in the Kitchin, and so continued with
throwing down the Pewter-Dishes, etc. great part of it all at
once coming clattering down, without the stroke of a Stone,
little or great, to move it. Then about Midnight this impious Operation not ceasing, but trespassing with a *continu-
ando*,[2] 2 very great Stones, weighing above 30 pound a piece
(that used to lye in the Kitchin, in or near the Chimny) were
in the former, wonted, rebounding manner, let fly against my
Door and Wall in the ante-Chamber, but with some little
distance of time. This thundring Noise must needs bring
up the Men from below, as before, (I need not say to wake me)
to tell me the Effect, which was the beating down several
Pictures, and displacing abundance of things about my Chamber: but the Repetition of this Cannon-Play by these great
rumbling Engines, now ready at hand for the purpose, and the
like additional disturbance by four Bricks that lay in the
outer-Room Chimney (one of which having been so imploy'd
the first Sunday Night, as has been said) made me despair
of taking Rest, and so forced me to rise from my Bed. Then
finding my Door burst open, I also found many Stones, and
great pieces of Bricks, to fly in, breaking the Glass-Windows,
and a Paper-Light, sometimes inwards, sometimes outwards:
So hitting the Door of my Chamber as I came through from
the ante-Chamber, lighting very near me as I was fetching
the Candlestick, and afterward the Candle being struck out,
as I was going to light it again. So a little after, coming up

was a Philadelphian; Thomas Maule, the Salem merchant who was later (1695)
to stir such fury in Massachusetts by his arraignment of the Puritan régime.
What Maule thought of| witchcraft must be gathered not only from his own
book, but from that of his Beverly neighbor, the Rev. John Hale, pp. 155–161.

[1] June.   [2] A "to be continued."

for another Candle, and being at the Stare-foot door, a wooden
Mortar with great Noise struck against the Floor, and was
just at my Feet, only not touching me, moving from the other
end of the Kitchin where it used to lye. And when I came up
my self, and two more of the same House, we heard a Whistling,
as it were near us in the outer Room, several times. Among
the rest of the Tools made use of to disturb us, I found an old
Card for dressing Flax in my Chamber. Now for *Monday*
Night, (*June* 26) one of the severest. The disturbance began
in the Kitchin with Stones; then as I was at Supper above in
the ante-Chamber, the Window near which I sate at Table
was broke in 2 or 3 parts of it inwards, and one of the Stones
that broke it flew in, and I took it up at the further end of the
Room. The manner is observable; for one of the squares
was broke into 9 or 10 small square pieces, as if it had been
regularly mark'd out into such even squares by a Workman,
to the end some of these little pieces might fly in my Face
(as they did) and give me a surprize, but without any hurt. In
the mean time it went on in the Kitchin, whither I went
down, for Company, all or most of the Family, and a Neighbour, being there; where many Stones (some great ones)
came thick and threefold among us, and an old howing Iron,[1]
from a Room hard by, where such Utensils lay. Then, as if
I had been the design'd Object for that time, most of the Stones
that came (the smaller I mean) hit me (sometimes pretty hard)
to the number of above 20, near 30, as I remember, and whether
I remov'd, sit, or walk'd, I had them, and great ones sometimes
lighting gently on me, and in my Hand and Lap as I sate,
and falling to the Ground, and sometimes thumping against
the Wall, as near as could be to me, without touching me.
Then was a- Room over the Kitchin infested, that had not
been so before, and many Stones greater than usual lumbring
there over our Heads, not only to ours, but to the great Disturbance and Affrightment of some Children that lay there.
And for Variety, there were sometimes three great, distinct
Knocks, sometimes five such sounds as with a great Maul,
reiterated divers times.

On *Tuesday* Night (*June* 28) we were quiet; but not so
on *Wednesday*, when the Stones were play'd about in the House.

---

[1] A hoeing-iron—the metal part of a hoe.

And on *Thursday* Morning I found some things that hung on
Nails on the Wall in my Chamber, *viz.* a Spherical Sun-Dial,
etc. lying on the Ground, as knock'd down by some Brick or
Stone in the ante-Chamber.   But my Landlord had the worst
of that Day, tho' he kept the Field, being there invisibly hit
above 40 times, as he affirm'd to me, and he receiv'd some
shrowd[1] hurtful Blows on the Back, and other Parts, which
he much complained of, and said he thought he should have
reason to do, even to his dying day; and I observ'd that he
did so, he being departed this Life since.[2]

Besides this, Plants of Indian Corn were struck up by the
Roots almost, just as if they had been cut with some edged
Instrument, whereas *re vera*[3] they were seen to be eradicated,
or rooted up with nothing but the very Stones, altho' the in-
jurious Agent was altogether unseen.   And a sort of Noise,
like that of Snorting and Whistling, was heard near the Men
at Work in the Fields many times, many whereof I my self,
going thither, and being there, was a Witness of; and parting
thence I receiv'd a pretty hard Blow with a Stone on the Calf
of my Leg.   So it continued that day in two Fields, where
they were severally at Work: and my Landlord told me, he
often heard likewise a humming Noise in the Air by him, as
of a Bullet discharg'd from a Gun; and so said a Servant of
his that work'd with him.

Upon *Saturday* (*July* 1), as I was going to visit my Neighbour Capt. Barefoot, and just at his Door, his Man saw, as
well as my self, 3 or 4 Stones fall just by us in the Field, or
Close, where the House stands, and not any other Person near
us.   At Night a great Stone fell in the Kitchin, as I was going
to Bed, and the Pewter was thrown down; many Stones flew
about, and the Candles by them put out 3 or 4 times, and the
Snorting heard; a Negro Maid hit on the Head in the Entry
between the Kitchin and Hall with a Porringer from the
Kitchin: also the pressing-Iron clattered against the Partition
Wall between the Hall and a Chamber beyond it, where I lay,
and Mr. Randolph,[4] His Majesty's Officer for the Customs, etc.

Some few Stones we had on *Sunday* Morning, (*July* 2)

---

[1] Shrewd, *i. e.*, sharp.   [2] Early in 1686.   [3] "In fact."

[4] Edward Randolph, arch-foe of the Massachusetts theocracy and for more
than a dozen years (1676–1689) chief inspirer of the royal policy as to the colonies.

none at Night. But on *Monday* Morning (the 3*d*) both Mr.
Walton, and 5 or 6 with him in the Field, were assaulted with
them, and their Ears with the old Snorting and Whistling.
In the Afternoon Mr. Walton was hit on the Back with Stones
very grievously, as he was in his Boat that lay at a Cove
side by his House. It was a very odd prank that was prac-
tis'd by the Devil a little while after this. One Night the
Cocks of Hay, made the Day before in the Orchard, was
spread all abroad, and some of the Hay thrown up into the
Trees, and some of it brought into the House, and scatter'd.
Two Logs that lay at the Door, laid, one of them by the
Chimny in the Kitchin; the other set against the Door of the
Room where Mr. Walton then lay, as on purpose to confine
him therein: A Form that stood in the Entry (or Porch)
was set along by the Fire side, and a joint Stool upon that,
with a Napking spread thereon, with two Pewter Pots, and
two Candlesticks: A Cheese-Press likewise having a Spit
thrust into one of the holes of it, at one end; and at the other
end of the Spit hung an Iron Kettle; and a Cheese was taken
out, and broke to pieces. Another time, I full well remember
'twas on a Sunday at Night, my Window was all broke with
a violent shock of Stones and Brick-bats, which scarce miss'd
my self: among these one huge one made its way through the
great square or shash of a Casement, and broke a great hole
in it, throwing down Books by the way, from the Window to a
Picture over-against it, on the other side of the Chamber,
and tore a hole quite through it about half a foot long, and the
piece of the Cloth hung by a little part of it, on the back-side
of the Picture.

After this we were pretty quiet,[1] saving now and then a
few Stones march'd about for Exercise, and to keep (as it
were) the Diabolical hand in use, till *July* 28, being *Friday*,
when about 40 Stones flew about, abroad, and in the House
and Orchard, and among the Trees therein, and a Window
broke before, was broke again, and one Room where they
never used before.

August 1. On *Wednesday* the Window in my ante-Chamber
was broke again, and many Stones were plaid about, abroad,

---

[1] It will be remembered that about this time Hannah Jones was put under
bond. See pp. 60–61, note 3.

and in the House, in the Day-time, and at Night. The same Day in the Morning they tried this Experiment; they did set on the Fire a Pot with Urin, and crooked Pins in it, with design to have it boil, and by that means to give Punishment to the Witch, or Wizard (that might be the wicked Procurer or Contriver of this Stone Affliction) and take off their own; as they had been advised. This was the Effect of it: As the Liquor begun to grow hot, a Stone came and broke the top or mouth of it, and threw it down, and spilt what was in it; which being made good again, another Stone, as the Pot grew hot again, broke the handle off; and being recruited and fill'd the third time, was then with a third Stone quite broke to pieces and split; and so the Operation became frustrate and fruitless.

On *August* 2, two Stones in the Afternoon I heard and saw my self in the House and Orchard; and another Window in the Hall was broke.   And as I was entring my own Chamber, a great square of a Casement, being a foot square, was broke, with the Noise as of a big Stone, and pieces of the Glass flew into the Room, but no Stone came in then, or could be found within or without.   At Night, as I, with others, were in the Kitchin, many more came in; and one great Stone that lay on a Spinning-Wheel to keep it steady, was thrown to the other side of the Room.   Several Neighbours then present were ready to testifie this Matter.

Upon *August* 3, On *Thursday* the Gate between my said Landlord and his Neighbour John Amazeen was taken off again, and thrown into Amazeen's Field, who heard it fall, and averr'd it then made a Noise like a great Gun.

On *Friday* the 4*th*, the Fence against Mr. Walton's Neighbour's Door, (the Woman of whom formerly there was great Suspicion, and thereupon Examination had, as appears upon Record;) this Fence being maliciously pull'd down to let in their Cattel into his Ground; he and his Servants were pelted with above 40 Stones as they went to put it up again; for she had often threatned that he should never injoy his House and Land.[1]   Mr. Walton was hit divers times, and all that Day in the Field, as they were Reaping, it ceas'd not, and their fell (by the Mens Computation) above an hundred Stones.

[1] See p. 37, note 1. Walton had doubtless fenced in the land in controversy.

A Woman helping to Reap (among the rest) was hit 9 or 10 times, and hurt to that degree, that her left Arm, Hip, Thigh, and Leg, were made black and blue therewith; which she showd to the Woman,[1] Mrs. Walton, and others. Mr. Woodbridge,[2] a Divine, coming to give me a Visit, was hit about the Hip, and one Mr. Jefferys a Merchant,[3] who was with him, on the Leg. A Window in the Kitchin that had been much batter'd before, was now quite broke out, and unwindow'd, no Glass or Lead at all being left: a Glass Bottle broke to pieces, and the Pewter Dishes (about 9 of them) thrown down, and bent.

On *Saturday* the 5*th*, as they were Reaping in the Field, three Sickles were crack'd and broke by the force of these lapidary Instruments of the Devil, as the Sickles were in the Reapers hands, on purpose (it seems) to obstruct their Labour, and do them Injury and Damage. And very many Stones were cast about that Day; insomuch, that some that assisted at that Harvest-Work, being struck with them, by reason of that Disturbance left the Field, but were follow'd by their invisible Adversaries to the next House.

On *Sunday*, being the 6*th*, there fell nothing considerable, nor on *Monday*, (7*th*) save only one of the Children hit with a Stone on the Back. We were quiet to *Tuesday* the 8*th*. But on *Wednesday* (9*th*) above 100 Stones (as they verily thought) repeated the Reapers Disquiet in the Corn-Field, whereof some were affirm'd by Mr. Walton to be great ones indeed, near as big as a Man's Head; and Mrs. Walton, his Wife being by Curiosity led thither, with intent also to make some Discovery by the most diligent and vigilant Observation she could use, to obviate the idle Incredulity some inconsiderate Persons might irrationally entertain concerning this venefical[4] Operation; or at least to confirm her own Sentiments and Belief of it. Which she did, but to her Cost; for she received an untoward Blow (with a Stone) on her Shoulder. There were likewise two Sickles bent, crack'd, and disabled with them, beating them violently out of their Hands that held them; and this reiterated three times successively.

[1] *I. e.*, to Hannah Jones.   [2] See p. 65, note 1.
[3] George Jeffrey, or Jaffrey, of Great Island.
[4] Sorcerous—from the Latin *venefica*, a witch.

After this we injoy'd our former Peace and Quiet, un-
molested by these stony Disturbances, that whole month of
August, excepting some few times; and the last of all in the
Month of September, (the beginning thereof) wherein Mr.
Walton himself only (the Original perhaps of this strange
Adventure, as has been declared) was the designed conclud-
ing Sufferer; who going in his Canoo (or Boat) from the Great
Island, where he dwelt, to Portsmouth, to attend the Council,
who had taken Cognizance of this Matter,[1] he being Summoned
thither, in order to his and the Suspect's Examination, and the
Courts taking Order thereabout, he was sadly hit with three
pebble Stones as big as ones Fist; one of which broke his Head,
which I saw him show to the President of the Council; the
others gave him that Pain on the Back, of which (with other
like Strokes) he complained then, and afterward to his Death.[2]

Who, that peruses these præternatural Occurrences, can
possibly be so much an Enemy to his own Soul, and irrefutable
Reason, as obstinately to oppose himself to, or confusedly
fluctuate in, the Opinion and Doctrine of Dæmons, or Spirits,
and Witches? Certainly he that do's so, must do two things

[1] See pp. 60–61, note 3.

[2] What order the courts took thereabout does not appear from the extant
records; but that Hannah Jones was not punished may be inferred from our
author's silence. As to the land dispute, it is recorded that in December, 1682,
John Amazeen, the constable, with his step-son Jeremiah Walford and others,
came with a warrant from Captain Stileman and arrested George Walton and his
helpers for wood-cutting on the lands granted him by Mason; and that, though
Walton carried it to the courts and offered evidence that some of the wood cut
for him had been seen in John Amazeen's yard, the jury found for the defendants'
cost of court. Walton appealed to the King in Council—Walford and Amazeen,
so wrote Secretary Chamberlain, claiming by a town grant of 1658 and "the jury
being all of them possessed of lands by virtue of town grants"; but, though he
gave Edward Randolph power of attorney to prosecute, the appeal was in 1684
dismissed. (Provincial Records, in N. H. Hist. Soc., *Collections*, VIII. 118, and
Calendar of State Papers, America and West Indies, 1681–1685, *passim*.) At
home, however, John Amazeen saw himself made an example of, his live-stock
levied on, and himself thrown into prison for his refusal of dues to Mason. Chamberlain lost his secretaryship with the change of government in 1686, but remained
as clerk of the courts till 1689, when, with the collapse of the Andros administration, he seems to have returned to England. (Vaughan's Journal, in N. H. Hist.
Soc., *Collections*, VIII. 187; *N. H. Prov. Papers*, I. 590, 600; Mass. Hist. Soc.,
Proceedings, XVII. 227.)

more: He must temerariously unhinge, or undermine the Fundamentals of the best Religion in the World; and he must disingenuously quit and abandon that of the Three Theologick Virtues or Graces, to which the great Doctor of the Gentils gave the Precedence, Charity, through his Unchristian and Uncharitable Incredulity.

Finis.

THE PENNSYLVANIA CASES OF MATTSON, HENDRICKSON, AND GUARD, 1684, 1701

INTRODUCTION

AT a first glance the utterances of the early Friends in Europe and America do not suggest a difference, in their beliefs as to witchcraft, from those of the Puritan world about them. George Fox thought himself endowed with a divine power for the detection of witches, and tells us himself how he turned from his path to tell a group of women that they were in the spirit of witchcraft or rebuked in open meeting those he discerned to be under the power of an evil spirit.[1] Richard Farnworth, long his chief lieutenant, put forth in 1655 a printed discourse "as a Judgment upon Witchcraft, and a deniall, testimony, and declaration against Witchcraft from those that the world reproachfully calleth Quakers,"[2] and Fox himself in 1657 devoted one largely to "the ground of Inchantings and seducing Spirits" and "of Nicromancy, which doth defile Witches and Wizards."[3] We have just met a New England Quaker as an accuser, and more than one gave testimony against the Salem witches. Even those

[1] See pp. 20–21 of the *Witchcraft and Quakerism* (Philadelphia, 1908) of Mrs. Amelia Mott Gummere, who quotes from the original MS. of Fox's journal.

[2] His anonymously published *Witchcraft Cast out from the Religious Seed and Israel of God* (London, 1655).

[3] His *A Declaration of the Ground of Error . . . and the Ground of Inchantings and Seducing Spirits, and the Doctrine of Devils, the Sons of Sorcerers, and the Seed of the Adulterer, and the Ground of Nicromancy, which doth defile Witches and Wizards* (London, 1657). But this book, like Farnworth's, is mainly a dissuasive from fortune-telling or the use of it. How slow was Fox's spirit to the darker suspicions of the witch-haters may best be gathered from his appeal "to the Masters of Ships and Seamen" (1676), wherein he dissuades them from the hasty ascription of storms to witchcraft; "and let New England professors [of religion] see whether or no they have not sometimes cast some poor simple people into the sea on pretence of being witches."

—a Bishop, a Whiting—who reviled their Puritan foes taunt them with Satan's besetments as if these were undoubted. It is only William Sewel, born and reared in Holland, whom we find translating into Dutch an English attack on the superstition.[1]

But at bottom, from the first, their gentle mysticism had in its universe no place for the arch-fiend of Orthodoxy. What Richard Farnworth so fiercely repudiates is only fortune-telling. If George Fox exclaims "Arise, children of God, and suffer not the Witch to live," it appears in a moment that by "the Witch" he means only the sin of divination, and that "every one that dwells in the spirit of God doth cut it off."

As for William Penn, born to wealth and culture, son of a Dutch mother and in closest touch with the enlightened mystics of the Continent, there is in his writings scarce a trace of the current demonology; and the motley crowd of heretics and free-thinkers whom his tolerant prospectus tempted to join his Quakers for the peopling of his colony on the Delaware were perhaps as little prone to faith in Satan. In the laws agreed upon in England between the proprietor and his colonists, in May of 1681, the long list of "Offences against God" which "draw his wrath upon magistrates" and "provoke his indignation against a country" contains no mention of those dealings with Satan so long deemed the direst insults to his majesty;[2] and the "Great Law" enacted by the

---

[1] *The Doctrine of Devils proved to be the Grand Apostacy of these Later Times* (London, 1676). The English original bears no author's name, but its Dutch title-page ascribes it to "N. Orchard, Predikant in Nieuw-Engeland." There is, however, nothing in the work to suggest an American authorship, unless it be the passage (p. 189) where, speaking of the vogue in Christendom of legends of the supernatural, the writer says that "the most part of Europe, Asia, and Africa resounded with them (and now yet too-taking in America)." If the author came to America, it was doubtless after writing it, and more probably to the middle or southern colonies, then often included by Europeans under the name of New England.

[2] *Gravissimum et omnium criminum maximum est, Crimen laesae Majestatis divinae*, "the gravest and greatest of all crimes is treason against God," says

provincial assembly, under Penn's presidency, in the winter of 1682–1683, though it regulates minutely the morals of the colonists, has never a word as to witchcraft. The charter indeed prescribed, as in the other colonies, that colonial laws should be agreeable, "so far as conveniently may be," with the laws of England; but this implied no validity for English statutes unless expressly adopted by the provincial legislature; and, as for witchcraft, it was not till 1717, with the fall of Penn's power, that under Governor Keith the statute of James I. was with other English criminal laws, by formal action of the Pennsylvania assembly, "put in execution in this province."

But the Swedish peasants who long before the arrival of Penn's colony had established themselves on the farther bank of the Delaware, and now came with their lands beneath his rule, knew little enough of the growing rationalism of the seventeenth century; and it was these (speaking still among themselves their own vernacular, and needing, as we shall see, an interpreter between them and their new landlord) who, during Penn's first visit, brought in his court at Philadelphia the one action for witchcraft known to Pennsylvania records.[1] The indictment, unhappily, is not preserved; but, as harm wrought by witchcraft to person or to property could of course,

---

Damhouder, the great Flemish jurist whose handbook of criminal law had been the prescribed authority in the colony on the Delaware until that colony fell into the hands of the English; and witchcraft he makes the culmination of this crime.

[1] The nationality of the accused is clear from their names, and "Lasse Cock," the councilman who served them as interpreter, is well known as a Swede. Of the witnesses named, "Vanculin" ("Coolin," "Cooling") was of course of Dutch stock, and Drystreet, Sanderlin, Ashcom, of English. All these names are familiar to the records of the "Court at Upland" (Chester), the tribunal for this district prior to Penn's coming; and its entries show these families established on the west bank of the Delaware a little above Chester. (See *Record of Upland Court, 1676–1681,* in vol. VII. of the *Memoirs of the Historical Society of Pennsylvania,* pp. 91–125.) As to the extraction of these colonists and the superstitions prevalent among them, see Amandus Johnson, *The Swedish Settlements on the Delaware, passim,* and especially pp. 28, 543–545.

like harm by any other means, be punished, if provable, under
the general statutes, it must be assumed that these, and not
the semi-religious law of James, were the basis of the prosecution.   It is the extant records of this case,[1] with that of a
more trifling later episode, which here must serve us for a
Pennsylvania narrative.

[1] Here reprinted from the *Minutes of the Provincial Council of Pennsylvania*,
I. (Philadelphia, 1852), pp. 93–96.   From this source they have been borrowed
by Smith, *History of Delaware County, Pennsylvania* (Philadelphia, 1862), pp.
152–153, and doubtless by others.

THE CASES OF MATTSON, HENDRICKSON, AND GUARD

Att a Councill held at Philadelphia the 7th 12th Mo., 1683.[1]

Present:

Wm. Penn, Prop'or[2] and Govr.

Lasse Cock,	Jno. Symcock,	Tho. Holmes.
Wm. Clayton.		

Margaret Mattson and Yeshro[3] Hendrickson, Examined and about to be proved Witches; whereupon, this board Ordered that Neels Matson should Enter into a recognizance of fifty pounds for his Wiff's appearance before this board the 27th Instant. Hendrick Jacobson[4] doth the same for his Wife.

Adjourned till the 20th 12th Mo., 83.

Att a Councill held at Philadelphia the 27th of the 12th month, 1683.[5]

Present:

Wm. Penn, Prop'or and Govr.

James Harrison,	Wm. Haigue,	Wm. Clayton,
Wm. Biles,	Chris. Taylor,	Tho: Holmes.
Lasse Cock,		

The Grand Jury being attested, The Govr gave them their Charge, and the Atturney Gen[er]all attended them with the presentmt; their names are as followed:

Robt Euer, foreman.	Rich. Orne,	Tho: Mosse,
Samll Carpenter,	Jno. Day,	Tho: Ducket,
Andrew Griscom,	Jno. Fisher,	Denis Lince,
Benj. Whitehead,	Jno. Barnes.	Tho: Phillyps,

---

[1] *I. e.*, February 7, 1684: March had by formal enactment been made "First Month."

[2] Proprietor.

[3] *I. e.*, Gertrude. *Cf.* p. 87.

[4] *I. e.*, Jacob Hendrickson—see p. 87.

[5] February 27, 1684.

85

Jno. Barnes,	Gunner Rambo,	Tho: Millard,
Samll Allen,	Enock Flower,	Jno. Yattman,
Jno. Parsons.	Henr: Drystreet.	Barnaby Wilcox.

Post Meridiem.

The Grand Jury made their returne, and found the Bill.

Ordered that those that were absent of the Petty Jury should be fined 40s each man.

Margarit Matson's Indictmt was read, and she pleads not Guilty, and will be tryed by the Countrey.

Lasse Cock attested Interpriter between the Prop'or and the Prisoner at the Barr.

The Petty Jury Impanneld; their names are as followed:

Jno. Hasting, foreman.	Albertus Hendrickson,	Robt Piles,
Robt Wade,	Nath. Evans,	Edwd Darter,
Wm Hewes,	Jer. Collet,	Jno. Kinsman,
Jno. Gibbons,	Walter Martin,	Edw Bezac.

Henry Drystreet attested, Saith he was told 20 years agoe, that the prisoner at the Barr was a Witch, and that severall Cows were bewitcht by her; also, that James Saunderling's mother tould him that she bewitcht her cow, but afterwards said it was a mistake, and that her Cow should doe well againe, for it was not her Cow but an Other Person's that should dye.

Charles Ashcom attested, saith that Anthony's Wife being asked why she sould her Cattle, was because her mother had Bewitcht them, having taken the Witchcraft of[1] Hendrick's[2] Cattle, and put it on their Oxon; She myght Keep[3] but noe Other Cattle, and also that one night the Daughter of the Prisoner called him up hastely, and when he came she sayd there was a great Light but Just before, and an Old woman with a Knife in her hand at the Bedd's feet, and therefore shee cryed out and desired Jno. Symcock to take away his Calves or Else she would send them to Hell.

James Claypoole attested Interpritor betwixt the Prop'or and the Prisoner.

The affidavid of Jno. Vanculin read, Charles Ashcom being a Witness to it.

---

[1] Off.   [2] Hendrickson's.

[3] Clearly a word is here omitted—perhaps "cows."

Annakey Coolin attested, saith her husband tooke the Heart of a Calfe that Dyed, as they thought, by Witchcraft, and Boyled it, wherupon the Prisoner at the Barr came in and asked them what they were doing; they said boyling of flesh; she said they had better they had Boyled the Bones, with severall other unseemly Expressions.

Magaret Mattson saith that she Vallues not Drystreet's Evidence; but if Sanderlin's mother had come, she would have answered her; also denyeth Charles Aschom's Attestation at her Soul, and Saith where is my Daughter; let her come and say so.

Annakey Cooling's attestation concerning the Gees, she denyeth, saying she was never out of her Conoo,[1] and also that she never said any such things Concerning the Calve's heart.

Jno. Cock attested, sayth he Knows nothing of the matter.

Tho: Balding's attestation was read, and Tho: Bracy attested, saith it is a True coppy.

The Prisoner denyeth all things, and saith that the Witnesses speaks only by hear say.

After wch the Govr gave the jury their Charge concerning the Prisoner at the Barr.

The jury went forth, and upon their Returne Brought her in Guilty of haveing the Comon fame of a witch, but not guilty in manner and forme as Shee stands Indicted.[2]

Neels Mattson and Antho. Neelson[3] Enters into a Recognizance of fifty pounds apeice, for the good behavior of Margaret Matson for six months.

Jacob Hendrickson Enters into the Recognizance of fifty pounds for the good behavior of Getro Hendrickson for six months.

Adjourned till the 20th day of the first Mo., 1684.[4]

[1] Canoe.

[2] The tact and quiet humor of this verdict should need no pointing out; but it has sometimes been oddly misunderstood.

[3] "Antho. Neelson" was very probably a son of Neels and Margaret Mattson: here still, as in the home-land, Scandinavian surnames were often not hereditary, but changed with every generation, so that a son of Neels (Cornelius) Mattson might be surnamed, not Mattson, but Neelson (the Swedish *Nilsson*, English *Nelson*). The assumption of Smith (*History of Delaware County*, pp. 153, 488) that he was a son-in-law is perhaps due only to ignorance of this usage.

[4] Thus ended in the colony, so far as Pennsylvania records show, the criminal prosecution of witches. But in 1696 a young Quaker who had incurred the

At a Council held at Philadelphia the 21st of 3 Mo,[1] 1701.

Present:

The Propritary and Governour.[2]

Edwd. Shippen, ⎱
Saml. Carpenter, ⎰ Esq'rs.
Griffith Owen,

Thos. Story, ⎱
Humpry Murray, ⎰ Esq'rs.
Caleb Pusey,

A Petition of Robt. Guard and his Wife being read, setting forth That a Certain Strange Woman lately arrived in this Town being Seized with a very Sudden illness after she had been in their Company on the 17th Instant, and Several Pins being taken out of her Breasts, One John Richards, Butcher, and his Wife Ann, charged the Petitrs with Witchcraft, and as being the Authors of the Said Mischief; and therefore, Desire their Accusers might be sent for, in Order either to prove their Charge, or that they might be acquitted, they Suffering much in their Reputation, and by that means in their Trade.

Ordered, that the Said John and Ann Richards be sent for; who appearing, the matter was inquired into, and being found trifling, was Dismissed.[3]

discipline of his Quarterly Meeting for practising divination was presented by the grand jury to the county court, fined by the court, and forbidden to repeat his magical practices (see Smith, *History of Delaware County*, pp. 192–194; Gummere, *Witchcraft and Quakerism*, Philadelphia, 1908, pp. 40–47). And in 1701, while Penn was once more in the colony (November, 1699–November, 1701), there occurred the episode next to be narrated. It is reprinted from the *Minutes of the Provincial Council of Pennsylvania*, II. 20.

[1] May 21.   [2] William Penn.

[3] That even in Pennsylvania there came a time when, under less calm guidance, a witch-panic was possible, is suggested by the following news item sent from Philadelphia on July 21, 1787, and published in the *Massachusetts Centinel* of August 1: "It must seriously affect every human mind that in consequence of the barbarous treatment lately suffered by the poor old woman, called a *witch*, she died on Wednesday last. It is to be hoped that every step will be taken to bring the offenders to punishment in justice to the wretched victim, as well as the violated laws of reason and society." The item is pointed out to the editor by a colleague just as this volume goes to press.

MEMORABLE PROVIDENCES, RELATING TO
WITCHCRAFTS AND POSSESSIONS, BY
COTTON MATHER, 1689

INTRODUCTION

MUCH less than even his illustrious father does the Rev. Cotton Mather (1662–1728) need here an introduction. His name and his personality are a commonplace in American history and literature. Opinion regarding him has indeed gone widely asunder; but, if he has found severe critics, he has also found able defenders. One of these, Mr. Barrett Wendell, has told his story almost wholly in his own words;[1] and the little book is not only of rare charm, but, though apology, of no small degree of frankness. It may be commended to all who would see Cotton Mather with his own eyes. His relations with witchcraft have been debated at especial length and with a wealth of knowledge by Mr. C. W. Upham and Mr. W. F. Poole.[2] But the reader of this volume hardly needs such help: the evidence in almost all its fullness lies before him.

The setting of Cotton Mather's life may be sketched in a word. Son of Increase Mather, grandson of John Cotton, precocious both in learning and in piety, he was from boyhood —if ever he had a boyhood—the rising hope of Massachusetts orthodoxy. All his life of answering to that hope was spent

---

[1] *Cotton Mather: the Puritan Priest* (Boston, 1891).

[2] By Mr. Upham in his *Salem Witchcraft* (Boston, 1867) and his "Salem Witchcraft and Cotton Mather" (*Historical Magazine*, V.); Mr. Poole in his "Cotton Mather and Salem Witchcraft" (*North American Review*, CVIII.) and his chapter on "Witchcraft at Boston" (*Memorial History of Boston*, II.). To these should perhaps be added Mr. George H. Moore's pungent *Notes on the Bibliography of Witchcraft in Massachusetts* (American Antiquarian Society, *Proceedings*, new series, V.); and of prime importance to the student is the *Diary of Cotton Mather* (Mass. Hist. Soc., *Collections*, seventh series, VII., VIII.), with the able notes of its editor, Mr. Worthington C. Ford.

in one long pastorate, that of the North Church, his father's church, his father his associate almost to the end. But pastor to him meant also student, politician, much besides.

The Memorable Providences was among his earliest books: he was only twenty-seven at its publication. It was twice reprinted—in 1691 at London, under the changed title of *Late Memorable Providences*, with an added " recommendation" by Richard Baxter, and in 1697 at Edinburgh, under the old title.[1]

---

[1] What seems in the list of Sibley (*Harvard Graduates*, III. 50) and in Sabin a reimpression of the book in 1690 with his *Speedy Repentance Urged* proves (on collation kindly made by the librarians of the John Carter Brown library) to be only a copy of the latter work bound up somewhat confusedly with a defective copy of the *Memorable Providences* (1689).

MEMORABLE PROVIDENCES

*Memorable Providences, Relating to Witchcrafts And Possessions.
A Faithful Account of many Wonderful and Surprising
Things, that have befallen several Bewitched and Possessed
Persons in New-England. Particularly, A Narrative of
the marvellous Trouble and Releef Experienced by a pious
Family in Boston, very lately and sadly molested with Evil
Spirits.*

*Whereunto is added, a Discourse delivered unto a Congregation
in Boston, on the Occasion of that Illustrious Providence.
As also a Discourse delivered unto the same Congregation;
on the occasion of an horrible Self-Murder Committed in the
Town. With an Appendix, in vindication of a Chapter in
a late Book of Remarkable Providences, from the Calumnies
of a Quaker at Pen-silvania.*

*Written by Cotton Mather, Minister of the Gospel, and Recom-
mended by the Ministers of Boston and Charleston.[1]*

*Printed at Boston in N. England by R. P. 1689. Sold by
Joseph Brunning, at his Shop at the Corner of the Prison-
Lane next the Exchange.[2]*

To the Honourable Wait Winthrop Esq;[3]

Sr.

By the special Disposal and Providence of the Almighty
God, there now comes abroad into the world a little History

---

[1] Charlestown.

[2] Title-page of the original.

[3] Wait Winthrop (1643–1717), son of Governor John Winthrop of Connecticut and grandson of Governor John Winthrop of Massachusetts, was himself a
man of weight in New England—jurist, member of the Massachusetts council,
major-general of the provincial forces. We shall meet him as a member of the
court at the Salem trials of 1692.

of several very astonishing Witchcrafts and Possessions, which partly my own Ocular Observation, and partly my undoubted Information, hath enabled me to offer unto the publick Notice of my Neighbours. It must be the Subject, and not the Manner or the Author of this Writing, that has made any people desire its Publication; For there are such obvious Defects in Both, as would render me very unreasonable, if I should wish about This or Any Composure of mine, O That it were printed in a book! But tho there want not Faults in the Discourse, to give me Discontent enough, my Displeasure at them will be recompensed by the Satisfaction I take in my Dedication of it; which I now no less properly than cheerfully make unto Your Self; whom I reckon among the Best of my Friends, and the Ablest of my Readers. Your Knowledge has Qualified You to make those Reflections on the following Relations, which few can Think, and tis not fit that all should See. How far the Platonic Notions of Dæmons which were, it may be, much more espoused by those primitive Christians and Scholars that we call The Fathers, than they seem countenanced in the ensuing Narratives, are to be allow'd by a serious man, your Scriptural Divinity, join'd with Your most Rational Philosophy, will help You to judge at an uncommon rate. Had I on the Occasion before me handled the Doctrin of Dæmons, or lanched forth into Speculations about magical Mysteries, I might have made some Ostentation, that I have read something and thought a little in my time; but it would neither have been Convenient for me, nor Profitable for those plain Folkes, whose Edification I have all along aimed at. I have therefore here but briefly touch't every thing with an American Pen; a Pen which your Desert likewise has further Entitled You to the utmost Expressions of Respect and Honour from. Though I have no Commission, yet I am sure I shall meet with no Crimination, if I here publickly wish You all manner of Happiness, in the Name of the great Multitudes whom you have laid under everlasting Obligations. Wherefore in the name of the many hundred Sick people, whom your charitable and skilful Hands have most freely dispens'd your no less generous than secret Medicines to; and in the name of Your whole Countrey, which hath long had cause to believe that you will succeed Your Honourable Father and Grandfather, in successful Endeavours for our Welfare; I say, In their Name, I now do wish you all the Prosperity of them that love Jerusalem. And whereas it hath been sometimes observed, That the Genius of an Author is commonly Discovered in the Dedicatory Epistle, I shall be content if this Dedicatory Epistle of mine, have now discovered me to be,

(Sir) Your sincere and very humble Servant,

C. MATHER.

To the Reader.

THE old Heresy of the sensual Sadducees, denying the Being of Angels either good or evil, died not with them; nor will it, whiles men (abandoning both Faith and Reason) count it their wisdom to credit nothing but what they see and feel. How much this fond opinion has gotten ground in this debauched Age is awfully observable; and what a dangerous stroak it gives to settle men in Atheism, is not hard to discern. God is therefore pleased (besides the witness born to this Truth in Sacred Writ) to suffer Devils sometimes to do such things in the world as shall stop the mouth of gainsayers, and extort a Confession from them.

It has also been made a doubt by some, whether there are any such things as Witches, i. e., Such as by Contract or Explicit Covenant with the Devil, improve, or rather are improved by him to the doing of things strange in themselves, and besides their natural Course. But (besides that the Word of God assures us that there have been such, and gives order about them) no Age passes without some apparent Demonstration of it. For, Though it be Folly to impute every dubious Accident, or unwonted Effect of Providence, to Witchcraft; yet there are some things which cannot be excepted against, but must be ascribed hither.

Angels and Men not being made for civil Converse together in this world; and all Communion with Devils being interdicted us; their Nature also being spiritual, and the Word of God having said so little in that particular concerning their way of Acting; hence it is that we can disclose but a little of those Mysteries of Darkness; all reports that are from themselves, or their Instruments, being to be esteemed as Illusions, or at least covered with Deceit, filled with the Impostures of the Father of Lies; and the effects which come under our consideration being Mysterious, rather Posing than Informing us.

The Secrets also of God's Providence, in permitting Satan and his Instruments to molest His children, not in their Estates only, but in their Persons and their Posterity too, are part of His Judgments that are unsearchable, and His Wayes that are past finding out; only this we have good Assurance for, that they are among the All things that work together for their good. Their Graces are hereby tried, their Uprightness is made known, their Faith and Patience have their perfect work.

Among the many Instances that have been of this kind, That which is Recorded in this Narrative, is worthy to be commended to the Notice of Mankind, it being a thing in it self full of Memorable passages, and faithfully recorded, according to the Truth in Matter of Fact, scarce any Instance being asserted in it, but what hath the Evidence of many credible Witnesses, did need require. Among others who had frequent Occasions to observe these things, the Reverend Author of this short History, was spirited to be more than ordinarily engaged in attending, and making particular Remarks upon the several passages occurring therein, and hath accordingly written very little besides what Himself was an eye-witness of, together with others, and the rest was gathered up with much Accuracy and Caution.

Its needless for us to insist upon the Commendation either of the Author or the Work; the former is known in the Churches, the latter will speak sufficiently for it self. All that we shall offer to stay the Reader from passing over to satisfy himself in that which follows, is only thus much, *Viz.*, That the following Account will afford to him that shall read with Observation, a further clear Confirmation, That, There is both a God, and a Devil, and Witchcraft: That, There is no out-ward Affliction, but what God may (and sometimes doth) permit Satan to trouble His people withal: That, The Malice of Satan and his Instruments, is very great against the Children of God · That, The clearest Gospel-Light shining in a place, will not keep some from entring hellish Contracts with infernal Spirits:

That, Prayer is a powerful and effectual Remedy against the malicious practises of Devils and those in Covenant with them: That, They who will obtain such Mercies of God, must pray unto Perseverance: That, God often gives to His people some apparent Encouragements to their Faith in Prayer, tho He does not presently perfect the Deliverance sought for: That, God's Grace is able to support His Children, and preserve their Grace firm, under sorest and Continuing Troubles: That, Those who refuse the Temptation to use doubtful or Diabolical Courses, to get the Assaults of the Devil and his Agents removed, Choosing to Recommend all to God, and rather to endure Affliction, than to have it Removed to His Dishonour, and the wounding of their own Consciences, never had cause to repent of it in the end.

And if these observations, together with the solemn Improvement made of this stupend[1] Providence, in the pertinent and Judicious Sermons annexed, may but obtain a due Impression on the hearts of such as shall peruse them, whether young or old; as therein will be their profit, so shall their Labour turn to the Praise of God, fully satisfie the Author for all his Care and Industry, and answer his sincere Aims: for which good Success we Commend it to the Blessing of God, to be followed with the importunate Prayers of us, who have been Eye- and Ear-witnesses of many of the most considerable things Related in the ensuing Narrative.

CHARLES MORTON.
JAMES ALLEN.
JOSHUA MOODEY.
SAMUEL WILLARD.[2]

The Introduction.

IT was once the Mistake of one gone to the Congregation of the Dead, concerning the Survivers, *If one went unto them*

---

[1] Stupendous: this shorter spelling (*cf.* "reverend") was then current.

[2] Morton was minister of Charlestown, Allen of the First Church in Boston, where Moodey, driven from Portsmouth (see pp. 31, 34, and 187, note 3), was now his associate, and Willard (see pp. 21, 22, 184, and 186, note 3) of the South Church. The North Church, the only other, was Mather's own; and his father, who was his colleague there, was now in England. Moodey had himself, in a letter to Increase Mather of October 4, 1688 (*Mather Papers*, pp. 367–368), written a brief account of the bewitchment of the Goodwin children.

from the dead, they will repent. The blessed God hath made some to come from the Damned, for the Conviction (may it also be for the Conversion) of us that are yet alive. The Devils themselves are by Compulsion come to confute the Atheism and Sadducism, and to reprove the Madness of ungodly men. Those condemned prisoners of our Atmosphære have not really sent Letters of Thanks from Hell, to those that are on Earth, promoting of their Interest, yet they have been forced, as of old, To confess that Jesus was the Holy one of God, so of late, to declare that Sin and Vice are the things which they are delighted in. But should one of those hideous Wights appear visibly with fiery chains upon him, and utter audibly his roarings and his warnings in one of our Congregations, it would not produce new Hearts in those whom the Scriptures handled in our Ministry do not affect. However it becomes the Embassadors of the L.[1] Jesus to leave no stroke untouch't that may conduce to bring men from the power of Satan unto God; and for this cause it is, that I have permitted the ensuing Histories to be published. They contain Things of undoubted Certainty, and they suggest Things of Importance unconceiveable. Indeed they are only one Head of Collections which in my little time of Observation I have made of Memorable Providences, with Reflections thereupon, to be reserved among other effects of my Diversion from my more stated and more weary Studies. But I can with a Contentment beyond meer Patience give these rescinded Sheets unto the Stationer, when I see what pains Mr. Baxter,[2] Mr. Glanvil,[3] Dr. More,[4] and several other Great Names have taken to publish Histories of Witchcrafts and Possessions unto the world. I said, Let me also run after them; and this with the more Alacrity because, I have tidings ready. Go then, my little Book, as a Lackey[5] to the more elaborate Essayes of

---

[1] Lord.

[2] Richard Baxter. His monograph on apparitions and witches, *The Certainty of the Worlds of Spirits*, was not published, indeed, until 1691; but, as he tells us in the preface to that work, "finding that almost all the Atheists, Sadducees, and Infidels did seem to profess that were they but sure of the Reality of the Apparitions and Operations of Spirits, it would cure them," he had for many years been inserting such evidence in his books.

[3] Joseph Glanvill (see p. 5, above).   [4] Henry More (see p. 5, above).

[5] *I. e.*, a footman, running behind their chariots.

those learned men. Go tell Mankind, that there are Devils and Witches; and that tho those night-birds least appear where the Day-light of the Gospel comes, yet New-Engl. has had Exemples of their Existence and Operation; and that not only the Wigwams of Indians, where the pagan Powaws[1] often raise their masters,[2] in the shapes of Bears and Snakes and Fires, but the Houses of Christians, where our God has had His constant Worship, have undergone the Annoyance of Evil spirits. Go tell the world, What Prayers can do beyond all Devils and Witches, and What it is that these Monsters love to do; and though the Dæmons in the Audience of several standers-by threatned much disgrace to thy Author, if he let thee come abroad, yet venture That, and in this way seek a just Revenge on Them for the Disturbance they have given to such as have called on the Name of God.

Witchcrafts and Possessions.

The First Exemple.

Section I. There dwells at this time, in the south part of Boston, a sober and pious man, whose Name is John Goodwin, whose Trade is that of a Mason, and whose Wife (to which a Good Report gives a share with him in all the Characters of Vertue) has made him the Father of six (now living) Children. Of these Children, all but the Eldest, who works with his Father at his Calling, and the Youngest, who lives yet upon the Breast of its mother, have laboured under the direful effects of a (no less palpable than) stupendous *Witchcraft.* Indeed that exempted Son had also, as was thought, some lighter touches of it, in unaccountable stabbs and pains now and then upon him; as indeed every person in the Family at some time or other had, except the godly Father, and the sucking Infant, who never felt any impressions of it. But these Four Children mentioned, were handled in so sad and strange a manner, as has given matter of Discourse and Wonder to all the Countrey, and of History not unworthy to be

---

[1] The "medicine men" of the Indians.

[2] *I. e.*, the devils: to the Puritans, as to the early Christians, all but Christian worship was devil worship.

considered by more than all the serious or the curious Readers in this New-English World.

Sect. II.   The four Children (whereof the Eldest was about Thirteen, and the youngest was perhaps about a third part so many years of age[1]) had enjoyed a Religious Education, and answered it with a very towardly Ingenuity.[2]   They had an observable Affection unto Divine and Sacred things; and those of them that were capable of it, seem'd to have such a Resentment[3] of their eternal Concernments as is not altogether usual.   Their Parents also kept them to a continual Employment, which did more than deliver them from the Temptations of Idleness, and as young as they were, they took a delight in it, it may be as much as they should have done.   In a word, Such was the whole Temper and Carriage of the Children, that there cannot easily be any thing more unreasonable, than to imagine that a Design to Dissemble could cause them to fall into any of their odd Fits; though there should not have happened,[4] as there did, a thousand Things, wherein it was perfectly impossible for any Dissimulation of theirs to produce what scores of spectators were amazed at.

Sect. III.   About Midsummer, in the year 1688, the Eldest of these Children, who is a Daughter, saw cause to examine their Washerwoman, upon their missing of some Linnen, which twas fear'd she had stollen from them; and of what use this linnen might bee to serve the Witchcraft intended, the Theef's Tempter knows!   This Laundress was the Daughter of an ignorant and a scandalous old Woman in the Neighbourhood; whose miserable Husband before he died, had sometimes complained of her, that she was undoubtedly a Witch, and that whenever his Head was laid, she would quickly arrive unto the punishments due to such an one.   This Woman in her daughters Defence bestow'd very bad Language upon the Girl that put her to the Question; immediately upon which, the

---

[1] Martha was 13, John 11, Mercy 7, Benjamin 5, the elder son (Nathaniel) 15, the baby (Hannah) six months old, when the narrative opens (midsummer, 1688).   (Savage, *Genealogical Dictionary*, and Boston records.)

[2] *I. e.*, with encouraging promise.

[3] *I. e.*, feeling, realization—in the religious cant of to-day, "a realizing sense."

[4] *I. e.*, even if there had not happened.

poor child became variously indisposed in her health, and visited with strange Fits, beyond those that attend an Epilepsy, or a Catalepsy, or those that they call The Diseases of Astonishment.[1]

Sect. IV.   It was not long before one of her Sisters, and two of her Brothers, were seized, in Order one after another, with Affects[2] like those that molested her.   Within a few weeks, they were all four tortured every where in a manner so very grievous, that it would have broke an heart of stone to have seen their Agonies.   Skilful Physicians were consulted for their Help, and particularly our worthy and prudent Friend Dr. Thomas Oakes,[3] who found himself so affronted[4] by the Distempers of the children, that he concluded nothing but an hellish Witchcraft could be the Original[5] of these Maladies. And that which yet more confirmed such Apprehension was, That for one good while, the children were tormented just in the same part of their bodies all at the same time together; and tho they saw and heard not one anothers complaints, tho likewise their pains and sprains were swift like Lightening, yet when (suppose) the Neck, or the Hand, or the Back of one was Rack't, so it was at that instant with t'other too.

Sect. V.   The variety of their tortures increased continually; and tho about Nine or Ten at Night they alwaies had a Release from their miseries, and ate and slept all night for the most part indifferently well, yet in the day time they were handled with so many sorts of Ails, that it would require of us almost as much time to Relate them all, as it did of them to Endure them.   Sometimes they would be Deaf, sometimes Dumb, and sometimes Blind, and often, all this at once.   One while their Tongues would be drawn down their Throats; another-while they would be pull'd out upon their Chins, to a prodigious length.   They would have their Mouths opened unto such a Wideness, that their Jaws went out of joint; and

---

[1] *I. e.*, stupefaction: diseases that rob one of his wits.   It should not be forgotten, here or later, that the author had once, while his stammering seemed to bar him from the ministry, begun the study of medicine.

[2] Affections, ailments.

[3] Dr. Oakes (1644–1719) was the locally eminent physician who in 1689 became speaker of the legislature and in 1690 was sent as a colonial deputy to England.

[4] Nonplussed, dumbfounded.   [5] Origin.

anon they would clap together again with a Force like that
of a strong Spring-Lock. The same would happen to their
Shoulder-Blades, and their Elbows, and Hand-wrists, and
several of their joints. They would at times ly in a benummed
condition; and be drawn together as those that are ty'd Neck
and Heels;[1] and presently be stretched out, yea, drawn Backwards, to such a degree that it was fear'd the very skin of their
Bellies would have crack'd. They would make most pitteous
out-cries, that they were cut with Knives, and struck with
Blows that they could not bear. Their Necks would be
broken, so that their Neck-bone would seem dissolved unto
them that felt after it; and yet on the sudden, it would become
again so stiff that there was no stirring of their Heads; yea,
their Heads would be twisted almost round; and if main
Force at any time obstructed a dangerous motion which they
seem'd to be upon, they would roar exceedingly. Thus they
lay some weeks most pittiful Spectacles; and this while as a
further Demonstration of Witchcraft in these horrid Effects,
when I went to Prayer by one of them, that was very desireous
to hear what I said, the Child utterly lost her Hearing till our
Prayer was over.

  Sect. VI. It was a Religious Family that these Afflictions
happened unto; and none but a Religious Contrivance to
obtain Releef, would have been welcome to them. Many
superstitious proposals were made unto them, by persons that
were I know not who, nor what, with Arguments fetch't from
I know not how much Necessity and Experience; but the distressed Parents rejected all such counsils, with a gracious Resolution, to oppose Devils with no other weapons but Prayers
and Tears, unto Him that has the Chaining of them; and to

---

[1] "Tied neck and heels" was doubtless at first, as the lexicographers understand it, only a phrase for the securest method of fettering; but it had now become a name for what was (in defiance of English law) a method of torture.
For its use at Salem see p. 363, note 2, below. Jardine says (*The Use of Torture in
the Criminal Law of England*, p. 37 ff.) that there is now shown in the Tower of
London a device "which compressed the neck of the sufferer down toward his
feet," and he thinks this may be that torture of "the manacles" often mentioned
in the English state trials of the sixteenth and seventeenth centuries and meant
by Shakespeare, when he makes Prospero say: "I'll manacle thy neck and feet
together." In Virginia tying neck and heels was in the seventeenth century a
penalty imposed by the courts.

try first whether Graces were not the best things to encounter
Witchcrafts with.   Accordingly they requested the four Ministers of Boston, with the Minister of Charlstown, to keep a
Day of Prayer at their thus haunted house; which they did
in the Company of some devout people there.   Immediately
upon this Day, the youngest of the four children was delivered,
and never felt any trouble as afore.   But there was yet a
greater Effect of these our Applications unto our God!

   Sect. VII.   The Report of the Calamities of the Family
for which we were thus concerned, arrived now unto the ears
of the Magistrates, who presently and prudently apply'd
themselves, with a just vigour, to enquire into the story.   The
Father of the Children complained of his Neighbour, the suspected ill woman, whose name was Glover; and she being
sent for by the Justices, gave such a wretched Account of her
self, that they saw cause to commit her unto the Gaolers Custody.   Goodwin had no proof that could have done her any
Hurt; but the Hag had not power to deny her interest in the
Enchantment of the Children; and when she was asked,
Whether she believed there was a God? her Answer was too
blasphemous and horrible for any Pen of mine to mention.
An Experiment was made, Whether she could recite the Lords
Prayer; and it was found, that tho clause after clause was most
carefully repeated unto her, yet when she said it after them
that prompted her, she could not possibly avoid making Nonsense of it, with some ridiculous Depravations.   This Experiment I had the curiosity since to see made upon two more,
and it had the same Event.   Upon the Commitment of this
extraordinary Woman, all the Children had some present ease;
until one (related unto her) accidentally meeting one or two
of them, entertain'd them with her Blessing, that is, Railing;
upon which Three of them fell ill again, as they were before.

   Sect. VIII.   It was not long before the Witch thus in the
Trap, was brought upon her Tryal; at which, thro' the Efficacy
of a Charm, I suppose, used upon her, by one or some of her
Crue,[1] the Court could receive Answers from her in none but
the Irish, which was her Native Language; altho she understood the English very well, and had accustomed her whole
Family to none but that Language in her former Conversa-

---

[1] Crew.

tion; and therefore the Communication between the Bench and the Bar,[1] was now cheefly convey'd by two honest and faithful men that were interpreters. It was long before she could with any direct Answers plead unto her Indictment; and when she did plead, it was with Confession rather than Denial of her Guilt. Order was given to search the old womans house, from whence there were brought into the Court, several small Images, or Puppets, or Babies, made of Raggs, and stuff't with Goat's hair, and other such Ingredients. When these were produced, the vile Woman acknowledged, that her way to torment the Objects of her malice, was by wetting of her Finger with her Spittle, and stroaking of those little Images. The abused Children were then present, and the Woman still kept stooping and shrinking as one that was almost prest to Death with a mighty Weight upon her. But one of the Images being brought unto her, immediately she started up after an odd manner, and took it into her hand; but she had no sooner taken it, than one of the Children fell into sad Fits, before the whole Assembly. This the Judges had their just Apprehensions at; and carefully causing the Repetition of the Experiment, found again the same event of it. They asked her, Whether she had any to stand by her: She replied, She had; and looking very pertly in the Air, she added, No, He's gone. And she then confessed, that she had One, who was her Prince, with whom she maintain'd, I know not what Communion. For which cause, the night after, she was heard expostulating with a Devil, for his thus deserting her; telling him that Because he had served her so basely and falsly, she had confessed all. However to make all clear, The Court appointed five or six Physicians one evening to examine her very strictly, whether she were not craz'd in her Intellectuals, and had not procured to her self by Folly and Madness the Reputation of a Witch. Diverse hours did they spend with her; and in all that while no Discourse came from her, but what was pertinent and agreeable: particularly, when they asked her, What she thought would become of her soul? she reply'd "You ask me a very solemn Question, and I cannot well tell what to say to it." She own'd her self a Roman Catholick; and could recite her Pater Noster in Latin very

---

[1] I. e., between the judges and the prisoner at the bar.

readily; but there was one Clause or two alwaies too hard for her, whereof she said, "She could not repeat it, if she might have all the world." In the up-shot, the Doctors returned her Compos Mentis;[1] and Sentence of Death was pass'd upon her.

Sect. IX. Diverse dayes were passed between her being Arraigned and Condemned. In this time one of her Neighbours had been giving in her Testimony of what another of her Neighbours had upon her Death related concerning her. It seems one Howen about Six years before, had been cruelly bewitched to Death; but before she died, she called one Hughes unto her, Telling her that she laid her Death to the charge of Glover; That she had seen Glover sometimes come down her Chimney; That she should remember this, for within this Six years she might have Occasion to declare it. This Hughes now preparing her Testimony, immediately one of her children, a fine boy, well grown towards Youth, was taken ill, just in the same woful and surprising manner that Goodwins children were. One night particularly, The Boy said he saw a Black thing with a Blue Cap in the Room, Tormenting of him; and he complained most bitterly of a Hand put into the Bed, to pull out his Bowels. The next day the mother of the boy went unto Glover, in the Prison, and asked her, Why she tortured her poor lad at such a wicked rate? This Witch replied, that she did it because of wrong done to her self and her daughter. Hughes denied (as well she might) that she had done her any wrong. "Well then," sayes Glover, "Let me see your child and he shall be well again." Glover went on, and told her of her own accord, "I was at your house last night." Sayes Hughes, "In what shape?" Sayes Glover, "As a black thing with a blue Cap." Sayes Hughes, "What did you do there?" Sayes Glover, "with my hand in the Bed I tryed to pull out the boyes Bowels, but I could not." They parted; but the next day Hughes appearing at Court, had her Boy with her; and Glover passing by the Boy, expressed her good wishes for him; tho' I suppose, his Parent had no design of any mighty Respect unto the Hag, by having him with her there. But the Boy had no more Indispositions after the Condemnation of the Woman.

[1] Of sound mind.

Sect. X.   While the miserable old Woman was under Condemnation, I did my self twice give a visit unto her.   She never
denyed the guilt of the Witchcraft charg'd upon her; but she
confessed very little about the Circumstances of her Confederacies with the Devils; only, she said, That she us'd to be at
meetings, which her Prince and Four more were present at.
As for those Four, She told who they were; and for her Prince,
her account plainly was, that he was the Devil.   She entertained me with nothing but Irish, which Language I had not
Learning enough to understand without an Interpreter; only
one time, when I was representing unto her That and How her
Prince had cheated her, as her self would quickly find; she
reply'd, I think in English, and with passion too, "If it be so,
I am sorry for that!"   I offer'd many Questions unto her,
unto which, after long silence, she told me, She would fain give
me a full Answer, but *they* would not give her leave.   It was
demanded, *"They!*   Who is that *They?"* and she return'd, that
They were her Spirits, or her Saints, (for they say, the same
Word in Irish signifies both).   And at another time, she included her two Mistresses, as she call'd them in that *They,*
but when it was enquired, Who those two were, she fell into
a Rage, and would be no more urged.

I Sett before her the Necessity and Equity of her breaking
her Covenant with Hell, and giving her self to the Lord Jesus
Christ, by an everlasting Covenant; To which her Answer
was, that I spoke a very Reasonable thing, but she could not
do it.   I asked her whether she would consent or desire to be
pray'd for; To that she said, If Prayer would do her any good,
shee could pray for her self.   And when it was again propounded, she said, She could not unless her spirits (or angels)
would give her leave.   However, against her will I pray'd
with her, which if it were a Fault it was in excess of Pitty.
When I had done, shee thank'd me with many good Words;
but I was no sooner out of her sight, than she took a stone, a
long and slender stone, and with her Finger and Spittle fell
to tormenting it; though whom or what she meant, I had the
mercy never to understand.

Sect. XI.   When this Witch was going to her Execution,
she said, the Children should not be relieved by her Death,
for others had a hand in it as well as she; and she named one

among the rest, whom it might have been thought Natural
Affection would have advised the Concealing of. It came to
pass accordingly, That the Three children continued in their
Furnace as before, and it grew rather Seven times hotter than
it was. All their former Ails pursued them still, with an addition of (tis not easy to tell how many) more, but such as
gave more sensible Demonstrations of an Enchantment growing very far towards a Possession by Evil spirits.

Sect. XII. The Children in their Fits would still cry
out upon *They* and *Them* as the Authors of all their Harm;
but who that *They* and *Them* were, they were not able to declare. At last, the Boy obtain'd at some times a sight of some
shapes in the room. There were Three or Four of 'em, the
Names of which the child would pretend at certain seasons to
tell; only the Name of One, who was counted a Sager Hag
than the rest, he still so stammered at, that he was put upon
some Periphrasis in describing her. A Blow at the place
where the Boy beheld the Spectre was alwaies felt by the Boy
himself in the part of his Body that answered what might be
stricken at; and this tho his Back were turn'd; which was
once and again so exactly tried, that there could be no Collusion in the Business. But as a Blow at the Apparition alwaies
hurt him, so it alwaies help't him too; for after the Agonies,
which a Push or Stab of That had put him to, were over, (as
in a minute or 2 they would be) the Boy would have a respite
from his Fits a considerable while, and the Hobgoblins dis-
appear. It is very credibly reported that a wound was this
way given to an Obnoxious woman in the town, whose name I
will not expose: for we should be tender in such Relations,
lest we wrong the Reputation of the Innocent by stories not
enough enquired into.

Sect. XIII. The Fits of the Children yet more arriv'd
unto such Motions as were beyond the Efficacy of any natural
Distemper in the World. They would bark at one another like
Dogs, and again purr like so many Cats. They would sometimes complain, that they were in a Red-hot Oven, sweating
and panting at the same time unreasonably: Anon they would
say, Cold water was thrown upon them, at which they would
shiver very much. They would cry out of dismal Blowes
with great Cudgels laid upon them; and tho' we saw no cud-

gels nor blowes, yet we could see the Marks left by them in
Red Streaks upon their bodies afterward.   And one of them
would be roasted on an invisible Spit, run into his Mouth, and
out at his Foot, he lying, and rolling, and groaning as if it had
been so in the most sensible manner in the world; and then he
would shriek, that Knives were cutting of him.   Sometimes
also he would have his head so forcibly, tho not visibly, nail'd
unto the Floor, that it was as much as a strong man could do
to pull it up.   One while they would all be so Limber, that it
was judg'd every Bone of them could be bent.   Another while
they would be so stiff, that not a joint of them could be stir'd.
They would sometimes be as though they were mad, and then
they would climb over high Fences, beyond the Imagination
of them that look'd after them.   Yea, They would fly like
Geese; and be carried with an incredible Swiftness thro the
air, having but just their Toes now and then upon the
ground, and their Arms waved like the Wings of a Bird.   One
of them, in the House of a kind Neighbour and Gentleman (Mr.
Willis) flew the length of the Room, about 20 foot, and flew
just into an Infants high armed Chair; (as tis affirmed) none
seeing her feet all the way touch the floor.

Sect. XIV.   Many wayes did the Devils take to make
the children do mischief both to themselves and others; but
thro the singular Providence of God, they always fail'd in the
attempts.   For they could never essay the doing of any harm,
unless there were some-body at hand that might prevent it;
and seldome without first shrieking out, "They say, I must do
such a thing!"   Diverse times they went to strike furious
Blowes at their tenderest and dearest friends, or to fling them
down staires when they had them at the Top, but the warnings
from the mouths of the children themselves, would still anticipate what the Devils did intend.   They diverse times were
very near Burning or Drowning of themselves, but the Children themselves by their own pittiful and seasonable cries for
Help, still procured their Deliverance: Which made me to
Consider, Whether the Little ones had not their Angels, in the
plain sense of Our Saviours Intimation.   Sometimes, When
they were tying their own Neck-clothes, their compelled hands
miserably strangled themselves, till perhaps, the standers-by
gave some Relief unto them.   But if any small Mischief hap-

pen'd to be done where they were; as the Tearing or Dirtying
of a Garment, the Falling of a Cup, the breaking of a Glass
or the like; they would rejoice extremely, and fall into a pleasure and Laughter very extraordinary.   All which things com-
par'd with the Temper of the Children, when they are themselves, may suggest some very peculiar Thoughts unto us.

Sect. XV.   They were not in a constant Torture for some
Weeks, but were a little quiet, unless upon some incidental
provocations; upon which the Devils would handle them like
Tigres, and wound them in a manner very horrible.   Particularly, Upon the least Reproof of their Parents for any unfit
thing they said or did, most grievous woful Heart-breaking
Agonies would they fall into.   If any useful thing were to be
done to them, or by them, they would have all sorts of Troubles
fall upon them.   It would sometimes cost one of them an Hour
or Two to be undrest in the evening, or drest in the morning.
For if any one went to unty a string, or undo a Button about
them, or the contrary; they would be twisted into such postures as made the thing impossible.   And at Whiles, they
would be so managed in their Beds, that no Bed-clothes could
for an hour or two be laid upon them; nor could they go to
wash their Hands, without having them clasp't so odly together, there was no doing of it.   But when their Friends were
near tired with Waiting, anon they might do what they would
unto them.   Whatever Work they were bid to do, they would
be so snap't in the member which was to do it, that they with
grief still desisted from it.   If one ordered them to Rub a
clean Table, they were able to do it without any disturbance;
if to rub a dirty Table, presently they would with many Torments be made uncapable.   And sometimes, tho but seldome,
they were kept from eating their meals, by having their Teeth
sett when they carried any thing unto their Mouthes.

Sect. XVI.   But nothing in the World would so discompose
them as a Religious Exercise.   If there were any Discourse of
God, or Christ, or any of the things which are not seen and are
eternal, they would be cast into intolerable Anguishes.   Once,
those two Worthy Ministers Mr. Fisk[1] and Mr. Thatcher,[2]
bestowing some gracious Counsils on the Boy, whom they then

[1] The Rev. Moses Fiske (1642–1708), minister at Braintree.
[2] The Rev. Peter Thacher (1651–1727), minister at Milton.

found at a Neighbours house, he immediately lost his Hearing, so that he heard not one word, but just the last word of all they said. Much more, All Praying to God, and Reading of His word, would occasion a very terrible Vexation to them: they would then stop their own Ears with their own Hands; and roar, and shriek; and holla, to drown the Voice of the Devotion. Yea, if any one in the Room took up a Bible to look into it, tho the Children could see nothing of it, as being in a croud of Spectators, or having their Faces another way, yet would they be in wonderful Miseries, till the Bible were laid aside. In short, No good thing must then be endured near those Children, Which (while they are themselves) do love every good thing in a measure that proclaims in them the Fear of God.

Sect. XVII. My Employments were such, that I could not visit this afflicted Family so often as I would; Wherefore, that I might show them what kindness I could, as also that I might have a full opportunity to observe the extraordinary Circumstances of the Children, and that I might be furnished with Evidence and Argument as a Critical Eye-Witness to confute the Saducism of this debauched Age; I took the Eldest of them home to my House. The young Woman continued well at our house, for diverse dayes, and apply'd her self to such Actions not only of Industry, but of Piety, as she had been no stranger to. But on the Twentieth of November in the Fore-noon, she cry'd out, "Ah, *They* have found me out! I thought it would be so!" and immediately she fell into her fits again. I shall now confine my Story cheefly to Her, from whose Case the Reader may shape some Conjecture at the Accidents of the Rest.

Sect. XVIII. Variety of Tortures now siez'd upon the Girl; in which besides the forementioned Ails returning upon her, she often would cough up a Ball as big as a small Egg, into the side of her Wind-pipe, that would near choak her, till by Stroking and by Drinking it was carried down again. At the beginning of her Fits usually she kept odly Looking up the Chimney, but could not say what she saw. When I bad her Cry to the Lord Jesus for Help, her Teeth were instantly sett; upon which I added, "Yet, child, Look unto Him," and then her Eyes were presently pulled into her head, so farr, that one might have fear'd she should never have us'd them more. When I prayed in the Room, first her Arms were with a strong, tho not seen Force clap't upon her ears; and when her hands were with violence pull'd away, she cryed out, "*They* make such a noise, I cannot hear a word!" She likewise complain'd, that Goody Glover's Chain was upon her Leg, and when she essay'd to go, her postures were exactly such as the chained Witch had before she died. But the manner still was, that her Tortures in a small while would pass over, and Frolicks succeed; in which she would continue many hours, nay, whole days, talking perhaps never wickedly, but alwaies wittily, beyond her self; and at certain provocations, her Tortures would renew upon her, till we had left off to give them. But she frequently told us, that if she might but steal, or be drunk, she should be well immediately.

Sect. XIX. In her ludicrous Fits, one while she would be for Flying; and she would be carried hither and thither, tho not long from the ground, yet so long as to exceed the ordinary power of Nature in our Opinion of it: another-while she would be for Diving, and use the Actions of it towards the Floor, on which, if we had not held her, she would have thrown her self. Being at this exercise she told us, That They said, she must go down to the Bottom of our Well, for there was Plate there, and They said, They would bring her safely up again. This did she tell us, tho she had never heard of any Plate there! and we ourselves who had newly bought the house, hardly knew of any; but the former Owner of the House just then coming in, told us there had been Plate for many years at the Bottom of the Well.

She had once a great mind to have eaten a roasted Apple, but whenever she attempted to eat it, her Teeth would be sett, and sometimes, if she went to take it up her Arm would be made so stiff, that she could not possibly bring her hand to her Mouth: at last she said, "Now They say, I shall eat it, if I eat it quickly"; and she nimbly eat it all up. Moreover,

There was one very singular passion that frequently attended her. An Invisible Chain would be clapt about her, and shee, in much pain and Fear, cry out, When They began to put it on. Once I did with my own hand knock it off, as it began to be fastned about her. But ordinarily, When it was

on, shee'd be pull'd out of her seat with such violence towards
the Fire, that it has been as much as one or two of us could
do to keep her out.   Her Eyes were not brought to be perpen-
dicular to her feet, when she rose out of her Seat, as the Mech-
anism of a Humane[1] Body requires in them that rise, but
she was one dragg'd wholly by other Hands: and once, When
I gave a stamp on the Hearth, just between her and the Fire,
she scream'd out, (tho I think she saw me not) that I Jarr'd
the Chain, and hurt her Back.

Sect. XX.   While she was in her Frolicks I was willing
to try, Whether she could read or no; and I found, not only
That If she went to read the Bible her Eyes would be strangely
twisted and blinded, and her Neck presently broken, but also
that if any one else did read the Bible in the Room, tho it
were wholly out of her sight, and without the least voice or
noise of it, she would be cast into very terrible Agonies.   Yet
once Falling into her Maladies a little time after she had read
the 59th Psalm, I said unto the standers by, "Poor child! she
can't now read the Psalm she readd a little while ago," she
listened her self unto something that none of us could hear and
made us be silent for some few Seconds of a minute.   Whereupon she said, "But I can read it, they say I shall!"   So I
show'd her the Psalm, and she readd it all over to us.   Then
said I, "Child, say Amen to it:" but that she could not do.   I
added, "Read the next:" but no where else in the Bible
could she read a word.   I brought her a Quakers Book; and
That she could quietly read whole pages of; only the Name of
God and Christ she still skip't over, being unable to pronounce
it, except sometimes with stammering a minute or two or
more upon it.   When we urged her to tell what the word was
that she missed, shee'd say, "I must not speak it; They say I
must not, you know what it is, it's G and O and D;" so shee'd
spell the Name unto us.   I brought her again one that I
thought was a Good Book; and presently she was handled
with intolerable Torments.   But when I show'd her a Jest-
Book, as, *The Oxford Jests*, or the *Cambridge Jests*, she could
read them without any Disturbance, and have witty Descants
upon them too.   I entertain'd her with a Book that pretends
to prove, That there are no Witches; and that she could read

---

[1] Human.   "Humane" was then the current spelling.

very well, only the Name Devils, and Witches, could not be uttered by her without extraordinary Difficulty. I produced a Book to her that proves, That there are Witches, and that she had not power to read. When I readd in the Room the Story of Ann Cole,[1] in my Fathers *Remarkable Providences,* and came to the Exclamation which the Narrative saies the Dæmons made upon her, "Ah she runs to the Rock!" it cast her into inexpressible Agonies; and shee'd fall into them whenever I had the Expression of, "Running to the Rock," afterwards. A popish Book also she could endure very well; but it would kill her to look into any Book, that (in my Opinion) it might have bin profitable and edifying for her to be reading of. These Experiments were often enough repeated, and still with the same Success, before Witnesses not a few. The good Books that were found so mortal to her were cheefly such as lay ever at hand in the Room. One was the *Guid to Heaven from the Word,* which I had given her. Another of them was Mr. Willard's little (but precious) *Treatise of Justification.* Diverse Books published by my Father I also tried upon her; particularly, his *Mystery of Christ;* and another small Book of his about Faith and Repentance, and the day of Judgement.

Once being very merrily talking by a Table that had this last Book upon it, she just opened the Book, and was immediately struck backwards as dead upon the floor. I hope I have not spoil'd the credit of the Books, By telling how much the Devils hated them. I shall therefore add, That my Grandfather Cottons Catechism called *Milk for Babes,* and *The Assemblies Catechism,* would bring hideous Convulsions on the Child if she look't into them; tho she had once learn't them with all the love that could be.

Sect. XXI. I was not unsensible that this Girls Capacity or incapacity to read, was no Test for Truth to be determin'd by, and therefore I did not proceed much further in this fanciful Business, not knowing What snares the Devils might lay for us in the Tryals. A few further Tryals, I confess, I did make; but what the event of 'em was, I shall not relate, because I would not offend. But that which most made me to wonder was, That one bringing to her a certain Prayer-Book, she not only could Read it very well, but also did read a large

---

[1] See pp. 18–21, above.

part of it over, and calling it Her Bible, she took in it a delight
and put on it a Respect more than Ordinary. If she were
going into her tortures, at the offer of this Book, she would
come out of her fits and read; and her Attendents were almost
under a Temptation to use it as a Charm, to make and keep
her quiet. Only, When she came to the Lords Prayer, (now
and then occurring in this Book) she would have her eyes put
out, so that she must turn over a new leaf, and then she could
read again. Whereas also there are Scriptures in that Book,
she could read them there, but if I shew'd her the very same
Scriptures in the Bible, she should sooner Dy than read them.
And she was likewise made unable to read the Psalms in an
ancient meeter, which this prayer-book had in the same vol-
umne with it. There were, I think I may say, no less than
Multitudes of Witnesses to this odd thing; and I should not
have been a faithful and honest Historian, if I had withheld
from the World this part of my History: But I make no
Reflections on it. Those inconsiderable men that are provoked at it (if any shall be of so little Sense as to be provoked)
must be angry at the Devils, and not at me; their Malice, and
not my Writing, deserves the Blame of any Aspersion which a
true History may seem to cast on a Book that some have
enough manifested their Concernment for.

Sect. XXII.   There was another most unaccountable
Circumstance which now attended her; and until she came to
our House, I think, she never had Experience of it. Ever now
and then, an Invisible Horse would be brought unto her, by
those whom she only called, "them," and, "Her Company":
upon the Approach of Which, her eyes would be still closed up;
for (said she) "They say, I am a Tell-Tale, and therefore they
will not let me see them." Upon this would she give a Spring
as one mounting an Horse, and Settling her self in a Riding-
Posture—she would in her Chair be agitated as one sometimes
Ambleing, sometimes Trotting, and sometimes Galloping very
furiously. In these motions we could not perceive that she
was stirred by the stress of her feet, upon the ground; for
often she touch't it not; but she mostly continued in her
Chair, though sometimes in her hard Trott we doubted she
would have been tossed over the Back of it. Once being
angry at his Dulness, When she said, she would cut off his

head if she had a knife, I gave her my Sheath, wherewith she suddenly gave her self a stroke on the Neck, but complain'd, it would not cut. When she had rode a minute or two or three, shee'd pretend to be at a Rendezvous with Them, that were Her Company; there shee'd maintain a Discourse with them, and asking many Questions concerning her self, (for we gave her none of ours) shee'd Listen much, and Received Answers from them that indeed none but her self perceived. Then would she return and inform us, how *They* did intend to handle her for a day or two afterwards, besides some other things that she enquired of *them*. Her Horse would sometimes throw her, with much Violence; but she would mount again; and one of the Standers-by once imagining *them* that were Her Company, to be before her (for she call'd unto them to stay for her) he struck with his Cane in the Air where he thought they were, and tho her eyes were wholly shutt, yet she cry'd out, that he struck her. Her Fantastic Journeyes were mostly performed in her Chair without removing from it; but sometimes would she ride from her Chair, and be carried odly on the Floor, from one part of the Room to another, in the postures of a Riding Woman. If any of us asked her, Who her Company were? She generally replyed, I don't know. But If we were instant in our Demand, she would with some witty Flout or other turn it off. Once I said, "Child, if you can't tell their Names, pray tell me what Clothes they have on;" and the Words were no sooner out of my mouth, but she was laid for dead upon the Floor.

Sect. XXIII. One of the Spectators once ask'd her, Whether she could not ride up stairs; unto which her Answer was, That she believe'd she could, for her Horse could do very notable things. Accordingly, when her Horse came to her again, to our Admiration she Rode (that is, was tossed as one that rode) up the stairs: there then stood open the Study of one belonging to the Family, into which entring, she stood immediately upon her Feet, and cry'd out, "They are gone; they are gone! They say, that they cannot,—God won't let 'em come here!" She also added a Reason for it, which the Owner of the Study thought more kind than true. And she presently and perfectly came to her self, so that her whole Discourse and Carriage was altered unto the greatest measure

of Sobriety, and she satt Reading of the Bible and Good
Books, for a good part of the Afternoon.   Her Affairs calling
her anon to go down again, the Dæmons were in a quarter of
a minute as bad upon her as before, and her Horse was Waiting for her.   I understanding of it, immediately would have
her up to the study of the young man where she had been at
ease before; meerly to try Whether there had not been a Fal-
lacy in what had newly happened: but she was now so twisted
and writhen, that it gave me much trouble to get her into my
Arms, and much more to drag her up the stairs.   She was
pulled out of my hands, and when I recovered my Hold, she
was thrust so hard upon me, that I had almost fallen backwards, and her own breast was sore afterwards, by their Com-
pressions to detain her; she seem'd heavier indeed than three
of her self.   With incredible Forcing (tho she kept Screaming,
"They say I must not go in!") at length we pull'd her in;
where she was no sooner come, but she could stand on her
Feet, and with an altered tone, could thank me, saying, "now
I am well."   At first shee'd be somewhat faint, and say, She
felt something go out of her; but in a minute or two, she could
attend any Devotion or Business as well as ever in her Life;
and both spoke and did as became a person of good Discretion.

I was loth to make a Charm of the Room; yet some
strangers that came to visit us, the Week after, desiring to see
the Experiment made, I permitted more than two or three
Repetitions of it; and it still succeded as I have declared.
Once when I was assisting 'em in carrying of her up, she was
torn out of all our hands; and to my self, she cry'd out, "Mr.
M., One of them is going to push you down the stairs, have a
care."   I remember not that I felt any Thrust or Blow; but
I think I was unaccountably made to step down backward
two or three stairs, and within a few hours she told me by
whom it was.

Sect. XXIV.   One of those that had bin concerned for
her Welfare, had newly implored the great God that the
young woman might be able to declare whom she apprehended
her self troubled by.   Presently upon this her Horse returned,
only it pestered her with such ugly paces, that she fell out with
her Company, and threatned now to tell all, for their so abusing her.   I was going abroad, and she said unto them that

were about her, "Mr. M. is gone abroad, my horse won't come back, till he come home; and then I believe" (said she softly,) "I shall tell him all." I staid abroad an hour or two, and then Returning, When I was just come to my Gate, before I had given the least Sign or Noise of my being there, she said, "My Horse is come!" and intimated, that I was at the Door. When I came in, I found her mounted after her fashion, upon her Aerial Steed; which carried her Fancy to the Journeys end. There (or rather then) she maintained a considerable Discourse with Her Company, Listening very attentively when she had propounded any Question, and receiving the Answers with impressions made upon her mind. She said; "Well what do you say? How many Fits more am I to have?—pray, can ye tell how long it shall be before you are hang'd for what you have done?—You are filthy Witches to my knowledge, I shall see some of you go after your sister; You would have killd me; but you can't, I don't fear you.—You would have thrown Mr Mather down stairs, but you could not.—Well! How shall I be To morrow?[1] Pray, What do you think of To morrow?— Fare ye well.—You have brought me such an ugly Horse, I am angry at you; I could find in my heart to tell all." So she began her homeward-paces; but when she had gone a little way, (that is a little while) she said, "O I have forgot one Question, I must go back again;" and back she rides. She had that day been diverse times warning us, that *they* had been contriving to do some harm to my Wife, by a Fall or a Blow, or the like; and when she came out of her mysterious Journeys, she would still be careful concerning Her. Accordingly she now calls to her Company again, "Hark you, One thing more before we part! What hurt is it you will do to Mrs Mather? will you do her any hurt?" Here she list'ned some time; and then clapping her hands, cry'd out, "O, I am glad on't, they can do Mrs. Mather no hurt: they try, but they say they can't." So she returns and at once, Dismissing her Horse, and opening her eyes, she call'd me to her, "Now Sir," (said she) "I'll tell you all. I have learn'd who they are that are the cause of my trouble, there's three of them," (and she named who) "if they were out of the way, I should be well. They

----

[1] [In the margin:] "Note, on To morrow, the Ministers of the Town were to keep a day of Prayer at her Fathers House."

say, they can tell now how long I shall be troubled, But they won't. Only they seem to think, their power will be broke this Week. They seem also to say, that I shall be very ill To morow, but they are themselves terribly afraid of to morrow; They fear, that to morrow we shall be delivered. They say too, that they can't hurt Mrs. Mather, which I am glad of. But they said, they would kill me to night, if I went to bed before ten a clock, if I told a word." And other things did she say, not now to be recited.

Sect. XXV. The Day following, which was, I think, about the twenty seventh of November, Mr. Morton of Charlestown, and Mr. Allen, Mr. Moody, Mr. Willard, and my self, of Boston, with some devout Neighbours, kept another Day of Prayer, at John Goodwin's house; and we had all the Children present with us there. The children were miserably tortured, while we laboured in our Prayers; but our good God was nigh unto us, in what we call'd upon Him for. From this day the power of the Enemy was broken; and the children, though Assaults after this were made upon them, yet were not so cruelly handled as before. The Liberty of the Children encreased daily more and more, and their Vexation abated by degrees; till within a little while they arrived to Perfect Ease, which for some weeks or months they cheerfully enjoyed. Thus Good it is for us to draw near to God.

Sect. XXVI. Within a day or two after the Fast, the young Woman had two remarkable Attempts made upon her, by her invisible Adversaries. Once, they were Dragging her into the Oven that was then heating, while there was none in the Room to help her. She clap't her hands on the Mantle-tree[1] to save her self; but they were beaten off; and she had been burned, if at her Out-cryes one had not come in from abroad for her Relief. Another time, they putt an unseen Rope with a cruel Noose about her Neck, Whereby she was choaked, until she was black in the Face; and though it was taken off before it had kill'd her, yet there were the red Marks of it, and of a Finger and a Thumb near it, remaining to be seen for a while afterwards.

Sect. XXVII. This was the last Molestation that they gave her for a While; and she dwelt at my house the rest of

---

[1] Mantelpiece, mantelshelf.

the Winter, having by an obliging and vertuous Conversation, made her self enough Welcome to the Family.   But within about a Fortnight, she was visited with two dayes of as Extraordinary Obsessions as any we had been the Spectators of. I thought it convenient for me to entertain my Congregation with a Sermon upon the memorable Providences which these Children had been concerned in.   When I had begun to study my Sermon, her Tormentors again seiz'd upon her; and all Fryday and Saturday, did they manage her with a special Design, as was plain, to disturb me in what I was about.   In the worst of her extravagancies formerly, she was more dutiful to my self, than I had reason to Expect, but now her whole carriage to me was with a Sauciness that I had not been us'd to be treated with.   She would knock at my Study Door, affirming, That some below would be glad to see me; when there was none that ask't for me.   She would call to me with multi-plyed Impertinencies, and throw small things at me wherewith she could not give me any hurt.   Shee'd Hector me at a strange rate for the work I was at, and threaten me with I know not what mischief for it.   She got a History that I had Written of this Witchcraft, and tho she had before this readd it over and over, yet now she could not read (I believe) one entire Sentence of it; but she made of it the most ridiculous Travesty in the World, with such a Patness and excess of Fancy, to supply the sense that she put upon it, as I was amazed at.   And she particularly told me, That I should quickly come to disgrace by that History.

Sect. XXVIII.   But there were many other Wonders be-held by us before these two dayes were out.   Few tortures at-tended her, but such as were provoked; her Frolicks being the things that had most possession of her.   I was in Latin telling some young Gentlemen of the Colledge, That if I should bid her Look to God, her Eyes would be put out, upon which her eyes were presently served so.   I was in some surprize, When I saw that her Troublers understood Latin, and it made me willing to try a little more of their Capacity.   We continu-ally found, that if an English Bible were in any part of the Room seriously look'd into, though she saw and heard nothing of it, she would immediately be in very dismal Agonies.   We now made a Tryal more than once or twice, of the Greek New-

Testament, and the Hebrew Old Testament; and We still found, That if one should go to read in it never so secretly and silently, it would procure her that Anguish, Which there was no enduring of. But I thought, at length, I fell upon one inferior Language which the Dæmons did not seem so well to understand.

Sect. XXIX. Devotion was now, as formerly, the terriblest of all the provocations that could be given her. I could by no means bring her to own, That she desired the mercies of God, and the prayers of good men. I would have obtained a Sign of such a Desire, by her Lifting up of her hand; but she stirr'd it not: I then lifted up her hand my self, and though the standers-by thought a more insignificant thing could not be propounded, I said, "Child, If you desire those things, let your hand fall, when I take mine away:" I took my hand away, and hers continued strangely and stifly stretched out, so that for some time, she could not take it down. During these two dayes we had Prayers oftener in our Family than at other times; and this was her usual Behavior at them. The man that prayed, usually began with Reading the Word of God; which once as he was going to do, she call'd to him, "Read of Mary Magdelen, out of whom the Lord cast seven Devils." During the time of Reading, she would be laid as one fast asleep; but when Prayer was begun, the Devils would still throw her on the Floor, at the feet of him that prayed. There would she lye and Whistle and sing and roar, to drown the voice of the Prayer; but that being a little too audible for Them, they would shutt close her Mouth and her ears, and yet make such odd noises in her Throat as that she her self could not hear our Cries to God for her. Shee'd also fetch very terrible Blowes with her Fist, and Kicks with her Foot at the man that prayed; but still (for he had bid that none should hinder her) her Fist and Foot would alwaies recoil, when they came within a few hairs breadths of him just as if Rebounding against a Wall; so that she touch'd him not, but then would beg hard of other people to strike him, and particularly she entreated them to take the Tongs and smite him; Which not being done, she cryed out of him, "He has wounded me in the Head." But before Prayer was out, she would be laid for Dead, wholly sensless and (unless to a severe Trial) Breathless; with her

Belly swelled like a Drum, and sometimes with croaking
Noises in it; thus would she ly, most exactly with the stiffness
and posture of one that had been two Days laid out for Dead.
Once lying thus, as he that was praying was alluding to the
words of the Canaanitess, and saying, "Lord, have mercy on
a Daughter vexed with a Devil;" there came a big, but low
voice from her, saying, "There's Two or Three of them" (or
us!) and the standers-by were under that Apprehension, as
that they cannot relate whether her mouth mov'd in speaking
of it. When Prayer was ended, she would Revive in a minute
or two, and continue as Frolicksome as before. She thus continued until Saturday towards the Evening; when, after this
man had been at Prayer, I charged all my Family to admit of
no Diversion by her Frolicks, from such exercises as it was
proper to begin the Sabbath with. They took the Counsel;
and tho she essayed, with as witty and as nimble and as various
an Application to each of them successively as ever I saw, to
make them laugh, yet they kept close to their good Books
which then called for their Attention. When she saw that,
immediately she fell asleep; and in two or three hours, she
waked perfectly her self; weeping bitterly to remember (for
as one come out of a dream she could remember) what had
befallen her.

Sect. XXX. After this, we had no more such entertainments. The Demons it may be would once or twice in a
Week trouble her for a few minutes with perhaps a twisting
and a twink[ling] of her eyes, or a certain Cough which did
seem to be more than ordinary. Moreover, Both she at my
house, and her Sister at home, at the time which they call
Christmas, were by the Dæmons made very drunk, though
they had no strong Drink (as we are fully sure) to make them
so. When she began to feel her self thus drunk, she complain'd, "O they say they will have me to keep Christmas
with them! They will disgrace me when they can do nothing
else!" And immediately the Ridiculous Behaviours of one
drunk were with a wonderful exactness represented in her
Speaking, and Reeling, and Spewing, and anon Sleeping, till
she was well again. But the Vexations of the Children otherwise abated continually.

They first came to be alwaies Quiet, unless upon Provoca-

tions. Then they got Liberty to work, but not to read: then
further on, to read, but not aloud, at last they were wholly
delivered; and for many Weeks remained so.

Sect. XXXI. I was not unsensible, that it might be an
easie thing to be too bold, and go too far, in making of Experiments: Nor was I so unphilosophical as not to discern many
opportunityes of Giving and Solving many Problems which
the pneumatic Discipline[1] is concerned in. I confess I have
Learn't much more than I sought, and I have bin informed of
some things relating to the invisible World, which as I did not
think it lawful to ask, so I do not think it proper to tell; yet
I will give a Touch upon one Problem commonly Discoursed
of; that is,

Whether the Devils know our Thoughts, or no?

I will not give the Reader my Opinion of it, but only my
Experiment. That they do not, was conjectured from this:
We could cheat them when we spoke one thing, and mean't
another. This was found when the Children were to be undressed. The Devils would still in wayes beyond the Force
of any Imposture, wonderfully twist the part that was to be
undress't, so that there was no coming at it. But, if we said,
untye his neckcloth, and the parties bidden, at the same time,
understood our intent to be, unty his Shooe! The Neckcloth,
and not the shooe, has been made strangely inaccessible. But
on the other side, That they do, may be conjectured from This.
I called the young Woman at my House by her Name, intending to mention unto her some Religious Expedient whereby
she might, as I thought, much relieve her self; presently her
Neck was broke, and I continued watching my Opportunity
to say what I designed. I could not get her to come out of her
Fit, until I had laid aside my purpose of speaking what I
thought, and then she reviv'd immediately. Moreover a
young Gentleman visiting of me at my Study to ask my advice about curing the Atheism and Blasphemy which he complained his Thoughts were more than ordinarily then infested
with; after some Discourse I carried him down to see this Girl
who was then molested with her unseen Fiends; but when he
came, she treated him very coursly and rudely, asking him
What he came to the house for? and seemed very angry at his

[1] The science of spirits, pneumatology, *i. e.*, the science of angels and demons.

being there, urging him to be gone with a very impetuous Importunity. Perhaps all Devils are not alike sagacious.

Sect. XXXII. The Last Fit that the young Woman had, was very peculiar. The Dæmons having once again seiz'd her, they made her pretend to be Dying; and Dying truly we fear'd at last she was: She lay, she tossed, she pull'd just like one Dying, and urged hard for some one to dy with her, seeming loth to dy alone. She argued concerning Death, in strains that quite amazed us; and concluded, That though she was loth to dy, yet if God said she must, she must; adding something about the state of the Countrey, which we wondred at. Anon, the Fit went over; and as I guessed it would be, it was the last Fit she had at our House. But all my Library never afforded me any Commentary on those Paragraphs of the Gospels, which speak of Demoniacs, equal to that which the passions of this Child have given me.

Sect. XXXIII. This is the Story of Goodwins Children, a Story all made up of Wonders! I have related nothing but what I judge to be true. I was my self an Eye-witness to a large part of what I tell; and I hope my neighbours have long thought, That I have otherwise learned Christ, than to ly unto the World. Yea, there is, I believe, scarce any one particular, in this Narrative, which more than one credible Witness will not be ready to make Oath unto. The things of most Concernment in it were before many Critical Observers; and the Whole happened in the Metropolis of the English America, unto a religious and industrious Family which was visited by all sorts of Persons, that had a mind to satisfy themselves. I do now likewise publish the History, While the thing is yet fresh and New; and I challenge all men to detect so much as one designed Falshood, yea, or so much as one important Mistake, from the Egg to the Apple of it. I have Writ as plainly as becomes an Historian, as truly as becomes a Christian, tho perhaps not so profitably as became a Divine. But I am resolv'd after this, never to use but just one grain of patience with any man that shall go to impose upon me a Denial of Devils, or of Witches. I shall count that man Ignorant who shall suspect, but I shall count him down-right Impudent if he Assert the Non-Existence of things which we have had such palpable Convictions of. I am sure he cannot be a Civil, (and some will question whether he can be an honest man) that shall go to deride the Being of things which a whole Countrey has now beheld an house of pious people suffering not a few Vexations by.   But if the Sadducee, or the Atheist, have no right Impressions by these Memorable Providences made upon his mind; yet I hope those that know what it is to be sober will not repent any pains that they may have taken in perusing what Records of these Witchcrafts and Possessions, I thus leave unto Posterity.[1]

Postscript.

You have seen the Trouble and the Relief of John Goodwins Children.   After which the Dæmons were let loose to make a fresh Attacque upon them, tho not in a manner altogether so terrible and afflictive as what they had before susteined.   All the Three Children were visited with some Return of their Calamities; but the Boy was the Child which endured most in this New Assault.[2]   He had been for some While kindly entertained with Mr. Baily[3] at Watertown, where he had enjoyed a long time of ease; the Devils having given him but little Disturbance, except what was for a short while after his first coming there.   He no sooner came Home, but he began to be ill again, with diverse peculiar Circumstances attending

---

[1] In 1697 the Boston merchant Calef wrote: "In the times of Sir Ed. Andros his Government, Goody Glover, a despised, crazy, ill-conditioned old Woman, an Irish Roman Catholick, was tried for afflicting Goodwins Children; by the Account of which Tryal, taken in Short-hand, for the use of the Jury, it may appear that the generality of her Answers were Nonsense, and her behaviour like that of one distracted.   Yet the Drs. finding her as she had been for many Years, brought her in *Compos Mentis*; and setting aside her crazy Answers to some insnaring questions, the proof against her was wholly deficient: The Jury brought her Guilty.

"Mr. Cotton Mather was the most active and forward of any Minister in the Country in those matters, taking home one of the Children, and managing such Intreagues with that Child, and after printing such an Account of the whole, in his Memorable Providences, as conduced much to the kindling those flames, that in Sir Williams time [1692] threatned the devouring this Country." (*More Wonders of the Invisible World*, pp. 151–152.)

[2] John, now aged 12.   The younger boy, Benjamin, it will be remembered, had early been "delivered" (§ 6, above).

[3] The Rev. John Bailey, then minister at Watertown.

of him.   There was this particularly remarkable; That the
Boy dream't he had a Bone within his skin growing cross his
Ribs; and when he awaked, he felt and found a thing there
which was esteem'd a Bone, by them that handled it; only
every one wondered how it should be lodged there.   An expert
Chirurgeon, Dr. John Clark, being advis'd with about it, very
dexterously took it out; and it prov'd not the imagined Bone,
but a considerable Pin; a brass Pin, which could not possibly
have come to ly there as it did, without the Prestigious[1]
Conveyance of a Misterious Witchcraft.   Another time, on a
Lord's Day his Father would have taken him to Meeting with
him; and when his Father spoke of going to some of the Assemblies in the Town (particularly both the North and the South)
the Boy would be cast into such Tortures and Postures, that
he would sooner Dy than go out of doors; but if his Father
spoke of going to others of the Assemblies in the Town, particularly the Quakers, the boy in a moment would be as well
as could be.   The tryal of this was more than five times repeated, and were it fully related, would be more than ten times
Admired.

Our Prayers for the Children were justly renewed, and I
hope not altogether unanswered.   Upon one Prayer over two
of them, they had about a Fortnights ease; and their Ails
again returning, Prayer was again awakened, with some Circumstances not proper to be exposed unto the World.   God
gave a present Abatement hereupon to the Maladies of the
Children, and caused their Invaders to retire; so that by degrees they were fully and quickly Delivered.   Two days of
Prayer obtained the Deliverance of two.   The Third, namely
the Boy, Remaining under some Annoyance by the evil spirits,
a third Day was employ'd for him, and he soon found the
blessed effects of it in his Deliverance also.   There were several very memorable things attending this Deliverance of the
Children, and the Vowes and the Pleas, used in the Prayers
which were thereby answerd, but they were all Private, yea,
in a sort, Secret; *Non est Religio ubi omnia patent;*[2] and I
understand (for I have some Acquaintance with him) That the

---

[1] *I. e.*, preternatural: the lying marvels of devils were counted "prestigious,"
not miraculous.

[2] "Where there is no mystery, there is no religion."

Friend of the Children,[1] whom God gave to be thus concerned and successful for them, desires me not to let Reports of those things go out of the Walls of a Study, but to leave them rather for the Notice of the other World. I think it will not be improper to tell the World, that one thing in the Childrens Deliverance was the strange Death of an horrible old Woman, who was presum'd to have a great hand in their Affliction.[2] Before her Death and at it, the Alms-House where she lived was terrified with fearful noises, and she seem'd to have her Death hastened by dismal Blowes received from the invisible World. But having mentioned this, all that I have now to publish is That Prayer and Faith was the thing which drove the Divels from the Children; and I am to bear this Testimony unto the world, That the Lord is nigh to all them, who call upon him in truth, and, That blessed are all they that wait for Him.

Finished, June 7th, 1689.[3]

Mantissa.

To the foregoing Narrative, we have added an account given us by the Godly Father of these Haunted Children; who upon his Reading over so much of our History, as was written of their Exercise before their full deliverance, was willing to express his Attestation to the Truth of it; with this further Declaration of the Sense which he had of the unusual Miseries, that then lay upon his Family. 'Tis in his own Style; but I suppose a Pen hath not commonly been managed with more cleanly Discourse by an Hand used only to the Trowel; and his Condition hath been such, that he may fairly have Leave to speak.

IN the year 1688, about Midsummer, it pleased the Lord to visit one of my children with a sore Visitation; and she was

---

[1] He is speaking, of course, of himself: the narrative (as must be inferred from § 27, above) was circulated in manuscript before its printing, and doubtless without the author's name. In revising it for the printer this page seems to have escaped his eye.

[2] Who this second old woman was does not appear.

[3] The story of the Goodwin children is retold by Mather in his *Magnalia* (1702), but without added details.

not only tormented in her Body, but was in great distress of
Mind, Crying out, That she was in the dark concerning her
Souls estate, and that she had mispent her precious time; She
and we thinking her time was near at an end.   Hearing those
Shrieks and Groans which did not only pierce the ears, but
Hearts of her poor Parents, now was a time for me to Consider
with my self, and to look into my own heart and life, and see
how matters did there stand between God and my own soul,
and see Wherefore the Lord was thus contending with me.
And upon Enquiry I found cause to judge my self, and to
justify the Lord.   This Affliction continuing some time, the
Lord saw good then to double the affliction in smiting down
another Child, and that which was most heart breaking of all,
and did double this double affliction was, it was apparent and
judged by all that saw them, that the Devil and his Instruments had a hand in it.

The consideration of this was most dreadful: I thought of
what David said, 2 Sam. 24. 14.   If he feared so to fall into
the hands of Men, oh! then to think of the Horror of our condition, to be in the Hands of Devils and Witches!   This our
doleful condition moved us to call to our Friends to have pity
on us, for Gods Hand had touched us.   I was ready to say,
that no ones affliction was like mine; That my little House
that should be a little Bethel for God to dwell in, should be
made a Den for Devils; that those little Bodies, that should
be Temples for the Holy Ghost to dwell in, should be thus
harrassed and abused by the Devil and ·his cursed Brood.
But now this twice doubled affliction is doubled again.   Two
more of my Children are smitten down, oh! the Cries, the
Shrieks, the Tortures of these poor Children!   Doctors cannot
help, Parents weep and lament over them, but cannot ease
them.   Now I considering my affliction to be more than ordinary, it did certainly call for more than ordinary Prayer.   I
acquainted Mr. Allen, Mr. Moodey, Mr. Willard, and Mr. C.
Mather, the four Ministers of the Town with it, and Mr.
Morton of Charlstown; earnestly desiring them, that they,
with some other praying people of God, would meet at my
house, and there be earnest with God, on the behalf of us and
our Children; which they (I thank them for it) readily attended
with great fervency of Spirit; but as for my part, my heart

was ready to sink to hear and see those doleful Sights.   Now
I thought that I had greatly neglected my duty to my Children,
in not admonishing and instructing of them; and that God
was hereby calling my sins to mind, to slay my Children.
Then I pondered of that place in Numb. 23. 23.   *Surely there
is no Inchantment against Jacob, neither is there any Devination
against Israel.*   And now I thought I had broke Covenant
with God, not only in one respect but in many, but it pleased
the Lord to bring that to mind in Heb. 8. 12.   *For I will be
merciful to their unrighteousness, and their Sins and Iniquities
will I remember no more.*   The Consideration how the Lord
did deal with Job, and his Patience and the End the Lord
made with him was some support to me.   I thought also, on
what David said, that He had sinned, but what have these
poor Lambs done?   But yet in the midd'st of my tumultous
Thoughts within me, it was Gods Comforts that did delight
my soul.   That in the 18 of Luke, and the Beginning, Where
Christ spake the Parable for that end, that men ought alwaies
to pray and not faint.   This, with many other places, bore up
my spirit.   I thought with Jonah that I would yet again Look
towards God's holy Temple; the Lord Jesus Christ.   And I
did greatly desire to find the Son of God with me in this
Furnace of Affliction, knowing hereby that no harm shall
befall me.   But now this solemn day of Prayer and Fasting
being at an End, there was an Eminent Answer of it: for one
of my Children was delivered, and one of the wicked instruments of the Devil discovered, and her own mouth condemned
her, and so accordingly Executed.   Here was Food for Faith,
and great encouragement still to hope and quietly wait for
the Salvation of the Lord; the Ministers still counselling and
encouraging me to labour to be found in Gods way, commiting
my case to him, and not to use any way not allowed in Gods
Word.   It was a thing not a little comfortable to us, to see
that the people of God was so much concerned about our
lamentable condition, remembering us at all times in their
prayers, which I did look at as a token for good; but you must
think it was a time of sore Temptation with us, for many did
say, (yea, and some good people too) were it their case, that
they would try some Tricks, that should give ease to their
Children: But I thought for us to forsake the counsel of

good old men, and to take the counsel of the young ones, it might ensnare our Souls, though for the present it might offer some relief to our Bodies; which was a thing I greatly feared; and my Children were not at any time free for doing any such thing. It was a time of sore affliction, but it was mixed with abundance of mercy, for my heart was many a time made glad in the house of Prayer. The Neighbourhood pitied us, and were very helpful to us: Moreover, though my Children were thus in every Limb and Joynt tormented by those Children of the Devil, they also using their tongues at their pleasure, sometimes one way, sometimes another; yet the Lord did herein prevent them, that they could not make them speak wicked words, though they did many times hinder them from speaking good ones; had they in these Fits blasphemed the Name of the Holy God, this you may think would have been an heart-breaking thing to us the poor Parents; but God in his mercy prevented them, a thing worth taking notice of. Likewise they slept well a nights: And the Ministers did often visit us, and pray with us, and for us; and their love and pity was so great, their Prayers so earnest and constant, that I could not but admire at it. Mr. Mather particularly; now his bowels so yearned towards us in this sad condition, that he not only pray's with us, and for us, but he taketh one of my Children home to his own house; which indeed was but a troublesome guest, for such an one that had so much work lying upon his hands and heart: He took much pains in this great Service, to pull this Child, and her Brother and Sister out of the hand of the Devil. Let us now admire and adore that Fountain the Lord Jesus Christ, from whence those streams come. The Lord himself will requite his labour of love. Our case is yet very sad, and doth call for more Prayer; and the good Ministers of this Town and Charlstown readily came, with some other good praying people to my house, to keep another Day of solemn Fasting and Prayer; which our Lord saith this kind goeth out by. My Children being all at home, the two biggest lying on the bed, one of them would fain have kicked the good men while they were wrestling with God for them, had not I held him with all my power and might; and sometimes he would stop his own ears. This you must needs think was a cutting thing to the poor parents. Now our hearts

were ready to sink, had not God put under his everlasting arms
of Mercy and helped us still to hope in his mercy, and to be
quiet, knowing that He is God, and that it was not for the
potsheards of the earth to strive with their Maker. Well
might David say, that had not the Law of his God been his
delight, he had perished in his Affliction. Now the Promises
of God are sweet; God having promised, to hear the prayer of
the destitute, and not to despise their prayer; and He will not
fail the Expectation of those that wait on Him; but He hear-
eth the cry of the poor and needy. These Jacobs came and
wrestled with God for a Blessing on this poor Family, which
indeed I hope they obtained, and may be now worthy of the
Name Israel, who prevailed with God, and would not let Him
go till He had blessed us. For soon after this, there were two
more of my children delivered out of this horrible pit. Here
was now a double mercy, and how sweet was it, knowing it
came in Answer of Prayer! Now we see and know, it is not
a vain thing to call on the name of the Lord. For He is a
present help in the time of trouble; and we may boldly say
the Lord has been our helper. I had sunk, but Jesus put forth
His hand and bore me up. My Faith was ready to fail, but
this was a support to me that Christ said to Peter, "I have
prayed for thee that thy faith fail not." And many other
Promises were as Cordials to my drooping soul. And the
Consideration of all those that ever came to Christ Jesus for
Healing, that He healed their bodies, pardoned their Sins,
and healed their Souls too; which I hope in God may be the
fruit of this present Affliction. If God be pleased to make
the Fruit of this Affliction to be to take away our sin, and
cleanse us from iniquity, and to put us on with greater diligence to make our Calling and election sure, then, happy
Affliction! The Lord said that I had need of this to awake me.
I have found a prosperous Condition a dangerous Condition.
I have taken notice and considered more of God's Goodness
in these few weeks of Affliction, than in many years of Prosperity. I may speak it with shame, so wicked and deceitful,
and ungrateful is my heart, that the more God hath been doing
for me, the less I have been doing for Him. My Returns have
not been according to my Receivings. The Lord help me now
to praise Him in heart, lip, and life. The Lord help us to see

by this Visitation, what need we have to get shelter under the wing of Christ, to hast to the Rock, where we may be safe. We see how ready the Devils are to catch us, and torment our Bodies, and he is as diligent to ensnare our Souls, and that many waies; but let us put on all our spiritual Armour, and follow Christ the Captain of our Salvation; and tho we meet with the Cross, let us bear it patiently and cheerfully, for if Jesus Christ be at the one end, we need not fear the Heaft[1] of it: if we have Christ we have enough; He can make His Rod as well as His Staffe to be a comfort to us; and we shall not want if we be the Sheep of Christ.   If we want Afflictions we shall have them, and sanctified Afflictions are choice mercies.

Now I earnestly desire the Prayer of all good people; That the Lord would be pleased to perfect that Work He hath begun, and make it to appear that Prayer is stronger than Witchcraft.

JOHN GOODWIN.

Decemb. 12, 1688.

This is our First Example; and it is This which has occasioned the Publication of the Rest.

Exemple II.

Among those Judgments of God, which are a great Deep, I suppose few are more unfathomable than this, That pious and holy men suffer sometimes by the Force of horrid Witch-crafts, and hellish Witches are permitted to break thorough the Hedge which our Heavenly Father has made about them that seek Him.   I suppose the Instances of this direful thing are Seldom, but that they are not Never we can produce very dismal Testimony.   One, and that no less Recent than Awful, I shall now offer: and the Reader of it will thereby learn, I hope, to work out his own Salvation with Fear and Trembling.

Sect. I.   Mr. Philip Smith, aged about Fifty years, a Son of eminently vertuous Parents, a Deacon of the Church at Hadley, a Member of our General Court, an Associate in their County Court, a Select-man for the affairs of the Town, a Lieutenant in the Troop, and, which crowns all, a man for

---

[1] Heft, weight.

Devotion and Gravity, and all that was Honest, exceeding exemplary; Such a man in the Winter of the Year 1684 was murdered with an hideous Witchcraft, which filled all those parts with a just astonishment. This was the manner of the Murder.

Sect. II.   He was concerned about Relieving the Indigencies of a wretched woman in the Town; who being dissatisfied at some of his just cares about her, expressed her self unto him in such a manner, that he declared himself apprehensive of receiving mischief at her hands; he said, he doubted she would attempt his Hurt.

Sect. III.   About the beginning of January he began to be very Valetudinarious,[1] labouring under those that seemed Ischiadick[2] pains. As his Illness increased on him, so his Goodness increased in him; the standers-by could in him see one ripening apace for another world; and one filled not only with Grace to an high degree, but also with Exceeding Joy. Such Weanedness from, and Weariness of the World, he shew'd, that he knew not (he said) whether he might pray for his continuance here. Such Assurance had he of the Divine Love unto him, that in Raptures he would cry out, "Lord, stay thy hand, it is enough, it is more than thy frail servant can bear!" But in the midst of these things, he uttered still an hard suspicion, That the ill Woman who had threatned him, had made impressions on him.

Sect. IV.   While he remained yet of a sound mind, he very sedately, but very solemnly charged his Brother to look well after him. Tho' he said he now understood himself, yet he knew not how he might be; "but be sure" (said he) "to have a care of me for you shall see strange things. There shall be a wonder in Hadley! I shall not be dead when it is thought I am!" This Charge he pressed over and over; and afterwards became Delirious.

Sect V.   Being become Delirious, he had a Speech Incessant and Voluble beyond all imagination, and this in divers Tones and sundry voices, and (as was thought) in various languages.

Sect. VI.   He cryed out not only of sore pain, but also of sharp Pins, pricking of him: sometimes in his Toe, sometimes

[1] Unwell.   [2] Sciatic.

in his Arm, as if there had been hundreds of them. But the
people upon search never found any more than One.

Sect. VII.   In his Distresses he exclaimed very much upon
the Woman afore-mentioned, naming her, and some others, and
saying, "Do you not see them; There, There, There they stand."

Sect. VIII.   There was a strong smell of something like
Musk, which was divers times in the Room where he was, and
in the other Rooms, and without the House; of which no
cause could be rendred. The sick-man as well as others,
complained of it; and once particularly, it so siez'd an Apple
Roasting at the Fire, that they were forced to throw it away.

Sect. IX.   Some that were about him, being almost at
their wits end, by beholding the greatness and the strangeness of his Calamities, did three or four times in one Night,
go and give Disturbance to the Woman that we have spoken
of: all the while they were doing of it, the good man was at
ease, and slept as a weary man; and these were all the times
they perceived him to take any sleep at all.

Sect. X.   A small Galley-Pot [1] of Alkermes,[2] that was near
full, and carefully look't after, yet unto the surprize of the
people was quite emptied, so that the sick man could not have
the Benefit of it.

Sect. XI.   Several persons that sat by him heard a Scratching, that seem'd to be on the Ticking near his feet, while his
Feet lay wholly still; nay, were held in the hands of others,
and his hands were far of [3] another way.

Sect. XII.   Sometimes Fire was seen on the Bed, or the
Covering, and when the Beholders began to discourse of it,
it would vanish away.

Sect. XIII.   Diverse people felt something often stir in the
Bed, at some distance from his Body. To appearance, the
thing that stirr'd was as big as a Cat: some try'd to lay hold
on it with their hands, but under the Covering nothing could
be found. A discreet and sober Woman, resting on the Beds
Feet, felt as it were a Hand, the Thumb and the Finger of it,
taking her by the side, and giving her a Pinch; but turning
to see What it might be, nothing was to be seen.

---

[1] A glazed earthen pot, such as apothecaries use.
[2] A once famous confect made from the kermes insect, then thought a berry.
[3] Off.

Sect. XIV.   The Doctor standing by the sick man, and seeing him ly still, he did himself try to lean on the Beds-head; but he found the Bed to shake so, that his head was often knocked against the Post, though he strove to hold it still; and others upon Tryal found the same.   Also, the sick man lying too near the side of the Bed, a very strong and stout man try'd to lift him a little further into the Bed; but with all his might he could not; tho' trying by and by, he could lift a Bed-stead, with a Bed, and man lying on it, all, without any strain to himself at all.

Sect. XV.   Mr. Smith dyes.   The Jury that viewed the Corpse found a Swelling on one Breast, which rendered it like a Womans.   His Privities were wounded or burned.   On his back, besides Bruises, there were several pricks, or holes, as if done with Awls or Pins.

Sect. XVI.   After the Opinion of all had pronounc'd him dead, his Countenance continued as Lively as if he had been Alive; his Eyes closed as in a slumber; and his nether Jaw not falling down.   Thus he remained from Saturday morning about Sun-rise, till Sabbath-Day in the After-noon, When those that took him out of the Bed found him still Warm, though the Season was as Cold as had almost been known in an Age.   On the Night after the Sabbath, his Countenance was yet as fresh as before; but on Monday Morning, they found the Face extremely tumified and discoloured; 'twas black and blue, and fresh blood seem'd to run down his Cheek in the Hairs.

Sect. XVII.   The night after he died, a very credible person, watching of the Corpse, perceived the Bed to move and stir, more than once; but by no means could find out the cause of it.

Sect. XVIII.   The second night, some that were preparing for the Funeral do say, That they heard diverse Noises in the Room, where the Corpse lay; as though there had been a great Removing and Clattering of stools and chairs.

Upon the whole, it appeared unquestionable that Witchcraft had brought a period unto the life of so good a man.[1]

[1] This story, too, is told again in the *Magnalia*, and in nearly the same words.

Exemple IV.

So Horrid and Hellish is the Crime of Witchcraft, that were Gods Thoughts as our thoughts, or Gods Wayes as our wayes, it could be no other but Unpardonable.   But that the Grace of God may be admired, and that the worst of Sinners may be encouraged, Behold, Witchcraft also has found a Pardon.   Let no man Despair of his own Forgiveness, but let no man also Delay about his own Repentance, how aggravated soever his Transgressions are.   From the Hell of Witchcraft our merciful Jesus can fetch a guilty Creature to the Glory of Heaven.   Our Lord hath sometimes Recovered those who have in the most horrid manner given themselves away to the Destroyer of their souls.

Sect. I.   There was one Mary Johnson tryed at Hartford, in this Countrey, upon an Indictment of Familiarity with the Devil.   She was found Guilty of the same, cheefly upon her own Confession, and condemned.

Sect. II.   Many years are past since her Execution; and the Records of the Court are but short; yet there are several Memorables that are found credibly Related and Attested concerning her.[1]

Sect. III.   She said, That a Devil was wont to do her many services.   Her Master once blam'd her for not carrying out the Ashes, and a Devil did clear the Hearth for her afterwards.   Her Master sending her into the Field, to drive out

---

[1] A Mary Johnson was indicted for witchcraft at Hartford in 1648; but the records of her case are now much shorter than in Mather's day, for they consist of a single entry of the Particular Court, December 7, 1648 (*Colonial Records of Connecticut*, I. 171), stating that "the Jury finds the Bill of Inditement against Mary Jonson, that by her owne confession shee is guilty of familiarity with the Devill." It has been inferred that she was of Wethersfield because an earlier passage (*Records*, I. 143) shows that in 1646 a woman of the name was sentenced, for thievery, to be whipped both at Hartford and at Wethersfield; and later passages (*Records*, I. 209, 222, 226, 332) providing (May 21, 1650) for the payment of "charges for Elizabeth Johnson's imprisonment to the first Thursday of next month, being 24 weeks," and for the care of "Goodwife Johnson's child, which was borne in the prison," have been supposed to refer to her, but Mather's account alone tells us of her execution and something of the evidence. The story is told by him again in his *Magnalia*, but in substantially the same words. His knowledge doubtless came through Mr. Stone.

the Hogs that us'd to break into it, a Devil would scowre them out, and make her laugh to see how he feaz'd 'em about.

Sect. IV.   Her first Familiarity with the Devils came by Discontent; and Wishing the Devil to take That and t'other Thing; and, The devil to do This and That; Whereupon a Devil appeared unto her, tendring her the best service he could do for her.

Sect. V.   She confessed that she was guilty of the Murder of a Child, and that she had been guilty of Uncleanness with Men and Devils.

Sect. VI.   In the time of her Imprisonment, the famous Mr. Samuel Stone[1] was at great pains to promote her Conversion unto God, and represent unto her both her Misery and Remedy; the Success of Which, was very desirable, and considerable.

Sect. VII.   She was by most Observers judged very Penitent, both before and at her Execution; and she went out of the World with many Hopes of Mercy through the Merit of Jesus Christ.   Being asked, what she built her hopes upon; She answered, on those Words, *Come to me all ye that labour and are heavy laden, and I will give you Rest*; and those, *There is a Fountain open for Sin and for Uncleanness*.   And she died in a Frame extremely to the Satisfaction of them that were Spectators of it.

Our God is a great Forgiver.

Exemple V.

The near Affinity between Witchcraft and Possession invites me to add unto the Foregoing Histories One that the Reader, I believe, will count worthy to be Related.   It is but a Fragment of what should have been a fuller Story; but I cannot without some Trouble or delay inconsistent with my present Designs put my self in a way to perfect it: and I was of the Opinion that, Let nothing be lost, was a Rule which I might very properly extend unto it.   The thing happened many (perhaps Thirty) years ago, and was then much discoursed of.   I don't Remember, that I have heard what became of the Boy concerned in the Narrative, but what I now pub-

[1] See above, p. 19, note 2.

lish, I find among the Papers of my Grand-father,[1] of Whom the World has had such a Character, that they cannot but judge, no Romance or Folly, nothing but what should be serious and weighty could be worthy of his Hand; and it is in his own Hand that I have the Manuscript, from whence I have caused it to be Transcribed. It runs in such Terms as these.

A Confession of a Boy at Tocutt; [2] *in the time of the Intermission of his Fits: and other Passages, which many were Eye-witnesses of.*

The Boy was for his natural Parts more than ordinary at seven years old. He with many others went to see a Conjurer play Tricks in Holland. There it was strongly suggested to him, He should be as good an Artist as he. From thence to eleven year old he used the Trade of inventing Lyes, and Stealing mony, Running away from his Father, spending of it at Dice, and with the vilest Company; and this Trade he used in that space (he confessed) above Forty times at least, and many strange Instances he gives of it. His Father following him with constant Instruction, and Correction, he was despertely hardned under all, and his heart sett in a way of Malice against the Word of God, and all his Father did to restrain him. When he was about ten or eleven years old, he ran away from Rotterdam, to Delph;[3] and the Devil appeared to him there in the shape of a Boy, counselling him not to hearken to the Word of God, nor unto any of his Father's Instructions, and propounding to him, to Enter into a Covenant with him. Being somewhat fearful at first, desired that he would not appear to him in a shape, but by a voice, and though his heart did inwardly consent, to what the Devil said, yet he was withheld that he could not then Enter into a Covenant with him. His Father not knowing this, but of his other Wickedness, being a godly Minister, procured many Christians to join with him in a day of Humiliation; confessed and bewailed his Sins, prayed for him, and sent him to New-E.[4] and so committed him to God. From that time to this, being now about Sixteen years old, the Devil hath constantly come to him by a voice; and he held a constant Discourse with him; and all about Entring into a Covenant with him: and still perswaded to have it written and sealed, making many promises to allure him, and telling him many Stories of Dr. Faustus,

---

[1] Whether his grandfather Mather or his grandfather Cotton does not appear. The contents suggest a suspicion that the original author was nearer the boy than either—perhaps the Rev. John Davenport, of New Haven.

[2] Later Branford—just east of New Haven and within its government.

[3] Delft.   [4] New England.

and other Witches, how bravely they have lived, and how he should live deliciously, and have Ease, Comfort, and Money; and sometimes threatning to tear him in pieces if he would not. But ordinarily his discourse was as loving and friendly as could be. He hath been strangely kept, by an hand of God, from making a Covenant to this day. For he still propounded many Difficulties to the Devil, which he could not satisfie his Reason in: and though, he saith, he was never well but when he was Discoursing with the devil, and his heart was strangely enclined to write and seal an Agreement, yet such dreadfull horrour did seiz upon him, at the very time, from the Word of God, and such fears of his Eternal Perishing, that he could not do it then. He put off the Devil still, that he was not in a fit Frame, but desired him to come again that he might have more Discourse, and he would consider of it. The Devil appeared to him a second time at New-haven, in the shape of a Boy, and a third time at Tocutt in the shape of a Fox; at which time, at first, they had loving discourse, as formerly; but at last, the Devil was urgent upon him, and told him, he had baffled with him so long, now he must enter into an agreement, or he would tear him in pieces: he saying, "How should I do it? would you have me write upon my hands?" "No," (saith the Devil) "Look here," and with that, set Paper, and Pen, and Ink like Blood before him. The former horrours, from the Word of God, and special passages, which he named, set in upon him so that he could not do it. Only before they parted, the Devil being so urgent upon him, telling him he had baffled with him, he set a year and half time for Consideration. The last quarter of a year is yet to come. The Devil told him, if he let him alone so long, he would baffle with him still: he answered, if he did not yeild then, he would give him leave to torment him whilst he lived. Still the Devil would not away, nor could he get from him. Then out of Fear he cryed out, "Lord, Jesus, rebuke the devil!" at which the Fox, Pen, Ink and Paper vanished. Yet he continued in his course of unheard-of Wickedness, and still his Will was bent to write and seal the Agreement, having his Discourse yet with Satan by Voice. His Brother with whom he lives at Tocut, having Convulsion Fits, he laughed and mocked at him, and acted the Convulsion Fits. A while after God sent Convulsion Fits on himself; in which time, his former Terrours, the Wrath of God, Death, Hell, Judgment, and Eternity were presented to him. He would fain then have confessed his sins, but when he was about to do it the Devil still held his mouth, that he could not. He entreated God, to release him, promising to confess and forsake his Sins, and the Lord did so; but he being well, grew as bad, or worse than ever. About six weeks since, his Convulsion Fits came again three times most dreadfully, with some Inter-

missions, and his former Horrours and Fears. He would have confessed his Sins but could not. It pleased God to put it into the
heart of one to ask him, Whether he had any Familiarity with the
Devil? he got out so much then as, Yes. He fetching Mr. Pierson,[1]
the Convulsion Fits left him, and he confessed all, how it had been
with him. That very night the Devil came to him, and told him,
Had he blabbed out such things? He would teach him to blabb!
and if he would not then write and seal the Agreement, he would
tear him in pieces, and he refusing, the Devil took a corporal Possession of him, and hath not ceased to torment him extremely ever
since. If any thing be spoken to him, the Devil answereth (and
many times he barks like a Fox, and hisseth like a Serpent) sometimes with horrible Blasphemies against the Name of Christ; and at
some other times the Boy is sensible. When he hath the Libertie of
his Voice, he tells what the Devil saith to him, urging him to seal the
Covenant still, and that he will bring Paper, Pen and Ink in the
night, when none shall see, pleading, that God hath cast him off, that
Christ cannot save him: That When He was upon earth He could
cast out devils, but now He is in Heaven He cannot. Sometimes he
is ready to yeild to all in a desperate way. Sometimes he breaks out
into Confession of his former sins, as they come into his mind; exceedingly judging himself and justifying God in His for ever leaving
of him in the hands of Satan. Once he was heard to Pray in such a
manner so sutable to his Condition, so Aggravating his Sin, and
pleading with God for mercy, and in such a strange, high enlarged
manner, as judicious godly persons then present, affirm they never
heard the like in their lives, that it drew abundance of tears from the
eyes of all present, being about twenty persons. But his torment
increased upon him worse after such a time; or if any thing were
spoken to him from the Word of God by others, or they pray with
him. The last week after he had confessed one strange Passage,
namely that once in Discourse he told the Devil, that if he would
make his Spittle to scald a dog, he would then go on in a way of
Lying and Dissembling, and believe that he should do it, which he
said, he did with all his heart, and so spit on the dog, and with that
a deal of Scalding Water did poure on the Dog. In pursuance of his
Promise, he went on in a way of Lying and Dissembling: That when
he was urged about it, that he had done some mischief to the dog,
then he fell down into a Swound, as if he had been dead. As soon as
he had confessed this, the Devil went out of him with an astonishing
Noise, to the terrour of those then present: and so he continued

---

[1] The Rev. Abraham Pierson (d. 1678), who was minister at Branford from
1644 to 1667.

one day. The next day being much troubled in himself for one special passage in his Discourse with the Devil, when he appeared to him as a Fox; saith he to the Devil, "I have formerly sought to God, and He hath been near unto me": With that the Devil enraged, said unto him then, "What, are you got hither?" and fell to threatning of him. He said to him again, "But I find no such Thoughts now, but do and will believe you now more than the Word of God which saith in Isa. 55, Seek the Lord," etc., and said further, "What comfort you shall afford me, I shall rely upon you for it." Remembring this Passage the Devil appeared to him, ready to enter into him again. Thereby much astonished, having the Bible in his hand, he opened it, and, as it were of it self, at that place of Isai. 55: his Eye was fixed upon it, and his Conscience accusing him for abusing the Word a year ago, his heart failing him, and the Devil entred into him again a Second time, railing upon him, and calling him, Blabtongue, and Rogue! he had promis'd to keep things secret, he would teach him to blabb, he would tear him in pieces. Since, he hath kept his Body in continual Motion, speaking in him, and by him, with a formidable Voice: sometimes singing of Verses wicked and witty, that formerly he had made against his Father's Ministry, and the Word of God, etc. When the Boy is come to himself, they tell him of them, and he owns them, that indeed such he did make. Mr. Eaton[1] being his Uncle, sent a Letter to him, which he told of before it came, saying also, it would be goodly stuff! Jeering at him. By and by the Letter came in, and none of the people knew of it before. He speaks of men coming to him before they come in Sight: and once, two being with him, their Backs turned, the Devil carried him away, they knew not how, and after search they found him in a Cellar, as dead, but after a little space he came to Life again. And another time, threw him up into a Chamber, stopped him up into a Hole, where they after found him. Another time he carried him about a Bow-Shot and threw him into a Hog-Stye amongst Swine, which ran away with a terrible noise.

Here is as much to be seen of the Venome of Sin, the Wrath of God against Sin, the Malice of the Devil, and yet his limited Power, and the Reasonings of Satan in an ocular Demonstration, as hath fallen out in any Age. Also the strange and High Expressions of a distressed Soul, in a way of Judging himself and pleading for Mercy, such as may be wondered at by all that hear of it; and more very observable passages could not be written for want of Time, which will after appear.

----

[1] Doubtless Theophilus Eaton, who was governor of the New Haven colony from 1639 till his death, in 1658.

Advertisement.

Of what did after appear, I have no Account; but what did then appear, is so undoubted and so wonderful, that it will sufficiently atone for my Publication of it.

Exemple VI. and VII.

Had there been Diligence enough used by them that have heard and seen amazing Instances of Witchcraft, our Number of Memorable Providences under this Head, had reached beyond the Perfect.   However, before I have done Writing, I will insert an Exemple or two, communicated unto me by a Gentleman of sufficient Fidelity to make a Story of his Relating Credible.   The Things were such as happened in the Town whereof himself is Minister; and they are but some of more which he favoured me with the Communication of.   But, it seems, I must be obliged to conceal the Names of the parties concerned, lest some should be Offended, tho None could be Injured by the mention of them.[1]

In a Town which is none of the youngest in this Countrey, there dwelt a very Godly and honest Man, who upon some Provocation, received very Angry and Threatning Expressions, from two women in the Neighbourhood; soon upon this, diverse of his Cattel in a strange manner dyed; and the man himself sometimes was haunted with sights of the women, as he thought, encountring of him.   He grew indisposed in his Body very unaccountably; and one day repaired unto a Church Meeting then held in the place, with a Resolution there to declare what he had met withal.   The man was one of such Figure and Respect among them, that the Pastor singled out him for to pray in the Assembly before their breaking up.   He pray'd with a more than usual measure of both Devotion and

---

[1] Who his informant was can only be guessed; but the description of the town as "none of the youngest in this Countrey" makes it impossible not to think of Salem, which was the oldest in the colony, and of the Rev. Nicholas Noyes, whose close acquaintance with Mather and whose sharing of his views on this subject are well known.

Discretion, but just as he was coming to that part of his Prayer, wherein he intended to petition Heaven for the Discovery of Witchcrafts which had been among them, he sank down Speechless and Senseless; and was by his Friends carried away to a Bed; where he lay for two or three hours in horrible Distress, fearfully starting, and staring and crying out "Lord, I am stab'd!" and now looking whistly to and fro, he said, "O here are wicked persons among us, even among *us*;" and he complained, "I came hither with a full purpose to tell what I knew, but now" (said he) "I ly like a Fool!" Thus he continued until the Meeting was over, and then his Fits left him; only he remained very sore. One or two more such Fits he had after that; but afterwards a more private sort of Torture was employ'd upon him. He was advised by a worthy man to apply himself unto a Magistrate; and warned, That he would shortly be murdered, if he did not. He took not the Counsil; but languished for some Weeks; yet able to Walk and Work; but Then, he had his Breath and Life suddenly taken away from him, in a manner of which no full Account could be given.

The man had a Son invaded with the like Fits, but God gave deliverance to him in answer to the Prayers of His people for him.

In the same Town, there yet lives a very pious Woman, that from another Woman of ill Fame, received a small gift, which was eaten by her. Upon the Eating of it, she became strangely altered and afflicted; and hindred from Sleeping at Night, by the Pulls of some invisible Hand for a long while together. A Shape or two of, I know not who, likewise haunted her, and gave her no little Trouble. At last, a Fit extraordinary Violent came upon her; wherein she pointed her Hand, and fixed her Eye, much upon the Chimney, and spake at a rate that astonished all about her. Anon, she broke forth into Prayer, and yet could bring out scarce more than a Syllable at a time. In her short Prayer she grew up to an high Act of Faith, and said, (by Syllables, and with Stammerings) "Lord, Thou hast been my Hope, and in Thee will I put my Trust; Thou hast been my Salvation here, and wilt be so for ever and ever!" Upon which her Fit left her; and she afterwards grew very well; still remaining so.

There were diverse other strange Things, which from the same Hand, I can both Relate and Believe, As, Of a Child bewitched into Lameness, and recovered immediately, by a Terrour given to the vile Authoress of the Mischief; but the exact Print, Image and Colour of an Orange made on the Childs Leg, presently upon the sending of an Orange to the Witch by the Mother of the Child, who yet had no evil design in making of the Present. And of other Children, which a palpable Witchcraft made its Impressions on; but *Manum de Tabula.*[1]

I entreat every Reader, to make such an Use of these things, as may promote his own well-fare and advance the Glory of God; and so answer the Intent of the Writer, who,

Hæc scribens studuit, bene de Pietate mereri.[2]

[1] "Hands off the slate!"—*i. e.*, stop writing.

[2] "In writing these things strove to deserve well of Piety." There follow, in the volume, the two sermons mentioned by the title-page, that occasioned by the affair of the Goodwin children coming last. It adds no information as to the episode, but calls itself "A Discourse on Witchcraft," and deals with the reality and nature of that sin. But at the end of it is this interesting "Notandum":

"Since the Finishing of the History which concerns Goodwin's Children, there has been a very wonderful Attempt made (probably by Witchcraft) on another Family in the Town. There is a poor Boy at this time under very terrible and amazing Circumstances which are a Repetition of, with not much Variation from those of the Children formerly molested. The person under vehement Suspicion to be the Authoress [of] this Boy's Calamities is one that was complain'd of by those Children in their Ails, and accordingly one or two of those Children has at this time some Renewal of their Afflictions also; which perhaps may be permitted by the Great God, not to disappoint our Expectations of their Deliverance, but for the Detection and the Destruction of more belonging to that hellish Knot, that has not yet perished as others of the Crue has done, before the poor prayers of them that Hope in God.

"The Book-sellers not being willing to stay the Event of these New Accidents, cause the Bridles here to be taken off."

A BRIEF AND TRUE NARRATIVE, BY DEODAT
LAWSON, 1692

INTRODUCTION

THE earliest account of the remarkable happenings at Salem, in the spring of 1692, which were to bring to a climax and then to a conclusion the quest of witches in New England, was that which here follows. The Rev. Deodat Lawson was singularly qualified to write it. He had himself, only a little earlier (1684-1688), served as pastor to Salem Village, the rural community in which these happenings took their rise; and, though dissensions in the parish prevented his longer stay, he seems to have been no party to these dissensions and must meanwhile have learned to know the scene and all the actors of that later drama which he here depicts. He was, too, a man of education, travel, social experience. Born in England, the son of a scholarly Puritan minister, and doubtless educated there, he first appears in New England in 1676, and at the time of his call to Salem Village was making his home in Boston. Thither he returned in 1688: Samuel Sewall, who on May 13 had him in at Sunday dinner, notes in his diary that he "came to Town to dwell last week," and often mentions him thereafter. How at the outbreak of the witch-panic he came to revisit the Village and to chronicle the doings there, he himself a dozen years later thus told his English friends :[1]

It pleased God in the Year of our Lord 1692 to visit the People at a place called Salem Village in New-England, with a very Sore and Grievous Affliction, in which they had reason to believe, that the Soveraign and Holy God was pleased to permit Satan and his Instruments, to Affright and Afflict those poor Mortals in such an Astonishing and Unusual manner.

[1] In the London edition of his Salem sermon. See below, p. 158, note 3.

Now, I having for some time before attended the work of the Ministry in that Village, the Report of those Great Afflictions came quickly to my notice; and the more readily because the first Person Afflicted was in the Minister's Family, who succeeded me, after I was removed from them; in pitty therefore to my Christian Friends, and former Acquaintance there, I was much concerned about them, frequently consulted with them, and fervently (by Divine Assistance) prayed for them; but especially my Concern was augmented, when it was Reported, at an Examination of a Person suspected for Witchcraft, that my Wife and Daughter, who Dyed Three Years before, were sent out of the World under the Malicious Operations of the Infernal Powers; as is more fully represented in the following Remarks. I did then Desire, and was also Desired, by some concerned in the Court, to be there present, that I might hear what was alledged in that respect; observing therefore, when I was amongst them, that the Case of the Afflicted was very amazing, and deplorable; and the Charges brought against the Accused, such as were Ground of Suspicions yet very intricate, and difficult to draw up right Conclusions about them; I thought good for the satisfaction of my self, and such of my Friends as might be curious to inquiry into those Mysteries of Gods Providence and Satans Malice, to draw up and keep by me, a Brief Account of the most Remarkable things, that came to my Knowledge in those Affairs; which Remarks were afterwards, (at my Request) Revised and Corrected by some who Sate Judges on the Bench, in those Matters; and were now Transcribed, from the same Paper, on which they were then Written.

A narrative so timely and so vouched for must have gone speedily into print.[1] The latest day named in it—"the 5th of April"— was probably the date both of its completion and of its going to press. In 1693 it was reprinted in London by John Dunton, who appended to it an anonymous "Further Account of the Tryals of the New-England Witches" (an extract from "a letter from thence to a Gentleman in London") bringing the story to February, 1693, and to both joined In-

---

[1] One of the acutest students of New England witchcraft, Mr. George H. Moore (in his "Notes on the Bibliography of Witchcraft in Massachusetts" in the *Proceedings* of the American Antiquarian Society, n. s., V. 248), has said of it: "I cannot resist the impression upon reading it, that it was promoted by Cotton Mather and that he wrote the 'Bookseller's' notice 'to the Reader.'" If so, he may well have inspired to the task both author and publisher.

crease Mather's *Cases of Conscience* (see pp. 377, 378, below), prefixing to the volume thus made up the title: *A Further Account of the Tryals of the New-England Witches. With the Observations of a Person who was upon the Place several Days when the suspected Witches were first taken into Examination. To which is added, Cases of Conscience*, etc.[1] In 1704 Lawson, himself now in England, cast it into a new form as an appendix to the English edition of his Salem sermon.[2] All names are now left out, that he "may not grieve any, whose Relations were either Accused or Afflicted, in those times of Trouble and Distress," and what had been a narrative is given a statistical form under "three Heads, viz. (1.) Relating to the Afflicted, (2.) Relating to the Accused, And (3.) Relating to the Confessing Witches."[3] On his own views, and the probable trend of his influence while at Salem, light is thrown by his introductory words:

After this,[4] I being by the Providence of God called over into England, in the Year 1696; I then brought that Paper of Remarks on the Witchcraft with me; upon the sight thereof, some Worthy Ministers and Christian Friends here desired me to Reprint the Sermon and subjoyn the Remarks thereunto, in way of Appendix, but for some particular Reasons I did then Decline it; But now, forasmuch as I my self had been an Eye and Ear Witness of most of those Amazing things, so far as they come within the Notice of Humane Senses; and the Requests of my Friends were Renewed since I came to Dwell in London; I have given way to the Publishing of them; that I may satisfy such as are not resolved to the Contrary, that there may be (and are) such Operations of the Powers of Darkness on the

[1] The contents of this volume were reprinted at London, in 1862, by John Russell Smith, in the volume of his *Library of Old Authors* which contains also Cotton Mather's *The Wonders of the Invisible World*. In this reprint they fill pp. 199–291, being described in its main title by only the misleading words, "A Farther Account of the Tryals of the New-England Witches, by Increase Mather."

[2] See below, p. 158, note 3.

[3] This revised form of his *Account* has been reprinted in full at the end of C. W. Upham's *Salem Witchcraft* (Boston, 1867), and, with but slight omissions, in the *Library of American Literature* edited by Stedman and Hutchinson (New York, 1891), II. 106–114.

[4] This passage immediately follows that above quoted.

Bodies and Minds of Mankind, by Divine Permission; and that those who Sate Judges in those Cases, may by the serious Consideration of the formidable Aspect and perplexed Circumstances of that Afflictive Providence be in some measure excused; or at least be less Censured, for passing Sentence on several Persons, as being the Instruments of Satan in those Diabolical Operations, when they were involved in such a Dark and Dismal Scene of Providence, in which Satan did seem to Spin a finer Thred of Spiritual Wickedness than in the ordinary methods of Witchcraft; hence the Judges desiring to bear due Testimony against such Diabolical Practices, were inclined to admit the validity of such a sort of Evidence as was not so clearly and directly demonstrable to Human Senses, as in other Cases is required, or else they could not discover the Mysteries of Witchcraft. . . .

One can not read these words without a suspicion that the reaction in New England against those held responsible for the procedure at Salem may have had to do with his return to England; and even in England, it is clear, his cause now needed defense. If any can wish him further ill, let them be appeased by our two glimpses of his after fate—a despairing letter in 1714,[1] begging from his New England friends meat, drink, and clothing for his sick and starving family, and the passing phrase of a writer who in 1727, mentioning Thomas Lawson, adds that "he was the father of the unhappy Mr. Deodate Lawson, who came hither from New England."[2]

But the reader should not enter on the study of the witch-panic of 1692 without knowing something of our other sources of knowledge. The contemporary narratives are practically all printed in the pages that follow, and a part of the trial records will be found embodied in Cotton Mather's *Wonders*;[3] but most of these must be sought otherwhere, and, alas, they are sadly scattered. Some Governor Hutchinson preserved in

---

[1] Published (from the Bodleian Library's Rawlinson MS. C. 128, fol. 12) by George H. Moore, in the *Proceedings* of the American Antiquarian Society, n. s., V. 268–269.

[2] Edmund Calamy, in his *Continuation*, II. 629 (II. 192 of Palmer's revision of 1775, *The Nonconformist's Memorial*).

[3] At pp. 215–244, below.

his wise and careful pages on this subject,[1] where alone a part
can now be found. Many have drifted into private hands—
like those which in 1860 came into the hands of the Massachusetts Historical Society and are in part printed in its *Proceedings* (1860–1862, pp. 31–37), or those published by Drake
in the foot-notes and appendices to his various histories and
editions,[2] or those now in the keeping of the Essex Institute at
Salem or of the Boston Public Library.[3] Such of these as are
in print are mentioned in the notes at the proper points. But
most are still in public keeping at Salem; and these in 1864
were printed by W. Elliot Woodward in the two volumes of
his *Records of Salem Witchcraft*, the work most fundamental
for the first-hand study of this episode. It is, however, imperfect and far from complete, and there is hope of a better:
the *Records and Files of the Quarterly Courts of Essex County*,
of which a third volume has just appeared, must in due
course include these witch-trials, and Mr. George Francis
Dow, their editor (who has already by his publication of the
witchcraft records relating to Topsfield [4] shown his keenness
in such work), has in mind the seizing of this opportunity
to print all obtainable papers relating to the Salem Witchcraft
episode. Precious documents too are published by Upham in
his classical *Salem Witchcraft* [5] and in the acute and learned
studies of Mr. Abner C. Goodell and Mr. George H. Moore.[6]

---

[1] *History of Massachusetts*, II., ch. I.

[2] In his *History and Antiquities of Boston* (Boston, 1856), pp. 497, 498, and
in his *The Witchcraft Delusion in New England*, III. 126, 169–197. All these
(the indictment and the testimony against Philip English, the examination of
Mary Clark and of the slave Tituba) are now in the New York Public Library,
as are also his documents of the Morse case, mentioned above, p. 31, note 1.

[3] As to the fate of the records in general see Upham, *Salem Witchcraft*, II. 462.

[4] In vol. XIII. of the *Historical Collections* of the Topsfield Historical Society
(1908).

[5] Boston, 1867, two vols.   [6] See p. 91, note 2; p. 373, note 3.

A BRIEF AND TRUE NARRATIVE

A Brief and True Narrative Of some Remarkable Passages Relating to sundry Persons Afflicted by Witchcraft, at Salem Village Which happened from the Nineteenth of March, to the Fifth of April, 1692.
Collected by Deodat Lawson.
Boston, Printed for Benjamin Harris and are to be Sold at his Shop, over-against the Old-Meeting-House. 1692.[1]

The Bookseller to the Reader.

The Ensuing Narrative, being a Collection of some Remarkables, in an Affair now upon the Stage, made by a Credible Eye-witness, is now offered unto the Reader, only as a Tast, of more that may follow in Gods Time. If the Prayers of Good People may obtain this Favour of God, That the Misterious Assaults from Hell now made upon so many of our Friends may be thoroughly Detected and Defeated, we suppose the Curious will be Entertained with as rare an History as perhaps an Age has had; whereof this Narrative is but a Forerunner.

BENJAMIN HARRIS.

ON the Nineteenth day of March last[2] I went to Salem Village,[3] and lodged at Nathaniel Ingersols near to the Min-

---

[1] Title-page of the original.

[2] 1692. This narrative may well be studied in close connection with the parallel narratives of Calef and Hale, printed at pp. 296 ff. and 399 ff. of this volume.

[3] Not Salem *town*, the present Salem city, but a rural district (what is now the township of Danvers, with parts of the townships adjoining it) which till 1672 had been a mere dependence of the town, but in that year, at the request of its inhabitants, was set off as a separate parish, though not as a distinct town. Despite the name of "village," there was in Salem Village no huddle of houses amounting to a hamlet, though about the meeting-house (where now is Danvers

ister Mr. P's. house,[1] and presently after I came into my Lodging Capt. Walcuts Daughter Mary[2] came to Lieut. Ingersols and spake to me, but, suddenly after as she stood by the door, was bitten, so that she cried out of her Wrist, and looking on it with a Candle, we saw apparently the marks of Teeth both upper and lower set, on each side of her wrist.

In the beginning of the Evening, I went to give Mr. P.[3] a visit. When I was there, his Kins-woman, Abigail Williams, (about 12 years of age,) had a grievous fit; she was at first hurryed with Violence to and fro in the room, (though Mrs. Ingersol endeavoured to hold her,) sometimes makeing as if she would fly, stretching up her arms as high as she could, and crying "Whish, Whish, Whish!" several times; Presently after she said there was Goodw. N.[4] and said, "Do you not see her? Why there she stands!" And the said Goodw. N. offered her The Book, but she was resolved she would not

Highlands) the farm-houses clustered more thickly than elsewhere. Prefixed to the Rev. Charles W. Upham's *Salem Witchcraft* is a map, which, on the basis of long and loving research, attempts to locate every house in all the region; and the text of that work will also be of constant use, as will the little volume of W. S. Nevins, *Witchcraft in Salem Village* (1892), with its views of sites and buildings (as "Stories of Salem Witchcraft" it had been printed in the *New England Magazine*, IV., V.) and the illustrated edition of John Fiske's *New France and New England* (1904).

[1] Nathaniel Ingersoll, deacon in the village church and perhaps its most devoted member, kept the tavern, or "ordinary," which was the recognized centre of the "Village." The meeting-house adjoined it to the east, to the west the parsonage, where lived Mr. Parris.

[2] Captain Jonathan Walcot, commander of the village militia, dwelt next beyond the parsonage. His daughter Mary was now seventeen.

[3] The Rev. Samuel Parris (1653–1720), whose part, and whose family's, in the Salem panic was to be so great, had been at Salem Village since 1688, succeeding Deodat Lawson as its spiritual head. Till then, though educated at Harvard, which is to say for the ministry, he had been engaged in the West Indian trade, and had lived for a time in Barbadoes, whence he had brought back with him the two slaves, John and Tituba, perhaps half negro, half native, with whom we must soon have to do. Abigail Williams, his niece, was a member of his household; and we shall meet also his little daughter Elizabeth, aged nine. The account of his life by S. P. Fowler (Essex Institute, *Proceedings*, II. 49–68) has been separately printed (Salem, 1857) and is appended to Drake's ed. of Mather and Calef (III. 198–222). But the student needs also Upham, *Salem Witchcraft*, and the documents reprinted by Calef, *More Wonders*, pp. 55–64.

[4] Rebecca Nurse, a matron of 71, wife of Francis Nurse, an energetic and prosperous farmer.

take it, saying Often, "I wont, I wont, I wont, take it, I do not know what Book it is: I am sure it is none of Gods Book, it is the Divels Book, for ought I know." After that, she run to the Fire, and begun to throw Fire Brands, about the house; and run against the Back, as if she would run up Chimney, and, as they said, she had attempted to go into the Fire in other Fits.

On Lords Day, the Twentieth of March, there were sundry of the afflicted Persons at Meeting, as, Mrs. Pope, and Goodwife Bibber, Abigail Williams, Mary Walcut, Mary Lewes, and Docter Griggs' Maid.[1] There was also at Meeting, Goodwife C.[2] (who was afterward Examined on suspicion of being a Witch:) They had several Sore Fits, in the time of Publick Worship, which did something interrupt me in my First Prayer; being so unusual. After Psalm was Sung, Abigail Williams said to me, "Now stand up, and Name your Text": And after it was read, she said, "It is a long Text." In the beginning of Sermon, Mrs. Pope, a Woman afflicted, said to me, "Now there is enough of that." And in the afternoon, Abigail Williams upon my referring to my Doctrine said to me, "I know no Doctrine you had, If you did name one, I have forgot it."

In Sermon time when Goodw. C was present in the Meetinghouse Ab. W. called out, "Look where Goodw. C sits on the Beam suckling her Yellow bird betwixt her fingers"! Anne Putnam another Girle afflicted said there was a Yellow-bird sat on my hat as it hung on the Pin in the Pulpit: but those that were by, restrained her from speaking loud about it.

On Monday the 21st of March, The Magistrates of Salem appointed to come to Examination of Goodw C.[3] And about

---

[1] Mrs. Pope was a woman of good social position and in early middle life; Sarah Bibber (or Vibber), aged 36, a loose-tongued creature, addicted to fits, who with her husband seems to have "worked out"; Mercy (not Mary) Lewes, a maid in the family of Thomas Putnam, whose wife and twelve-year-old daughter, both named Ann, were also to have a leading part among "the afflicted." "Doctor Griggs' maid," Elizabeth Hubbard, aged 17, was a niece of his wife. It was probably Dr. Griggs, the physician of the Village, who had first pronounced the girls bewitched.

[2] Martha Corey, wife of Giles Corey. She too was advanced in years.

[3] For the official report of this examination, as of those to follow, and for all the legal documents connected with these cases, the student must of course

twelve of the Clock, they went into the Meeting-House, which was Thronged with Spectators: Mr. Noyes[1] began with a very pertinent and pathetic Prayer; and Goodwife C. being called to answer to what was Alledged against her, she desired to go to Prayer, which was much wondred at, in the presence of so many hundred people: The Magistrates told her, they would not admit it; they came not there to hear her Pray, but to Examine her, in what was Alledged against her. The Worshipful Mr. Hathorne[2] asked her, Why she Afflicted those Children? she said, she did not Afflict them. He asked her, who did then? she said, "I do not know; How should I know?" The Number of the Afflicted Persons were about that time Ten, viz. Four Married Women, Mrs. Pope, Mrs. Putman,[3] Goodw. Bibber, and an Ancient Woman, named Goodall, three Maids, Mary Walcut, Mercy Lewes, at Thomas Putman's, and a Maid at Dr. Griggs's, there were three Girls from 9 to 12 Years of Age, each of them, or thereabouts, viz. Elizabeth Parris, Abigail Williams and Ann Putman; these were most of them at G. C's Examination, and did vehemently accuse her in the Assembly of afflicting them, by Biting, Pinching, Strangling, etc. And that they did in their Fit see her Likeness coming to them, and bringing a Book to them, she said, she had no Book; they affirmed, she had a Yellow-Bird, that used to suck betwixt her Fingers, and being asked about it, if she had any Familiar Spirit, that attended her, she said, She had no Familiarity with any such thing. She was a Gospel Woman: which Title she called her self by; and the Afflicted Persons told her, ah! She was, A Gospel Witch. Ann Putman did there affirm, that one day when Lieutenant Fuller was at

turn to the publications embodying such court records (see p. 151, above). Those of Goodwife Corey's case may be found in Woodward's *Records of Salem Witchcraft*, I. 50–60. Especially interesting is the evidence as to her rational attitude: "shee told us," testify those who went to arrest her, "that shee did not thinke that there were any witches." They add that it "was said of her that shee would open the eyes of the magistrates and ministers."

[1] The Rev. Nicholas Noyes, minister at Salem town.

[2] John Hathorne, or Hawthorne, a magistrate of the colony, and, as a member of the highest court, a local magistrate as well, had his home on his farm in Salem Village and must have known personally all these neighbors. It must be remembered, and may well be pointed out here, that Massachusetts magistrates were not men trained to the law, but only respected laymen.

[3] Putnam: this misspelling was common.

Prayer at her Fathers House, she saw the shape of Goodw. C. and she thought Goodw. N. Praying at the same time to the Devil, she was not sure it was Goodw. N. she thought it was; but very sure she saw the Shape of G. C. The said C. said, they were poor, distracted Children, and no heed to be given to what they said. Mr. Hathorne and Mr. Noyes replyed, it was the judgment of all that were present, they were Bewitched, and only she, the Accused Person said, they were Distracted. It was observed several times, that if she did but bite her Under lip in time of Examination the persons afflicted were bitten on their armes and wrists and produced the Marks before the Magistrates, Ministers and others. And being watched for that, if she did but Pinch her Fingers, or Graspe one hand hard in another, they were Pinched and produced the Marks before the Magistrates, and Spectators. After that, it was observed, that if she did but lean her Breast against the Seat, in the Meeting House, (being the Barr at which she stood,) they were afflicted. Particularly Mrs. Pope complained of grievous torment in her Bowels as if they were torn out. She vehemently accused said C. as the instrument, and first threw her Muff at her; but that flying not home, she got off her Shoe, and hit Goodwife C. on the head with it. After these postures were watched, if said C. did but stir her feet, they were afflicted in their Feet, and stamped fearfully. The afflicted persons asked her why she did not go to the company of Witches which were before the Meeting house mustering? Did she not hear the Drum beat? They accused her of having Familiarity with the Devil, in the time of Examination, in the shape of a Black man whispering in her ear; they affirmed, that her Yellow-Bird sucked betwixt her Fingers in the Assembly; and order being given to see if there were any sign, the Girl that saw it said, it was too late now; she had removed a Pin, and put it on her head; which was found there sticking upright.

They told her, she had Covenanted with the Devil for ten years, six of them were gone, and four more to come. She was required by the Magistrates to answer that Question in the Catechism, "How many persons be there in the God-Head?" she answered it but oddly, yet was there no great thing to be gathered from it; she denied all that was charged upon her,

and said, They could not prove a Witch; she was that Afternoon Committed to Salem-Prison; and after she was in Custody, she did not so appear to them, and afflict them as before.

On Wednesday the 23 of March, I went to Thomas Putmans, on purpose to see his Wife: I found her lying on the
Bed, having had a sore fit a little before. She spake to me, and
said, she was glad to see me; her Husband and she both desired
me to pray with her, while she was sensible; which I did,
though the Apparition said, I should not go to Prayer. At the
first beginning she attended; but after a little time, was taken
with a fit: yet continued silent, and seemed to be Asleep:
when Prayer was done, her Husband going to her, found her
in a Fit; he took her off the Bed, to set her on his Knees; but
at first she was so stiff, she could not be bended; but she afterwards set down; but quickly began to strive violently with her
Arms and Leggs; she then began to Complain of, and as it
were to Converse personally with, Goodw. N., saying, "Goodw.
N. Be gone! Be gone! Be gone! are you not ashamed, a Woman
of your Profession, to afflict a poor Creature so? what hurt did
I ever do you in my life! you have but two years to live, and
then the Devil will torment your Soul, for this your Name is
blotted out of Gods Book, and it shall never be put in Gods
Book again, be gone for shame, are you not afraid of that which
is coming upon you? I Know, I know, what will make you
afraid; the wrath of an Angry God, I am sure that will make
you afraid; be gone, do not tourment me, I know what you
would have (we judged she meant, her Soul) but it is out of
your reach; it is Clothed with the white Robes of Christs
Righteousness." After this, she seemed to dispute with the
Apparition about a particular Text of Scripture. The Apparition seemed to deny it, (the Womans eyes being fast closed
all this time); she said, She was sure there was such a Text;
and she would tell it; and then the Shape would be gone, for
said she, "I am sure you cannot stand before that Text!"
then she was sorely Afflicted; her mouth drawn on one side,
and her body strained for about a minute, and then said, "I will
tell, I will tell; it is, it is, it is!" three or four times, and then
was afflicted to hinder her from telling, at last she broke forth
and said, "It is the third Chapter of the Revelations." I did
something scruple the reading it, and did let my scruple ap-

pear, lest Satan should make any Superstitious lie to improve the Word of the Eternal God. However, tho' not versed in these things, I judged I might do it this once for an Experiment. I began to read, and before I had near read through the first verse, she opened her eyes, and was well; this fit continued near half an hour. Her Husband and the Spectators told me, she had often been so relieved by reading Texts that she named, something pertinent to her Case; as Isa. 40. 1, Isa. 49. 1, Isa. 50. 1, and several others.

On Thursday the Twenty fourth of march, (being in course the Lecture Day, at the Village,) Goodwife N. was brought before the Magistrates Mr. Hathorne and Mr. Corwin,[1] about Ten of [the] Clock, in the Fore Noon, to be Examined in the Meeting House; the Reverend Mr. Hale[2] begun with Prayer, and the Warrant being read, she was required to give answer, Why she aflicted those persons? she pleaded her owne innocency with earnestness. Thomas Putman's Wife, Abigail Williams and Thomas Putmans daughter accused her that she appeared to them, and afflicted them in their fitts: but some of the other said, that they had seen her, but knew not that ever she had hurt them; amongst which was Mary Walcut, who was presently after she had so declared bitten, and cryed out of her in the meeting-house; producing the Marks of teeth on her wrist. It was so disposed, that I had not leisure to attend the whole time of Examination,[3] but both Magistrates

[1] Jonathan Corwin was, like Hathorne, a member of the Court of Assistants, the highest legislative and judicial body of the colony, and like him the son of one of its founders. They were the men of highest note in the Salem region. Corwin lived in the town.

[2] Of Beverly. As to him see p. 397, below.

[3] What drew Mr. Lawson away from the examinations was doubtless the need to complete his preparation for the important sermon of that day; and it must have been this on which he was pondering when (as he records a few lines later) the shrieks of the afflicted reached him as he walked, "a little distance from the meeting-house." That sermon was, however, no extempore production, but a studied disquisition on the power and malice of the Devil, who "Contracts and Indents with Witches and Wizzards, that they shall be the Instruments by whom he may more secretly Affect and Afflict the Bodies and Minds of others." "And the Devil," taught Lawson, committing himself wholly to belief in the worth of that "spectral evidence" which was to play such a part in the Salem episode, "having them in his subjection, by their Consent, he will use their Bodies and Minds, Shapes and Representations, to Affright and Afflict others at his pleasure." The magistrates were present at the sermon; and to them he dedicated the ser-

and Ministers told me, that the things alledged by the afflicted, and defences made by her, were much after the same manner, as the former was. And her Motions did produce like effects as to Biteing, Pinching, Bruising, Tormenting, at their Breasts, by her Leaning, and when, bended Back, were as if their Backs was broken. The afflicted persons said, the Black Man whispered to her in the Assembly, and therefore she could not hear what the Magistrates said unto her. They said also that she did then ride by the Meeting-house, behind the Black Man. Thomas Putman's wife had a grievous Fit, in the time of Examination, to the very great Impairing of her strength, and wasting of her spirits, insomuch as she could hardly move hand, or foot, when she was carryed out. Others also were there grievously afflicted, so that there was once such an hideous scrietch and noise, (which I heard as I walked, at a little distance from the Meeting house,) as did amaze me, and some that were within told me the whole assembly was struck with consternation, and they were afraid, that those that sate next to them, were under the influence of Witchcraft. This woman also was that day committed to Salem Prison. The Magistrates and Ministers also did informe me, that they apprehended a child of Sarah G.[1] and Examined it, being between 4 and 5 years of Age, And as to matter of Fact, they did Unanimously affirm, that when this Child did but cast its eye upon the afflicted persons, they were tormented, and they held her Head, and yet so many as her eye could fix upon were afflicted. Which they did several times make careful observation of: the afflicted complained, they had often been Bitten by this child, and produced the marks of a small set of teeth, accordingly, this was also committed to Salem Prison; the child looked hail, and well as other Children. I saw it at Lieut. Ingersols.[2] After the commitment of Goodw. N., Tho: Putmans wife was much better, and had no violent fits

mon when, in the following year, he gave it to the press under the title of *Christ's Fidelity the only Shield against Satan's Malignity.* A second edition was printed under his eye at London in 1704 (see p. 149, above).

[1] Sarah Good, who with Sarah Osburn and Parris's slave-woman Tituba had been examined and committed to jail on March 1, before Lawson's visit (see p. 343, below).

[2] Little Dorcas Good, thus sent to prison "as hale and well as other children," lay there seven or eight months, and "being chain'd in the dungeon was

at all from that 24th of March to the 5th of April. Some others also said they had not seen her so frequently appear to them, to hurt them.

On the 25th of March, (as Capt. Stephen Sewal,[1] of Salem, did afterwards inform me) Eliza. Paris had sore Fits, at his house, which much troubled himself, and his wife, so as he told me they were almost discouraged. She related, that the great Black Man came to her, and told her, if she would be ruled by him, she should have whatsoever she desired, and go to a Golden City. She relating this to Mrs. Sewall, she told the child, it was the Divel, and he was a Lyar from the Beginning, and bid her tell him so, if he came again: which she did accordingly, at the next coming to her, in her fits.

On the 26th of March, Mr. Hathorne, Mr. Corwin, and Mr. Higison[2] were at the Prison-Keepers House, to Examine the Child,[3] and it told them there, it had a little Snake that used to Suck on the lowest Joynt of it[s] Fore-Finger; and when they inquired where, pointing to other places, it told them, not there, but there, pointing on the Lowest point of Fore-Finger; where they Observed a deep Red Spot, about the Bigness of a Flea-bite, they asked who gave it that Snake? whether the great Black man, it said no, its Mother gave it.

The 31 of March there was a Publick Fast kept at Salem on account of these Afflicted Persons. And Abigail Williams said, that the Witches had a Sacrament that day at an house in the Village, and that they had Red Bread and Red Drink. The first of April, Mercy Lewis, Thomas Putman's Maid, in her fitt, said, they did eat Red Bread like Mans Flesh, and

so hardly used and terrifyed" that eighteen years later her father alleged "that she hath ever since been very chargeable, haveing little or no reason to govern herself." See his petition for damages, September 13, 1710 (printed in the *N. E. Hist. and Gen. Register*, XXXV. 253—the MS. is now in the President White Library at Cornell University). He was allowed £30.

[1] Stephen Sewall, clerk of the courts at Salem, in whose home the Rev. Mr. Parris had now placed his daughter Elizabeth—a fact which may have some connection with his being one of the most ardent furtherers of the trials. It was from him that Cotton Mather later asked the materials for his account of them (see p. 206, below). He must, of course, not be confused with his more eminent brother, Samuel Sewall, of Boston, whom we shall soon meet as a judge in the Salem trials.

[2] The Rev. John Higginson, the aged senior minister of the church in Salem.

[3] Dorcas Good, of course, not Elizabeth Parris.

would have had her eat some: but she would not; but turned away her head, and Spit at them, and said, "I will not Eat, I will not Drink, it is Blood," etc. She said, "That is not the Bread of Life, that is not the Water of Life; Christ gives the Bread of Life, I will have none of it!" This first of April also Marcy Lewis aforesaid saw in her fitt a White man and was with him in a Glorious Place, which had no Candles nor Sun, yet was full of Light and Brightness; where was a great Multitude in White glittering Robes, and they Sung the Song in the fifth of Revelation the Ninth verse, and the 110 Psalm, and the 149 Psalm; and said with her self, "How long shall I stay here? let me be along with you": She was loth to leave this place, and grieved that she could tarry no longer. This Whiteman[1] hath appeared several times to some of them, and given them notice how long it should be before they had another Fit, which was sometimes a day, or day and half, or more or less: it hath fallen out accordingly.

The third of April, the Lords-Day, being Sacrament-day, at the Village, Goodw. C.[2] upon Mr. Parris's naming his Text, John 6, 70, *One of them is a Devil,* the said Goodw. C. went immediately out of the Meeting-House, and flung the door after her violently, to the amazement of the Congregation: She was afterward seen by some in their Fits, who said, "O Goodw. C., I did not think to see you here!" (and being at their Red bread and drink) said to her, "Is this a time to receive the Sacrament, you ran-away on the Lords-Day, and scorned to receive it in the Meeting-House, and, Is this a time to receive it? I wonder at you!" This is the summ of what I either saw my self, or did receive Information from persons of undoubted Reputation and Credit.

Remarks of things more than ordinary about the Afflicted Persons.

1. They are in their Fits tempted to be Witches, are shewed the List of the Names of others, and are tortured, because they will not yield to Subscribe, or meddle with, or touch the Book, and are promised to have present Relief if they would do it.

---

[1] White man.

[2] Not Goodwife Corey, but Goodwife Sarah Cloyse, sister of Rebecca Nurse. For an explanation of the slammed door, see p. 346, below.

2. They did in the Assembly mutually Cure each other, even with a Touch of their Hand, when Strangled, and otherwise Tortured; and would endeavour to get to their Afflicted, to Relieve them.

3. They did also foretel when anothers Fit was a-coming, and would say, "Look to her! she will have a Fit presently," which fell out accordingly, as many can bear witness, that heard and saw it.

4. That at the same time, when the Accused Person was present, the Afflicted Persons saw her Likeness in other places of the Meeting-House, suckling her Familiar, sometimes in one place and posture, and sometimes in another.

5. That their Motions in their Fits are Preternatural, both as to the manner, which is so strange as a well person could not Screw their Body into; and as to the violence also it is preternatural, being much beyond the Ordinary force of the same person when they are in their right mind.

6. The eyes of some of them in their fits are exceeding fast closed, and if you ask a question they can give no answer, and I do believe they cannot hear at that time, yet do they plainely converse with the Appearances, as if they did discourse with real persons.

7. They are utterly pressed against any persons Praying with them, and told by the appearances, they shall not go to Prayer, so Tho. Putmans wife was told, I should not Pray; but she said, I should: and after I had done, reasoned with the Appearance, "Did not I say he should go to Prayer?"

8. The forementioned Mary W.[1] being a little better at ease, the Afflicted persons said, she had signed the book; and that was the reason she was better. Told me by Edward Putman.[2]

Remarks concerning the Accused.

1. For introduction to the discovery of those that afflicted them, It is reported Mr. Parris's Indian Man and Woman made a Cake of Rye Meal, and the Childrens water, baked it

---

[1] Walcot.

[2] Deacon Edward Putnam, a pillar of the village church, was brother and close neighbor to Thomas Putnam, whose wife, daughter, and maid were leaders among "the afflicted."

in the Ashes, and gave it to a Dogge, since which they have discovered, and seen particular persons hurting of them.

2. In Time of Examination, they seemed little affected, though all the Spectators were much grieved to see it.

3. Natural Actions in them produced Preternatural actions in the Afflicted, so that they are their own Image without any Poppits of Wax or otherwise.[1]

4. That they are accused to have a Company about 23 or 24 and they did Muster in Armes, as it seemed to the Afflicted Persons.

5. Since they were confined, the Persons have not been so much Afflicted with their appearing to them, Biteing or Pinching of them, etc.

6. They are reported by the Afflicted Persons to keep dayes of Fast and dayes of Thanksgiving, and Sacraments; Satan endeavours to Transforme himself to an Angel of Light, and to make his Kingdom and Administrations to resemble those of our Lord Jesus Christ.

7. Satan Rages Principally amongst the Visible Subjects of Christ's Kingdom and makes use (at least in appearance) of some of them to Afflict others; that Christ's Kingdom may be divided against it self, and so be weakened.

8. Several things used in England at Tryal of Witches, to the Number of 14 or 15, which are wont to pass instead of or in Concurrence with Witnesses, at least 6 or 7 of them are found in these accused: see Keebles Statutes.[2]

[1] *I. e.*, these witches have no need, as do others (see p. 104), to make images, or puppets, in the likeness of those they wish to torment, and then by torturing the puppets to inflict the same tortures on those they represent: these witches have only to act, and their victims are preternaturally compelled to the same action.

[2] What is meant is clearly not the collection of English statutes compiled by Joseph Keeble, or Keble, (1632–1710). Often printed (1676, 1681, 1684, 1695, 1706), this seems to have been standard in the colonies as at home; but it contains absolutely nothing but the text of the statutes in force, "with the titles of such as are expired, repealed, altered, or out of use," and at the end an analytical table of subjects. The work really meant is Keble's *An Assistance to Justices of the Peace* (London, 1683, 1689). This work, however, borrows its pages on witchcraft (pp. 217–220) from the older manuals of Lambarde, West, and Dalton; and the passage in question is one compiled by Michael Dalton, for the later editions of his *The Countrey Justice*, from Thomas Potts's *Discoverie of Witches* (1613) and Richard Barnard's *Guide to Grand-Jury Men* (1627). For aid in this identification, and for a transcript of these pages from the Harvard copy of Keble, the editor is indebted to Mr. David M. Matteson.

9. Some of the most solid Afflicted Persons do affirme the same things concerning seeing the accused out of their Fitts as well as in them.

10. The Witches had a Fast, and told one of the Afflicted Girles, she must not Eat, because it was Fast Day, she said, she would: they told her they would Choake her then; which when she did eat, was endeavoured.

Finis.

LETTER OF THOMAS BRATTLE, F. R. S., 1692

INTRODUCTION

FROM that April day when Mr. Lawson closed his account it was long before another eye-witness undertook a narrative. Yet great things were doing. At Salem accusation and hearing went on apace, and the jails grew crowded, awaiting the session of a court. On May 14 arrived from England President Increase Mather, bringing the new charter, and with him the new governor, Sir William Phips. What the governor thought of the emergency and how he dealt with it we shall presently learn from his own pen. But other pens were earlier busy. Perhaps the most notable was that of Thomas Brattle, who early in October addressed the following letter to some clerical correspondent. Who this divine may have been whose questions the letter answers is unknown: our document is not the original, but a copy without superscription, and from its contents we can infer no more than that he lived or had lived in the colony. But Thomas Brattle we know well. "He was," wrote President Leverett of Harvard at his death, "a gentleman by his birth and education of the first order in this country." Born at Boston, in 1658, of wealthy parentage, a graduate and a master of arts of Harvard, then a traveller and a student abroad, he won such distinction as a mathematician, and notably as an astronomer, as to be made a member of the Royal Society, and was in close touch with the world of scholars; but his career was that of an opulent and cultivated Boston merchant, and for twenty years, from 1693 to his death in 1713, he was treasurer of Harvard College. "In the Church," said of him the Boston *News-Letter*, "he was known and valued for his Catholick Charity to all of the reformed

Religion, but more especially his great Veneration for the Church of England, although his general and more constant communion was with the Nonconformists." In other words, he was of the liberal party in religion and politics, an eminent opponent of the Puritan theocracy, and he did not escape the epithets "apostate" and "infidel."

The letter here printed did not see print in his own day; but that the present copy exists suggests that it may have been meant to circulate in manuscript,[1] and it is not impossible that it was even written for that purpose. Yet if so, we may be sure it was used with discretion. It was his grand-nephew, the then well-known Thomas Brattle, Esq., of Cambridge, who late in the eighteenth century communicated it to the Massachusetts Historical Society.[2] From that manuscript copy it is here reprinted.

[1] The suggestion is that of Sibley, in his sketch of Brattle's life (*Harvard Graduates*, II. 489–498), the best summary of what is known of him. That the extant copy is without superscription, and signed by initials only, may point to such a use. It must not be forgotten that it was written on the eve of the session of the General Court.

[2] It was first published in that society's *Collections*, V. 61–79.

LETTER OF THOMAS BRATTLE, F. R. S., 1692

October 8, 1692.

Reverend Sir,

YOUR's I received the other day, and am very ready to serve you to my uttmost. I should be very loath to bring myself into any snare by my freedom with you, and therefore hope that you will put the best construction on what I write, and secure me from such as would interprett my lines otherwise than they are designed. Obedience to lawfull authority I evermore accounted a great duty; and willingly I would not practise any thing that might thwart and contradict such a principle. Too many are ready to despise dominions, and speak evil of Dignities; and I am sure the mischiefs, which arise from a factious and rebellious spirit, are very sad and notorious; insomuch that I would sooner bite my finger's ends than. willingly cast dirt on authority, or any way offer reproach to it: Far, therefore, be it from me, to have any thing to do with those men your letter mentions, whom you acknowledge to be men of a factious spirit, and never more in their element than when they are declaiming against men in public place, and contriving methods that tend to the disturbance of the common peace. I never accounted it a credit to my cause, to have the good liking of such men. *My son!* (says Solomon) *fear thou the Lord and the King, and meddle not with them that are given to change.* Prov. xxiv. 21. However, Sir, I never thought Judges infallible; but reckoned that they, as well as private men, might err; and that when they were guilty of erring, standers by, who possibly had not half their judgment, might, notwithstanding, be able to detect and behold their errors. And furthermore, when errors of that nature are thus detected and observed, I never thought it an interfering with dutifullness and subjection for one man to communicate his thoughts to another thereabout; and with modesty and due reverence to debate the premised failings; at least, when errours are fundamental, and palpably pervert the great end of authority and government: for as to circumstantial errours, I must confesse my principle is, that it is the duty of a good subject to cover with his silence a multitude of them. But I shall no longer detain you with my preface, but passe to some things you look for, and whether you expect such freedome from me, yea or no, yet shall you find, that I am very open to communicate my thoughts unto you, and in plain terms to tell you what my opinion is of the Salem proceedings.

First, as to the method which the Salem Justices do take in their examinations, it is truly this: A warrant being issued out to apprehend the persons that are charged and complained of by the afflicted children, (as they are called); said persons are brought before the Justices, (the afflicted being present.) The Justices ask the apprehended why they afflict those poor children; to which the apprehended answer, they do not afflict them. The Justices order the apprehended to look upon the said children, which accordingly they do; and at the time of that look, (I dare not say by that look, as the Salem Gentlemen do) the afflicted are cast into a fitt. The apprehended are then blinded, and ordered to touch the afflicted; and at that touch, tho' not by the touch, (as above) the afflicted ordinarily do come out of their fitts. The afflicted persons then declare and affirm, that the apprehended have afflicted them; upon which the apprehended persons, tho' of never so good repute, are forthwith committed to prison, on suspicion for witchcraft. One of the Salem Justices[1] was pleased to tell Mr. Alden,[2] (when upon his examination) that truly he had been acquainted with him these many years; and had always accounted him a good man; but indeed now he should be obliged to change his opinion. This, there are more than one or two did hear, and are ready to swear to, if not in so many words, yet as to its natural and plain meaning. He saw reason to change his opinion of Mr. Alden, because that at the time he touched the poor child, the poor child came out of her fitt.

---

[1] Bartholomew Gedney.

[2] Captain John Alden, of Boston, son of the John Alden of the *Mayflower* and of Longfellow's poem. For Alden's own account of this episode see pp. 353–355, below.

I suppose his Honour never made the experiment, whether there was not as much virtue in his own hand, as there was in Mr. Alden's, to cure by a touch. I know a man that will venture two to one with any Salemite whatever, that let the matter be duly managed, and the afflicted person shall come out of her fitt upon the touch of the most religious hand in Salem. It is worthily noted by some, that at some times the afflicted will not presently come out of their fitts upon the touch of the suspected; and then, forsooth, they are ordered by the Justices to grasp hard, harder yet, etc. insomuch that at length the afflicted come out of their fitts; and the reason is very good, because that a touch of any hand, and processe of time, will work the cure; infallibly they will do it, as experience teaches.

I cannot but condemn this method of the Justices, of making this touch of the hand a rule to discover witchcraft; because I am fully persuaded that it is sorcery, and a superstitious method, and that which we have no rule for, either from reason or religion. The Salem Justices, at least some of them, do assert, that the cure of the afflicted persons is a natural effect of this touch; and they are so well instructed in the Cartesian philosophy, and in the doctrine of *effluvia*, that they undertake to give a demonstration how this touch does cure the afflicted persons; and the account they give of it is this; that by this touch, the venemous and malignant particles, that were ejected from the eye, do, by this means, return to the body whence they came, and so leave the afflicted persons pure and whole. I must confesse to you, that I am no small admirer of the Cartesian philosophy; but yet I have not so learned it. Certainly this is a strain that it will by no means allow of.

I would fain know of these Salem Gentlemen, but as yet could never know, how it comes about, that if these apprehended persons are witches, and, by a look of the eye, do cast the afflicted into their fitts by poisoning them, how it comes about, I say, that, by a look of their eye, they do not cast others into fitts, and poison others by their looks; and in particular, tender, fearfull women, who often are beheld by them, and as likely as any in the whole world to receive an ill impression from them. This Salem philosophy, some men may call the new philosophy; but I think it rather deserves the name of Salem superstition and sorcery, and it is not fitt to be named in a land of such light as New-England is. I think the matter might be better solved another way; but I shall not make any attempt that way, further than to say, that these afflicted children, (as they are called,) do hold correspondence with the devill, even in the esteem and account of the S. G.;[1] for when the black man, *i. e.* (say these gentlemen,) the Devill, does appear to them, they ask him many questions, and accordingly give information to the inquirer; and if this is not holding correspondence with the devill, and something worse, I know not what is.

But furthermore, I would fain know of these Salem Justices what need there is of further proof and evidence to convict and condemn these apprehended persons, than this look and touch, if so be they are so certain that this falling down and arising up, when there is a look and a touch, are natural effects of the said look and touch, and so a perfect demonstration and proof of witchcraft in those persons. What can the Jury or Judges desire more, to convict any man of witchcraft, than a plain demonstration, that the said man is a witch? Now if this look and touch, circumstanced as before, be a plain demonstration, (as their Philosophy teaches,) what need they seek for further evidences, when, after all, it can be but a demonstration?

But let this pass with the S. G. for never so plain and natural a demonstration; yet certain is it, that the reasonable part of the world, when acquainted herewith, will laugh at the demonstration, and conclude that the said S. G. are actually possessed, at least, with ignorance and folly.

I most admire[2] that Mr. N. N.[3] the Reverend Teacher at Salem, who was educated at the School of Knowledge, and is certainly a learned, a charitable, and a good man, though all the devils in Hell, and all the possessed girls in Salem, should say to the contrary; at him, (I say,) I do most admire; that he should cry up the above mentioned philosophy after the manner that he does. I can assure you, that I can bring you more than two, or twice two, (very credible persons) that will

---

[1] *I. e.*, Salem gentlemen—and so hereafter.

[2] Marvel, am surprised.   [3] Nicholas Noyes.

affirm, that they have heard him vindicate the above mentioned demonstration as very reasonable.

Secondly, with respect to the confessours, (as they are improperly called,) or such as confesse themselves to be witches, (the second thing you inquire into in your letter), there are now about fifty of them in Prison; many of which I have again and again seen and heard; and I cannot but tell you, that my faith is strong concerning them, that they are deluded, imposed upon, and under the influence of some evill spirit; and therefore unfitt to be evidences either against themselves, or any one else. I now speak of one sort of them, and of others afterward.

These confessours, (as they are called,) do very often contradict themselves, as inconsistently as is usual for any crazed, distempered person to do. This the S. G. do see and take notice of; and even the Judges themselves have, at some times, taken these confessours in flat lyes, or contradictions, even in the Courts; By reason of which, one would have thought, that the Judges would have frowned upon the said confessours, discarded them, and not minded one tittle of any thing that they said; but instead thereof, (as sure as we are men,) the Judges vindicate these confessours, and salve their contradictions, by proclaiming, that the Devill takes away their memory, and imposes upon their brain. If this reflects any where, I am very sorry for it: I can but assure you, that, upon the word of an honest man, it is truth, and that I can bring you many credible persons to witnesse it, who have been eye and ear wittnesses to these things.

These confessours then, at least some of them, even in the Judges' own account, are under the influence of the Devill; and the brain of these Confessours is imposed upon by the Devill, even in the Judges' account. But now, if, in the Judges' account, these confessours are under the influence of the Devill, and their brains are affected and imposed upon by the Devill, so that they are not their own men, why then should these Judges, or any other men, make such account of, and set so much by, the words of these Confessours, as they do? In short, I argue thus:

If the Devill does actually take away the memory of them at some times, certainly the Devill, at other times, may very reasonably be thought to affect their fancyes, and to represent false ideas to their imagination. But now, if it be thus granted, that the Devill is able to represent false ideas (to speak vulgarly) to the imaginations of the confessours, what man of sense will regard the confessions, or any of the words, of these confessours?

The great cry of many of our neighbours now is, What, will you not believe the confessours? Will you not believe men and women who confesse that they have signed to the Devill's book? that they were baptized by the Devill; and that they were at the mock-sacrament once and again? What! will you not believe that this is witchcraft, and that such and such men are witches, altho' the confessours do own and assert it?

Thus, I say, many of our good neighbours do argue; but methinks they might soon be convinced that there is nothing at all in all these their arguings, if they would but duly consider of the premises.

In the mean time, I think we must rest satisfyed in it, and be thankfull to God for it, that all men are not thus bereft of their senses; but that we have here and there considerate and thinking men, who will not thus be imposed upon, and abused, by the subtle endeavours of the crafty one.

In the next place, I proceed to the form of their inditements, and the Trials thereupon.

The Inditement runs for sorcery and witchcraft, acted upon the body of such an one, (say M. Warren), at such a particular time, (say April 14, '92,) and at divers other times before and after, whereby the said M. W. is wasted and consumed, pined, etc.

Now for the proof of the said sorcery and witchcraft, the prisoner at the bar pleading not guilty.

1. The afflicted persons are brought into Court; and after much patience and pains taken with them, do take their oaths, that the prisoner at the bar did afflict them: And here I think it very observable, that often, when the afflicted do mean and intend only the appearance and shape of such an one, (say G. Proctour) yet they positively swear that G. Proctour did afflict them; and they have been allowed so to do; as tho' there was no real difference between G. Proctour and the shape of G.

Proctour. This, methinks, may readily prove a stumbling block to the Jury, lead them into a very fundamental errour, and occasion innocent blood, yea the innocentest blood imaginable, to be in great danger. Whom it belongs unto, to be eyes unto the blind, and to remove such stumbling blocks, I know full well; and yet you, and every one else, do know as well as I who do not.[1]

2. The confessours do declare what they know of the said prisoner; and some of the confessours are allowed to give their oaths; a thing which I believe was never heard of in this world; that such as confesse themselves to be witches, to have renounced God and Christ, and all that is sacred, should yet be allowed and ordered to swear by the name of the great God! This indeed seemeth to me to be a grosse taking of God's name in vain. I know the S. G. do say, that there is hopes that the said Confessours have repented; I shall only say, that if they have repented, it is well for themselves; but if they have not, it is very ill for you know who. But then,

3. Whoever can be an evidence against the prisoner at the bar is ordered to come into Court; and here it scarce ever fails but that evidences, of one nature and another, are brought in, tho', I think, all of them altogether aliene to the matter of inditement; for they none of them do respect witchcraft upon the bodyes of the afflicted, which is the alone matter of charge in the inditement.

4. They are searched by a Jury; and as to some of them, the Jury brought in, that [on] such or such a place there was a preternatural excrescence. And I wonder what person there is, whether man or woman, of whom it cannot be said but that, in some part of their body or other, there is a preternatural excrescence. The term is a very general and inclusive term.

Some of the S. G. are very forward to censure and condemn the poor prisoner at the bar, because he sheds no tears: but such betray great ignorance in the nature of passion, and as great heedlessnesse as to common passages of a man's life. Some there are who never shed tears; others there are that ordinarily shed tears upon light occasions, and yet for their lives cannot shed a tear when the deepest sorrow is upon their hearts; and who is there that knows not these things? Who

---

[1] He means, of course, the judges.

knows not that an ecstasye of Joy will sometimes fetch teares, when as the quite contrary passion will shutt them close up? Why then should any be so silly and foolish as to take an argument from this appearance? But this is by the by. In short, the prisoner at the bar is indited for sorcery and witchcraft acted upon the bodyes of the afflicted. Now, for the proof of this, I reckon that the only pertinent evidences brought in are the evidences of the said afflicted.

It is true, that over and above the evidences of the afflicted persons, there are many evidences brought in, against the prisoner at the bar; either that he was at a witch meeting, or that he performed things which could not be done by an ordinary natural power; or that she sold butter to a saylor, which proving bad at sea, and the seamen exclaiming against her, she appeared, and soon after there was a storm, or the like. But what if there were ten thousand evidences of this nature; how do they prove the matter of inditement! And if they do not reach the matter of inditement, then I think it is clear, that the prisoner at the bar is brought in guilty, and condemned, merely from the evidences of the afflicted persons.

The S. G. will by no means allow, that any are brought in guilty, and condemned, by virtue of spectre Evidence, (as it is called,) *i. e.* the evidence of these afflicted persons, who are said to have spectral eyes; but whether it is not purely by virtue of these spectre evidences, that these persons are found guilty, (considering what before has been said,) I leave you, and any man of sense, to judge and determine. When any man is indited for murthering the person of A. B. and all the direct evidence be, that the said man pistolled the shadow of the said A. B. tho' there be never so many evidences that the said person murthered C. D., E. F. and ten more persons, yet all this will not amount to a legal proof, that he murthered A. B.; and upon that inditement, the person cannot be legally brought in guilty of the said inditement; it must be upon this supposition, that the evidence of a man's pistolling the shadow of A. B. is a legal evidence to prove that the said man did murther the person of A. B. Now no man will be so much out of his witts as to make this a legal evidence; and yet this seems to be our case; and how to apply it is very easy and obvious.

As to the late executions,[1] I shall only tell you, that in the opinion of many unprejudiced, considerate and considerable spectatours, some of the condemned went out of the world not only with as great protestations, but also with as good shews of innocency, as men could do.

They protested their innocency as in the presence of the great God, whom forthwith they were to appear before: they wished, and declared their wish, that their blood might be the last innocent blood shed upon that account. With great affection[2] they intreated Mr. C. M.[3] to pray with them: they prayed that God would discover what witchcrafts were among us; they forgave their accusers; they spake without reflection on Jury and Judges, for bringing them in guilty, and condemning them: they prayed earnestly for pardon for all other sins, and for an interest in the pretious blood of our dear Redeemer; and seemed to be very sincere, upright, and sensible of their circumstances on all accounts; especially Proctor and Willard, whose whole management of themselves, from the Goal to the Gallows, and whilst at the Gallows, was very affecting and melting to the hearts of some considerable Spectatours, whom I could mention to you:—but they are executed, and so I leave them.

Many things I cannot but admire and wonder at, an account of which I shall here send you.

And 1. I do admire that some particular persons, and particularly Mrs. Thatcher of Boston,[4] should be much complained of by the afflicted persons, and yet that the Justices should never issue out their warrants to apprehend them,

---

[1] The names presently mentioned would seem to show that he has especially in mind the executions of August 19, and his words suggest that he was present on this occasion. Those then executed, besides John Proctor and John Willard, were the Rev. George Burroughs, George Jacobs, and Martha Carrier. For two other accounts of their death, both perhaps by eye-witnesses, see below, pp. 360–364. But there had been executions also on June 10, July 19, and September 22.

[2] Emotion, earnestness.

[3] Cotton Mather.

[4] Mrs. Margaret Thacher (1625–1694), widow of the Rev. Thomas Thacher (d. 1678), first minister of the Old South Church. She was the only child of the wealthy Boston merchant Henry Webb, and had been left by a first marriage the widow of Jacob Sheafe, then the richest man in Boston.

when as upon the same account they issue out their warrants for the apprehending and imprisoning many others.

This occasions much discourse and many hot words, and is a very great scandal and stumbling block to many good people; certainly distributive Justice should have its course, without respect to persons; and altho' the said Mrs. Thatcher be mother in law to Mr. Corwin,[1] who is one of the Justices and Judges, yet if Justice and conscience do oblige them to apprehend others on the account of the afflicted their complaints, I cannot see how, without injustice and violence to conscience, Mrs. Thatcher can escape, when it is well known how much she is, and has been, complained of.

2. I cannot but admire that Mr. H. U.[2] (whom we all think innocent,) should yet be apprehended on this account, and ordered to prison, by a mittimus under Mr. Lynd's[3] his hand, and yet that he should be suffered, for above a fortnight, to be in a private house; and after that, to quitt the house, the town, and the Province, and yet that authority should not take effectual notice of it. Methinks that same Justice, that actually imprisoned others, and refused bail for them on any terms, should not be satisfyed without actually imprisoning Mr. U. and refusing bail for him, when his case is known to be the very same with the case of those others.

If he may be suffered to go away, why may not others? If others may not be suffered to go, how in Justice can he be allowed herein?

3. If our Justices do think that Mrs. C.[4] Mr. E.[5] and his wife, Mr. A.[6] and others, were capital offenders, and justly imprisoned on a capital account, I do admire that the said Justices should hear of their escape from prison, and where they are gone and entertained, and yet not send forthwith to the said places,[7] for the surrendering of them, that Justice might be done them. In other Capitalls[8] this has been prac-

[1] Jonathan Corwin, of Salem.

[2] Hezekiah Usher (1639–1697), a prominent Boston merchant.

[3] Doubtless Joseph Lynde (1637–1727), of Charlestown—since June a member of the Council under the new Mather charter.

[4] Mrs. Nathaniel Cary, of Charlestown. See pp. 349–352.

[5] Philip English, of Salem. See p. 371 and note 1.

[6] John Alden, of Boston. See p. 170, note 2.

[7] *I. e.*, to New York.   [8] *I. e.*, capital cases.

tised; why then is it not practised in this case, if really judged
to be so heinous as is made for?

4. I cannot but admire, that any snould go with their distempered friends and relations to the afflicted children, to
know what their distempered friends ayl; whether they are
not bewitched; who it is that afflicts them, and the like. It
is true, I know no reason why these afflicted may not be consulted as well as any other, if so be that it was only their
natural and ordinary knowledge that was had recourse to:
but it is not on this notion that these afflicted children are
sought unto; but as they have a supernatural knowledge; a
knowledge which they obtain by their holding correspondence
with spectres or evill spirits, as they themselves grant. This
consulting of these afflicted children, as abovesaid, seems to
me to be a very grosse evill, a real abomination, not fitt to be
known in N. E.[1] and yet is a thing practised, not only by
Tom and John—I mean the ruder and more ignorant sort—
but by many who professe high, and passe among us for some
of the better sort. This is that which aggravates the evil,
and makes it heinous and tremendous; and yet this is not the
worst of it, for, as sure as I now write to you, even some of our
civil leaders, and spiritual teachers, who, (I think,) should
punish and preach down such sorcery and wickedness, do
yet allow of, encourage, yea, and practise this very abomination.

I know there are several worthy Gentlemen in Salem, who
account this practise as an abomination, have trembled to
see the methods of this nature which others have used, and
have declared themselves to think the practise to be very evill
and corrupt; but all avails little with the abettours of the
said practice.

A person from Boston, of no small note, carried up his child
to Salem, (near 20 miles,) on purpose that he might consult
the afflicted about his child; which accordingly he did; and
the afflicted told him, that his child was afflicted by Mrs.
Cary and Mrs. Obinson.[2] The man returned to Boston, and
went forthwith to the Justices for a warrant to seise the said

---

[1] New England.

[2] Mrs. Obinson was probably the wife of William Obinson, or Obbinson, a
Boston tanner.

Obinson, (the said Cary being out of the way); but the Boston Justices saw reason to deny a warrant. The Rev. Mr. I. M.[1] of Boston, took occasion severely to reprove the said man; asking him whether there was not a God in Boston, that he should go to the Devill in Salem for advice; warning him very seriously against such naughty practices; which, I hope, proved to the conviction and good of the said person; if not, his blood will be upon his own head.

This consulting of these afflicted children, about their sick, was the unhappy begining of the unhappy troubles at poor Andover: Horse and man were sent up to Salem Village, from the said Andover, for some of the said afflicted; and more than one or two of them were carried down to see Ballard's wife,[2] and to tell who it was that did afflict her. I understand that the said B. took advice before he took this method; but what pity was it, that he should meet with, and hearken to such bad Counsellours? Poor Andover does now rue the day that ever the said afflicted went among them; they lament their folly, and are an object of great pity and commiseration. Capt. B.[3] and Mr. St.[4] are complained of by the afflicted, have left the town, and do abscond. Deacon Fry's wife, Capt'n Osgood's wife, and some others, remarkably pious and good people in repute, are apprehended and imprisoned; and that that is more admirable, the forementioned women are become a kind of confessours, being first brought thereto by the urgings and arguings of their good husbands, who, having taken up that corrupt and highly pernicious opinion, that whoever were accused by the afflicted, were guilty, did break charity with their dear wives, upon their being accused, and urge them to confesse their guilt; which so far prevailed with them as to make them say, they were afraid of their being in the snare of the Devill; and which, through the rude and bar-

---

[1] Increase Mather.

[2] Mrs. Joseph Ballard. See below, pp. 371–372; and, for more as to this Andover episode, pp. 241–244, 418–420. The records of the Andover cases are printed by Woodward in his *Records of Salem Witchcraft* (Roxbury, 1864), and there are chapters on the episode in Abiel Abbot's *History of Andover* (Andover, 1829) and Sarah Loring Bailey's *Historical Sketches of Andover* (Boston, 1880).

[3] Dudley Bradstreet. See p. 372.

[4] Stevens? The conjecture is Mrs. Bailey's (*Historical Sketches of Andover*, p. 228).

barous methods* that were afterwards used at Salem, issued
in somewhat plainer degrees of confession, and was attended
with imprisonment. The good Deacon and Captain are now
sensible of the errour they were in; do grieve and mourn bitterly, that they should break their charity with their wives,
and urge them to confesse themselves witches. They now
see and acknowledge their rashnesse and uncharitablenesse,
and are very fitt objects for the pity and prayers of every
good Christian. Now I am writing concerning Andover, I
cannot omit the opportunity of sending you this information;
that Whereas there is a report spread abroad the country, how
that they were much addicted to Sorcery in the said town,
and that there were fourty men in it that could raise the Devill
as well as any astrologer, and the like; after the best search
that I can make into it, it proves a mere slander, and a very
unrighteous imputation.

The Rev'd Elders of the said place were much surprized
upon their hearing of the said Report, and faithfully made inquiry about it; but the whole of naughtiness, that they could
discover and find out, was only this, that two or three girls
had foolishly made use of the sieve and scissors,[2] as children
have done in other towns. This method of the girls I do not
Justifye in any measure; but yet I think it very hard and
unreasonable, that a town should lye under the blemish and

---

* You may possibly think that my terms are too severe; but should I
tell you what a kind of Blade was employed in bringing these women to their
confession; what methods from damnation were taken; with what violence
urged; how unseasonably they were kept up; what buzzings and chuckings of
the hand were used, and the like, I am sure that you would call them, (as I
do), rude and barbarous methods.[1] [Marginal note in the original.]

[1] What Brattle may mean by "methods from *damnation*" is a puzzle to the
editor. Perhaps "damnation" is only a euphemism for "hell." Possibly he
thinks of that clause in the Massachusetts laws (*Body of Liberties of* 1641, art. 45;
Lawes and Libertyes, 1660, p. 67; 1672, p. 129) which permits a prisoner "in some
capital case, when he is first fully convicted by clear and sufficient evidence to
be guilty," to be tortured for the discovery of his accomplices, yet not with such
tortures as are barbarous and inhuman. What he means by "buzzings and chuckings of the hand," *i. e.*, whisperings and wheedlings, will grow clear if one turn
to pp. 374–376, and read what these Andover women themselves tell of the methods
used with them.

[2] A mode of divination much in vogue in New England as in Old. Called
also "sieve and shears" or "riddle and shears": the learned name is *coscinomancy.*

scandal of sorceryes and conjuration, merely for the inconsiderate practices of two or three girls in the said town.

5. I cannot but admire that the Justices, whom I think to be well-meaning men, should so far give ear to the Devill, as merely upon his authority to issue out their warrants, and apprehend people. Liberty was evermore accounted the great priviledge of an Englishman; but certainly, if the Devill will be heard against us, and his testimony taken, to the siezing and apprehending of us, our liberty vanishes, and we are fools if we boast of our liberty. Now, that the Justices have thus far given ear to the Devill, I think may be mathematically demonstrated to any man of common sense: And for the demonstration and proof hereof, I desire, only, that these two things may be duly considered, *viz.*

1. That several persons have been apprehended purely upon the complaints of these afflicted, to whom the afflicted were perfect strangers, and had not the least knowledge of imaginable, before they were apprehended.

2. That the afflicted do own and assert, and the Justices do grant, that the Devill does inform and tell the afflicted the names of those persons that are thus unknown unto them. Now these two things being duly considered, I think it will appear evident to any one, that the Devill's information is the fundamental testimony that is gone upon in the apprehending of the aforesaid people.

If I believe such or such an assertion as comes immediately from the Minister of God in the pulpitt, because it is the word of the everliving God, I build my faith on God's testimony: and if I practise upon it, this my practice is properly built on the word of God: even so in the case before us,

If I believe the afflicted persons as informed by the Devill, and act thereupon, this my act may properly be said to be grounded upon the testimony or information of the Devill. And now, if things are thus, I think it ought to be for a lamentation to you and me, and all such as would be accounted good Christians.

If any should see the force of this argument, and upon it say, (as I heard a wise and good Judge once propose,) that they know not but that God almighty, or a good spirit, does give this information to these afflicted persons; I make answer thereto, and say, that it is most certain that it is neither almighty God, nor yet any good Spirit, that gives this information; and my Reason is good, because God is a God of truth; and the good Spirits will not lye; whereas these informations have several times proved false, when the accused were brought before the afflicted.

6. I cannot but admire that these afflicted persons should be so much countenanced and encouraged in their accusations as they are: I often think of the Groton woman, that was afflicted, an account of which we have in print, and is a most certain truth, not to be doubted of.[1] I shall only say, that there was as much ground, in the hour of it, to countenance the said Groton woman, and to apprehend and imprison, on her accusations, as there is now to countenance these afflicted persons, and to apprehend and imprison on their accusations. But furthermore, it is worthy of our deepest consideration, that in the conclusion, (after multitudes have been imprisoned, and many have been put to death,) these afflicted persons should own that all was a mere fancy and delusion of the Devill's, as the Groton woman did own and acknowledge with respect to herself; if, I say, in after times, this be acknowledged by them, how can the Justices, Judges, or any else concerned in these matters, look back upon these things without the greatest of sorrow and grief imaginable? I confesse to you, it makes me tremble when I seriously consider of this thing. I have heard that the chief judge[2] has expressed himself very hardly of the accused woman at Groton, as tho' he believed her to be a witch to this day; but by such as knew the said woman, this is judged a very uncharitable opinion of the

---

[1] "The Groton woman" was Elizabeth Knapp, and the "account in print" probably that of Increase Mather reprinted above, pp. 21–23, though possibly Willard's sermon (see p. 21, note 4) is meant.

[2] William Stoughton, the new lieutenant-governor. He had been educated for the ministry in the Harvard class of 1650, and went to England, where he preached for some ten years, receiving meanwhile at Oxford his mastership in arts and the honor of a fellowship; but, ejected at the Restoration, he returned to New England, and there, though counted an able preacher, declined a settlement and drifted into public life. He seems to have set store by his learning in theology, and to the end to have maintained the Devil's impotence to personate by a spectre any but a guilty witch. As to his career see the careful study by Sibley, in his *Harvard Graduates* (I. 194–208).

said Judge, and I do not understand that any are proselyted thereto.

Rev'd Sir, these things I cannot but admire and wonder at. Now, if so be it is the effect of my dullness that I thus admire, I hope you will pity, not censure me: but if, on the contrary, these things are just matter of admiration, I know that you will join with me in expressing your admiration hereat.

The chief Judge is very zealous in these proceedings, and says, he is very clear as to all that hath as yet been acted by this Court, and, as far as ever I could perceive, is very impatient in hearing any thing that looks another way. I very highly honour and reverence the wisdome and integrity of the said Judge, and hope that this matter shall not diminish my veneration for his honour; however, I cannot but say, my great fear is, that wisdome and counsell are withheld from his honour as to this matter, which yet I look upon not so much as a Judgment to his honour as to this poor land.

But altho' the Chief Judge, and some of the other Judges, be very zealous in these proceedings, yet this you may take for a truth, that there are several about the Bay, men for understanding, Judgment, and Piety, inferiour to few, (if any,) in N. E. that do utterly condemn the said proceedings, and do freely deliver their Judgment in the case to be this, *viz.* that these methods will utterly ruine and undoe poor N. E. I shall nominate some of these to you, *viz.* The hon'ble Simon Bradstreet, Esq. (our late Governor); the hon'ble Thomas Danforth, Esq. (our late Deputy Governor); the Rev'd Mr. Increase Mather, and the Rev'd Mr. Samuel Willard. Major N. Saltonstall, Esq. who was one of the Judges, has left the Court, and is very much dissatisfyed with the proceedings of it. Excepting Mr. Hale, Mr. Noyes, and Mr. Parris, the Rev'd Elders, almost throughout the whole Country, are very much dissatisfyed. Several of the late Justices, *viz.* Thomas Graves, Esq. N. Byfield, Esq. Francis Foxcroft, Esq. are much dissatisfyed; also several of the present Justices; and in particular, some of the Boston Justices, were resolved rather to throw up their commissions than be active in disturbing the liberty of their Majesties' subjects, merely on the accusations of these afflicted, possessed children.

Finally; the principal Gentlemen in Boston, and there-about, are generally agreed that irregular and dangerous methods have been taken as to these matters.

Sir, I would not willingly lead you into any errour, and therefore would desire you to note,

1. That when I call these afflicted "the afflicted children," I would not be understood as though I meant, that all that are afflicted are *children*: there are several young men and women that are afflicted, as well as children: but this term has most prevailed among us, because of the younger sort that were first afflicted, and therefore I make use of it.

2. That when I speak of the Salem Gentlemen, I would not be understood as tho' I meant every Individual Gentleman in Salem; nor yet as tho' I meant, that there were no men but in Salem that run upon these notions: some term they must have, and this seems not improper, because in Salem this sort of Gentlemen does most abound.

3. That other Justices in the Country, besides the Salem Justices, have issued out their warrants, and imprisoned, on the accusations of the afflicted as aforesaid; and therefore, when I speak of the Salem Justices, I do not mean them exclusively.

4. That as to the above mentioned Judges, that are commissionated for this Court at Salem, five of them do belong to Suffolk county; four of which five do belong to Boston;[1] and therefore I see no reason why Boston should talk of Salem, as tho' their own Judges had had no hand in these proceedings at Salem.

Nineteen persons have now been executed, and one pressed to death for a mute: seven more are condemned; two of which are reprieved, because they pretend their being with child; one, *viz.* Mrs. Bradbury of Salisbury, from the intercession of some friends; and two or three more, because they are confessours.[2]

The Court is adjourned to the first Tuesday in November, then to be kept at Salem; between this and then will be [the]

---

[1] See p. 355. Richards, Sargent, Sewall, Winthrop, were of Boston; Stoughton of Dorchester, close by. Only Gedney was of Salem, till Corwin was called in to replace Saltonstall (who was of Haverhill).

[2] As to all these see below, pp. 360–374.

great assembly,[1] and this matter will be a peculiar matter of their agitation. I think it is matter of earnest supplication and prayer to almighty God, that he would afford his gracious presence to the said assembly, and direct them aright in this weighty matter. Our hopes are here; and if, at this Juncture, God does not graciously appear for us, I think we may conclude that N. E. is undone and undone.

I am very sensible, that it is irksome and disagreeable to go back, when a man's doing so is an implication that he has been walking in a wrong path: however, nothing is more honourable than, upon due conviction, to retract and undo, (so far as may be,) what has been amiss and irregular.

I would hope that, in the conclusion, both the Judges and Justices will see and acknowledge that such were their best friends and advisers as disswaded from the methods which they have taken, tho' hitherto they have been angry with them, and apt to speak very hardly of them.

I cannot but highly applaud, and think it our duty to be very thankfull, for the endeavours of several Elders,[2] whose lips, (I think,) should preserve knowledge, and whose counsell should, I think, have been more regarded, in a case of this nature, than as yet it has been: in particular, I cannot but think very honourably of the endeavours of a Rev'd person in Boston,[3] whose good affection to his countrey in general,

---

[1] The General Court. It convened on October 12. Its attitude as to the Salem trials is thus tersely intimated in Judge Sewall's diary: "Oct. 26, 1692. A Bill is sent in about calling a Fast and Convocation of Ministers, that [we] may be led in the right way as to the Witchcrafts. The season and manner of doing it, is such, that the Court of Oyer and Terminer count themselves thereby dismissed. 29 Nos and 33 yeas to the Bill." The bill itself has been printed (from the Mass. Archives, XI. 70) by G. H. Moore, in the *Proceedings* of the American Antiquarian Society (n. s., II. 172); and that those of Brattle's mind had not relied alone on prayer to influence the assembly may be seen by the petition printed in the *N. E. Hist. and Gen. Register*, XXVII. 55, and in the *Proceedings* of the American Antiquarian Society, n. s., V. 246 (see also *Proceedings*, n. s., II. 171).

[2] The ministers, now practically the only "elders."

[3] It has been generally assumed, and with reason, that this "Rev'd person" was the Rev. Samuel Willard. Three of the judges (Sargent, Sewall, and Winthrop) were members of his church (the Old South) and, unless one suspect Brattle of intent to mislead, "spiritual relation" must here mean a pastor's. The phrase "good affection to the country" suggests, too, one who, like Willard,

and spiritual relation to three of the Judges in particular, has made him very solicitous and industrious in this matter; and I am fully persuaded, that had his notions and proposals been hearkened to, and followed, when these troubles were in their birth, in an ordinary way, they would never have grown unto that heigth which now they have. He has as yet mett with little but unkindness, abuse, and reproach from many men; but I trust that, in after times, his wisdome and service will find a more universal acknowledgment; and if not, his reward is with the Lord.

Two or three things I should have hinted to you before, but they slipped my thoughts in their proper place.

Many of these afflicted persons, who have scores of strange fitts in a day, yet in the intervals of time are hale and hearty, robust and lusty, as tho' nothing had afflicted them. I Remember that when the chief Judge gave the first Jury their charge, he told them, that they were not to mind whether the bodies of the said afflicted were really pined and consumed, as was expressed in the inditement; but whether the said afflicted did not suffer from the accused such afflictions as naturally

shared Brattle's political views. We have seen already (p. 23) what caution in 1671 he used in the case of Elizabeth Knapp; and, if the "notions and proposals" meant by Brattle are now lost, we have from his pen what puts his position in 1692 beyond all question—a little dialogue, published anonymously while the troubles were at their height, which with fairness and courtesy, but with striking clearness and boldness, argues against the iniquity of the procedure. Its title runs: *Some Miscellany Observations on our Present Debates respecting Witchcrafts, in a Dialogue between S. and B. By P. E. and J. A. Philadelphia, Printed by William Bradford, for Hezekiah Usher.* 1692. "S." and "B." undoubtedly mean Salem and Boston. Philadelphia and Bradford probably had as little to do with the book (the type is not Bradford's) as did Hezekiah Usher, P. E. (Philip English), or J. A. (John Alden), three notable fugitives from Salem justice. All alike were merely remote enough to bear in safety the imputation of such a book. John Alden and Hezekiah Usher were members of Willard's church; and Philip English and his wife he visited while in custody at Boston, and probably was a party to their escape. At least the Rev. William Bentley, of Salem, recording in his diary, May 21, 1793, what their great-granddaughter Susanna Hathorne had told him, relates that Willard and Moodey "visited them and invited them to the public worship on the day before they were to return to Salem for trial. Their text was that they that are persecuted in one city, let them flee to another. After Meeting the Ministers visited them at the Gaol, and asked them whether they took notice of the discourse, and told them their danger and urged them to escape since so many had suffered. Mr. English replied, 'God *tended* to their being pined and consumed, wasted, etc.   This, (said he,) is a pining and consuming in the sense of the law. I add not.

Furthermore: These afflicted persons do say, and often have declared it, that they can see Spectres when their eyes are shutt, as well as when they are open.   This one thing I evermore accounted as very observable, and that which might serve as a good key to unlock the nature of these mysterious troubles, if duly improved by us.   Can they see Spectres when their eyes are shutt?   I am sure they lye, at least speak falsely, if they say so; for the thing, in nature, is an utter impossibility.   It is true, they may strongly fancye, or have things represented to their imagination, when their eyes are shutt; and I think this is all which ought to be allowed to these blind, nonsensical girls; and if our officers and Courts have apprehended, imprisoned, condemned, and executed our guiltlesse neighbours, certainly our errour is great, and we shall rue it in the conclusion.   There are two or three other things that I have observed in and by these afflicted persons, which make me strongly suspect that the Devill imposes upon their brains, and deludes their fancye and imagination; and that

will not permit them to touch me.' Mrs. English said: 'Do you not think the sufferers innocent?' He (Moody) said 'Yes.' She then added, 'Why may we not suffer also?' The Ministers then told him if he would not carry his wife away they would." (Quoted by R. D. Paine, in his *Ships and Sailors of Old Salem*, from Bentley's privately printed diary, which seems to give the tale in a more primitive form than his letter to Alden, in the Mass. Hist. Soc., *Collections*, X.) "It ought never to be forgotten," said Willard's colleague, Ebenezer Pemberton, preaching in 1707 his funeral sermon, "with what Prudence, Courage and Zeal he appeared for the Good of this People in that Dark and Mysterious Season when we were assaulted from the Invisible World. And how singularly Instrumental he was in discovering the Cheats and Delusions of Satan, which did threaten to stain our Land with Blood and to deluge it with all manner of Woes." True, Judge Sewall, mentioning in 1696 (*Diary*, I. 433) Willard's sermon at the day of public prayer, says that he spake smartly "at last" about the Salem witchcraft; but "at last" here means "at the end," "as the peroration of his sermon." It is clearly Willard whom Cotton Mather has especially in mind when in his life of Phips and again in his *Magnalia* (bk. II., p. 62) he sets forth the views of those "who from the beginning were very much dissatisfied with these proceedings," having "already known of one at the Town of Groton" who had falsely accused a neighbor. The strange suggestion of W. F. Poole that Brattle here means Cotton Mather himself, is adequately answered by Upham, in his *Salem Witchcraft and Cotton Mather.*

the Devill's book (which they say has been offered them) is a mere fancye of theirs, and no reality: That the witches' meeting, the Devill's Baptism, and mock sacraments, which they oft speak of, are nothing else but the effect of their fancye, depraved and deluded by the Devill, and not a Reality to be regarded or minded by any wise man. And whereas the Confessours have owned and asserted the said meetings, the said Baptism, and mock Sacrament, (which the S. G. and some others, make much account of) I am very apt to think, that, did you know the circumstances of the said Confessours, you would not be swayed thereby, any otherwise than to be confirmed, that all is perfect Devilism, and an Hellish design to ruine and destroy this poor land: For whereas there are of the said Confessours 55 in number, some of them are known to be distracted, crazed women, something of which you may see by a petition lately offered to the chief Judge, a copy whereof I may now send you;[1] others of them denyed their guilt, and maintained their innocency for above eighteen hours, after most violent, distracting, and draggooning[2] methods had been used with them, to make them confesse. Such methods they were, that more than one of the said confessours did since tell many, with teares in their eyes, that they thought their very lives would have gone out of their bodyes; and wished that they might have been cast into the lowest dungeon, rather than be tortured with such repeated buzzings and chuckings and unreasonable urgings as they were treated withal.

They soon recanted their confessions, acknowledging, with sorrow and grief, that it was an hour of great temptation with them; and I am very apt to think, that as for five or six of the said confessours, if they are not very good Christian women, it will be no easy matter to find so many good Christian women in N. E. But, finally, as to about thirty of these fifty-five Confessours, they are possessed (I reckon) with the Devill, and afflicted as the children are, and therefore not fitt to be regarded as to any thing they say of themselves or others. And whereas the S. G. do say that these confessours made

---

[1] The paper meant is doubtless that printed at pp. 374–375, below.

[2] The attempt of Louis XIV. to force his Protestant subjects to abandon their faith by turning loose his dragoons upon them had already furnished the English language with this new word.

their Confessions before they were afflicted, it is absolutely contrary to universal experience, as far as ever I could understand. It is true, that some of these have made their confession before they had their falling, tumbling fitts, but yet not absolutely before they had any fitts and marks of possession, for (as the S. G. know full well) when these persons were about first confessing, their mouths would be stopped, and their throats affected, as tho' there was danger of strangling, and afterward (it is true) came their tumbling fitts. So that, I say, the confessions of these persons were in the beginning of their fitts, and not truly before their fitts, as the S. G. would make us believe.

Thus, (Sir,) I have given you as full a narrative of these matters as readily occurs to my mind, and I think every word of it is matter of fact; the several glosses and descants whereupon, by way of Reasoning, I refer to your Judgment, whether to approve or disapprove.

What will be the issue of these troubles, God only knows; I am afraid that ages will not wear off that reproach and those stains which these things will leave behind them upon our land. I pray God pity us, Humble us, Forgive us, and appear mercifully for us in this our mount of distress: Herewith I conclude, and subscribe myself,

Reverend Sir, your real friend and humble servant,

T. B.

LETTERS OF GOVERNOR PHIPS TO THE HOME GOVERNMENT, 1692–1693

INTRODUCTION

SIR WILLIAM PHIPS, who arrived in May as the royal governor under the new charter, was no stranger to New England. Born in 1651 at a hamlet on the Maine coast, just beyond the Kennebec, where his father, a Bristol gunsmith, had become a settler, he had early turned from sheep-herding to ship-carpentry, and then coming up to Boston, where at twenty-two he first learned to read and write, he had by thrift become the master of a vessel and had found a path to fortune in the rescue of lost treasure from Spanish galleons sunken in West Indian waters. These ventures had brought him into partnership with some of the most powerful of English nobles, and even with royalty itself, and his sturdy honesty (or perhaps a wise use of his wealth) won him from the King in 1687 the honor of knighthood and in 1688 appointment as high sheriff of New England. The hostility of Governor Andros brought the sheriffship to nothing; but the English revolution overturned Andros in 1689, and the emancipated colonies made Sir William head of the expedition that conquered Nova Scotia, and then sent him with another against Quebec. Meanwhile President Increase Mather was laboring in England, as the agent of Massachusetts, for the restoration of the ancient charter; and when Sir William (who during his absence had, as his son's convert, become a member of his church) turned up there too, and just in time to support him against the other New England commissioners in accepting from the King what could be got, though not what could be wished, he was the natural nominee for the new governorship.

But the new governor was little trained for such an emergency as awaited him in New England. What more natural in such a crisis, which to the thought of that day seemed to need the divine more than the statesman, than to turn for counsel to his pastor and patron, or to his colleague the new lieutenant-governor,[1] who had enjoyed precisely that training in theology which seemed now his own chief lack? Stoughton was made chief justice of a special court created by the governor to try the witch-cases,[2] and during the latter's repeated absences[3] at the frontier became the acting governor. The ministers of Boston were "consulted by his Excellency and the Honourable Council" as to the conduct of the trials. Their "Return," bearing date of June 15, was drawn by Cotton Mather;[4] and it was perhaps now that that divine, who had early (May 31) furnished the judges a body of instructions,[5] was inspired by "the Direction of His Excellency the Governor"[6] to undertake that "Account of the Sufferings brought

[1] William Stoughton (see above, p. 183 and note 2) was of course also a nominee of Mather's. He had not been forward in the revolution which overthrew the Andros government, but he had rallied to it, and Cotton Mather had written his father wishing he might "do anything to restore him to the favor of the country."

[2] In the last week of May, at his first meetings with the new Council. The court began its sessions at Salem on June 2.

[3] He was present in Boston at meetings of the Council on June 13, 18, July 4, 8, 15, 18, 21, 22, 25, 26, September 5, 12, 16, and again on October 14 (Moore, in American Antiquarian Society, *Proceedings*, n. s., V. 251 note). Sewall on September 29 notes in his diary: "Governor comes to Town."

[4] A summary of it may be found on pp. 356–357, below; the full text is appended to Increase Mather's *Cases of Conscience* (1693) and has been often reprinted, both with that work and in later books. It is Cotton Mather himself (in his life of Phips) who tells us that he drafted it.

[5] In his letter of May 31 to his parishioner John Richards, a member of the court (*Mather Papers*, pp. 391–397). It is endorsed—with reason—"Mr Cotton Mather, an Essay concerning Witchcraft"; for an essay it really is. A supplement, and an interesting one, is his letter of August 17 to John Foster, a member of the Council (printed by Upham in his *Salem Witchcraft and Cotton Mather*, pp. 39–40).

[6] It has been questioned (by Upham and again by G. H. Moore) whether "the Governor" whose "commands" Mather alleges (see p. 206) may not be Stoughton instead of Phips; but his discrimination between the two is too clear and too constant to admit the suspicion, and still less can Stoughton and

upon the Countrey by Witchcraft," which was ready for submission to Sir William on his return from the east in early October, and with which, under its title of *The Wonders of the Invisible World*, we must soon make acquaintance. The opening clauses of the governor's letter show plainly the influence of that book;[1] and the change in tone between its earlier and its later portion, and yet more between the letter of October and that of February, is not the least interesting feature of these documents.[2]

Sewall (see pp. 251, 378) have been inexact. A doubt as to who consulted the clergy must be similarly answered. Yet Stoughton may well have been behind both acts.

[1] His phrases are taken almost bodily from the book (see, in Drake's edition, pp. 102–109, not here reprinted); and his statement as to the methods of the court echoes Mather's. It has been suggested (by Moore) that Mather himself drafted the letter; but neither the style nor the matter of its later portion can be his.

[2] Cotton Mather, in his life of Phips, names as one of the causes of the governor's changing attitude, the reply of "the Dutch and French Ministers of the Province of New York," who had "their Judgement asked by the Chief Judge of that Province"—the Massachusetts Tory, Joseph Dudley. These questions (now printed with the answers in the *Proceedings* of the Mass. Hist. Soc., second series, I, 348–358) throw a vivid light on the problems then agitating the public mind. They are dated at New York on October 5, and the answers, dated October 11, cannot have reached Boston before the middle of that month. More distinctly than the Boston clergy they reject "spectral evidence." According to the Anglican rector at New York, John Miller (commenting on Mather's statement as borrowed by the geographer Hermann Moll), "the advice of the established English Minister was also asked and generously given"; "but," he adds, "they were not so civill as to thank him for it, nor do they here acknowledge it, although it was much to their purpose, and stood them in good stead." It may be found, however, written out by his own hand in his copy of Moll's *Atlas* (now in the New York Public Library); and it is summarized at pp. 274–276 of the New York Historical Society's *Collections* for 1869 and in the edition of Miller's *New York considered* (1695) by Mr. Paltsits (1903), to whom the editor owes suggestion of the matter. Miller's answers are, indeed, somewhat less credulous than those of his Calvinist colleagues; but (as appears from a "Memorandum" of his own) it is by no means certain that they reached New England.

LETTERS OF GOVERNOR PHIPS

WHEN I first arrived I found this Province miserably harrassed with a most Horrible witchcraft or Possession of Devills
which had broke in upon severall Townes, some scores of poor
people were taken with preternaturall torments some scalded
with brimstone some had pins stuck in their flesh others hurried into the fire and water and some dragged out of their
houses and carried over the tops of trees and hills for many
Miles together; it hath been represented to mee much like
that of Sweden about thirty years agoe,[1] and there were many
committed to prison upon suspicion of Witchcraft before my
arrivall. The loud cries and clamours of the friends of the
afflicted people with the advice of the Deputy Governor and
many others prevailed with mee to give a Commission of Oyer
and Terminer for discovering what witchcraft might be at
the bottome or whether it were not a possession. The chief
Judge in this Commission was the Deputy Governour and the
rest were persons of the best prudence and figure that could
then be pitched upon. When the Court came to sitt at Salem
in the County of Essex they convicted more than twenty persons of being guilty of witchcraft, some of the convicted were
such as confessed their Guilt, the Court as I understand began
their proceedings with the accusations of the afflicted and then
went upon other humane[2] evidences to strengthen that. I was
almost the whole time of the proceeding abroad in the service
of Their Majesties in the Eastern part of the Country and depended upon the Judgement of the Court as to a right method
of proceeding in cases of Witchcraft but when I came home I
found many persons in a strange ferment of dissatisfaction which
was increased by some hott Spiritts that blew up the flame,[3] but

---

[1] The famous case at Mohra in 1669–1670. Cotton Mather had appended
to his *Wonders* an account of it. [2] Human.

[3] He thinks perhaps of the Baptist preacher, William Milborne, one of the
leaders in the later revolution, who on June 25 was called before the Council

on enquiring into the matter I found that the Devill had taken upon him the name and shape of severall persons who were doubtless inocent and to my certain knowledge of good reputation for which cause I have now forbidden the committing of any more that shall be accused without unavoydable necessity, and those that have been committed I would shelter from any Proceedings against them wherein there may be the least suspition of any wrong to be done unto the Innocent.   I would also wait for any particular directions or commands if their Majesties please to give mee any for the fuller ordering this perplexed affair.   I have also put a stop to the printing of any discourses one way or other, that may increase the needless disputes of people upon this occasion, because I saw a likelyhood of kindling an inextinguishable flame if I should admitt any publique and open Contests and I have grieved to see that some who should have done their Majesties and this Province better service have so far taken Councill of Passion as to desire the precipitancy of these matters, these things have been improved by some to give me many interuptions in their Majesties service and in truth none of my vexations have been greater than this, than that their Majesties service has been hereby unhappily clogged, and the Persons who have made soe ill improvement of these matters here are seeking to turne it all upon mee,[1] but I hereby declare that as soon as I came from fighting against their Majesties Enemyes and understood what danger some of their innocent subjects might be exposed to, if the evidence of the afflicted persons only did prevaile either to the committing or trying any of them, I did before

because of two papers subscribed by him and several others, "containing very high reflections upon the administration of public justice within this their Majesty's Province" (Moore, *Notes on Witchcraft*, p. 12; *Final Notes*, p. 72). What seems one of these papers, addressed "to the Grave and Juditious the Generall Assembly of the Province," has been found (see it in *N. E. Hist. and Gen. Register*, XXVII. 55, and reprinted by Moore in American Antiquarian Society, *Proceedings*, n. s., V. 246) and proves a protest against the conviction "upon bare specter testimonie" of "persons of good fame and of unspotted reputation." It must have been in circulation before the detection of its author, and was very possibly the reason for the consultation of the clergy.

[1] It must be remembered that the new charter, by opening the suffrage to those who were not church members, had greatly strengthened the party opposed to the theocracy—and to the theocracy's governor. More than once it has been said, too, that the Salem witchcraft was the rock on which the theocracy shattered.

any application was made unto me about it put a stop to the
proceedings of the Court and they are now stopt till their
Majesties pleasure be known.   Sir I beg pardon for giving you
all this trouble, the reason is because I know my enemies are
seeking to turn it all upon me and I take this liberty because
I depend upon your friendship, and desire you will please to
give a true understanding of the matter if any thing of this
kind be urged or made use of against mee.   Because the just-
nesse of my proceeding herein will bee a sufficient defence.   Sir

I am with all imaginable respect

Your most humble Servt

WILLIAM PHIPS.

Dated at Boston
   the 12th of october 1692.[1]

Mem'dm
   That my Lord President be pleased to acquaint his Ma'ty
in Councill with the account received from New England from
Sir Wm. Phips the Governor there touching Proceedings against
severall persons for Witchcraft as appears by the Governor's
letter concerning those matters.

BOSTON in New England Febry 21st, 169¾.

May it please yor. Lordshp.
   BY the Capn. of the *Samuell and Henry* I gave an account
that att my arrivall here I found the Prisons full of people

---

[1] This letter, with its memorandum, has been printed in the *Essex Institute
Historical Collections*, IX. 86–88, from a copy made in the British archives ("Colonial Entry Book, vol. 62, p. 414," now C. O. 5: 905, p. 414).   It has since
been printed also in the *Calendar of State Papers, Colonial*, 1689–1692 (no. 2551,
p. 720), which uses not only this MS. (mistakenly called "an extract") but
another ("Board of Trade, New England, 6, no. 7," now C. O. 5: 857, no. 7);
but the editor has corrected and paraphrased.   The last-named MS. (C. O.
5 : 857, no. 7) is, however, the original letter; and the present impression has
been carefully collated with it at London, many corrections resulting.   October
14, in the Essex Institute's reprint, is only a printer's error for October 12.
The letter was addressed to William Blathwayt, clerk of the Privy Council, and
it is he who added the memorandum (to the Entry Book copy).

committed upon suspition of witchcraft and that continuall
complaints were made to me that many persons were grievously
tormented by witches and that they cryed out upon severall
persons by name, as the cause of their torments.   The number
of these complaints increasing every day, by advice of the
Lieut Govr. and the Councill I gave a Commission of Oyer
and Terminer to try the suspected witches and at that time
the generality of the People represented the matter to me as
reall witchcraft and gave very strange instances of the same.
The first in Commission was the Lieut. Govr. and the rest persons of the best prudence and figure that could then be pitched
upon and I depended upon the Court for a right method of
proceeding in cases of witchcraft.   At that time I went to
command the army at the Eastern part of the Province, for
the French and Indians had made an attack upon some of our
Fronteer Towns.   I continued there for some time but when
I returned I found people much disatisfied at the proceedings
of the Court, for about Twenty persons were condemned and
executed of which number some were thought by many persons to be innocent.   The Court still proceeded in the same
method of trying them, which was by the evidence of the
afflicted persons who when they were brought into the Court
as soon as the suspected witches looked upon them instantly
fell to the ground in strange agonies and grievous torments,
but when touched by them upon the arme or some other part
of their flesh they immediately revived and came to themselves,
upon [which] they made oath that the Prisoner at the Bar did
afflict them and that they saw their shape or spectre come from
their bodies which put them to such paines and torments:
When I enquired into the matter I was enformed by the
Judges that they begun with this, but had humane testimony
against such as were condemned and undoubted proof of their
being witches, but at length I found that the Devill did take
upon him the shape of Innocent persons and some were accused
of whose innocency I was well assured and many considerable
persons of unblameable life and conversation were cried out
upon as witches and wizards.   The Deputy Govr. notwithstanding persisted vigorously in the same method, to the great
disatisfaction and disturbance of the people, untill I put an

end to the Court and stopped the proceedings, which I did because I saw many innocent persons might otherwise perish and at that time I thought it my duty to give an account thereof that their Ma'ties pleasure might be signifyed, hoping that for the better ordering thereof the Judges learned in the law in England might give such rules and directions as have been practized in England for proceedings in so difficult and so nice a point; When I put an end to the Court[1] there were at least fifty persons in prison in great misery by reason of the extream cold and their poverty, most of them having only spectre evidence against them, and their mittimusses being defective, I caused some of them to be lett out upon bayle and put the Judges upon considering of a way to reliefe others and prevent them from perishing in prison, upon which some of them were convinced and acknowledged that their former proceedings were too violent and not grounded upon a right foundation but that if they might sit againe, they would proceed after another method, and whereas Mr. Increase Mathew[2] and severall other Divines did give it as their Judgment that the Devill might afflict in the shape of an innocent person and that the look and the touch of the suspected persons was not sufficient proofe against them, these things had not the same stress layd upon them as before, and upon this consideration I permitted a spetiall Superior Court[3] to be held at Salem

---

[1] It was on October 29, three days after the passage by the General Court of the bill calling for a fast and a convocation of ministers for guidance "as to the witchcrafts," and, as Judge Sewall tells us (see p. 186, note 1, above) in such "season and manner" that "the Court of Oyer and Terminer count themselves thereby dismissed," that in the Council, when "Mr. Russel asked whether the Court of Oyer and Terminer should sit, expressing some fear of Inconvenience by its fall," the "Governour said it must fall." (Sewall's *Diary*, I. 368.)

[2] Mather. Undoubtedly an error of the English copyist. The advice meant was that of the twelve ministers of Boston and vicinity on June 15. See introduction.

[3] The Superior Court was created by act of the General Court of the province—of course with the concurrence of the governor—on November 25, 1692; but its session at Salem would, under the law, have come in the next November, and a supplementary act was passed on December 16, providing, "upon consideration that many persons charged capital offenders are now in custody within the county of Essex," for a court of assize and general jail delivery there on January 3.

in the County of Essex on the third day of January, the Lieut
Govr. being Chief Judge.　Their method of proceeding being
altered, all that were brought to tryall to the number of fifety
two, were cleared saving three, and I was enformed by the
Kings Attorny Generall that some of the cleared and the condemned were under the same circumstances or that there was
the same reason to clear the three condemned as the rest
according to his Judgment.　The Deputy Govr. signed a Warrant for their speedy execucion and also of five others who
were condemned at the former Court of Oyer and terminer,
but considering how the matter had been managed I sent a
reprieve whereby the execucion was stopped untill their Maj.
pleasure be signified and declared.　The Lieut. Gov. upon this
occasion· was inraged and filled with passionate anger and refused to sitt upon the bench in a Superior Court then held at
Charles Towne,[1] and indeed hath from the beginning hurried
on these matters with great precipitancy and by his warrant
hath caused the estates, goods and chattles of the executed to
be seized and disposed of without my knowledge or consent.
The stop put to the first method of proceedings hath dissipated
the blak cloud that threatened this Province with destruccion;
for whereas this delusion of the Devill did spread and its dis-
mall effects touched the lives and estates of many of their
Ma'ties Subjects and the reputacion of some of the principall
persons here,[2] and indeed unhappily clogged and interrupted
their Ma'ties affaires which hath been a great vexation to me,
I have no new complaints but peoples minds before divided

[1] For this episode see pp. 382–383.

[2] A "letter from Boston" printed in the British *Calendar of State Papers,
Colonial*, 1693–1696, p. 63, says that "The witchcraft at Salem went on vigorously . . . until at last members of Council and Justices were accused"; and the
Boston merchant Calef in 1697 wrote: "If it be true what was said at the Counsel-
board in answer to the commendations of Sir William, for his stopping the proceedings about Witchcraft, *viz.* That it was high time for him to stop it, his own
Lady being accused; if that Assertion were a truth, then New-England may
seem to be more beholden to the accusers for accusing of her, and thereby necessi-
tating a stop, than to Sir William" (*More Wonders*, p. 154).　Lady Phips had
earned an accusation by daring, in Sir William's absence, herself to issue a warrant for the discharge of an accused woman.　The keeper lost his place.　(MS.
letter quoted by Hutchinson, II. 61, note; the writer had it from the keeper himself and had seen the document.)

and distracted by differing opinions concerning this matter
are now well composed.

I am

Yor. Lordships most faithfull

humble Servant

WILLIAM PHIPS

[Addressed:]   To the Rt. Honble
the Earle of Nottingham
att Whitehall
London
[Indorsed:]   R [*i. e.*, received] May 24, 93
abt. Witches[1]

<hr>

[1] This letter is here reprinted from the Massachusetts Historical Society's
Proceedings, second ser., I. 340–342, where the original, in the British archives,
is described as "America and West Indies, No. 591" and "also in Colonial Entry
Book, No. 62, p. 426"; but the *Calendar of State Papers, Colonial*, 1693–1696,
which again prints it, though in abridged form, ascribes it to "America and West
Indies, 561, nos. 28, 29," and mentions the duplicate as "Col. Entry Bk., Vol.
LXII, pp. 426–430," and as "entered as addressed to William Blathwayt." It
may also be found in G. H. Moore's *Final Notes on Witchcraft in Massachusetts*
(New York, 1885), pp. 90–93, with his annotations. Examination at the British
Public Record Office shows that the original letter (formerly America and West
Indies, 561, no. 28) is now C. O. 5 : 51, no. 28, and is plainly addressed to the
Earl of Nottingham.

FROM "THE WONDERS OF THE INVISIBLE
WORLD," BY COTTON MATHER, 1693

INTRODUCTION

How *The Wonders of the Invisible World* came to be written we have already seen.[1] Its author had "a talent for sudden composures." We have seen what a scrap-bag was his *Memorable Providences*; and the pigeon-holes of his desk must for months have been gathering materials that could now be put to use. What these materials were is suggested by his title-page; but the title-page description is not exact. There is first an essay, entitled "Enchantments Encountered," on New England as a home of the saints and the plot of the Devil against her, especially as revealed by the witches now confessing; next an abstract of the rules of Perkins, Gaule, and Bernard for the detection of witches. Then follows "A Discourse on the Wonders of the Invisible World, uttered (in part) on Aug. 4, 1692." It is a sermon on Rev. xii. 12, depicting in apocalyptic phrase the Devil's wrath and its present manifestation. Next comes "An Hortatory and Necessary Address, to a Country now extraordinarily alarum'd by the Wrath of the Devil"—this, too, doubtless written for a sermon. "Having thus discoursed on the Wonders of the Invisible World," says then the author, "I shall now, with God's help, go on to relate some Remarkable and Memorable Instances of Wonders which that World has given to ourselves." Yet he still inserts "A Narrative of an Apparition which a Gentleman in Boston had of his Brother," before proceeding to those Salem trials, the kernel of his book, which are reprinted below.

Doubtless these were meant, as the title-page suggests, to form a part of the "Enchantments Encountered," but failed

---

[1] See pp. 194–195.

to arrive in time. Mather had long been begging them from Stephen Sewall (brother of Judge Sewall), the clerk of the court; but the clerk was then very busy. On September 20 Mather wrote: "That I may be the more capable to assist in lifting up a standard against the infernal enemy, I must renew my most importunate request." What he asks is "a narrative of the evidence given in at the trials of half a dozen, or if you please, a dozen, of the principal witches that have been condemned." He pleads not only Sewall's promise, but that "his Excellency, the Governor, laid his positive commands upon me to desire this favor of you"; "and the truth is," he adds, "there are some of his circumstances with reference to this affair, which I need not mention, that call for the expediting of your kindness." He wants also some of the clerk's "observations about the confessors, and the credibility of what they assert, or about things evidently preternatural in the witchcrafts"; but, "assure yourself," he concludes, "I shall not wittingly make what you write prejudicial to any worthy design which those two excellent persons, Mr. Hale and Mr. Noyes, may have in hand." But the clerk took counsel before he acted. His brother's *Diary* records, on Thursday, September 22, that "William Stoughton, Esqr., John Hathorne, Esqr., Mr. Cotton Mather, and Capt. John Higginson, with my brother St., were at our house, speaking about publishing some Trials of the Witches." These had been received and utilized by early October (see p. 247), and the book, thus far complete, could before October 11 be laid before the judges (see p. 251) and by the 12th could furnish material for the governor's letter (see p. 195).

Before the book was out of press there was time to add the narrative of the Swedish witches and the sermon on "the Devil discovered"; but these could not seriously have delayed the printing, for the book, complete and printed, must have gone to London by the same ship which in mid-October took

Sir William's letter. A copy of the book was doubtless sent, with this letter, to the home government; and it was perhaps precisely for this use that the volume had been hurried into existence and into print. What is certain is that such a copy had before December 24 reached the hands of John Dunton, the London publisher; for on that day he announced its speedy publication, and by December 29 it was already in print, though with "1693" on its title-page.[1] A "second edition," much abridged (though not by the omission of the Salem trials), he issued in February 1693, and reprinted it as a "third" in June.

The news-letter, with imprint of 1692, calling itself *A True Account of the Tryals . . . at Salem, in New England . . . in a Letter to a Friend in London* and signed at end "C. M." is only a bookseller's fraud, compiled from the *Wonders* by some hack (who has not even taken the trouble to imitate its style) and printed in 1693.

The *Wonders* was reprinted at Salem in 1861 (with Calef's *More Wonders*), by Mr. S. P. Fowler, in a volume called *Salem Witchcraft*; but, alas, from the abridged "third edition" and with serious further abridgment. In 1862 the first London edition was embodied in a volume of John Russell Smith's *Library of Old Authors* (*cf.* p. 149, note 1); and in 1866 the work was again reprinted, and with much more exactness,[2] as

---

[1] That this London edition was printed, not from a manuscript copy, but from the printed Boston edition, broken up for the compositors, is clear to any printer who compares the two. See, for details, a paragraph in the N. Y. *Nation* for November 5, 1908 (LXXXVII. 435), or the descriptive note of G. F. Black in the New York Library's *List of Works relating to Witchcraft in the United States* (*Bulletin*, 1908, XII. 666). All extant copies of the Boston edition seem to have the title-page date "1693" (an alleged exception proves to be a myth); and this probably means that till January, at least, the book was withheld from circulation. As to all the early editions, see Moore, *Notes on the Bibliography of Witchcraft in Massachusetts* (American Antiquarian Society, *Proceedings*, n. s., V.), and the New York Library's *List*, as above.

[2] The type being set from the first London edition, but the proofs read by the Boston one. (See Drake's preface, p. vii, and his postscript, p. 247.)

no. V. of the *Historical Series* of W. Elliot Woodward (Roxbury, Mass.), being again coupled with Calef's *More Wonders* (forming nos. VI., VII., of the same series) under a common title, *The Witchcraft Delusion in New England*, and a common editor, S. G. Drake, who contributes elaborate introductions and notes. An alleged reprint by J. Smith, London, 1834 (and again by H. Howell in 1840), as an addition to Baxter's, *Certainty of the World of Spirits* is not Mather's *Wonders* at all, but only the witchcraft pages of his *Magnalia*.

THE WONDERS OF THE INVISIBLE WORLD

The Wonders of the Invisible World. Observations As well His-
torical as Theological, upon the Nature, the Number, and
the Operations of the Devils. Accompany'd with
I. *Some Accounts of the Grievous Molestations, by Dæmons and*
Witchcrafts, which have lately annoy'd the Countrey; and the
Trials of some eminent Malefactors Executed upon occasion
thereof: with several Remarkable Curiosities therein occurring.
II. *Some Counsils, Directing a due Improvement of the terrible*
things, lately done, by the Unusual and Amazing Range of
Evil Spirits, in Our Neighbourhood: and the methods to pre-
vent the Wrongs which those Evil Angels may intend against
all sorts of people among us; especially in Accusations of the
Innocent.
III. *Some Conjectures upon the great Events, likely to befall*
the World in General, and New-England in Particular; as
also upon the Advances of the time, when we shall see Better
Dayes.
IV. *A short Narrative of a late Outrage committed by a knot of*
Witches in Swedeland, very much Resembling, and so far
Explaining, That under which our parts of America have
laboured!
V. *The Devil Discovered: In a Brief Discourse upon those*
Temptations, which are the more Ordinary Devices of the
Wicked One.
By Cotton Mather.
Boston, Printed, by Benjamin Harris for Sam. Phillips. 1693.[1]
Published by the Special Command of His Excellency, the Gover-
nour of the Province of the Massachusetts-Bay in New-En-
gland.[2]

[1] Title-page of original.

[2] Reverse of title-page. Governor Sir William Phips. We have just read,
indeed, his own assertion (p. 197, above) that he had "put a stop to the printing
of any discourses one way or other," and this may explain why, though this

The Author's Defence.

'TIS, as I remember, the Learned Scribonius,[1] who Reports, that One of his Acquaintance, devoutly making his Prayers on the behalf of a Person molested by Evil Spirits, received from those Evil Spirits an horrible Blow over the Face: And I may my self Expect not few or small Buffetings from Evil Spirits, for the Endeavours wherewith I am now going to Encounter them. I am far from Insensible, That at this Extraordinary Time of the Devils Coming down in Great Wrath upon us, there are too many Tongues and Hearts thereby Set on Fire of Hell; that the various Opinions about the Witchcrafts which of Later Time have Troubled us, are maintained by some with so much Cloudy Fury, as if they could never be sufficiently Stated, unless written in the Liquor wherewith Witches use to write their Covenants; and that he who becomes an Author at such a Time, had need be Fenced with Iron, and the Staff of a Spear. The unaccountable Frowardness, Asperity, Untreatableness, and Inconsistency of many persons, every Day gives a Visible Exposition of that passage, *An Evil Spirit from the Lord came upon Saul*; and Illustration of that Story, *There met him two Possessed with Devils, exceeding Fierce, so that no man might pass by that way.* To send abroad a Book, among such Readers, were a very unadvised Thing, if a man had not such Reasons to give, as I can bring, for such an Undertaking. Briefly, I hope it cannot be said, They are all so; No, I hope the Body of this People, are yet in such a Temper, as to be capable of Applying their Thoughts, to make a Right Use of the Stupendous and prodigious Things that are happening among us: and because I

book was complete in October, it was not published before January, as well as why, when it did appear, it thus bore the express sanction of the governor. As to the suggestion of Upham and Moore that not Phips but Stoughton may be here meant, see p. 194, note 6.

[1] Wilhelm Adolf Scribonius, a Hessian scholar, is best known in the literature of witchcraft as the chief advocate of the water ordeal (see p. 21, above) for the detection of witches. This story is told on ff. 82–83 of his *Physiologia Sagarum* (Marburg, 1588—the full title is *De Sagarum Natura et Potestate, deque his recte cognoscendis et puniendis Physiologia*), and in English by Baxter, *Worlds of Spirits*, p. 104.

was concern'd, when I saw that no Abler Hand Emitted any
Essayes to Engage the Minds of this People in such Holy,
Pious, Fruitful Improvements, as God would have to be made
of His Amazing Dispensations now upon us, Therefore it is,
that One of the Least among the Children of New-England,
has here done, what is done. None, but the Father, who sees
in Secret, knows the Heart-breaking Exercises, wherewith I
have Composed what is now going to be Exposed, Lest I should
in any One Thing miss of Doing my Designed Service for His
Glory, and for His People; But I am now somewhat comforta-
bly Assured of His favourable Acceptance; and, I will not
Fear; what can a Satan do unto me!

Having Performed Something of what God Required, in
labouring to suit His Words unto His Works, at this Day
among us, and therewithal handled a Theme that has been
sometimes counted not unworthy the Pen, even of a King, it
will easily be perceived, that some subordinate Ends have
been considered in these Endeavours.

I have indeed set my self to Countermine the whole Plot
of the Devil against New-England,[1] in every Branch of it, as
far as one of my Darkness can comprehend such a Work of
Darkness. I may add, that I have herein also aimed at the
Information and Satisfaction of Good men in another Countrey, a Thousand Leagues off, where I have, it may be, More,
or however, more Considerable Friends, than in My Own;[2]
And I do what I can to have that Countrey, now as well as
alwayes, in the best Terms with My Own. But while I am

[1] As to this "plot of the Devil," see Mather's own words (*Wonders*, pp. 16–19,
25, not here reprinted): "we have been advised . . . that a Malefactor, accused
of Witchcraft as well as Murder, and Executed in this place more than Forty
Years ago, did then give Notice of An Horrible Plot against the Country by
Witchcraft, and a Foundation of Witchcraft then laid, which if it were not
seasonably discovered would probably Blow up, and pull down all the Churches
in the Country." "We have now with Horror," he adds, "seen the Discovery of
such a Witchcraft!" and from the confessions at Salem he learns that "at prodigious Witch-Meetings the Wretches have proceeded so far as to Concert and
Consult the Methods of Rooting out the Christian Religion from this Country"
and setting up instead of it a "Diabolism." Not even this is all: "it may be
fear'd that, in the Horrible Tempest which is now upon ourselves, the design of
the Devil is to sink that Happy Settlement of Government wherewith Almighty
God has graciously enclined Their Majesties to favour us."

[2] It is of England, of course, that he speaks.

doing these things, I have been driven a little to do something likewise for My self; I mean, by taking off the false Reports and hard Censures about my Opinion in these matters, the Parters Portion, which my pursuit of Peace has procured me among the Keen. My hitherto Unvaried Thoughts are here Published; and, I believe, they will be owned by most of the Ministers of God in these Colonies; nor can amends be well made me, for the wrong done me, by other sorts of Representations.

In fine, For the Dogmatical part of my Discourse, I want no Defence; for the Historical part of it, I have a very Great One. The Lieutenant-Governour of New-England, having perused it, has done me the Honour of giving me a Shield,[1] under the Umbrage whereof I now dare to walk Abroad.

Reverend and Dear Sir,

You Very much Gratify'd me, as well as put a kind Respect upon me, when you put into my hands, Your Elaborate and most seasonable Discourse, entituled, *The Wonders of the Invisible World.* And having now Perused so fruitful and happy a Composure, upon such a Subject, at this Juncture of Time, and considering the Place that I Hold in the Court of Oyer and Terminer, still Labouring and Proceeding in the Trial of the persons Accused and Convicted for Witchcraft, I find that I am more nearly and highly concerned than as a meer Ordinary Reader, to Express my Obligation and Thankfulness to you for so great Pains; and cannot but hold my self many ways bound, even to the utmost of what is proper for me, in my present Publick Capacity, to declare my Singular Approbation thereof. Such is Your Design, most plainly expressed throughout the whole; such Your Zeal for God, Your Enmity to Satan and his Kingdom, Your Faithfulness and Compassion to this poor people; Such the Vigour, but yet great Temper of your Spirit; Such your Instruction and Counsel, your Care of Truth, Your Wisdom and Dexterity in allaying and moderating that among us, which needs it; Such your Clear Discerning of Divine Providences and Periods, now running on apace towards their Glorious Issues in the World; and finally, Such your Good News of The Shortness of the Devils Time, That all Good Men must needs Desire the making of this your Dis-

---

[1] As to Lieutenant-Governor Stoughton, head of the court which had tried the witch cases, see above, p. 183 and note 2, and pp. 196–201. His "shield" means the following letter.

course Publick to the World; and will greatly Rejoyce that the Spirit of the Lord has thus Enabled you to Lift up a Standard against the Infernal Enemy, that hath been Coming in like a Flood upon us.   I do therefore make it my particular and Earnest Request unto you, that as soon as may be, you will Commit the same unto the Press accordingly.   I am,

Your Assured Friend,

WILLIAM STOUGHTON.

I Live by Neighbours that force me to produce these Undeserved Lines.   But now, as when Mr. Wilson,[1] beholding a great Muster of Souldiers, had it by a Gentleman then present said unto him, "Sir, I'l tell you a great Thing: here is a mighty Body of People; and there is not Seven of them all but what Loves Mr. Wilson;" that Gracious Man presently and pleasantly Reply'd, "Sir, I'll tell you as good a thing as that; here is a mighty Body of People, and there is not so much as One among them all, but Mr. Wilson Loves him." Somewhat so: 'Tis possible that among this Body of People there may be few that Love the Writer of this Book; but give me leave to boast so far, there is not one among all this Body of People, whom this Mather would not Study to Serve, as well as to Love.   With such a Spirit of Love, is the Book now before us written: I appeal to all this World; and if this World will deny me the Right of acknowledging so much, I Appeal to the Other, that it is Not written with an Evil Spirit: for which cause I shall not wonder, if Evil Spirits be Exasperated by what is Written, as the Sadducees doubtless were with what was Discoursed in the Days of our Saviour.   I only Demand the Justice, that others Read it, with the same Spirit wherewith I writ it.[2]

.   .   .   .

But I shall no longer detain my Reader, from His expected entertainment, in a Brief Account of the Trials which have passed upon some of the Malefactors Lately Executed at Salem, for the Witchcrafts whereof they stood Convicted.

---

[1] Doubtless the Rev. John Wilson (d. 1667), the first minister of Boston.

[2] There now follow the miscellaneous matters described in the introduction, making up more than half of his volume.

For my own part, I was not Present at any of Them;[1] nor ever Had I any personal prejudice at the persons thus brought upon the Stage; much less at the Surviving Relations of those persons, with and for whom I would be as Hearty a mourner as any man Living in the World: The Lord Comfort them! But having Received a Command so to do,[2] I can do no other than shortly Relate the Chief Matters of fact, which occurr'd in the Trials of some that were Executed, in an Abridgment collected out of the Court-Papers, on this occasion put into my Hands.[3] You are to take the Truth, just as it was; and the Truth will hurt no good man. There might have been more of these, if my Book would not thereby have been swollen too big; and if some other worthy hands did not perhaps intend something further in these Collections;[4] for which cause I have only singled out Four or Five, which may serve to Illustrate the way of dealing, wherein Witchcrafts use to be concerned; and I Report matters not as an Advocate but as an Historian.

They were some of the Gracious Words inserted in the Advice, which many of the Neighbouring Ministers did this Summer humbly lay before our Honorable Judges, "We cannot but with all thankfulness acknowledge the success which the Merciful God has given unto the Sedulous and Assiduous endeavours of Our Honourable Rulers, to detect the abominable Witchcrafts which have been committed in the Country; Humbly Praying that the discovery of those mysterious and mischievous wickednesses, may be perfected." [5] If in the midst of the many Dissatisfactions among us, the publication of these Trials may promote such a pious Thankfulness unto God, for Justice being so far executed among us, I shall Re-

---

[1] He must at least have been present at some of the examinations (like those described by Lawson) preceding the trials; for in his *Diary* (I. 151), commending the judges, he adds, "and my Compassion, upon the Sight of their Difficulties, raised by my Journeyes to Salem, the chief Seat of these diabolical Vexations, caused mee yett more to do so." From attending the trials he had excused himself (see the letter mentioned on p. 194, note 5) on the score of ill health.

[2] From the governor; see above, p. 194, and p. 250.   [3] See introduction.

[4] Meaning, doubtless, Hale and Noyes. See p. 206, above.

[5] This is the second paragraph in the reply of the ministers of Boston, June 15, 1692, to the request of the governor and Council for advice. (See p. 194, above.) It was drawn up by Cotton Mather himself.

joyce that God is Glorified; and pray that no wrong steps of
ours may ever sully any of His Glorious Works.[1]

* * * * * * * *

I. The Tryal of G. B.[2] At a Court of Oyer and Terminer,
Held in Salem, 1692.

Glad should I have been, if I had never known the Name
of this man; or never had this occasion to mention so much
as the first Letters of his Name.[3]   But the Government re-
quiring some Account of his Trial to be Inserted in this Book,
it becomes me with all Obedience to submit unto the Order.
I. This G. B. was indicted for Witch-crafts, and in the
Prosecution of the Charge against him, he was Accused by
five or six of the Bewitched, as the Author of their Miseries;
he was Accused by eight of the Confessing Witches, as being
an Head Actor at some of their Hellish Randezvouzes, and one

[1] What next follows, very cleverly ensuring a friendly attitude toward the
Salem court, is an account of the English witch-trial of 1664 before Sir Matthew
Hale.   It is abridged from the well-known booklet (*A Tryal of Witches at the
Assizes held at Bury St. Edmonds*, etc.) published at London in 1682, which had
been a guide to the Salem judges (see p. 416, below).

[2] The Rev. George Burroughs, the most notable of the victims at Salem.
A graduate of Harvard in the class of 1670, he preached in Maine for some years,
and in 1680 became pastor at Salem Village, where he fell heir to a parish quarrel,
and, becoming involved in it, found it wise to remove in 1683—Deodat Lawson
succeeding him.   Burroughs returned to Maine, and was a pastor there at Wells,
when his accusation by the "afflicted" at Salem caused his arrest.   He was
brought back to Salem on May 4, committed on May 9, tried on August 5, executed on August 19.   As to his story see especially Upham, *Salem Witchcraft*,
Sibley, *Harvard Graduates* (II. 323–334), Moore, "Notes on the Bibliography of
Witchcraft in Massachusetts" (in American Antiquarian Society, *Proceedings*,
n. s., V.), pp. 270–273, but, first of all, the mentions of Calef, reprinted below (pp.
301, 360–365, 378–379).

[3] It is not improbable that Mather had already begun to find himself blamed
for his harsh words as to Burroughs.   On August 5, the day of his trial, he had
written to a friend: "Our Good God is working of Miracles.   Five Witches were
Lately Executed, impudently demanding of God a Miraculous Vindication of
their Innocency.   Immediately upon this, Our God Miraculously sent in Five
Andover-Witches, who made a most ample, surprising, amazing Confession, of
all their Villainies and declared the Five newly executed to have been of their
Company; discovering many more; but all agreeing in Burroughs being their
Ringleader, who, I suppose, this day receives his Trial at Salem, whither a Vast
Concourse of people is gone; My Father this morning among the Rest."

who had the promise of being a King in Satans Kingdom, now going to be Erected: he was Accused by nine persons for extraordinary Lifting, and such Feats of Strength, as could not be done without a Diabolical Assistance.   And for other such Things he was Accused, until about Thirty Testimonies were brought in against him; nor were these judg'd the half of what might have been considered for his Conviction: however they were enough to fix the Character of a Witch upon him according to the Rules of Reasoning, by the Judicious Gaule,[1] in that Case directed.

II.   The Court being sensible, that the Testimonies of the Parties Bewitched use to have a Room among the Suspicions or Presumptions, brought in against one Indicted for Witchcraft, there were now heard the Testimonies of several Persons, who were most notoriously Bewitched, and every day Tortured by Invisible Hands, and these now all charged the Spectres of G. B. to have a share in their Torments.   At the Examination of this G. B. the Bewitched People were grievously harassed with Preternatural Mischiefs, which could not possibly be Dissembled; and they still ascribed it unto the Endeavours of G. B. to kill them.   And now upon his Trial, one of the Bewitched Persons testify'd, That in her Agonies, a little Black hair'd man came to her, saying his Name was B. and bidding her set her hand unto a Book which he show'd unto her; and bragging that he was a Conjurer, above the ordinary Rank of Witches; That he often persecuted her with the offer of that Book, saying, She should be well, and need fear no body, if she would but Sign it; but he inflicted cruel Pains and Hurts upon her, because of her Denying so to do. The Testimonies of the other Sufferers concurred with these; and it was Remarkable, that whereas Biting was one of the ways which the Witches used for the vexing of the Sufferers, when they cry'd out of G. B. biting them, the print of the Teeth would be seen on the Flesh of the Complainers, and just

---

[1] John Gaule, rector of Great Stoughton, in Huntingdonshire, was the first to oppose openly the witch-finder Hopkins, and wrote a little book, *Select Cases of Conscience touching Witches and Witchcrafts* (London, 1646), to lay bare his outrages and suggest saner methods.   (See Notestein, *Witchcraft in England*, pp. 186–187, 236–237.)   His rules for the detection of witches are published (though not without serious garbling) earlier in Mather's volume.

such a sett of Teeth as G. B's would then appear upon them, which could be distinguished from those of some other mens. Others of them testify'd, That in their Torments, G. B. tempted them to go unto a Sacrament, unto which they perceived him with a sound of Trumpet Summoning of other Witches, who quickly after the Sound would come from all Quarters unto the Rendezvouz. One of them falling into a kind of Trance, afterwards affirmed, That G. B. had carried her into a very high Mountain, where he show'd her mighty and glorious Kingdoms, and said, He would give them all to her, if she would write in his Book; but she told him, They were none of his to give; and refused the motions, enduring of much misery for that Refusal.

It cost the Court a wonderful deal of Trouble, to hear the Testimonies of the Sufferers; for when they were going to give in their Depositions, they would for a long time be taken with fitts, that made them uncapable of saying any thing. The Chief Judge asked the prisoner, who he thought hindred these witnesses from giving their testimonies? and he answered, He supposed it was the Divel. That Honourable person then reply'd, How comes the Divel so loathe to have any Testimony born against you? Which cast him into very great confusion.

III. It has been a frequent thing for the Bewitched people to be entertained with Apparitions of Ghosts of murdered people, at the same time that the Spectres of the witches trouble them. These Ghosts do always affright the Beholders more than all the other spectral Representations; and when they exhibit themselves, they cry out, of being Murdered by the witchcrafts or other violences of the persons who are then in spectre present. It is further considerable, that once or twice, these Apparitions have been seen by others at the very same time that they have shewn them selves to the Bewitched; and seldom have there been these Apparitions but when something unusual and suspected had attended the Death of the party thus Appearing. Some that have bin accused by these Apparitions, accosting of the Bewitched People, who had never heard a word of any such persons ever being in the world, have upon a fair examination freely and fully confessed the murders of those very persons, altho' these also did not know how the Apparitions had complained of them. Accordingly several of the Bewitched had given in their Testimony, that they had been troubled with the Apparitions of two women, who said that they were G. B's two wives, and that he had been the Death of them; and that the Magistrates must be told of it, before whom if B. upon his trial deny'd it, they did not know but that they should appear again in the Court.   Now, G. B. had been infamous for the Barbarous usage of his two successive wives, all the Country over.   Moreover, It was testify'd, the spectre of G. B. threatning of the sufferers told them, he had killed (besides others) Mrs. Lawson and her Daughter Ann.[1]   And it was noted, That these were the vertuous wife and Daughter of one at whom this G. B. might have a prejudice for his being serviceable at Salem-village, from whence himself had in Ill Terms removed some years before: and that when they dy'd, which was long since, there were some odd circumstances about them, which made some of the Attendents there suspect something of witchcraft, tho' none Imagined from what Quarter it should come.

Well, G. B. being now upon his Triall, one of the Bewitched persons was cast into Horror at the Ghosts of B's two deceased wives then appearing before him, and crying for Vengeance against him.   Hereupon several of the Bewitched persons were successively called in, who all not knowing what the former had seen and said, concurred in their Horror of the Apparition, which they affirmed that he had before him.   But he, tho' much appalled, utterly deny'd that he discerned any thing of it; nor was it any part of his Conviction.

IV.   Judicious Writers have assigned it a great place in the Conviction of witches, when persons are Impeached by other Notorious witches, to be as Ill as themselves; especially, if the persons have been much noted for neglecting the Worship of God.   Now, as there might have been Testimonies Enough of G. B's Antipathy to Prayer and the other Ordinances of God, tho' by his profession singularly obliged thereunto; so, there now came in against the prisoner the Testimonies of several persons, who confessed their own having been Horrible Witches, and ever since their confessions had been themselves terribly Tortured by the Devils and other

[1] The wife and the daughter of Deodat Lawson; see p. 148.

Witches, even like the other Sufferers; and therein undergone
the pains of many Deaths for their Confessions.

These now Testify'd, that G. B. had been at Witch-meetings
with them; and that he was the Person who had Seduc'd
and Compell'd them into the snares of Witchcraft: That he
promised them Fine Cloaths, for doing it; that he brought
Poppets to them, and thorns to stick into those Poppets, for
the afflicting of other People; And that he exhorted them,
with the rest of the Crue, to bewitch all Salem-Village, but
be sure to do it Gradually, if they would prevail in what
they did.

When the Lancashire Witches[1] were condemn'd, I don't
Remember that there was any considerable further Evidence,
than that of the Bewitched, and then that of some that confessed. We see so much already against G. B. But this
being indeed not Enough, there were other things to render
what had already been produced credible.

V. A famous Divine[2] recites this among the Convictions
of a Witch; The Testimony of the Party Bewitched, whether
Pining or Dying; together with the Joint Oathes of Sufficient
Persons that have seen certain Prodigious Pranks or Feats
wrought by the party Accused. Now God had been pleased
so to leave this G. B. that he had ensnared himself by several
Instances, which he had formerly given of a Preternatural
strength, and which were now produced against him. He was
a very Puny man;[3] yet he had often done things beyond the
strength of a Giant. A Gun of about seven foot barrel, and
so heavy that strong men could not steadily hold it out with
both hands; there were several Testimonies, given in by Persons of Credit and Honour, that he made nothing of taking up
such a Gun behind the Lock, with but one hand, and holding
it out like a Pistol, at Arms-end. G. B. in his Vindication was
so foolish as to say, That an Indian was there, and held it out
at the same time: Whereas, none of the Spectators ever saw

---

[1] *I. e.*, those tried and executed in 1612, and famous through the *Discoverie*
of Potts (London, 1613), which Mather seems here to use, and the play of Shad-
well.

[2] John Gaule again: this is the fifth of his "more certain" signs. (*Select
Cases*, p. 82.)

[3] But see, on the contrary, page 301.

any such Indian; but they suppos'd the Black man (as the Witches call the Devil; and they generally say he resembles an Indian) might give him that Assistence. There was Evidence likewise brought in, that he made nothing of Taking up whole Barrels fill'd with Malasses or Cider, in very Disadvantagious Postures, and Carrying of them through the Difficultest Places out of a Canoo to the Shore.

Yea, there were Two Testimonies that G. B. with only putting the Fore-Finger of his Right hand into the Muzzel of an heavy Gun, a Fowling-piece of about six or seven foot Barrel, did Lift up the Gun, and hold it out at Arms end; a Gun which the Deponents though strong men could not with both hands Lift up, and hold out at the Butt end, as is usual. Indeed, one of these Witnesses was over perswaded by some persons to be out of the way upon G. B's Trial; but he came afterwards with sorrow for his withdraw, and gave in his Testimony: Nor were either of these Witnesses made use of as evidences in the Trial.

VI.   There came in several Testimonies relating to the Domestick Affayrs of G. B. which had a very hard Aspect upon him; and not only prov'd him a very ill man; but also confirmed the Belief of the Character, which had been already fastned on him.

'Twas testifyed, That keeping his two Successive Wives in a strange kind of Slavery, he would when he came home from abroad pretend to tell the Talk which any had with them; That he has brought them to the point of Death, by his Harsh Dealings with his Wives, and then made the People about him to promise that in Case Death should happen, they would say nothing of it; That he used all means to make his Wives Write, Sign, Seal, and Swear a Covenant, never to Reveal any of his Secrets; That his Wives had privately complained unto the Neighbours about frightful Apparitions of Evil Spirits, with which their House was sometimes infested; and that many such things have been Whispered among the Neighbourhood. There were also some other Testimonies, relating to the Death of People, whereby the Consciences of an Impartial Jury were convinced that G. B. had Bewitched the persons mentioned in the Complaints. But I am forced to omit several passages, in this, as well as in all the succeeding

Trials, because the Scribes who took Notice of them, have not Supplyed me.

VII.   One Mr. Ruck, Brother in Law to this G. B., Testify'd, that G. B. and he himself, and his Sister, who was G. B's Wife, going out for Two or three Miles to gather Straw-Berries, Ruck with his Sister the Wife of G. B. Rode home very Softly, with G. B. on Foot in their Company.   G. B. stept aside a little into the Bushes; Whereupon they Halted and Halloo'd for him.   He not answering, they went away homewards, with a Quickened pace, without any expectation of seeing him in a considerable while; and yet when they were got near home, to their Astonishment they found him on foot with them, having a Basket of Straw-Berries.   G. B. immediately then fell to chiding his Wife, on the account of what she had been speaking to her Brother, of him, on the Road: which when they wondred at, he said, He knew their thoughts.   Ruck being startled at that, made some Reply, intimating that the Devil himself did not know so far; but G. B. answered, My God makes known your Thoughts unto me.   The prisoner now at the Barr had nothing to answer, unto what was thus Witnessed against him, that was worth considering.   Only he said, Ruck and his Wife left a Man with him, when they left him.   Which Ruck now affirm'd to be false; and when the Court asked G. B. What the Man's Name was? his countenance was much altered; nor could he say, who 'twas.   But the Court began to think, that he then step'd aside, only that by the assistance of the Black Man, he might put on his Invisibility, and in that Fascinating Mist, gratifie his own Jealous humour, to hear what they said of him.   Which trick of rendring themselves Invisible, our Witches do in their confessions pretend that they sometimes are Masters of; and it is the more credible, because there is Demonstration that they often render many other things utterly Invisible.

VIII.   Faltring, Faulty, unconstant, and contrary Answers upon Judicial and deliberate examination, are counted some unlucky symptoms of guilt, in all crimes, Especially in Witchcrafts.[1]   Now there never was a prisoner more Eminent for them, than G. B. both at his Examination and on his Trial.

---

[1] He is quoting John Gaule—the first of his "more certain" signs (*Select Cases*, pp. 80–81).

His Tergiversations, Contradictions, and Falsehoods, were very sensible: he had little to say, but that he had heard some things that he could not prove, Reflecting upon the Reputation of some of the witnesses.   Only he gave in a paper to the Jury; wherein, altho' he had many times before granted, not only that there are Witches, but also that the present sufferings of the Countrey are the Effect of horrible Witchcrafts, yet he now goes to evince it, That there neither are, nor ever were Witches, that having made a compact with the Divel, Can send a Divel to Torment other people at a distance.   This paper was Transcribed out of Ady;[1] which the Court presently[2] knew, as soon as they heard it.   But he said, he had taken none of it out of any Book; for which, his evasion afterwards was, that a Gentleman gave him the discourse in a manuscript, from whence he Transcribed it.

IX.   The Jury brought him in guilty: But when he came to Dy, he utterly deny'd the Fact, whereof he had been thus convicted.[3]

[1] Thomas Ady, *A Candle in the Dark* (London, 1656)—reprinted in 1661 as *A Perfect Discovery of Witches*.   In neither edition are precisely these words to be found; but their substance occurs often.   How bold and thoroughgoing a skeptic is Ady, and why Mather counts it answer enough that the passage was taken from his book, may be guessed from his opening sentence in which he gives "The Reason of the Book": "The Grand Errour of these latter Ages is ascribing power to Witches, and by foolish imagination of mens brains, without grounds in the Scriptures, wrongfull killing of the innocent under the name of Witches." "When one Mr. Burroughs, a Clergyman, who some few years since was hang'd in New-England as a Wizzard, stood upon his Tryal," wrote Dr. Hutchinson in 1718 in the book that was to end the controversy (*Historical Essay concerning Witchcraft*, p. xv), "he pull'd out of his Pocket a Leaf that he had got of Mr. Ady's Book, to prove that the Scripture Witchcrafts were not like ours: And as that Defence was not able to save him, I humbly offer my Book as an Argument on the Behalf of all such miserable People."

[2] "Presently" then meant "at once."

[3] For details as to his execution see above, p. 177, and below, pp. 360-361. Before accepting in perfect faith Mather's account of his trial, one should weigh not only the comments of Calef (see pp. 378-380, below) and the severer criticisms of Upham (*Salem Witchcraft and Cotton Mather*) but the extant records (*Records of Salem Witchcraft*, II. 109-128; Mass. Hist. Soc., *Proceedings*, 1860-1862, pp. 31-37; indictment, Calef, p. 113).

II. *The Tryal of Bridget Bishop,*[1] *alias Oliver, At the Court of Oyer and Terminer Held at Salem, June 2, 1692.*

I. She was Indicted for Bewitching of several persons in the Neighbourhood, the Indictment being drawn up, according to the Form in such Cases usual. And pleading, Not Guilty, there were brought in several persons, who had long undergone many kinds of Miseries, which were preternaturally Inflicted, and generally ascribed unto an horrible Witchcraft. There was little Occasion to prove the Witchcraft, it being Evident and Notorious to all Beholders. Now to fix the Witchcraft on the Prisoner at the Bar, the first thing used, was the Testimony of the Bewitched; whereof several Testify'd, That the Shape of the Prisoner did oftentimes very grievously pinch them, choak them, Bite them, and Afflict them; urging them to write their Names in a Book, which the said Spectre called, Ours. One of them did further Testify, that it was the Shape of this Prisoner, with another, which one Day took her from her Wheel, and carrying her to the River side, threatned there to Drown her, if she did not Sign to the Book mentioned: which yet she refused. Others of them did also Testify, that the said Shape did in her Threats brag to them that she had been the Death of sundry persons, then by her Named; that she had Ridden a man then likewise Named. Another Testify'd the Apparition of Ghosts unto the Spectre of Bishop, crying out, You Murdered us! About the Truth whereof, there was in the matter of Fact but too much Suspicion.

II. It was Testify'd, That at the Examination of the Prisoner before the Magistrates, the Bewitched were extreamly Tortured. If she did but cast her Eyes on them, they were presently struck down; and this in such a manner as there could be no Collusion in the Business. But upon the Touch of her Hand upon them, when they lay in their Swoons, they would immediately Revive; and not upon the Touch of any ones else. Moreover, upon some Special Actions of her Body,

---

[1] As to Bridget Bishop see also pp. 249, 356, below. She was of Salem Village, where she kept a sort of wayside tavern, but had long lived in the town, and still held property there. She was the first witch to be tried (June 2) and executed (June 10)—perhaps because she had so long been under suspicion. The records of her case are printed in *Records of Salem Witchcraft,* I. 135-172.

as the shaking of her Head, or the Turning of her Eyes, they presently and painfully fell into the like postures. And many of the like Accidents now fell out, while she was at the Bar. One at the same time testifying, That she said, She could not be Troubled to see the Afflicted thus Tormented.

III.   There was Testimony likewise brought in, that a man striking once at the place, where a Bewitched person said, the Shape of this Bishop stood, the Bewitched cried out, that he had Tore her Coat, in the place then particularly specify'd; and the Womans Coat was found to be Torn in that very place.

IV.   One Deliverance Hobbs, who had Confessed her being a Witch, was now Tormented by the Spectres, for her Confession. And she now Testify'd, That this Bishop tempted her to Sign the Book again, and to Deny what she had Confess'd. She affirmed, that it was the Shape of this Prisoner, which whipped her with Iron Rods, to compel her thereunto. And she affirmed, that this Bishop was at a General Meeting of the Witches, in a Field at Salem-Village, and there partook of a Diabolical Sacrament in Bread and Wine then Administred!

V.   To render it further Unquestionable, that the prisoner at the Bar was the Person truly charged in *this* Witchcraft, there were produced many Evidences of *other* Witchcrafts, by her perpetrated. For Instance, John Cook testify'd, that about five or six years ago, One morning, about Sun-Rise, he was in his Chamber assaulted by the Shape of this prisoner: which Look'd on him, grin'd at him, and very much hurt him with a Blow on the side of the Head: and that on the same day, about Noon, the same Shape walked in the Room where he was, and an Apple strangely flew out of his Hand, into the Lap of his Mother, six or eight foot from him.

VI.   Samuel Gray testify'd, That about fourteen years ago, he wak'd on a Night, and saw the Room where he lay full of Light; and that he then saw plainly a Woman between the Cradle and the Bed-side, which look'd upon him. He Rose, and it vanished; tho' he found the Doors all fast. Looking out at the Entry-Door, he saw the same Woman, in the same Garb again; and said, In Gods Name, what do you come for? He went to Bed, and had the same Woman again assaulting him. The Child in the Cradle gave a great schreech, and the Woman Disappeared. It was long before the Child could be quieted; and tho' it were a very likely thriving Child, yet from this time it pined away, and after divers months dy'd in a sad Condition. He knew not Bishop, nor her Name; but when he saw her after this, he knew by her Countenance, and Apparrel, and all Circumstances, that it was the Apparition of this Bishop which had thus troubled him.

VII. John Bly and his Wife testify'd, that he bought a sow of Edward Bishop, the Husband of the prisoner; and was to pay the price agreed, unto another person. This Prisoner being Angry that she was thus hindred from fingring the money, Quarrell'd with Bly. Soon after which, the Sow was taken with strange Fits, Jumping, Leaping, and knocking her head against the Fence; she seem'd Blind and Deaf, and would neither eat nor be suck'd. Whereupon a neighbour said, she believed the Creature was Over-Looked; and sundry other circumstances concurred, which made the Deponents Belive that Bishop had Bewitched it.

VIII. Richard Coman testify'd, that eight years ago, as he lay Awake in his Bed, with a Light Burning in the Room, he was annoy'd with the Apparition of this Bishop, and of two more that were strangers to him, who came and oppressed him so, that he could neither stir himself, nor wake any one else, and that he was the night after molested again in the like manner; the said Bishop taking him by the Throat, and pulling him almost out of the Bed. His kinsman offered for this cause to lodge with him; and that Night, as they were Awake, Discoursing together, this Coman was once more visited by the Guests which had formerly been so troublesome; his kinsman being at the same time strook speechless and unable to move Hand or Foot. He had laid his sword by him, which these unhappy spectres did strive much to wrest from him; only he held too fast for them. He then grew able to call the People of his house; but altho' they heard him, yet they had not power to speak or stir; until at last, one of the people crying out, what's the matter? the spectres all vanished.

IX. Samuel Shattock testify'd, That in the Year 1680, this Bridget Bishop often came to his house upon such frivolous and foolish errands, that they suspected she came indeed with a purpose of mischief. Presently whereupon his eldest child, which was of as promising Health and Sense as any child of its Age, began to droop exceedingly; and the oftener that Bishop came to the House, the worse grew the Child. As the Child would be standing at the Door, he would be thrown and bruised against the Stones, by an Invisible Hand, and in like sort knock his Face against the sides of the House, and bruise it after a miserable manner. Afterwards this Bishop would bring him things to Dy, whereof he could not Imagine any use; and when she paid him a piece of Money, the Purse and Money were unaccountably conveyed out of a Lock'd box, and never seen more. The Child was immediately hereupon taken with terrible fits, whereof his Friends thought he would have dyed: indeed he did almost nothing but cry and Sleep for several Months together; and at length his understanding was utterly taken away. Among other Symptoms of an Inchantment upon him, one was, that there was a Board in the Garden, whereon he would walk; and all the invitations in the world could never fetch him off. About Seventeen or Eighteen years after, there came a Stranger to Shattocks House, who seeing the Child, said, "This poor Child is Bewitched; and you have a Neighbour living not far off, who is a Witch." He added, "Your Neighbour has had a falling out with your Wife; and she said in her Heart, your Wife is a proud Woman, and she would bring down her Pride in this Child." He then Remembred, that Bishop had parted from his Wife in muttering and menacing Terms, a little before the Child was taken Ill. The abovesaid Stranger would needs carry the Bewitched Boy with him to Bishops House, on pretence of buying a pot of Cyder. The Woman Entertained him in furious manner; and flew also upon the Boy, scratching his Face till the Blood came; and saying, "Thou Rogue, what, dost thou bring this Fellow here to plague me?" Now it seems the Man had said, before he went, that he would fetch Blood of *her*. Ever after the Boy was follow'd with grievous Fits, which the Doctors themselves generally ascribed unto Witchcraft; and wherein he would be thrown still into the Fire or the Water, if he were not constantly look'd after; and it was verily believed that Bishop was the cause of it.

X. John Louder testify'd, that upon some little controversy with Bishop about her fowles, going well to Bed, he did awake in the Night by moonlight, and did see clearly the likeness of this woman grievously oppressing him; in which miserable condition she held him, unable to help him self, till near Day. He told Bishop of this; but she deny'd it, and threatned him very much. Quickly after this, being at home on a Lords day, with the doors shutt about him, he saw a Black Pig approach him; at which he going to kick, it vanished away. Immediately after, sitting down, he saw a Black thing Jump in at the Window, and come and stand before him. The Body was like that of a Monkey, the Feet like a Cocks, but the Face much like a mans. He being so extreemly affrighted, that he could not speak, this Monster spoke to him, and said, "I am a Messenger sent unto you, for I understand that you are in some Trouble of Mind, and if you will be ruled by me, you shall want for nothing in this world." Whereupon he endeavoured to clap his hands upon it; but he could feel no substance, and it jumped out of the window again; but immediately came in by the Porch, though the Doors were shut, and said, "You had better take my Counsel!" He then struck at it with a stick, but struck only the Groundsel, and broke the Stick. The Arm with which he struck was presently Disenabled, and it vanished away. He presently went out at the Back-Door, and spyed this Bishop, in her Orchard, going toward her House; but he had not power to set one foot forward unto her. Whereupon returning into the House, he was immediately accosted by the Monster he had seen before; which Goblin was now going to Fly at him; whereat he cry'd out, "The whole Armour of God be between me and you!" So it sprang back, and flew over the Apple Tree, shaking many Apples off the Tree, in its flying over. At its Leap, it flung Dirt with its Feet against the Stomach of the Man; whereon he was then struck Dumb, and so continued for three Days together. Upon the producing of this Testimony, Bishop deny'd that she knew this Deponent: yet their two Orchards joined, and they had often had their Little Quarrels for some years together.

XI. William Stacy Testifyed, That receiving Money of this Bishop, for work done by him, he was gone but a matter of Three Rods from her, and looking for his money, found it unaccountably gone from him. Some time after, Bishop asked him, whether his Father would grind her grist for her? He demanded why? she Reply'd, "Because Folks count me a Witch." He answered, "No Question, but he will grind it for you." Being then gone about six Rods from her, with a small Load in his Cart, suddenly the Off-wheel slump't and sunk down into an Hole upon plain ground, so that the Deponent was forced to get help for the Recovering of the wheel. But stepping Back to look for the Hole which might give him this disaster, there was none at all to be found. Some time after, he was waked in the Night; but it seem'd as Light as Day, and he perfectly saw the shape of this Bishop in the Room, Troubling of him; but upon her going out, all was Dark again. He charg'd Bishop afterwards with it, and she deny'd it not; but was very angry. Quickly after, this Deponent having been threatned by Bishop, as he was in a dark Night going to the Barn, he was very suddenly taken or lifted from the ground, and thrown against a stone wall; After that, he was again hoisted up and thrown down a Bank, at the end of his House. After this again, passing by this Bishop, his Horse with a small load, striving to Draw, all his Gears flew to pieces, and the Cart fell down; and this deponent going then to lift a Bag of corn, of about two Bushels, could not budge it with all his might.

Many other pranks of this Bishops this Deponent was Ready to testify. He also testify'd, that he verily Believed, the said Bishop was the Instrument of his Daughter Priscilla's Death; of which suspicion, pregnant Reasons were assigned.

XII.   To Crown all, John Bly and William Bly Testify'd, That being Employ'd by Bridget Bishop, to help take down the Cellar-wall of the old House, wherein she formerly Lived, they did in Holes of the said old Wall find several Poppets,[1] made up of Rags and Hogs Brussels, with Headless Pins in them, the Points being outward. Whereof she could give no Account unto the Court, that was Reasonable or Tolerable.

XIII.   One thing that made against the Prisoner was, her being evidently convicted of Gross Lying in the Court, several Times, while she was making her Plea. But besides this, a

---

[1] Supposed, of course, by her accusers to be such "images" as witches were alleged to make of their victims, for the sake of torturing them by proxy. (See above, p. 163, note 1, p. 219, and below, p. 440, note 1.)

Jury of Women found a preternatural Teat upon her Body;[1] but upon a second search, within Three or four hours, there was no such thing to be seen. There was also an account of other people whom this woman had afflicted. And there might have been many more, if they had been enquired for. But there was no need of them.

XIV. There was one very strange thing more, with which the Court was newly Entertained. As this Woman was, under a Guard, passing by the Great and Spacious Meeting-House of Salem, she gave a Look towards the House. And immediately a Dæmon Invisibly Entring the Meeting-house, Tore down a part of it; so that tho' there were no person to be seen there, yet the people at the Noise running in, found a Board, which was strongly fastned with several Nails, transported unto another quarter of the House.

III.	*The Tryal of Susanna Martin,*[2] *At the Court of Oyer and Terminer, Held by Adjournment at Salem, June* 29, 1692.

I. Susanna Martin, pleading Not Guilty to the Indictment of Witchcraft brought in against her, there were produced the evidences of many persons very sensibly and grievously Bewitched; who all complaned of the prisoner at the Bar, as the person whom they Believed the cause of their Miseries. And now, as well as in the other Trials, there was an extraordinary endeavour by Witchcrafts, with Cruel and Frequent Fits, to hinder the poor sufferers from giving in their complaints; which the Court was forced with much patience to obtain, by much waiting and watching for it.

II. There was now also an Account given, of what passed at her first examination before the Magistrates. The cast of her eye then striking the Afflicted People to the ground, whether they saw that Cast or no; there were these among other passages between the Magistrates and the Examinate.

Magistrate.	Pray, what ails these People?
Martin.	I don't know.

---

[1] See below, p. 436, and note 1.

[2] Of Amesbury. She too had been long accused. For the trial records see *Records of Salem Witchcraft*, I. 193–233. She was executed on July 19.

Magistrate.   But what do you think ails them?

Martin.   I don't desire to spend my Judgment upon it.

Magistrate.   Don't you think they are Bewitch'd?

Martin.   No, I do not think they are.

Magistrate.   Tell us your thoughts about them then.

Martin.   No, my thoughts are my own when they are in, but when they are out, they are anothers.   Their Master——

Magistrate.   Their Master? who do you think is their Master?

Martin.   If they be dealing in the Black Art, you may know as well as I.

Magistrate.   Well, what have you done towards this?

Martin.   Nothing at all.

Magistrate.   Why, tis you or your Appearance.

Martin.   I cannot help it.

Magistrate.   Is it not Your Master? How comes your Appearance to hurt these?

Martin.   How do I know?   He that appeared in the shape of Samuel, a Glorify'd Saint, may Appear in any ones shape.

It was then also noted in her, as in others like her, that if the Afflicted went to approach her, they were flung down to the Ground.   And, when she was asked the Reason of it, she said, "I cannot tell; it may be, the Devil bears me more Malice than another."

III.   The Court accounted themselves Alarum'd by these things, to Enquire further into the Conversation of the Prisoner; and see what there might occur, to render these Accusations further credible.   Whereupon, John Allen, of Salisbury, testify'd, That he refusing, because of the weakness of his Oxen, to Cart some Staves, at the request of this Martin, she was displeased at it; and said, "It had been as good that he had; for his Oxen should never do him much more Service."   Whereupon this Deponent said, "Dost thou threaten me, thou old Witch?   I'l throw thee into the Brook": Which to avoid, she flew over the Bridge, and escaped.   But, as he was going home, one of his Oxen Tired, so that he was forced to Unyoke him, that he might get him home.   He then put his Oxen, with many more, upon Salisbury Beach, where Cattle did use to get Flesh.   In a few days, all the Oxen upon the Beach were found by their Tracks, to have run unto the mouth of

Merrimack-River, and not returned; but the next day they were found come ashore upon Plum-Island. They that sought them used all imaginable gentleness, but they would still run away with a violence that seemed wholly Diabolical, till they came near the mouth of Merrimack-River; when they ran right into the Sea, swimming as far as they could be seen. One of them then swam back again, with a swiftness amazing to the Beholders, who stood ready to receive him, and help up his Tired Carcass: But the Beast ran furiously up into the Island, and from thence, through the Marishes, up into New-bury Town, and so up into the Woods; and there after a while found near Amesbury. So that, of Fourteen good Oxen, there was only this saved: the rest were all cast up, some in one place, and some in another, Drowned.

IV. John Atkinson Testify'd, That he Exchanged a Cow with a Son of Susanna Martins, whereat she muttered, and was unwilling he should have it. Going to Receive this Cow, tho' he Hamstring'd her, and Halter'd her, she of a Tame Creature grew so mad, that they could scarce get her along. She broke all the Ropes that were fastned unto her, and though she were Ty'd fast unto a Tree, yet she made her Escape, and gave them such further Trouble, as they could ascribe to no cause but Witchcraft.

V. Bernard Peache testify'd, That being in Bed on a Lords-day Night, he heard a scrabbling at the Window, whereat he then saw Susanna Martin come in, and jump down upon the Floor. She took hold of this Deponents Feet, and drawing his Body up into an Heap, she lay upon him near Two Hours; in all which time he could neither speak nor stirr. At length, when he could begin to move, he laid hold on her Hand, and pulling it up to his mouth, he bit three of her Fingers, as he judged, unto the Bone. Whereupon she went from the Chamber, down the Stairs, out at the Door. This Deponent thereupon called unto the people of the House, to advise them of what passed; and he himself did follow her. The people saw her not; but there being a Bucket at the Left-hand of the Door, there was a drop of Blood found on it; and several more drops of Blood upon the Snow newly fallen abroad. There was likewise the print of her two Feet just without the Threshold; but no more sign of any Footing further off.

At another time this Deponent was desired by the Prisoner, to come unto an Husking of Corn, at her House; and she said, If he did not come, it were better that he did! He went not; but the Night following, Susanna Martin, as he judged, and another came towards him. One of them said, "Here he is!" but he having a Quarter-staff, made a Blow at them. The Roof of the Barn broke his Blow; but following them to the Window, he made another Blow at them, and struck them down; yet they got up, and got out, and he saw no more of them.

About this time, there was a Rumour about the Town, that Martin had a Broken Head; but the Deponent could say nothing to that.

The said Peache also testify'd the Bewitching of Cattle to Death, upon Martin's Discontents.

VI. Robert Downer testifyed, That this Prisoner being some years ago prosecuted at Court for a Witch,[1] he then said unto her, He believed she was a Witch. Whereat she being dissatisfied, said, That some Shee-Devil would Shortly fetch him away! Which words were heard by others, as well as himself. The Night following, as he lay in his Bed, there came in at the Window the likeness of a Cat, which Flew upon him, took fast hold of his Throat, lay on him a considerable while, and almost killed him. At length he remembred what Susanna Martin had threatned the Day before; and with much striving he cryed out, "Avoid, thou Shee-Devil! In the Name of God the Father, the Son, and the Holy Ghost, Avoid!" Whereupon it left him, leap'd on the Floor, and Flew out at the Window.

And there also came in several Testimonies, that before ever Downer spoke a word of this Accident, Susanna Martin and her Family had related, How this Downer had been Handled!

VII. John Kembal testifyed, that Susanna Martin, upon a Causeless Disgust, had threatned him, about a certain Cow of his, That she should never do him any more Good: and it

---

[1] In 1669. She was then bound over to the Superior Court, but was discharged without trial. (Hutchinson, *History of Massachusetts*, II., ch. I., as published from an earlier draft, with notes by W. F. Poole, in *N. E. Hist. and Gen. Register*, XXIV.)

came to pass accordingly. For soon after the Cow was found stark Dead on the dry Ground, without any Distemper to be discerned upon her. Upon which he was followed with a strange Death upon more of his Cattle, whereof he lost in One Spring to the value of Thirty Pounds. But the said John Kembal had a further Testimony to give in against the Prisoner which was truly admirable.

Being desirous to furnish himself with a Dog, he applied himself to buy one of this Martin, who had a Bitch with Whelps in her House. But she not letting him have his Choice, he said, he would supply himself then at one Blezdels. Having mark'd a puppy which he lik'd at Blezdels, he met George Martin, the Husband of the prisoner, going by, who asked him, Whether he would not have one of his Wives Puppies? and he answered, No. The same Day, one Edmund Eliot, being at Martins House, heard George Martin relate, where this Kembal had been, and what he had said. Whereupon Susanna Martin replyed, "If I live, I'll give him Puppies enough!" Within a few Dayes after, this Kembal coming out of the Woods, there arose a little Black Cloud in the N.W. and Kembal immediately felt a Force upon him, which made him not able to avoid running upon the stumps of Trees, that were before him, albeit he had a broad, plain Cart way, before him; but tho' he had his Ax also on his Shoulder to endanger him in his Falls, he could not forbear going out of his way to tumble over them. When he came below the Meeting-House, there appeared unto him a little thing like a Puppy, of a Darkish Colour; and it shot backwards and forwards between his Legs. He had the Courage to use all possible Endeavours of Cutting it with his Ax; but he could not Hit it; the Puppy gave a jump from him, and went, as to him it seem'd, into the Ground. Going a little further, there appeared unto him a Black Puppy, somewhat bigger than the first, but as Black as a Cole. Its motions were quicker than those of his Ax; it Flew at his Belly, and away; then at his Throat; so, over his Shoulder one way, and then over his Shoulder another way. His heart now began to fail him, and he thought the Dog would have Tore his Throat out. But he recovered himself, and called upon God in his Distress; and Naming the Name of Jesus Christ, it Vanished away at once. The Deponent Spoke

not one Word of these Accidents, for fear of affrighting his
wife. But the next Morning, Edmond Eliot going into Martins House, this woman asked him where Kembal was? He
Replyed, At home, a bed, for ought he knew. She returned,
"They say, he was frighted last Night." Eliot asked, "With
what?" She answered, "With Puppies." Eliot asked, Where
she heard of it, for he had heard nothing of it? She rejoined,
"About the Town." Altho' Kembal had mentioned the
Matter to no Creature Living.

VIII. William Brown testify'd, that Heaven having
blessed him with a most Pious and prudent wife, this wife of
his one day mett with Susanna Martin; but when she ap-
proch'd just unto her, Martin vanished out of sight, and left
her extremely affrighted. After which time, the said Martin
often appear'd unto her, giving her no little trouble; and
when she did come, she was visited with Birds that sorely
peck't and Prick'd her; and sometimes a Bunch, like a pullets
egg, would Rise in her throat, ready to Choak her, till she cry'd
out, "Witch, you shan't choak me!" While this good Woman
was in this Extremity, the Church appointed a Day of Prayer,
on her behalf; whereupon her Trouble ceas'd; she saw not
Martin as formerly; and the Church, instead of their Fast,
gave Thanks for her Deliverance. But a considerable while
after, she being Summoned to give in some Evidence at the
Court, against this Martin, quickly thereupon this Martin
came behind her, while she was milking her Cow, and said
unto her, "For thy defaming me at Court, I'l make thee the
miserablest Creature in the World." Soon after which, she
fell into a strange kind of Distemper, and became horribly
Frantick, and uncapable of any Reasonable Action; the
Physicians declaring, that her Distemper was preternatural,
and that some Devil had certainly Bewitched her; and in that
Condition she now remained.

IX. Sarah Atkinson testify'd, That Susanna Martin came
from Amesbury to their House at Newbury, in an extraordinary
Season, when it was not fit for any one to Travel. She came
(as she said unto Atkinson) all that long way on Foot. She
brag'd and show'd how dry she was; nor could it be perceived
that so much as the Soles of her Shoes were wet. Atkinson
was amazed at it; and professed, that she should her self have

been wet up to the knees, if she had then came so far; but Martin reply'd, She scorn'd to be Drabbled! It was noted, that this Testimony upon her Trial cast her in a very singular Confusion.

X. John Pressy testify'd, That being one Evening very unaccountably Bewildred, near a field of Martins, and several times, as one under an Enchantment, returning to the place he had left, at length he saw a marvellous Light, about the Bigness of an Half-Bushel, near two Rod out of the way. He went, and struck at it with a Stick, and laid it on with all his might. He gave it near forty blows; and felt it a palpable substance. But going from it, his Heels were struck up, and he was laid with his Back on the Ground, Sliding, as he thought, into a Pit; from whence he recover'd, by taking hold on the Bush; altho' afterwards he could find no such Pit in the place. Having, after his Recovery, gone five or six Rod, he saw Susanna Martin standing on his Left-hand, as the Light had done before; but they changed no words with one another. He could scarce find his House in his Return; but at length he got home, extreamly affrighted. The next day, it was upon Enquiry understood, that Martin was in a miserable condition by pains and hurts that were upon her.

It was further testify'd by this Deponent, That after he had given in some Evidence against Susanna Martin, many years ago, she gave him foul words about it; and said, He should never prosper more; particularly, That he should never have more than two Cows; that tho' he were never so likely to have more, yet he should never have them. And that from that very Day to this, namely for Twenty Years together, he could never exceed that Number; but some strange thing or other still prevented his having of any more.

XI. Jervis Ring testifyed, that about seven years ago, he was oftentimes and grievously Oppressed in the Night, but saw not who Troubled him, until at last he, Lying perfectly Awake, plainly saw Susanna Martin approach him. She came to him, and forceably Bit him by the Finger; so that the Print of the Bite is now so long after to be seen upon him.

XII. But besides all of these Evidences, there was a most wonderful Account of one Joseph Ring, produced on this Occasion.

This man has been strangely carried about by Dæmons, from one Witch-Meeting to another, for near two years together; and for one Quarter of this Time, they have made him and kept him Dumb, tho' he is now again able to speak. There was one T. H.[1] who having, as tis judged, a Design of engaging this Joseph Ring in a Snare of Devillism, contrived a wile, to bring this Ring two Shillings in Debt unto him.

Afterwards, this poor man would be visited with unknown shapes, and this T. H. sometimes among them; which would force him away with them, unto unknown Places, where he saw meetings, Feastings, Dancings; and after his Return, wherein they hurried him along thro' the Air, he gave Demonstrations to the Neighbours, that he had indeed been so transported. When he was brought unto these Hellish meetings, one of the First things they still [2] did unto him, was to give him a knock on the Back, whereupon he was ever as if Bound with Chains, uncapable of Stirring out of the place, till they should Release him. He related, that there often came to him a man, who presented him a Book, whereto he would have him set his Hand; promising to him, that he should then have even what he would; and presenting him with all the Delectable Things, persons, and places, that he could imagine. But he refusing to subscribe, the business would end with dreadful Shapes, Noises and Screeches, which almost scared him out of his witts. Once with the Book, there was a Pen offered him, and an Inkhorn with Liquor in it, that seemed like Blood: but he never toucht it.

This man did now affirm, that he saw the Prisoner at several of those Hellish Randezvouzes.

Note, This Woman was one of the most Impudent, Scurrilous, wicked creatures in the world; and she did now throughout her whole Trial discover herself to be such an one. Yet when she was asked, what she had to say for her self? her Cheef Plea was, That she had Led a most virtuous and Holy Life!

[1] Thomas Hardy, of Great Island, near Portsmouth. See *Records*, I. 216.
[2] Always.

IV. The Trial of Elizabeth How,[1] *at the Court of Oyer and Terminer, Held by Adjournment at Salem, June 30, 1692.*

I. Elizabeth How pleading Not Guilty to the Indictment of Witchcrafts, then charged upon her, the Court, according to the usual proceeding of the Courts in England, in such Cases, began with hearing the Depositions of Several Afflicted People, who were grievously Tortured by sensible and evident Witchcrafts, and all complained of the Prisoner, as the cause of their Trouble. It was also found that the Sufferers were not able to bear her Look, as likewise, that in their greatest Swoons, they distinguished her Touch from other peoples, being thereby raised out of them.

And there was other Testimony of people to whom the shape of this How gave trouble Nine or Ten years ago.

II. It has been a most usual thing for the Bewitched persons, at the same time that the Spectres representing the Witches Troubled them, to be visited with Apparitions of Ghosts, pretending to have bin Murdered by the Witches then represented. And sometimes the confessions of the witches afterwards acknowledged those very Murders, which these Apparitions charged upon them; altho' they had never heard what Informations had been given by the Sufferers.

There were such Apparitions of Ghosts testified by some of the present Sufferers, and the Ghosts affirmed that this How had Murdered them: which things were Fear'd but not prov'd.

III. This How had made some Attempts of Joyning to the Church, at Ipswich, several years ago; but she was deny'd an Admission into that Holy Society, partly through a suspicion of witchcraft, then urged against her. And there now came in Testimony, of Preternatural Mischiefs, presently befalling some that had been Instrumental to Debar her from the Communion, whereupon she was Intruding.

[1] Of Ipswich. For the touching story of her trial and of the loyalty of her blind husband and her daughters, see especially Upham, *Salem Witchcraft*, II. 216–223, and, in the *Historical Collections* of the Topsfield Historical Society, XIII. (1908), the study on "Topsfield in the Witchcraft Delusion," by Mrs. Towne and Miss Clark. In the same volume (pp. 107–126) Mr. G. F. Dow has published the records of her case more completely than has Woodward in *Records of Salem Witchcraft* (II. 69–94). She was executed on July 19.

IV.   There was a particular Deposition of Joseph Safford,
That his Wife had conceived an extream Aversion to this How,
on the Reports of her Witchcrafts: but How one day, taking
her by the hand, and saying, "I believe you are not Ignorant
of the great Scandal that I ly under, by an evil Report Raised
upon me," She immediately, unreasonably, and unperswade-
ably, even like one Enchanted, began to take this Womans
part.   How being soon after propounded, as desiring an Admission to the Table of the Lord, some of the pious Brethren
were unsatisfy'd about her.   The Elders appointed a Meeting
to hear Matters objected against her; and no Arguments in
the world could hinder this Goodwife Safford from going to
the Lecture.   She did indeed promise, with much ado, that
she would not go to the Church-Meeting, yet she could not
refrain going thither also.   How's Affayrs there were so
Canvased, that she came off rather Guilty than Cleared; nevertheless Goodwife Safford could not forbear taking her by the
Hand, and saying, "Tho' you are Condemned before men,
you are Justify'd before God."   She was quickly taken in a
very strange manner, Frantick, Raving, Raging and Crying
out, "Goody How must come into the Church; she is a precious
Saint; and tho' she be Condemned before Men, she is Justify'd before God."   So she continued for the space of two or
three Hours; and then fell into a Trance.   But coming to her
self, she cry'd out, "Ha! I was mistaken"; and afterwards
again repeated, "Ha! I was mistaken!"   Being asked by a
stander by, "Wherein?" She replyed, "I thought Goody How
had been a Precious Saint of God, but now I see she is a Witch.
She has Bewitched me, and my Child, and we shall never be
well, till there be Testimony for her, that she may be taken
into the Church."   And How said afterwards, that she was
very Sorry to see Safford at the Church-Meeting mentioned.
Safford after this declared herself to be afflicted by the Shape
of How; and from that Shape she endured many Miseries.
   V.   John How, Brother to the Husband of the prisoner
testifyed, that he refusing to accompany the prisoner unto her
Examination, as was by her desired, immediately some of his
Cattle were Bewitched to Death, Leaping three or four foot
high, turning about, Squeaking, Falling, and Dying, at once;
and going to cut off an Ear, for an use that might as well per-

haps have been Omitted,[1] the Hand wherein he held his knife was taken very Numb, and so it remained, and full of Pain, for several Dayes; being not well at this very Time. And he suspected this prisoner for the Author of it.

VI. Nehemiah Abbot testify'd, that unusual and mischievous Accidents would befal his cattle, whenever he had any Difference with this Prisoner. Once, Particularly, she wished his Oxe Choaked; and within a Little while that Oxe was Choaked with a Turnip in his Throat. At another time, refusing to lend his horse, at the Request of her Daughter, the horse was in a Preternatural manner abused. And several other Odd Things of that kind were testify'd.

VII. There came in Testimony, that one goodwife Sherwin, upon some Difference with How, was Bewitched, and that she Dy'd, Charging this How of having an Hand in her Death. And that other People had their Barrels of Drink unaccountably mischieved, spoilt, and spilt, upon their Displeasing of her.

The things in themselves were Trivial; but there being such a Course of them, it made them the more to be considered. Among others, Martha Wood gave her Testimony, that a Little after her Father had been employ'd in gathering an Account of Howes Conversation, they once and again Lost Great Quantities of Drink out of their Vessels, in such a manner, as they could ascribe to nothing but Witchcraft. As also, that How giving her some Apples, when she had eaten of them she was taken with a very strange kind of a maze, insomuch that she knew not what she said or did.

VIII. There was Likewise a cluster of Depositions, that one Isaac Cummings refusing to lend his Mare unto the Husband of this How, the mare was within a Day or two taken in a strange condition. The Beast seemed much Abused; being

---

[1] What this purpose may have been does not appear in the evidence: John How testifies merely that a neighbor who had laughed at him for thinking the sow bewitched told him to cut off her ear, "the which I did." It was doubtless to burn it, as a means to detect the witch. So, Perkins and Gaule say, in England it was a practice to burn the thing bewitched; and so at New Haven, in 1657, Thomas Mullener cut off the tail and ear of a pig and threw them into the fire to find out the witch (*Records of the Colony of New Haven*, II. 224). The belief was that the person who then first came to the fire was the witch (see below, p. 411).

Bruised, as if she had been Running over the Rocks, and marked where the Bridle went, as if burnt with a Red hot Bridle. Moreover, one using a Pipe of Tobacco for the Cure of the Beast, a blew Flame issued out of her, took hold of her Hair, and not only Spread and Burnt on her, but it also flew upwards towards the Roof of the Barn, and had like to have set the Barn on Fire. And the Mare dy'd very suddenly.

IX. Timothy Perley and his Wife Testify'd, not only that unaccountable Mischiefs befel their Cattle, upon their having of Differences with this Prisoner: but also, that they had a Daughter destroy'd by Witchcrafts; which Daughter still charged How as the cause of her Affliction; and it was noted, that she would be struck down, whenever How were spoken of. She was often endeavoured to be Thrown into the Fire, and into the Water, in her strange Fits: tho' her Father had Corrected her for Charging How with Bewitching her, yet (as was testify'd by others also) she said, she was sure of it, and must dy standing to it. Accordingly she Charged How to the very Death; and said, Tho' How could Afflict and Torment her Body, yet she could not Hurt her Soul: and, That the Truth of this matter would appear, when she should be Dead and Gone.

X. Francis Lane testify'd, That being hired by the Husband of this How to get him a parcel of Posts and Rails, this Lane hired John Pearly to assist him. This Prisoner then told Lane, that she believed the Posts and Rails would not do, because John Perley helped him; but that if he had got them alone, without John Pearlies help, they might have done well enough. When James How came to receive his Posts and Rails of Lane, How taking them up by the ends, they, tho' good and sound, yet unaccountably broke off, so that Lane was forced to get Thirty or Forty more. And this Prisoner being informed of it, she said, she told him so before; because Pearly help'd about them.

XI. Afterwards there came in the Confessions of several other (penitent) Witches, which affirmed this How to be one of those, who with them had been baptized by the Devil in the River at Newbery-Falls: before which, he made them there kneel down by the Brink of the River and Worship him.

V.   The Trial of Martha Carrier,[1] *at the Court of Oyer and Terminer, Held by Adjournment at Salem, August 2, 1692.*

I.   Martha Carrier was Indicted for the Bewitching of certain Persons, according to the Form usual in such Cases. Pleading Not Guilty, to her Indictment, there were First brought in a considerable number of the Bewitched Persons; who not only made the Court sensible of an horrid Witchcraft committed upon them, but also deposed, That it was Martha Carrier, or her Shape, that Grievously Tormented them, by Biting, Pricking, Pinching, and Choaking of them.   It was further deposed, that while this Carrier was on her Examination, before the Magistrates, the Poor People were so Tortured that every one expected their Death upon the very Spott; but that upon the binding of Carrier they were eased.   Moreover the Look of Carrier then laid the Afflicted People for Dead; and her Touch, if her Eye at the same Time were off them, raised them again.   Which things were also now seen upon her Trial.   And it was Testifyed, that upon the mention of some having their Necks twisted almost round, by the Shape of this Carrier, she replyed, "Its no matter, tho' their Necks had been twisted quite off."

II.   Before the Trial of this prisoner, several of her own Children had frankly and fully confessed, not only that they were Witches themselves, but that this their Mother had made them so.   This Confession they made with great shows of Repentance, and with much Demonstration of Truth.   They Related Place, Time, Occasion; they gave an account of Journeyes, Meetings, and Mischiefs by them performed; and were very credible in what they said.   Nevertheless, this Evidence was not produced against the Prisoner at the Bar, inasmuch as there was other Evidence enough to proceed upon.

III.   Benjamin Abbot gave in his Testimony, that last March was a twelve month, this Carrier was very Angry with

[1] Of Andover. She was executed, like Burroughs, on August 19, the day when Mather himself was present and said "all died by a righteous sentence" (Sewall, *Diary,* I. 363).   "All of them," says Judge Sewall, "said they were innocent, Carrier and all."   Important for her case are, beside the *Records of Salem Witchcraft* (II. 54–68, 198–199), the documents preserved by Hutchinson (*Massa-*

him, upon laying out some Land, near her Husbands: Her Expressions in this Anger, were, That she would stick as close to Abbot, as the Bark stuck to the Tree, and that he should Repent of it afore seven years came to an end, so as Doctor Prescot should never cure him. These words were heard by others, besides Abbot himself; who also heard her say, She would hold his Nose as close to the Grindstone, as ever it was held since his Name was Abbot. Presently after this, he was taken with a swelling in his Foot, and then with a pain in his side, and exceedingly Tormented. It bred into a sore, which was Lanced by Doctor Prescot, and several Gallons of Corruption ran out of it. For six weeks it continued very bad; and then another sore bred in his Groin, which was also Lanc'd by Doctor Prescot. Another Sore then bred in his Groin, which was likewise Cut, and put him to very great Misery. He was brought unto Deaths Door, and so remained until Carrier was taken, and carried away by the Constable; from which very day, he began to mend, and so grew better every day, and is well ever since.

Sarah Abbot also, his Wife, testify'd, that her Husband was not only all this while Afflicted in his Body, but also that strange, extraordinary and unaccountable Calamities befel his Cattel; their Death being such as they could guess at no Natural Reason for.

IV. Allin Toothaker testify'd, That Richard, the Son of Martha Carrier, having some Difference with him, pull'd him down by the Hair of the Head. When he Rose again, he was going to strike at Richard Carrier; but fell down flat on his Back to the ground, and had not power to stir hand or foot, until he told Carrier he yielded; and then he saw the Shape of Martha Carrier go off his Breast.

This Toothaker had Received a Wound in the Wars; and he now testify'd, that Martha Carrier told him, He should never be Cured. Just afore the Apprehending of Carrier, he could thrust a knitting Needle into his Wound, four Inches

chusetts, II., ch. I., and the draft edited by Poole in *N. E. Hist. and Gen. Register*, XXIV.). They are reprinted in Abbot's *History of Andover* (Andover, 1829), and Mrs. Bailey, in her *Historical Sketches of Andover* (Boston, 1880) has added others and told the story in detail (pp. 194–237). On Goodwife Carrier and her Andover neighbors see also pp. 180–182, 363, 371–375, 418–421.

Deep; but presently after her being Siezed, he was thoroughly Healed.

He further testify'd, That when Carrier and he sometimes were at variance, she would clap her hands at him, and say, He should get nothing by it; Whereupon he several times lost his Cattle, by strange Deaths, whereof no Natural Causes could be given.

V.   John Rogger also testifyed, That upon the threatning words of this malicious Carrier, his Cattle would be strangely Bewitched; as was more particularly then described.

VI.   Samuel Preston testify'd, that about two years ago, having some Difference with Martha Carrier, he lost a Cow in a strange Preternatural unusual manner; and about a month after this, the said Carrier, having again some Difference with him, she told him, He had lately lost a Cow, and it should not be long before he Lost another! which accordingly came to Pass; for he had a Thriving and well-kept Cow, which without any known cause quickly fell down and Dy'd.

VII.   Phebe Chandler testify'd, that about a Fortnight before the apprehension of Martha Carrier, on a Lords-Day, while the Psalm was singing, in the Church, this Carrier then took her by the shoulder and shaking her, asked her, where she Lived? she made her no Answer, although as Carrier, who lived next door to her Fathers House, could not in reason but know who she was.   Quickly after this, as she was at several times crossing the Fields, she heard a voice, that she took to be Martha Carriers, and it seem'd as if it was over her Head. The voice told her, she should within two or three days be Poisoned.   Accordingly, within such a Little time, One Half of her Right Hand became greatly swollen, and very painful; as also part of her Face; whereof she can give no account how it came.   It continued very Bad for some dayes; and several times since, she has had a great pain in her Breast; and been so siezed on her Legs, that she has hardly been able to go. She added that lately, going well to the House of God, Richard, the Son of Martha Carrier, Look'd very earnestly upon her, and immediately her hand, which had formerly been poisoned, as is abovesaid, began to pain her greatley, and she had a strange Burning at her stomach; but was then struck deaf, so that she could not hear any of the prayer, or singing, till the two or three last words of the Psalme.

VIII.   One Foster, who confessed her own Share in the Witchcraft for which the Prisoner stood indicted, affirm'd, That she had seen the Prisoner at some of their Witch-Meetings, and that it was this Carrier, who perswaded her to be a Witch. She confessed, That the Devil carry'd them on a Pole, to a Witch-Meeting; but the Pole broke, and she hanging about Carriers Neck, they both fell down, and she then Received an Hurt by the Fall, whereof she was not at this very time Recovered.

IX.   One Lacy, who likewise confessed her share in this Witchcraft, now Testify'd, That she and the Prisoner were once Bodily present at a Witch-meeting in Salem-Village; and that she knew the Prisoner to be a Witch, and to have been at a Diabolical Sacrament, and that the Prisoner was the undoing of her and her Children, by Enticing them into the Snare of the Devil.

X.   Another Lacy, who also Confessed her share in this Witchcraft, now Testify'd, That the Prisoner was at the Witch-Meeting, in Salem Village, where they had Bread and Wine Administred unto them.

XI.   In the Time of this Prisoner's Trial, one Susanna Shelden in open Court had her Hands Unaccountably Ty'd together with a Wheel-band, so fast that without Cutting it could not be Loosed: It was done by a Spectre; and the Sufferer affirm'd, it was the Prisoners.

Memorandum.   This Rampant Hag, Martha Carrier, was the Person, of whom the Confessions of the Witches, and of her own Children among the rest, agreed, That the Devil had promised her, she should be Queen of Hell.

Having thus far done the Service imposed upon me, I will further pursue it, by relating a few of those Matchless Curiosities, with which the Witchcraft now upon us has entertained us.   And I shall Report nothing but with Good Authority, and what I would Invite all my Readers to examine, while tis yet Fresh and New, that if there be found any mistake, it may be as willingly Retracted, as it was unwillingly Committed.

The First Curiositie.

I. Tis very Remarkable to see what an Impious and Impudent Imitation of Divine Things is Apishly affected by the Devil, in several of those matters, whereof the Confessions of our Witches and the Afflictions of our Sufferers have informed us.

That Reverend and Excellent Person, Mr. John Higginson,[1] in My Conversation with him, Once invited me to this Reflection; That the Indians which came from far to settle about Mexico, were in their Progress to that Settlement, under a Conduct of the Devil, very strangely Emulating what the Blessed God gave to Israel in the Wilderness.

Acosta[2] is our Author for it, that the Devil in

their Idol Vitzlipultzli governed that mighty Nation. He commanded them to leave their Country, promising to make them Lords over all the Provinces possessed by Six other Nations of Indians, and give them a Land abounding with all precious things. They went forth, carrying their Idol with them, in a Coffer of Reeds, supported by Four of their Principal Priests; with whom he still Discoursed, in secret, Revealing to them the Successes, and Accidents of their way. He advised them, when to March, and where to Stay, and without his Commandment they moved not. The first thing they did, wherever they came, was to Erect a Tabernacle, for their False God; which they set always in the midst of their Camp, and there placed the Ark upon an Altar. When they, Tired with pains, talked of proceeding no further in their Journey, than a certain pleasant Stage, whereto they were arrived, this Devil in one night horribly kill'd them that had started this Talk, by pulling out their Hearts. And so they passed on, till they came to Mexico.

The Devil which then thus imitated what was in the Church of the Old Testament, now among Us would Imitate the Affayrs

---

[1] Senior minister at Salem Town. See also p. 248, note 2, and pp. 398, 399–402.

[2] It is the Spanish Jesuit, Joseph Acosta, who in his *Natural and Moral History of the Indies* (bk. VII., ch. 4) relates this. Mather seems to have used the English version of Grimston (London, 1604), paraphrasing and abridging after a free fashion and inserting from the following chapter what is in his last two sentences.

of the Church in the New. The Witches do say, that they
form themselves much after the manner of Congregational
Churches; and that they have a Baptism and a Supper, and
Officers among them, abominably Resembling those of our
Lord.

But there are many more of these Bloody Imitations, if
the Confessions of the Witches are to be Received; which I
confess, ought to be but with very much of Caution.

What is their striking down with a fierce Look? What is
their making of the Afflicted Rise, with a touch of their Hand?
What is their Transportation thro' the Air? What is their
Travelling in Spirit, while their Body is cast into a Trance?
What is their causing of Cattle to run mad and perish? What
is their Entring their Names in a Book? What is their coming
together from all parts, at the Sound of a Trumpet? What is
their Appearing sometimes Cloathed with Light or Fire upon
them? What is their Covering of themselves and their Instruments with Invisibility? But a Blasphemous Imitation
of certain Things recorded about our Saviour, or His Prophets,
or the Saints in the Kingdom of God.

A Second Curiositie.

II.   In all the Witchcraft which now Grievously Vexes us,
I know not whether any thing be more Unaccountable, than
the Trick which the Witches have, to render themselves and
their Tools Invisible. Witchcraft seems to be the Skill of
Applying the Plastic Spirit of the World[1] unto some unlawful
purposes, by means of a Confederacy with Evil Spirits. Yet
one would wonder how the Evil Spirits themselves can do
some things: especially at Invisibilizing of the Grossest Bodies.
I can tell the Name of an Ancient Author, who pretends to
show the way, how a man may come to walk about Invisible,
and I can tell the Name of another Ancient Author, who pretends to Explode that way. But I will not speak too plainly,
Lest I should unawares Poison some of my Readers, as the

---

[1] This phrase shows the influence of Ralph Cudworth (see his *Intellectual
System*, bk. I., ch. III., § 37) and through him of Cambridge Platonism—whose
demonology (*e. g.*, Cudworth, bk. I., ch. V., at end) must also be remembered
here.

Pious Hemingius did one of his Pupils, when he only by way
of Diversion recited a Spell, which, they had said, would cure
Agues.[1] This much I will say; The notion of procuring Invisibility, by any Natural Expedient yet known, is, I Believe,
a meer Plinyism; How far it may be obtained by a Magical
Sacrament, is best known to the Dangerous Knaves that have
Try'd it. But our Witches do seem to have got the Knack:
and this is one of the Things, that make me think, Witchcraft
will not be fully understood, until the Day when there shall
not be one Witch in the World.

There are certain people very Dogmatical about these
matters; but I'l give them only these Three Bones to Pick.

First, One of our Bewitched people was cruelly assaulted
by a Spectre, that, she said, ran at her with a Spindle: tho' no
body else in the Room, could see either the Spectre or the
Spindle. At last, in her miseries, giving a Snatch at the Spectre, she pull'd the Spindle away; and it was no sooner got
into her hand, but the other people then present beheld, that
it was indeed a Real, Proper, Iron Spindle, belonging they
knew to whom; which when they Lock'd up very safe, it was
nevertheless by Dæmons unaccountably stole away, to do
further mischief.

Secondly, Another of our Bewitched People was haunted
with a most abusive Spectre, which came to her, she said,
with a Sheet about her. After she had undergone a deal of
Teaze, from the Annoyances of the Spectre, she gave a Violent
Snatch at the Sheet that was upon it; wherefrom she tore a
Corner, which in her Hand immediately became Visible to a
Roomful of Spectators; a Palpable Corner of a Sheet. Her
Father, who was now holding her, Catch'd that he might Keep
what his Daughter had so strangely Seized, but the unseen
Spectre had like to have pull'd his Hand off, by Endeavouring
to wrest it from him; however he still held it, and I suppose
has it still to show; it being but a few Hours ago, namely
about the Beginning of this October, that this Accident happened; in the family of one Pitman, at Manchester.

Thirdly, A young man, delaying to procure Testimonials

[1] It is the great Danish theologian Nicholas Hemming (Niels Hemmingsen)
who tells this story of himself in his *Admonitio de Superstitionibus Magicis vitandis*
(Copenhagen, 1575), fol. C2 verso.

for his Parents, who being under confinement on Suspicion of Witchcraft, required him to do that Service for them, was quickly pursued with odd Inconveniences. But once above the Rest, an Officer going to put his Brand on the Horns of some Cows, belonging to these people, which tho' he had Siez'd for some of their Debts, yet he was willing to leave in their Possession, for the Subsistence of the poor Family; this young man help'd in holding the Cows to be thus Branded. The three first Cows he held well enough; but when the hot Brand was clap't upon the Fourth, he winc'd and shrunk at such a rate, as that he could hold the Cow no longer. Being afterwards Examined about it, he Confessed, That at that very Instant when the Brand entred the Cows Horn, exactly the like burning Brand was clap'd upon his own Thigh; where he has Exposed the Lasting Marks of it, unto such as asked to see them.

Unriddle these Things,—*Et Eris mihi magnus Apollo*.[1]

A Third Curiositie.

III. If a Drop of Innocent Blood should be shed, in the Prosecution of the Witchcrafts among us, how unhappy are we! For which cause, I cannot express my self in better terms, than those of a most Worthy Person, who lives near the present Center of these things.[2] "The Mind of God in these matters, is to be carefully look'd into, with due Circumspection, that Satan deceive us not with his Devices, who transforms himself into an Angel of Light, and may pretend Justice and yet intend Mischief." But on the other side, if the Storm of Justice do now fall only on the Heads of those Guilty Witches and Wretches which have defiled our Land, How Happy!

The Execution of some that have lately Dyed has been immediately attended with a strange Deliverance of some, that had lain for many years in a most sad Condition, under

---

[1] "And thou shalt be to me a great Apollo"—*i. e.*, a great revealer of mysteries. For their unriddling see p. 370, below.

[2] It has been suggested that this means the Rev. John Higginson, the venerable senior minister at Salem, whose hesitation as to the proceedings may be inferred from Brattle's words (p. 184, above)—and from all else we know. See below, p. 398.

they knew not whose Evil Hands. As I am abundantly satisfy'd, That many of the Self-Murders committed here, have
been the effects of a Cruel and Bloody Witchcraft, letting fly
Dæmons upon the miserable Seneca's;[1] thus, it has been admirable unto me to see, how a Devillish Witchcraft, sending
Devils upon them, has driven many poor people to Despair,
and persecuted their minds with such Buzzes[2] of Atheism and
Blasphemy, as has made them even run Distracted with Terrors: and some long Bow'd down under such a Spirit of In-
firmity, have been marvelously Recovered upon the Death of
the Witches.

One Whetford particularly ten years ago, challenging of
Bridget Bishop (whose Trial you have had) with Stealing of a
Spoon, Bishop threatned her very direfully: presently after
this was Whetford in the Night, and in her Bed, visited by
Bishop, with one Parker, who making the Room Light at their
coming in, there discoursed of several mischiefs they would
inflict upon her. At last, they pull'd her out, and carried her
unto the Sea-side, there to drown her; but she calling upon
God, they left her, tho' not without Expressions of their Fury.
From that very Time, this poor Whetford was utterly spoilt,
and grew a Tempted, Froward, Crazed sort of a Woman; a
vexation to her self, and all about her; and many ways unreasonable. In this Distraction she lay, till those women were
Apprehended, by the Authority; then she began to mend;
and upon their Execution, was presently and perfectly Recovered, from the ten years madness that had been upon her.

A Fourth Curiositie.

IV. 'Tis a thousand pitties, that we should permit our
Eyes to be so Blood-shot with passions, as to loose the sight
of many wonderful Things, wherein the Wisdom and Justice
of God, would be Glorify'd. Some of those Things, are the
frequent Apparitions of Ghosts, whereby many Old Murders
among us, come to be considered. And, among many Instances
of this kind, I will single out one, which concerned a poor man,

---

[1] The philosopher Seneca, it will be remembered, was an advocate of suicide
and ended his own life thus.

[2] Whisperings.

lately Prest unto Death, because of his Refusing to Plead for his Life.[1] I shall make an Extract of a Letter, which was written to my Honourable Friend, Samuel Sewal, Esq.,[2] by Mr. Putman,[3] to this purpose;

The Last Night my Daughter Ann was grievously Tormented by Witches, Threatning that she should be Pressed to Death, before Giles Cory. But thro' the Goodness of a Gracious God, she had at last a little Respite. Whereupon there appeared unto her (she said) a man in a Winding Sheet; who told her that Giles Cory had Murdered him, by Pressing him to Death with his Feet; but that the Devil there appeared unto him, and Covenanted with him, and promised him, He should not be Hanged. The Apparition said, God Hardened his Heart, that he should not hearken to the Advice of the Court, and so Dy an easy Death; because as it said, "It must be done to him as he has done to me." The Apparition also said, That Giles Cory was carry'd to the Court for this, and that the Jury had found the Murder, and that her Father knew the man, and the thing was done before she was born. Now Sir, This is not a little strange to us; that no body should Remember these things, all the while that Giles Cory was in Prison, and so often before the Court. For all people now Remember very well, (and the Records of the Court also mention it,) That about Seventeen Years ago, Giles Cory kept a man in his House, that was almost a Natural Fool: which Man Dy'd suddenly. A Jury was Impannel'd upon him, among whom was Dr. Zorobbabel Endicot;[4] who found the man bruised to Death, and having clodders of Blood about his Heart. The Jury, whereof several are yet alive, brought in the man Murdered; but as if some Enchantment had hindred the Prosecution of the Matter, the Court Proceeded not against Giles Cory, tho' it cost him a great deal of Mony to get off.

Thus the Story.

The Reverend and Worthy Author, having at the Direction of His Excellency the Governour, so far Obliged the Publick, as to give some Account of the Sufferings brought upon the

[1] As to the case of Giles Corey see below, pp. 366–367.

[2] Judge Sewall, of the court.

[3] Thomas Putnam, of Salem Village, whose wife and daughter played so large a part as accusers.

[4] Of Salem Village. A son of John Endicott, the first governor of the Bay colony, and himself much honored as a physician.

Countrey by Witchcraft; and of the Trials which have passed upon several Executed for the Same:

Upon Perusal thereof, We find the Matters of Fact and Evidence, Truly reported. And a Prospect given, of the Methods of Conviction, used in the Proceedings of the Court at Salem.

Boston Octob 11.   WILLIAM STOUGHTON
         1692.   SAMUEL SEWALL.

A BRAND PLUCK'D OUT OF THE BURNING, BY
COTTON MATHER, 1693

INTRODUCTION

THE *Wonders of the Invisible World* was not yet issued, the General Court was still debating its course toward the accused who filled the jails, and Judge Sewall (on November 22, 1692) was just imploring God to "bless the Assembly in their debates" and (if "consisting with his Justice and Holiness") to "vindicate the late Judges," when there fell into the hands of the Rev. Cotton Mather an opportunity to show the province and the world how a case of bewitchment should be handled. It is likely enough that he had known Mercy Short from the time of her first seizure, in the early summer; but from November, and especially from the day when she fell into a paroxysm while attending his church, and was carried into a neighbor's, where for weeks she lay at his door, till her "deliverance" on March 16, he gave the case the attention that fruited in the following journal. The journal was doubtless soon thereafter completed, and, like his earlier narrative of the case of the Goodwin children,[1] and his later one of Margaret Rule's,[2] put into circulation among his friends.

The manuscript, still extant in his own handwriting, bears on its cover-page, in his hand, "To be returned unto Cotton Mather." And in the possession of Cotton Mather and his family it seems to have remained until 1814, when his granddaughter, Mrs. Hannah (Mather) Crocker, presented it, with many other papers, to the American Antiquarian Society at Worcester, Massachusetts.[3] "About ten years ago," writes

---

[1] See p. 119 and p. 126, note 1.   [2] See p. 306, note 3, p. 307, note 1.

[3] "The manuscript," writes Mr. Brigham, the present librarian of that society, "unquestionably came to the Society in December, 1814, under which

255

W. F. Poole in the second volume (1881) of the *Memorial History of Boston*, "Dr. Samuel F. Haven, the accomplished librarian of the American Antiquarian Society, in looking through the Mather manuscripts in that library, found one entitled, *A Brand Pluckt out of the Burning*, and on examination it proved to be the long-lost Mercy Short narrative." "Dr. Haven, in announcing the discovery," he adds, "promised to print it with notes; but he has not yet found leisure to fulfil his promise." That leisure never came. A transcript of the booklet was made and lent to Poole, who made it the basis of his careful summary of the case,[1] and this transcript has since been used by other scholars; but when, after Dr. Haven's death (in 1881), his successor was frequently asked, "When

date is the following entry in the Donation Book: 'Above Nine Hundred Sermons, in manuscript and separate, written and preached by the Mathers. Together with a number of manuscript books and papers which were in the Mather Library. Presented to the Society by Mrs. Hannah Crocker of Boston.' "

The vicissitudes, earlier and later, of the papers and books of the Mathers have been related in much detail by Mr. Julius H. Tuttle ("The Libraries of the Mathers," in the *Proceedings* of the American Antiquarian Society, n. s., XX. 269–356), and he narrates (p. 310) how in October, 1831, another body of old papers, which "nobody could read," found their way from the garret once Samuel Mather's to the Antiquarian Society. But it is the hand of President Isaiah Thomas (d. April, 1831), who received the gift of Mrs. Crocker, that has written on the cover-page of our MS. its title of "Brand Plucked out of the Burning"; and it was doubtless while looking over the "*débris* from the drawers and pigeon-holes of a student's desk, that came to this Society with the family library from Mrs. Hannah Mather Crocker," that Librarian Haven (see his report, p. 36 in the *Proceedings* of the American Antiquarian Society, April, 1869) first noticed it.

The original manuscript is $7\frac{3}{4}$ inches high by 6 inches wide. It contains 20 leaves, of which the first is blank. The remaining pages are numbered from 1 to 38, p. 26 having nothing upon it and therefore no numbering. At the end of p. 38 the text breaks off abruptly, after the opening words (printed below, p. 286) of section 29. These suffice to show the section merely a postscript and to convince us that few words are missing. The manuscript shows marks of much use; many words are blotted or erased, and there are some interlineations in a different ink, some in the same ink, but practically all in the same hand. The most important marks of the writer's later thought are in the shape of marginal additions.

For this careful description of the MS. thanks are due to Librarian Brigham and to Dr. Charles H. Lincoln, who has prepared the copy for the printer.

[1] *Memorial History of Boston*, II. 147–152.

shall you publish Cotton Mather's account of the trial of Mercy Short?" he could only reply that it "should see the light at an early day, under the editorial supervision of such students of the witchcraft problem as Drs. Poole and Moore."[1] Poole seriously thought of the task. "His study of the witchcraft problem and literature," said Librarian Barton at his death,[2] "had led him to hope that he might edit with notes our Cotton Mather manuscript account of the case of Mercy Short"; but he seems never to have taken it in hand, and no other has since attempted it.

The importance of the narrative lies not only in its contemporaneity with the Salem trials and the side-lights it gives us on that episode and its environment, but yet more in the clearness with which it shows just what its author stood for in the matter. To him the case of Mercy Short was not only identical in kind with those of "the Bewitched people then tormented by Invisible Furies in the County of Essex": it was itself one of those cases. And from first to last he was conscious that he was making his treatment of it an object lesson. The present editor is far, indeed, from finding in it, like Mr. Poole, "the principles and methods of the Boston ministers" in general, and yet farther from his conviction that Mather meant his method to be a rival of the court's. He can not overlook that author's own explanation that, "had wee not studiously suppressed all clamours and Rumours that might have touched the Reputacion of people exhibited in this Witchcraft, there might have ensued most uncomfortable uproar";[3] or that, if he himself used prayer and fasting, he had a little earlier reminded the court how in Sweden a fast "was immediately [followed] with a remarkable Smile of God upon the endeavours of the Judges to discover and Extirpate the Authors of that Execrable witchcraft";[4] or that, if he found

---

[1] Report of Librarian Barton, April, 1885, in *Proceedings*, n. s., III. 385–386.
[2] See his report for April, 1894 (*ibid.*, IX. 184).   [3] See p. 276, below.
[4] Mass. Hist. Soc., *Collections*, fourth series, VIII. 392.

in Mercy Short's revelations confirmation of his view that the
Devil may sometimes personate the innocent, he found confirmation also for his faith that such a "dark dispensation"
must be rare and that God could find a way to shelter the
guiltless;[1] or that, if he restrained the bewitched girl from betraying to any but himself the names of her tormentors, he
was ready himself to betray them to justice as fast as they
seemed to him "dangerous and damnable" and as there could
be found "more cause," *i. e.*, such added evidence as he had
again and again declared satisfactory in the Salem convictions.[2]
But for these conclusions, as for Mr. Poole's, the present narrative must serve pre-eminently as a criterion; and for the
precise nature and limits of his method, for the appraisal of
his credulity and of his rôle as exorcist and as dupe, no other
can compare with it, not even that of Margaret Rule.[3]   And,
unlike the latter, it does not come to us through the hand of a
foe.   It is in the light of such contemporary utterances that
one must read those pages of his *Diary* which there is so much
reason to believe the work of later years.[4]

---

[1] P. 274, below.   [2] *Ibid.*   [3] Pp. 308–323, below.

[4] That *A Brand pluck'd out of the Burning* was written before *Another Brand
pluckt out of the Burning* is clear from their titles; and the mention, in the latter,
of Mercy Short's experiences, "whereof a Narrative has been already given,"
as ending "about half a year" earlier, before Margaret Rule's began—*i. e.*, before
September 10, 1693—gives us March of that year as a *terminus a quo*.   March
16, 1693, is the latest date mentioned in the manuscript itself; and it is clear from
the hope with which it ends that its author then lost little time in closing his
record and sharing it with his friends—if, in a less complete form, it was not
already known to them.

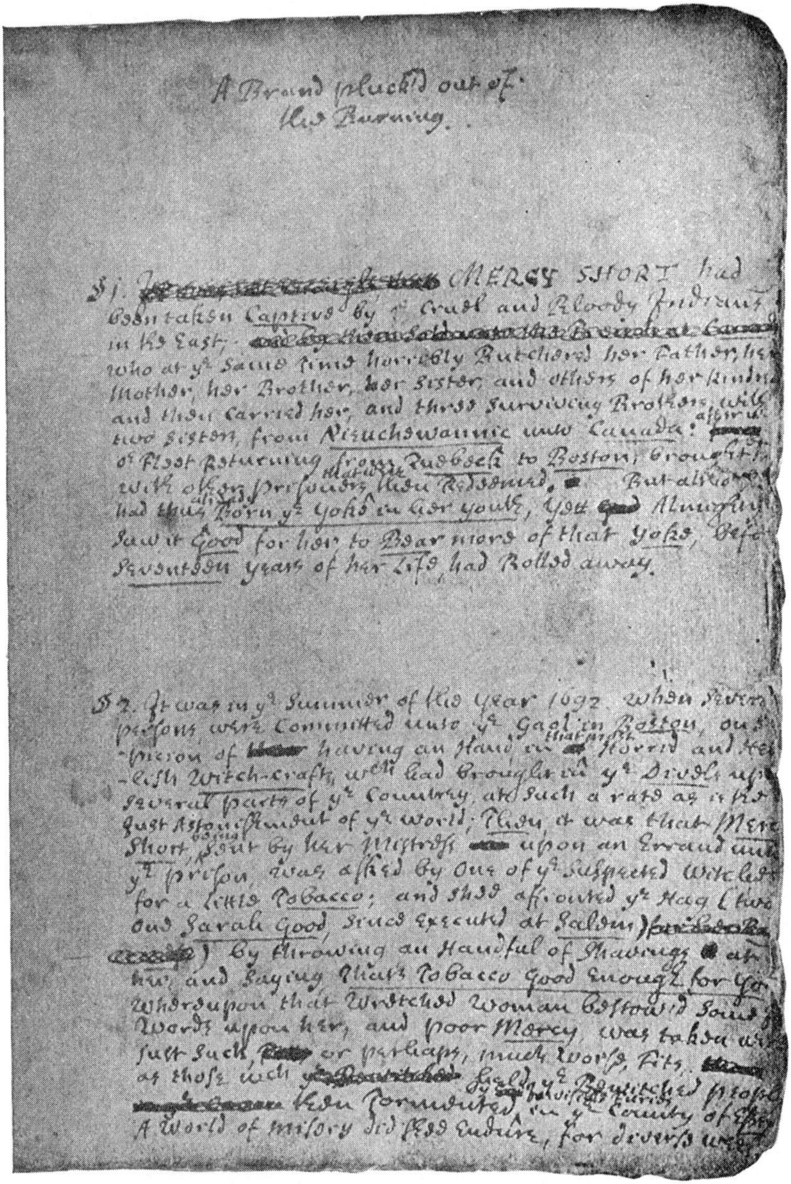

A BRAND PLUCK'D OUT OF THE BURNING

§ 1. MERCY SHORT had been taken Captive by our cruel and Bloody Indians in the East, who at the same time horribly Butchered her Father, her Mother, her Brother, her Sister, and others of her Kindred and then carried her, and three surviving Brothers with two Sisters, from Nieuchewannic[2] unto Canada: after which our Fleet Returning from Quebeck to Boston, brought them with other prisoners that were then Redeemed. But altho she had then already Born the Yoke in her youth, Yett God Almighty saw it Good for her to Bear more of that Yoke, before seventeen years of her Life had Rolled away.

§ 2. It was in the Summer of the Year 1692, when sever[al] persons were committed unto the Gaol in Boston on suspicion of having an Hand in that most Horrid and Hellish Witchcraft, which had brought in the Divels upon several parts of the Country, at such a rate as is the just Astonishment of the world; Then it was that Mercy Short, being sent by her Mistress upon an Errand unto the prison, was asked by one of the Suspected Witches for a little Tobacco; and she affronted the

---

[1] A cover-page of the manuscript bears the inscription (by a later hand): "Brand Plucked out of the Burning, being an Account of Mercy Short who was supposed to suffer by Witchcraft 1692." And in the hand of Cotton Mather himself are written the words: "To be returned unto Cotton Mather."

[2] Or Salmon Falls, a New Hampshire settlement on the river dividing that province from Maine, where now on the Maine side is the village of Berwick. In his *Magnalia* (bk. VII., art. 6) Mather has told in detail the story of this taking of Salmon Falls by the French and Indians (March 18, 1690) and what share in this calamity "fell to the family of one Clement Short": "This honest man, with his pious wife, and three children, were kill'd; and six or seven of their children were made prisoners." His knowledge of the episode was doubtless gathered from Mercy Short. The fleet, which brought her to Boston, arrived November 19, 1690. She probably went into domestic service, and, as we shall see, in a neighborhood where were "people of quality."

Hag (t'was one Sarah Good, since executed at Salem)[1] by throwing an Handful of Shavings at her and saying, That's Tobacco good enough for you. Whereupon that Wretched Woman bestowed some ill words upon her, and poor Mercy was taken with just such, or perhaps much worse, Fits as those which held the Bewitched people then Tormented by Invisible Furies in the County of Essex. A world of misery did shee endure, for diverse weeks together, and such as could not possibly bee inflicted upon her without the Immediate efficiency of some Agent, or Rational or Malicious; until God was pleased at length to hear the multiply'd prayers of His people for her Deliverance. There were many Remarkable Things in the molestations then given her; Whereof one was that they made her Fast for Twelve Days together.

§ 3. Being happily Delivered, shee for diverse months remained so; even until the Winter following. But then shee suddenly fell into a swoon wherein shee lay for Dead many hours together; and it was not long before the Distinct and Formal Fits of Witchcraft return'd upon her.[2] Shee continued variously Tortured and Harassed by Evil Spirits; and in the same circumstances that had been upon her formerly until one of the ministers in the Town[3] took a little company of his praying Neighbors, and kept a Day of prayer with her and for her. On which day shee lay wholly insensible of the people that were thus concerned on her behalf and entertained with none but the cursed Spectres, whom alone shee saw, shee heard, shee felt; nevertheless while that minister was preaching on Marc. 9. 28, 29, shee flew upon him and shee tore a leaf of his Bible.[4] For some days after This Day shee continued

---

[1] Sarah Good (see pp. 343 ff., 414) was sent to the Boston jail on March 7, condemned at Salem June 30, executed on July 19. As she is here spoken of as only "suspected," the interview with Mercy Short was as early as June.

[2] The event is noted by Sewall (*Diary*, I. 370) under November 22: "Now about, Mercy Short grows ill again, as formerly." This he probably added when about to write the following entry: "November 25. Mr. Mather sent for to her."

[3] Mather himself, of course.

[4] Then doubtless it was—"Nov. 29. 1692"—that Mather wrote in his Bible: "While I was preaching at a private fast (kept for a possessed young woman)—on Mark 9. 28, 29.—the Devel in the Damsel flew upon mee, and tore the Leaf, as it is now torn over against the Text." A facsimile of this autograph note is

in her grievous vexations; but then, after what was little short of an Entire and a Total Fast for about Nine Dayes together, in those miseries, at length shee gained about Three Dayes Remission. In this Intermission of her Anguishes, shee did eat a little, and but a very little, Victuals; and shee was able on the Lords Day to visit the Lords House, near half a mile from the place of her abode.[1]

§ 4. While shee was in the congregation shee so fell under the Arrest of her Invisible Troublers that shee now Saw and Heard nothing but those horrid Fiends, but when the Assembly was just broke up, they fell to Tormenting of her at such a rate, that many strong men with an united Force, could not well carry her any Further than the House of a kind Neighbour, who charitably took her in. T'was by the singular Providence of God, that shee was thus cast amo[ng] a Neighborhood whose Hearts Hee stirred up to pitty her, to releeve her, to pray for her, and with a most christian compassion do all that could piously bee done, for her Deliverance. There shee lay for diverse weeks; and you shall now bee told in what manner handled! A manner differing Little or Nothing from that wherein shee had been thus long already Tortured.

§ 5. There exhibited himself unto her a Divel having the Figure of A Short and a Black Man; and it was remarkable that altho' shee had no sort of Acquaintance with Histories of what has happened elswhere, to make any Impressions upon her Imagination, yett the Divel that visited her was just of the same Stature, Feature, and complexion with what the Histories of the Witchcrafts beyond-sea ascribe unto him; he was a wretch no taller than an ordinary Walking-Staff; hee was not of a Negro, but of a Tawney, or an Indian colour; hee wore an high-crowned Hat, with strait Hair; and had one Cloven-Foot. This Divel still brought with him unto her a considerable Number of Spectres, most exactly resembling the persons of several people in the countrey, some of whose Names were

---

prefixed by Sparks to the life of Cotton Mather in his *Library of American Biography* (at p. 161), and the tracing made by him for it is treasured, with his others, in the library of Cornell University.

[1] *I. e.*, to come to Mather's church on Sunday, December 4: her nine days' fast, if begun on November 22, ended on December 1, and "three days' remission" had followed.

either formerly known, or now by their companions told unto her. And these wicked Spectres assisted, or obeyed, their Divellish Master, who brought them to infest her with such hideous Assaults, as were the Astonishment of all the standers-by.

§ 6. When this Divel with his confederate and concomitant Spectres came unto this our poor Neighbour, it was their custom to cast her into such horrible Darkness that shee still imagined herself in a desolate cellar, where Day or Night could not bee distinguished. Her eyes were open, moving to and fro after the Hellish Harpyes that were now fluttering about her; but so little able to see any thing else, that altho wee made as if wee would strike at her eyes, it would not make her wink. If wee laid our Hands upon them it hindred her from a view of those Fiends which troubled her; but shee gave us afterwards to understand, that it put her unto much pain to bee so hindred. Her ears were altogether stopt unto all of our Noises, being wholly engrossed by the Invisible Assailants; insomuch that tho' wee sometimes halloo'd extremely loud in her ears, yett shee heard nothing of it. And it was particularly considerable that altho shee could bee no other than utterly ignorant of what the European Books relate concerning such matters, nevertheless the Voice of these Dæmons was exactly such as you shall read in Glanvils collections[1] and elsewhere; twas Big, Low, Thick, and such as ordinarily caused her to say Haah! or How! or What do you say? and listen and oblige them to Repeat before shee could understand. *Note.* That wee the standers-by could neither see nor Hear the things which thus entertained this young woman, and I hope wee never shall; but wee were informed partly from the Speeches that fell from her in these Trances; partly from the Accounts by her afterwards given unto us; and partly by a multitude of other concurrant circumstances.

§ 7. The Divel, and his crew, having thus forced her senses from conversing with their ordinary objects, and captivated them unto this communion with The Powers of Darkness, Their manner was in the first place, to make her a tender of a Book, somewhat long and thick (Like the wast-books of many Traders), butt bound and clasp't, and filled not only with the

---

[1] As to Joseph Glanvill and his "collections," see above, pp. 5–6.

Names or Marks, but also with the explicit (short) Covenants of such as had listed themselves in the Service of Satan, and the Design of Witchcraft; all written in Red characters; many whereof shee had opportunity to read when they opened the Book before her. This Book of Death did they Tempt her to sign; and condescended so far in their sollicitacions, as to tell her, That if shee would only Touch it with her Finger it should bee enough. Only the received signification of this little ceremony should bee That shee now became the Devoted Vassal of the Divel. This was the Temptacion with which they still persecuted her; and it was the very same, that the Evil Spirits were at the same time using upon far more than a Score of miserable people so posessed in several other parts of the countrey. Whether this Book bee indeed a Real Book or no I dispute not. Mercy herself shee thinks it is; and gives this reason for it, That a Touch of it (they told her) would have cured her. Besides They diverse times made her Eyes very sore by thrusting it hard upon them, to make her Touch it when shee should unawares lift up her Hands to save her Eyes. And they at last gave her to understand, That they thought they should bee forced shortly to drop it.

§ 8. As the Bewitched, in other parts of the world, have commonly had no other style for their Tormentors but only *They* and *Them*; so had Mercy Short. Wherefore to consult Brevity, wee shall Note the Divel, and those that accompanied him in this Business, by that style. And so I go on to say That *They* first used a thousand Flatteries and Allurements to induce her unto a compliance with the Desire of the Divel. They showed her very splendid garments, and thence proceeded unto greater glories, which they promised her if shee would sign to Their Book. They engag'd unto her, I know not how many more conveniences, if shee would but so much as Touch it. When all these persuasives were ineffectual, They terrify'd her with horrible Threatnings of miseries which they would inflict upon her, and then They as cruelly Inflicted a great part of what They Threatened.

But that which added unto the Horror of the matter was that when those Tygres were addressing themselves to some of their Furious Inflictions, They would so cloathe themselves in Flames of Fire (a Divellish and most impudent imitation, sure, of something mentioned in the Scripture!) as to render themselves beyond measure formidable; and accordingly, just before They fell upon her with any Torments of a more than ordinary Account, shee would sometims, by the fright of what shee perceived them doing, fall a Trembling so that the very Bed would shake under her. *Memorandum.* That one evening I had with mee a Lanthorn accomodated with a glass-Ball, which rendered the Light so extremely glaring that one could hardly bear to look upon it, but one might thereby read a very small print a very great way off; and shee being then able to see and speak, told us That *Hee* (meaning The Black Man) sometimes came to her with Eyes Flaming like the Light of that Lanthorn.

§ 9. T'would bee a long work to Recite all the Tortures with which They plagued her. I shall only Touch upon the principal. Besides the Thousands of cruel pinches given her by those Barbarous Visitants, they stuck innumerable pins into her. Many of those pins They did themselves pluck out again; and yett They left the Bloody Marks of them, which would bee as tis the strange Property of most Witch-wounds to bee, cured, perhaps in less than a Minute. But some of the Pins They left in her, and those wee took out, with Wonderment. Yea, sometimes They would force Pins into her Mouth, for her to swallow them; and tho' Shee strove all shee was able to keep them out, yett They were too hard for her. Only before they were gott into her Throat, the Standers-by would by some Dexterity gett hold of them, and fetch them away. When this mischief was over, They would then come and sitt upon her Breast, and pull open her Jaw, and keep her without fetching one sensible Breath, sometimes for Half-an-hour, and sometimes for several whole Hours together. At last, when wee came to understand that it was the Sitting of the Spectres upon her, which cast her into those doleful Postures, wee would with main Force, (and so heavy shee was beyond her Ordinary Weight, that the lifting of her called for a more than Ordinary Force) lift her upright, and the Spectres would imediately then so fall off, that her Breath return'd unto her. At other times there would be heard, it may bee, by more than seven Witnesses at a time, the Scratches of the Spectres on the Bed and on the Wall.

§ 10. Moreover, They would sometimes bring her a little Cup that had a Whitesh Liquor in it (unto Us, wholly invisible), which They would pour down her Throat, holding her Jawes wide open in spite of all the Shriekings and Strivings wherewith shee expressed a Reluctancy to Taking of it. Wee saw her swallow this Poison, tho wee saw not the Poison; and immediately shee would swell prodigiously, and bee just like one poisoned with a Dose of Rats-bane. After these Potions, shee was capable ordinarily to beg of us, that wee would help her to some Sallet Oyl.[1] Upon the Taking whereof, the swelling would in a little while abate. Behold, a proper Venefic Witchcraft![2]   Because the Name for Sorcerers in the Bible may signify Poisoners, tis a foolish Thing thence to infer that by Witches, the Scripture means no more than such as committ Murders by Poisons. One great Skill, and way of Afflicting People in Witchcraft, is by another sort of Poisoning than what may bee seen by common Eyes. Yea I suppose, all the Bewitched have undergone such a Spirituous Infection that wee may count them in a manner poisoned.

Notandum, That Sometimes our laying our Hands on the Mouth of Mercy Short, when wee perceived the Spectres forcing their Poisons into her Mouth, did keep her from taking of them in.

§ 11. Another of the Miseries Whereto They putt her was an Extreme Fasting for many Days together. Shee having obtained a Liberty of Eating for Three Dayes, after a Fast of Nine Dayes, was immediately compelled unto another Fast, which lasted for about Fifteen Dayes together. In all this Time, shee was permitted scarce to swallow one bitt or drop of any Victuals. One Raw Pear shee ate, and now and then an Apple, and some Hard Cider shee drank, things that would rather sett an Edge upon the Severity of her Fast: Sometimes also a Chestnut might go down into her Craving Stomach and sometimes a little Cold Water. If anything else were offered her, her Teeth would bee sett, and Shee thrown into hideous

---

[1] Salad-oil, olive oil.

[2] Weyer (and after him many other opponents of witch persecution) had maintained that *venefica*, the name for witch in the Latin Bible, meant only "a poisoner."

Torments: and it must bee usually for two or three Dayes together, that such poor Things as These also must bee deny'd her. Breefly, Shee scarce took any jot of Sustenance, but what wee suppos'd would rather increase the Tortures and Mischiefs of her Fast. How shee was all this while supported I pretend not now to guess. But the famous Henricus ab Heer,[1] in his Observacions, affirms upon Oath, That a Bewitched Girl, residing in his House, kept just such another Fast; and That for Fifteen Dayes and Nights together shee took neither Meat nor Drink. And yett, this Fast was not so long as that mentioned by Dr Plott,[2] in his Natural History of Oxford-shire; who affirms, That in the Year 1671, one Rebecka Smith, who was thought Bewitched, continued without Eating or Drinking for Ten Weeks together; and afterwards lived only upon warm Broaths taken in Small Quantities for a whole Twelvemonth. It seems that Long Fasting is not only Tolerable, but strangely Agreeable to such as have something more than Ordinary to do with the Invisible World.

§ 12. But Burning seem'd the cruellest of all her Tortures. They would Flash upon her the Flames of a Fire, that was to Us indeed (tho not unto her) Invisible; but unto us all, in the Mischiefs and Effects of it, the most sensible Thing that could bee. The Agonies of One Roasting a Faggot at the Stake were not more Exquisite, than what Shee underwent, in the Scalds which those Hell-hounds gave unto her, sometimes for near a Quarter of an Hour together. Wee saw not the Flames, but Once the Room smelt of Brimstone, and at other, yea, at many Times, wee saw her made Excessively Sore by these Flames, and wee saw Blisters thereby Raised upon her. To cure the Soreness which this Fiery Trial would give unto her, wee were forced sometimes to apply the Oyle commonly used for the cure of Scalds, and yett (Like other Witch-wounds) in a Day or Two all would bee well again: Only the marks of some Wounds thus given her, shee will probably carry to her Grave. I may add, That once They thrust an hot Iron down her

---

[1] Henricus ab Heer (Hendrik van Heer), c. 1570–c. 1636, many years private physician of the prince-archbishops of Cologne.

[2] Robert Plot (1640–1696), a Kentish antiquary, published in 1676 his *Natural History of Oxfordshire*. It won him a place in the Royal Society, of which in 1682 he became secretary.

Throat; which tho' it were to us Invisible, yett wee saw the
Skin fetch'd off her Tongue and Lips.

§ 13. Reader, If thou hadst a Desire to have seen a Picture
of Hell, it was visible in the doleful Circumstances of Mercy
Short! Here was one lying in Outer Darkness, haunted with
the Divel and his Angels, deprived of all common Comforts,
tortured with most cruciating Fires, Wounded with a thousand
Pains all over, and cured immediately, that the Pains of those
Wounds might bee repeated. It was of old said, If One went
unto them from the Dead, they will Repent. As for us, wee
have had not only the Damned coming to us from the Dead,
in this Witchcraft, but the very State of the Damned itself
represented most visibly before our eyes: Hard-hearted Wee,
if wee do not Repent of the Things which may expose us to an
Eternal Durance in such a State!

§ 14. Her Discourses to *Them* were some of the most Surprising Things imaginable, and incredibly beyond what might
have been expected, from one of her small Education or Experience. In the Times of her Tortures, Little came from her,
besides direful Shrieks, which were indeed so frightful, as to
make many people Quitt the Room. Only now and then any
Expression of marvellous Constancy would bee heard from her;
e. g. "Tho' you kill mee, I'l never do what you would have mee.
—Do what you will, yett with the Help of Christ, I'l never
touch your Book.—Do, Burn mee then, if you will; Better
Burn here, then [than] Burn in Hell." But when her Torturer
went off, Then t'was that her senses being still detained in a
Captivity to Spectres, as the only object of them, Wee were
Ear-witnesses to Disputacions that amazed us. Indeed Wee
could not hear what They said unto her; nor could shee herself hear them ordinarily without causing them to say over
again: But Wee could Hear Her Answers, and from her
Answers Wee could usually gather the Tenour of Their Assaults. One very Frequent Theam with Them was Railing
and Slander against a certain Person in the Town,[1] Whom
shee often quoted in her Arguments against the Divel, and at
Whom, shee thought, the Divel had a very particular Provoca-

[1] This "certain person," like the "one man" of the following sentence,
was of course Mather himself: it must be remembered that this account was
meant to seem anonymous.

tion and Malignity. Yea, There was One Man Who on a certain Sabbath had solemnly prayed for her (I think hee said) no less than Ten Times. Four of which Times, were with her too, and yett wee perceived the Divel at Night Reviling that man unto her, with telling her, That hee had not in the Day past pray'd for her so much as Once! But the cheef Argument held between Her and Them, was upon the Business of Signing the *Book*, by Them tendred unto Her.—In the Handling of this Argument, innumerable Things were uttered by her which would have been more Agreeable to[1] One of a greater Elevation in Christianity; but omitting multitudes of such passages, I shall record a few, which were to This Purpose.

Oh You horrid Wretch! You make my very Heart cold within mee. It is an Hell to mee, to hear You speak so! What? Are You *God?* No, bee gone, You Divel! Don't pester mee any more with such horrid Blasphemies!

You! Do You say that You are *Christ!* No, You are a Divel, and I hope that Christ will shortly deliver mee from such a Divel.— The Christ of God came to seek and to save that which is Lost, such as I am; but as for You, You come to seek and confound all that you can light upon.

If You are *Christ,* Pray how came you by that Cloven Foot?— If You are a Christ I am sure you are a very odious One; You shall bee no Christ for mee.—Pray, go about Your Business; if You are Christ, yett I tell you plainly, You shall bee none of my Christ. I know of a Better Christ; and Him will I follow.—You, a Christ! No, You are a Beast. If You had not been a Beast, would You have asked of our Lord that Hee would give You leave to enter into an Herd of Swine!—I think truly, That Hogs are the fittest company for You!—Would You know my mind? Why then, I say this:— When You have become a Man, and have suffered a cruel Death on a Cross for me; and when you have Reconciled me to God, and been some Ages in Heaven powerfully Interceding for my Salvation from the Divel,—Then come to mee again, and I shall have something further to say to You.—In the meantime I say to You, In the Name of the Lord Jesus Christ, the Son of God, Beegone!

You pretend a precious deal of Love to mee indeed! If You Love mee so much, pray, why do you Starve mee? I am een famished; It is Nine Dayes now, that I have not eaten one bitt of Victuals.

---

[1] More suitable for.

Fine Promises! You'l bestow an Husband upon mee, if I'l bee your Servant. An Husband! What? A Divel! I shall then bee finely fitted with an Husband: No I hope the Blessed Lord Jesus Christ will marry my Soul to Himself yett before Hee has done with mee, as poor a Wretch as I am!—Fine Clothes! What? Such as Your Friend Sarah Good[1] had, who hardly had Rags to cover her! Pray why did you not provide better for Her Then?—Never Dy! What? Is my Life in Your Hands? No, if it had, You had killed mee long before this Time!—Whats that?—So You can!—Do it then, if You can. Come, I dare You; here, I challenge You to do it. Kill mee if You can.—Poor Fool!—But hark Yee! If you can keep your Servants alive, the more false Wretch you, to lett the Halter choke the Witches that were hanged the t'other Day! tho' You promised them, that when the Halters were about their Necks, You would come and Rescue them!

You talk of carrying mee to Heaven! It makes mee think of Goody Carrier;[2] pray whither did you carry her?—Heaven! What a foolish Question is that? Was I ever there? No, I never was there; but I hope I shall be there; and I believe what I have heard and read in the Word of God concerning it. I confess, You were once in Heaven; but God for Your Pride, hurled you thence; and You shall never come there again.—They that follow You, will mistake the Way to Heaven, I'l promise 'em. Hee that has the Divel for his Leader must bee content with Hell for his Lodging.—Hell! Yee Lying Wretch, I have catch'd you in an hundred Lyes; Who would beleeve one Word You say? Yesterday or t'otherday, You told mee there was no Hell; and now You tell mee, that One may come out of Hell when they will. Pray then, Lett Sarah Good come; if I could see her, I am confident shee would tell mee that Hell is a terrible place; and I know there is no coming out.—But if all the Wood in this World were laid in One Fire, it would not bee so dreadful as Hell; that Hell, whither You carry all that follow You. They are out of there Wits that will serve such a Divel.

Well if You do Burn mee, I had better Burn for an Hour or Two here then in Hell forever.—What? Will you Burn all Boston and shall I bee Burnt in that Fire?—No, tis not in Your Power. I hope God won't lett you do that. (*Memorandum,* The Night after these Words were spoken, the Town had like to have been burn't; but God wonderfully prevented it.) What?—Germany?—Was that Place in Germany as big as Boston?—Well, I hope that in spite of You, Boston shall stand until the Great Burning of all; and I pray what will come of You Then!—Safe enough!—How, Safe enough?—

[1] See pp. 343 ff., 414.   [2] See pp. 241 ff.

Among the Jews!—Why, what will you do among Them? They'l
have none such as You among them, I warrant yee!

Stay, One at once!—Well, And is that all that You have to say?
—Pray then, Hear what I have to say.—I say this, That when You,
yee filthy Witches, first gave yourselves to your Black Master there,
it was the worst Dayes work that ever You did in Your Lives. And
I seriously advise you all, to Repent of what You have done. I hope
tis not altogether Too late, at least for some of you, to Repent.—
Tho' you have done mee so much Wrong, yett I heartily wish you so
much Good, as Repentance and Conversion.—O that you would fall
down before the God against Whom you have sinned, and beg of
Him, that for the sake of Jesus Christ, Hee would pardon your horrible sin.—If You won't take this Counsil, I think, twil bee no Hurt
to wish that God would bring you out, and that you may Dy for what
you have done and that the World may be no longer troubled with you.

Whats that? Must the Younger Women, do yee say, hearken to
the Elder?—They must bee another Sort of Elder Women than You
then! they must not bee Elder Witches, I am sure. Pray, do you
for once Hearken to mee.—What a dreadful Sight are You! An
Old Woman, an Old Servant of the Divel! You, that should instruct
such poor, young, Foolish Creatures as I am, to serve the Lord Jesus
Christ, come and urge mee to serve the Divel! Tis an horrible Thing!
—And pray, how durst You, after You had given yourself to the Divel,
come to the Table of the Lord: I profess I wonder the Divel did not
come and fetch you away alive!—But God is a long-suffering God!

Well; and what if I am Fatherless? How often have you told
mee of That? No, I been't Fatherless. I have God for my Father
and I don't Question but Hee'l provide well for me. Has not Hee
upheld mee all the while? I had signed your Book before now, if
God had not kept mee with His Grace. You had before now made
an end of mee, if God had not stood by mee. And I beleeve that
God will yett deliver mee out of your Cruel Hands.

You are Wicked Wretches. What do you show mee the Shape
of that good Woman for? I know her. Shee's a good Woman.
Shee never did mee any Hurt. Yett you would fain have mee cry
out of her. But I will bee so far from crying out of Her that I will
not cry out of You; I don't know what Tricks you have gott; but
I hope God will keep mee from letting fall one word that may blast
the Name of any Person in the World. I will never tell any body,
who you are that have Tormented mee, only it may bee I may tell
One Gentleman[1] who will be as careful, that no Harm should come
on't, as I can desire him.—How ever I hope God will find you out.

---

[1] The "one Gentleman" hinted at is of course to be understood as Mather.

Truly I am in a very miserable Condicion. Tis a sad Thing to ly starving in the Dark one Day after another, and to see none but Hellish Fiends all the While, and suffer all manner of cruelties from them.—You tell me, that some do but Laugh at mee; I am sure, they would do better to Pray for mee.—You say, that such and such are in the Room; Why won't you lett mee see them then?

Well, I am perswaded, that yett for all this I shall bee gloriously delivered, and God will have a great deal of Glory. Had I not belonged unto God, I can't think that you would have made such a Deal of aDo to gett mee into your Hands. And if God had not a purpose to make mee one of His own Servants, I can't but think Hee would have left mee before now to become one of Yours.—What a blessed thing will this bee! I can't butt think that You are very shortly to loose mee, both Body and Soul too, and that what You have been doing to my Body, will but help forward the Everlasting Salvacion of my Soul. It makes my Heart Rejoice, to think how finely You'l bee cheated!

Memorandum. T'was an ordinary thing for the Divel to persecute her with Stories of what this and that Body in the Town spoke against her. The Unjust and Absurd Reflections cast upon her by Rash People in the coffee-houses or elsewhere, Wee discerned that the Divel Reported such Passages unto her in her Fitts, to discourage her. But shee bore those Trials as well as the rest.

§ 15. But when shee had so much Release from the captivating Impressions of the Wretches that haunted her, as to bee able to see and hear the Good People about her in the Room, Shee underwent another sort of plague, which I don't Remember that ever I observed in more than One or Two Bewitched person[s] besides her. Her Tortures were turned into Frolicks; and Shee became as extravagant as a Wild-cat. Shee now had her Imaginacion so strangely disordered, that shee must not Acknowledge any of her Friends; but tho' shee Retained a Secret Notion, Who wee were, yett shee might by no means confess it. Shee would sometimes have diverse of these Fitts in a Day, and shee was always excessively Witty in them; never downright Profane, but yett sufficiently Insolent and Abusive to such as were about her. And in these Fitts also shee took an extraordinary Liberty (which I have likewise noted in some other possessed Persons) to animadvert upon all

People, that had any thing in their Apparrel that savoured
of Curiosity or Ornament. Her Apprehension, Understanding,
and Memory, were now Riper than ever in her Life; and yett,
when shee was herself, Shee could Remember the other Accidents of her Afflictions but Forgot almost everything that
passed in these Ludicrous Intervals.

§ 16. There was this Remarkable in these Frolicks, that altho' shee could Hear and Make all manner of other Discourse,
yett shee might bee partaker of None that had anything of
Religeon in it: Her Ear would immediately bee stop'd, if
wee spoke any good Thing, and her Mouth, if shee went to
speak any such Thing. Nevertheless, the charms upon her
were so circumstanced, that wee were able by little Tricks and
Signs to make her sensible of many Devout Things, after which
her Cravings were so greedy that shee would sometimes cry
for vexation (as Frolicksome as shee was) if shee missed of
presently comprehending us. If any Prayers or Psalms were
used in the Room, shee could not Hear a Word; and yett could
hear the least Whisper of any thing else that passed, even in
that very Instant. Shee would importunately require us to
Pray; yett shee might not utter that Word but say "Do—
You know what"; or, "Do, what You use to do." And when
wee had any thing to say unto her about Prayer, wee could
make her hear tho' not the Word itself (much less the Thing)
yett the Letters of the Word seve[rally] mentioned. The Spel
upon her was not such but that a good Word might bee Spelt,
when it could not bee Spoke unto her. I give One Specimen
of the way wee took to convey unto her mind, those Religious
Notions, whereto shee had a manifested Inclination. Shee
cry'd unto a Minister,[1] that hee would tell her what shee should
say to *Them*, When They should again assault her. Hee thereupon advised her, "Mercy, tell 'em, That the Lord Jesus Christ
has broke the Old Serpents Head." And the communication
that follow'd, was after this fashion.

Mer. What do you say?
Min. I say, Tell 'em, That the Lord Jesus Christ has broken
the Old Serpents Head.—Can you hear?
Mer. No. I can't hear a Word.

---

[1] Mather of course again means himself.

Min. Well, then; mind mee and you shall Know what you can't Hear.—A Snake.—Mercy, can you hear?

Mer. Yes.

Min. Well,—An Old Snake.—can you hear?

Mer. Yes,—well, what of an old snake?

Min. (Striking with his Finger on his Forhead) Why, His Head broke.—D'ye Hear?

Mer. Yes; and what then?

Min. (Pointing up to Heaven.) Why, Who broke it? D'yee mind?

Mer. Oh! I understand.—Well, what else shall I tell them?

After this rate, a Minister in two or three Minutes once made her apprehend about Seven or Eight Things Wherewith shee might [maintain] herself against the Spectres. And when They came next upon her, shee had all of them up unto her Troublers with a Readiness and Exactness beyond what the minister supposed hee could himself have had if hee had been putt upon Repeating them. I mention This with the more of particularity, because it affords a Matter of Curious Reflection.

Moreover, While shee was in these Frolicks, it seems that shee was able still to see what Spectres were hovering about her chamber, and how They were employed. Shee shook for fear, when shee saw them once preparing an Image in the Room; wherefrom shee foretold, That the Image being formed in order to her Torment, Shee should have a Terrible Evening on't. And so shee had! But shee afterwards told one in whose custody that Image might bee found. At an other time, Shee fell a Laughing at One in the Room,[1] and asked him, Whether hee had not a Gold Ring about him? Hee knew hee had, and look'd for it in the pocket where hee knew it was, but it was missing; and Shee, laughing, told him, That a Spectre had newly taken it out; but, said shee, "Look in such a Place and you shall find it." Accordingly, hee Look'd and Found. Shee added, "They said, that if hee putt it on, They would have it off his Finger again before hee gott home." Hee, to spite Them, Try'd; but tho' hee diverse times between That and Home, thought his Finger taken with an odd Numbness, yett hee kept it on.

[1] Unquestionably himself again.

§ 17. As for the Spectres that Visited and Afflicted Mercy Short, there were among them such as wore the shape of several, who are doubtless Innocent as to the Crime of Witchcraft; it would bee a great Iniquity in Mee, to judge them otherwise; and the World, I hope, shall neither by My means, nor by Hers, ever know, who they were. But there is Cause to fear that some few of the persons thus Represented, are as Dangerous and as Damnable Witches as ever were in the World; altho These also must bee covered until there bee more Cause for their being made obnoxious. However, tis a very dark Dispensacion of Divine Providence, and such as carries much Humilliation in it, that an Innocent Person should bee, tho' but in Effigie, Randevouz'd among these Fiends of Darkness. And concerning these Diabolical Spectres, wee mark'd sundry other Things that were beyond measure Odd. One was This: The Honest man, who had given entertainment unto this distressed Mercy, observing that when shee lay, as to us wholly senseless, the motion of her Eyes did intimate whereabouts the Spectres cheefly play'd, hee silently fetch'd a Sword, with a purpose to make a pass at them. Nevertheless, if hee did but go at any time to take the Sword into his hand, tho' shee could not possibly discern any thing of it, yett her Eyes would presently bee shutt, and her Head pull'd into Bed, so that hee must loose the Direction which her Looke had given him. I cannot say that This Oddity would bear an Inference that the Witches were any of them Corporeally tho' Invisibly present in the Chamber. But there was Another, that would make one suspect they might. On the twenty-fifth of December it was,[1] that Mercy said, They were going to have a Dance; and immediately those that were attending her, most plainly Heard and Felt a Dance, as of Barefooted People, upon the Floor; whereof they are willing to make oath before any Lawful Authority. If I should now venture to suppose, That the Witches do sometimes come in person to do their Mischiefs, and yett have the horrible skill of cloathing themselves with Invisibilities, it would seem Romantic. And yett I am inclinable to think it, upon Reasons more than tis here a Place to mention. But in my Opinion, Tis not more Incredible, or Inscrutable, than what

---

[1] Modern readers may need to be reminded of the Puritan horror of the celebration of Christmas, and even of the use of its name.

I am going to Relate; namely, That altho' wee have all the
Demonstration a Reasonable man can desire, that Mercy Short
could not in the least measure Hear, when wee were perhaps
Half an Hundred of us together singing of a Psalm in the
Room; nevertheless, at that very Time, shee could Hear a
little Knock of a little Child at the Door.   I say, the Philosophy that can give an Account for the One of these may do
it for t'other too!

§ 18.   There were some strange things attending of Mercy
Short, whereof some were at some Loss about the Original,
whence they should proceed.   It was marvellous to Hear how
much her Answers to the Spectres transcended her ordinary
capacity.   That shee should so patiently and resolutely undergo
her Intolerable Torments, when one Stroke of her Finger
would have eased them all, is yet more marvellous.   But that
which carries most of marvel in it, is, The Impulse which
directed her unto the Scriptures that might have assisted or
quickened us in our Devotions, If wee had seen Cause to have
made that Use of them.   In her Trances, a Bible Happening
to ly on her Bed, shee has taken it up, and without ever casting her Eye upon it, shee has Turned over many Leaves, at
last folding down a Leaf to a Text, I holding up the Text unto
the Spectres; but of all the Texts in the Bible, which do you
think it was?   T'was That, in Rev. 12. 12, *The Divel is come
down unto you, having great Wrath, because hee knows hee hath
but a short Time.*   Again, in her Humours, calling for a Psalm-
book, shee has, in the Dark, turned over many Leaves, and at
length, without Reading a Syllable, shee has turn'd down a
Leaf to a Psalm, advising us to go sing it, on her behalf.   I do
affirm That no man living ever could have singled out Psalms
more expressive of, and suitable to, her circumstances, than
those that shee pitch'd upon.   One of them, I remember, was
the Beginning of the Hundred and second.   And when One
present said, "No, Lett us not sing that psalm: it may bee
tis They direct it; and it won't bee good for us to follow Their
Direction"; She reply'd with Indignacion, "They, Fool! No,
Tis not They direct mee; Do you think They would go to
to direct a fitt psalm for my Condicion?   No, My Direction
comes from another Quarter; If you would know Whence, the
first letter of the Name is G"— (it seems, that shee could not

speak out the Word.) When shee came to herself, shee told mee, her manner was to Turn the Leaves, till t'was Darted into her Mind that shee had the Place; and there shee folded. Moreover, shee did sometimes with much vehemency exclaim, That there were (three perhaps, or six) persons in the Room, that never pray'd so much as once in all their Lives: and shee was importunate that a Minister then in the Room[1] would go drive those Prayerless Wretches out of the Room. The Minister chid her, and said, If there were any such, hee knew not how to distinguish them, and hee would not ask her to do it for him. "Well, its no matter," said shee, "take but a Candle then and look in their Faces, and you'l know by their Blushing who they are; Turn them out that Blush." But all that the Minister did, was to warn the Company, That if any of them had the guilt of a Prayerless Life upon their Consciences, they must Repent of it, or know who was well acquainted with it. Nevertheless there was cause given to fear too much of Truth in the Accusacion.

§ 19. The Methods that were taken for the Deliverance of Mr. Goodwins afflicted Family, four years ago,[2] were the very same that wee now follow'd for Mercy Short; and Shee would herself most affectionately express her own Desires, that none but Such might bee taken. Had wee not studiously suppressed all Clamours and Rumours that might have touched the Reputacion of people exhibited in this Witchcraft, there might have ensued most uncomfortable Uproars. But Prayer with Fasting wee knew to bee a course against which none but men most bruitishly Atheistical (and yett such there are among us) could make Exceptions. Wherefore a number of Pious People did ordinarily every Day go in and Pray with her; and whereas many of our People had some singularly grounded perswasions, that no Exercise of Religion did give so much Vexacion unto the Spectres in the Haunted Chamber, as the Singing of Psalms, they commonly sang between almost every Prayer. But they judg'd it necessary to Fast as well as Pray: and as I have had opportunity to see, in some former Dispossessions, the People of God usually speed not, until they do what may bee called A Beseech[ing of] the Lord Thrice; Thus the Christians here were putt upon spending Three Dayes in Fasting and Prayer

---

[1] Again himself, of course.   [2] For that story see pp. 99 ff., above.

one quickly after another: And indeed, it was the special Grace of God, that carried the Faith of His poor Servants thro' the Difficulty of beholding the Rage of the Divel to grow under and against all their Prayer for the conquering of that Rage.

Some of us had fearful Suggestions of Unbeleef now and then buzz'd into our Minds; and (which was a little suprizing!) the Divel in the Next Fitts would sometimes tell Mercy Short what they were. It was also remarkable that when wee were intending a Day of Prayer, the Spectres would ussually advise her of our Intention, and brag that They would hinder the People from coming: According to which Brag of Theirs, t'was wonderful to see how many Pious Christians that were desirous to have been with us were hindered of their Desires, by unexpected occasions pressing in upon them. However, Many of the Children of God in the Neighbourhood were helped by Him to an extraordinary exercise of Grace, and while some in the Town who by their profession were under obligacion to better things, kept Scoffing, Railing, Raving, These kept Praying, Fasting and Beleeving. Until at Length, Meat came out of the Eater!—As her Deliverance drew near, it was with her as I have seen in one more Possessed Person. A strange Fancy of Dying Possessed her, and her Discourse ran much upon her Funeral. Wee then quickly saw the Death and Burial of the Trouble now upon her.

§ 20. It was not long after the Third Fast, that on the evening before the Sabbath, which began this New-Year, 1693, Mercy Short fell into a Fitt of Despair wherein her Anguishes exceeded any that had bin yett upon her. The Spectres kept continually howling in her Ears, That God had utterly cast her off, and that shee was to bee Damned after all. But that which made all the misery was, that in this point they so gain'd upon her, as they had never done before; that is, they made her almost conclude that what they said of this matter, had something of Truth in it. And the dolours now Raised in her were inexpressible! Shee Shriek'd, shee Roar'd, shee Cry'd out, "This is worse than all the Rest! What? must I bee Banished from the Favour of God after all?" Yea, shee imagined that the Spectres were indeed fetching of her away! In this Agony, shee call'd for a Minister in the Neighbourhood; upon whose coming in, shee quickly called for her Clothes, dressed herself, and came to him, with a Countenance marvellously altered into a Look of Discretion and Gravity; and shee said, "Now, Go, and Give to the Great God, the greatest Thanks you can devise; for I am gloriously delivered! My Troubles are gone, and I hope they'l visit mee no more." It seems *They* left her, just before, in very Raging Terms, and said, They had no further Power over her. Shee has ever since continued free from her Invisible Troublers; only they left her extremely Faint and Weak. But the Neighbourhood then returned solemn Thanks to that Faithful God, who thus gave them to *Tread upon the Lion, and to Trample the Dragon underfoot.*

§ 21. Mercy Short having obtained this Deliverance, did for a Sabbath of Weeks Enjoy What shee had obtained; yett not without frequent Fainting and Swooning Fits, that seem'd the Effect of the weakness wherein the Torments of her former Enchantment left her. But at the End of Seven Weeks, her Invisible Tormentors again siezed her on a Lords Day, in the midst of the Assembly then meeting at North Boston, for the Worship of God; just before which unhappy siezure shee thought shee felt the Threatnings of it, in unaccountable Disorders, and in a scent of Brimstone haunting of her Lodgings. The Spectres now under the Conduct of their Black Leader, handled the poor Young Woman for the most part just as they did in the former Visitation; but rather with more Vigour and Fury, and such as wee judged could not but putt a Speedy End unto her Life.

§ 22. The Impudence of the Troublesome Spectres was now somewhat more Daring and Broad-faced than formerly. It grew common with them to snatch from her such Apples and Biskets, as were given her to Try whether shee could eat them; so that no more could ever bee seen of them. And Mercy Short affirm'd, That shee saw the Spectres (tho' wee could not,) eating them in the Room, what wee perceived they had stolen from her. And whether it were from the Mistake or from the Malice of the Spectres, it was no Rare Thing for the Standers-by to have their Arms cruelly scratch'd, and Pins thrust into their Flesh, by these Fiends, while they were molesting of Mercy Short. Yea, several Persons did sometimes actually lay their Hands upon these Fiends; the Wretches

were Palpable, while yett they were not Visible, and several of
our People, tho' they Saw nothing, yett Felt a Substance that
seem'd like a Cat, or Dog, and tho' they were not Fanciful,
they Dy'd away at the Fright! This Thing was too Sensible
and Repeated a Thing, to bee pure Imaginacion. I suspected,
That one Thing which more heightened the Boldness of the
Spectres, was the Freedom used by some of our Folks in striking
with swords, at the parts of the Room where they conjectured
Them to bee Hovering. It was particularly remarkable, That
some who were very Busy in this method of treating the Spectres, upon a presumption that they might bee corporally present, (tho' covered with such a Cloud of Invisibilitie as Virgil,
I remember, gave once unto his Eneas), were terribly scared
with Apparitions in their journeyes home, whereof, tho' they
made no manner of Report, yett Mercy Short was presently
after able to tell her Attendents; as having heard the Spectres
brag unto her, and unto one another, how They had paid such
and such for striking at them. They were another sort of
Weapons, unto which therefore I advised my Neighber; even
the Ancient Arms of the Church.

§ 23. In the new Assault, They did not make the poor Damsels Fast extend much above a Week; tho' about so long They
did. After That, shee gott Liberty once in Two or Three Days,
or so, to swallow a Mouthful or Two of some Refreshment.
Her other Fits were such as formerly attended her; but in her
Frolicks, I found the Charms upon her so feeble that altho' shee
might not Hear a Word of Religion, (after the hearing whereof
her Longings were nevertheless very passionate), yett there
was No Word, but what wee could make her Hear, by spelling
it unto her. Even those words, *God, Christ, Lord, Jesus, Soul,
Sin, Heaven, Hell, Angels, Divels, Witches*, which They would
never permitt her to Hear in any kind of Discourse what ever,
yett wee could make her Hear by Spelling of them. Moreover One of her Neighber[s] using a little Ingenuity, related
a great part of the Histories in the Bible unto her, while shee
was in these Humors, and helped her to apply them unto her
own comfortable Direction and Encouragement; but hee was
forced still to disguise these Histories with a Sort of Air that
could not so well have been given them, upon any other Occasion.

§ 24. The Thing still prest upon her, was to Sign, or to Touch Their *Book*; and about that Book, wee now had several Odd Entertainments, beyond what we had before. Shee said They have had Three Books, whereof the Third was newly begun; and This was the Book which they now offered her in her Temptacions; tho' they sometimes also show'd her the Second, which it seems wanted but a Leaf or two, to bee fill'd in her former Visitacion. While shee lay in her Extatic Circumstances, Two or Three of us diverse Times Heard her to Read in one or t'other of these Books, upon her demanding of it, as proper for her to See the Books, before they could imagine it Reasonable for her to sett her hand unto any of them. What she read, I do for some just causes, forbear fully to relate; but, in general, the Book seem'd a Journal of the cheef things acted or design'd at Their great Witch-meetings; not without some circumstances that carried an odd Resemblence of the Alcoran; it had in it the Methods to bee used in seducing of people unto the service of the Divel, and the Names of them that had been seduced, with the Terms which they were to serve. It particularly surprised some in the Room, on the Eve of March 9, 1693, to overhear her, in the Book then opened unto her, spelling a Word that was too hard for her; but from the best Judgment that could bee made of the Letters that shee recited, it was Quadragesima. And several more such odd Things were overheard: whereof One was a Discourse to bee used by Witchmakers unto their Proselytes, of this purport, That when Paul and Silas were in prison, they sang; but it was unto the Divel that they sang; an Earthquake then came, and the Prison-doors were opened. But it was the Divel that made that Earthquake and opened those prison-doors. Accordingly, if the Servants of the Divel should come at any time to bee clap'd up in Goal they might Expect a like Deliverance. Horrible stuff! But I'l tell no more. Shee one Day sent a Request unto His Excellency, the Governer,[1] and unto a Minister in the Neighbourhood,[2] that shee might Receive a Visit from them; in which Visit, shee inform'd them, That the Spectres had newly confessed unto her, that they had been compelled, a Day or two before, to Drop Their Second Book, in the Cockloft of a Garret belonging to the House of a person

----

[1] Sir William Phips.   [2] Mather, of course.

of Quality, not far off. But Their Difficulty to Beleave, that
there was any Corporeal (or any more than a Mystical) Book
in the Business, caused them to bee Negligent in the Search
of it; however, They did after some Dayes, upon mature consideration, permitt a Discreet Servant privately to go see
whether there were any Thing in that place or no. When the
Servant was Examining the place directed, a great Black Cat,
never before known to bee in the House, jumping over him,
threw him into such a Fright and Sweat, that altho' hee were
one otherwise of Courage enough, hee desisted at that Time
from looking any further. Mercy Short presently after sent
for the Minister, and expressed an extreme Discontent and
Vexation for his minding so little, what Informacion shee had
given about the Book; adding (tho' her Attendents affirm'd
shee had never been told a Word of What had happened)
That the Spectres had pray'd and beg'd of their Black-man so
hard, that their Book might not yett come to light, hee had
at length permitted one of them, to putt on the Shape of a
Cat and fetch the Book away; which was done (shee said)
just as the Servant had almost laid his hand upon it; but that
hee had been so scared by the Cat as to give over the Search.
However shee beleeved They must shortly Drop it again.
For my own part, I look'd upon these Things as having much
of Diabolical Delusion in them; and as intended partly to
make Diversion for Divels that love to play upon mankind.
Whether the Cat were what was pretended, I shall give no
Opinion: tho' I know the Assertion of some, That every Spirit
is endued with an Innate Power by which it can attract suitable matter out of all Things for a Covering or Body, of a
proportionable Form and Nature to itself: which Assertion,
Well stated, Proved, and Applyed, would solve some of the
hardest Phenomena that belong to the uncouth and horrid
Shapes, wherein mischiefs are done by Witchcraft.

§ 25. But there were some strange Occurrence about another
Book, which, whether there lay any thing in the bottom of
them, further than a Trick of the Divels, to decoy us into some
Inconveniences, wee could not Conclude, but thought it not
amiss to Beware. One who was Executed at Salem for Witchcraft had confessed That at their Cheef Witch-meetings, there
had been present some French canadians, and some Indian

Sagamores, to concert the methods of ruining New England. Now tho' Mercy Short had never heard, as far as I have learn't, of any such Confession, yett the Spectres now, as it were clapping a Chain upon her, would leave her sometimes in a Stupid, Sottish, Senseless Condicion, for many Hours together: out of which Condition when shee came, shee told us, That at such Times the Spectres went away to Their Witch-meetings; but that when They Returned, the whole Crew, besides her daily Troublers, look'd in upon her, to see how the work was carried on; That there were French Canadiens and Indian Sagamores among them, diverse of whom shee knew, and particularly Nam'd em: And, that They show'd her a Book, out of which, they said, they took their Directions for the Devotions perform'd at their Meetings; and they added, That they did use to fetch that Book from the Study of a certain Person in the Neighbourhood;[1] Yea, that •they had, unbeknown to him, gott the Book away to their conventions more than an hundred times; moreover to confirm her in the Beleef of what They said, they folded a Leaf of it, before her eyes. These Things did shee tell us, and shee described unto us the Colour, the Breadth, and Length, and Thickness, and other Circumstances of the Book, with all the Exactness Imaginable: saying also, That there were Psalms in it. Accordingly the person mentioned, tho' Hee were owner of a Library furnished with Books of all sorts, yett quickly found in it, the Book with which these Theevish Divels had made so bold; and Mercy, having it shown unto her, immediately knew it from any other. It was a Book that indeed came from Canada; a French Book of Idolatrous Devotions, entituled, *Les Saints Devoirs de L'Ame Devote. Avec L'Office de La Vierge, pour tous Les Temps De L'Année: Et L'Office Des Morts, de La Croix, et Autres; reformez au Saint Concile de Trente.*[2] But that which added unto the surprise was, That hee found a Leaf doubled down in the Book, which hee could not conceive how it should come: and when a Night or Two after, just as hee went unto his Rest, hee left this Book on his Table in his Study, carefully

---

[1] Mather's own.

[2] An ordinary book of Catholic devotion: "The Holy Duties of the Devout Soul. With the Devotions due the Virgin throughout the Year: and the Office of the Dead, of the Cross, and others; reformed at the Holy Council of Trent."

seeing that there should not bee one Leaf at all folded in it; yett the next morning hee found Three Leaves unaccountably Folded, and then Visiting Mercy, hee perceived the Spectres bragging, That tho' shee had [said] shee would warrant them, that Gentleman would keep his Book out of their Hands, yett they had Last Night stole the Book again unto one of their meetings, and folded sundry Leaves in it.   They also told her afterwards, That the said person had another Book standing by this, with a Gray Cover, a Little Bigger than This, but much akin to it, and having many pictures in it; which Book they sometimes Likewise used at their meetings; and that they had newly used it, but returning it they had sett it up the Backside outwards.   Now to increase our surprize, tho' what they said about using the Book abroad might bee all a Ly, yett all the rest was very True, The Title of the Book was *L'Office de La Semaine Sainte, et de L'Octave de Pasque, à L'usage de Rome, et du Diocese de Paris.*[1]   These Things very Naturally Raised in mee, a Contemplacion of the proper *Enchantments* whereby *Popery* was at first Begun, and has been Maintain'd; and of the Confusion with which the Divels may probably bee cast, from an Apprehension of the Total Dissolution that is quickly to bee given unto all the Charms, which have hitherto Intoxicated the Nations in that Superstition.   But if I should so far forget myself, as to Lay before my Readers, the several Reflections which I found myself invited still to make on these Occasions, I should perform a Work, which for a thousand Reasons I choose rather to Reserve.

§ 26.   Whether I ask my Readers to do it, or no, I know they will variously spend their Judgments upon one of the strangest Things that has occured in our Story, now to bee Related.   Mercy Short was attended with another Spirit, besides those which were her continual Tormentors; a Spirit, which indeed never was Visible nor, I think, properly Audible, any further than in Whisper, unto her; but which managed his Communion with her cheefly by an Impulse, most powerfully and sensibly making Impressions upon her Mind.   This Wonderful Spirit would suggest unto her, How to Answer the Temptacions of the Diabolical Spectres, and comfort her with Assurances that shee should at last bee Victorious over Them.

[1] This too is but a Catholic book of devotion—the offices of Holy Week.

T'was by the Guidance of this Spirit that shee would sometimes take a Bible into her Hands, and without even casting
an Eye so much as once upon it, after Turning over Scores of
Leaves, Turn down a Leaf at last, unto the most pertinent
Place that could bee thought of, and from thence Argue
against the Wretches that molested her.

For Instance, Once when They were urging her to write
her Name in Their Book, shee did in that unaccountable
Manner Turn to Rev. 13. 8. *All that dwell upon Earth shall
worship him, whose Names are not written in the Book of Life of
the Lamb*: and tho' shee saw not the Text herself, yett Folding
down a Leaf unto it, shee held it up unto the Spectres, for Them
to Read it; adding withal, That her Name was already in that
Book of the Lamb, and therefore it should never come into
Their cursed Book!   To which They Reply'd, Shee had shown
them a Scripture which one (they named)[1] had never yett
preached upon: and in That, they spoke True. Another Time
shee did in that marvellous Manner, Folding a Leaf, without
any Looking, show the Spectres that Place in Luc. 7. 21. *And
in that same Hour, Hee cured many of their Infirmities, and
plagues and of Evil Spirits.*   Thus also, After They had been
trying to perswade her, that there would bee no Day of Judgment, shee did in the same astonishing manner show them that
place in Act. 1. 11. *This same Jesus Which is taken up from
you into Heaven, shall so come, in Like Manner, as yee have seen
Him go into Heaven.*   Well, When the young Woman had lain
under her miseries about Three Weeks, this Notable Spirit,
in the Beginning of the Fourth Week, bid her, Bee of Good
Cheer and Hold her Integrity against all the Rage of the Divel
and his Witches, for the Next Thursday in the Evening about
Nine or Ten a clock, shee should bee gloriously delivered,
And accordingly, some Dayes a forehand, shee desired that I
would, with my Brother, bee There at the Time.   I suppose
many of my Readers will bee at as much Loss to Determine,
what sort of Spirit this is, as the New-foundlanders are, what
to think of that spirit by them called White-Hat! who ordinarily appears on the Shore, in a White-hat, crying out, Hale
up!   Hale up! a little before some dangerous Tempest.

§ 27. The people of God in the Neighbourhood still kept

[1] Of course again Mather.

themselves close unto the unexceptionable way of Continual and Importunate *Prayer*, for the Deliverance of the Afflicted Maid. For my part, I did all I could, that not so much· as the Name of any one good person in the World might suffer the least Ill-Report on this occasion; but unwearied Prayer, wee thought, was our only Way now to Resist the Divel. Accordingly, the Pious People in the North-part of Boston, did very much Pray With the young Woman as well as For her. There are, in that vicinage, several meetings of Young Folks (both sexes apart) who every week meet, that they may Pray with one another; and These now Adjourned their meetings, at the Seasons of them, unto the Haunted Chamber. Yea, There was, I think, scarce a Night for near a Month together, which was not All spent in the Exercise of Devotion, by those that Watched. Indeed, in this New Molestacion of Mercy Short, the Good people kept not any Whole Dayes for Prayer with Fasting on her behalf, as they did before, yett I have understood that shee had a Friend or Two, who did so; but behold, the Lord must bee again Besought Thrice! The First and the Second of the Dayes thus kept had not their full Answer; the Third was no sooner kept, but the Answer came; whereof You are now to bee Informed.

§ 28. The Young Woman on the Thursday Evening which had been by her mentioned (namely March 16, 1693) lay very free from her usual Torments. Wee perceived from her, That the Spectres Try'd all the Evening long to inflict their Tortures upon her, but still They found her so Hedged by some unseen Defence, that they were unable to Touch her; and the Black Man would thereupon Kick Them, Cuff Them, and Maul Them, for Their so failing in all Their Attempts to wound her. Whereupon with a sort of Bravery shee Insulted over Them; and at last, when the Hour came, Shee said in a way of Derision, "Well, I see you are going; What good counsil have you to give mee, before you go?" They then spoke, I know not what pestiferous Things unto her; but, giving them an Angry Interruption, Shee bid them Hear Her counsil to Them. So, Telling the Black Man that shee had nothing to say unto him, for his Condition was beyond Repentance and Forgiveness, unto the rest shee gave such savoury Admonitions, about endeavouring their own Recovery out of the Snare of the Divel,

as might have broke an Heart of Stone to have heard Them.
They at last bid her leave off, and now, Take their Blessing;
which it seems was of this Tenour, "Go and bee Damned, Wee
can do no more!" Whereunto Shee Reply'd, "O yee cursed
Wretches; Is that Your Blessing? Well After all the wrong
that you have done to mee, I do not wish that any one of you
may bee Damned; I wish you may bee all saved, if that bee
possible. However, In the Name of the Blessed Lord Jesus
Christ, bee gone, and lett mee bee no more Troubled with
you." Upon That, they flew away Immediately, Striking another young Woman down for Dead upon the Floor as they
went along; and so, with a Raised Soul, shee bore a Part with
us, in Giving Thanks to God for her Deliverance; Nor have
her Troublers ever since troubled her with any further Visits.
Upon her first Rescue from these evil Hands, altho' her Eyes
were seemingly Fair, yett the poisons they had used upon
them were such, that shee was as blind as one that had been
struck with Lightning; but in a few Dayes her sight Returned. They also left her under a very Ill Habit of Body,
whereof shee could not bee cured without some Time and Care;
but in That also shee experienced much of the Divine Goodness. Nor am I without Hope, that God will enable her to
walk answerable to the great obligations, which Hee has thus
laid upon her, by bringing her up out of an Horrible Pitt!

§ 29. My Reader must excuse mee, that I so much Forbear
to give my Opinion about the true Nature and Meaning of
these preternatural occurrences. If God, the Father of Lights,
graciously should grant unto any of His poor Servants (as I
beleeve to some Hee hath!) a System of Consistent Thoughts
about such Works of Darkness, yett such is the froward, flout-
ing sidred,[1] and proud Humour, whereunto the people are
now Enchanted, no man in his Wits would fully expose his
Thoughts unto them, till the charms which enrage the people
are a little better Dissipated. I remember an Odd Relation,
in the German *Ephemerides*, for[2] . . .

---

[1] Cidered, *i. e.*, soured.

[2] Here, with the end of its thirty-eighth page, the manuscript breaks abruptly
off. The "*Ephemerides*" at the close means the *Miscellanea Curiosa*, or *Ephemerides Medico-physicae*, which since 1670 had been published yearly in Germany.
The best postscript for this narrative is that inserted by Mather himself

into his diary for 1693, after the entry for February 12: "About this Time, I had many wonderful Entertainments, from the Invisible World, in the Circumstances of a Young Woman, horribly possessed with Divels. The Damsel was cast into my cares, by the singular Providence of God; and accordingly besides my Cares to releeve her, to advise her, to observe the prodigious things that befel her (whereof I have written a Narrative) I procured some of my devout Neighbours, to join with mee in praying for her. Wee kept Three Successive Dayes of Prayer with Fasting on her behalf, and then wee saw her Delivered; for which, wee kept a Time of solemn Thanksgiving. But after a while, her Tormentors returned, and her Miseries renewed; and my Neighbours being now either too weary or too busy, to do as afore, tho' they made much Prayer daily with her as well as for her, I did alone in my Study fast and pray for her Deliverance. And, unto my Amazement, when I had kept my third Day for her, shee was finally and for-ever delivered from the hands of evil Angels; and I had afterwards the Satis-faction of seeing not only her so brought home unto the Lord, that shee was ad-mitted unto our Church, but also many other, even some scores, of young People, awakened by the Picture of Hell, exhibited in her Sufferings, to flee from the Wrath to come."

It was perhaps more nearly at the time that, to the entry of March 28 recording the birth of his malformed and short-lived babe, he added: "I had great Reason to suspect a Witchcraft, in this præternatural Accident; because my Wife, a few weeks before her Deliverance, was affrighted with an horrible Spectre, in our Porch, which Fright caused her Bowels to turn within her; and the Spectres which, both before and after, tormented a young Woman in our Neighbourhood, brag'd of their giving my Wife that Fright, in hopes, they said, of doing Mischief unto her Infant at least, if not unto the Mother: and besides all this, the Child was no sooner born, but a suspected Woman sent unto my Father, a Letter full of railing against myself, wherein shee told him, Hee little knew, what might quickly befall some of his Posterity."

From this passage it is clear that Mercy Short was not at the end of her besetments; and one should not turn from her story, or from that of Margaret Rule, next to be told, without reading (at p. 384, below) what in 1697 a contem-porary writes of "their vicious courses since."

FROM "MORE WONDERS OF THE INVISIBLE
WORLD," BY ROBERT CALEF, 1700

INTRODUCTION

Of Robert Calef almost nothing is known except what can be learned from his book. There has even been doubt as to whether, of the two Robert Calefs known to us in Boston at this time, the writer was the father or the son. In 1692, the time of the Salem witchcraft, the father's age was 44, the son's 18.[1] It is unlikely that anybody would have thought of the son but for a note copied into one of the memorandum-books of Dr. Jeremy Belknap (1744–1798).[2] This note, of unknown source, reads: "Robert Calef, author of 'More Wonders of the Invisible World,' printed at London in 1700, was a native of England; a young man of good sense, and free from superstition; a merchant in Boston. He was furnished with materials for his work by Mr. Brattle, of Cambridge; and his brother, of Boston; and other gentlemen, who were opposed to the Salem proceedings.—E. P." The writer speaks as if with knowledge; and that so sound a historian as Dr. Belknap should have copied the note speaks for its worth. Able scholars have by it been led to ascribe the book to the younger Robert; but more careful study seems to show the objections insuperable. The author never adds "Jr." to his name, as a son would have done, and as seems to have been the younger Robert's custom.[3] He never pleads youth, even

[1] S. G. Drake, in the introduction to his edition of Calef, would make his age 14; but the genealogist of the family, Mr. Matthew A. Stickney, says 18. Yet Mr. Stickney urges the father's authorship (*N. E. Hist. and Gen. Register*, XXX. 461; XLIX. 224). He died in 1894, leaving this genealogy, alas, unpublished, and his heirs decline to let it be consulted.

[2] Mass. Hist. Soc., *Proceedings*, 1858, p. 288.

[3] Thus in 1706 "Robt. Calef, Jun.," was chosen a clerk of the market (*Boston Record Commissioners' Reports*, VIII. 36); thus in 1708 "Robert Calef,

when most apologetic; and, what weighs more, his indignant
foes, seeking all ways to discredit him, never hint at such a
thing. His matter and style have in them nothing of boyish-
ness; and once, in words suggestive of a migrant and a man
of years, he speaks (p. 297, below) of "sound Reason, which is
what I have been long seeking for in this Country in vain."
Most serious of all, his handwriting seems that found in documents clearly the elder Calef's, and is that of a mature and even
by 1700 that of an aging man; while that of the younger Robert
was in 1719–1722 still firm and flexible—and notably different.[1]

Robert Calef the elder came to America at some time before
1688. He was a cloth-merchant, and doubtless a maker as

jun[r]." becomes a constable (id., VIII. 45), and gains permission to erect a
house (id., XI. 68, XXIX. 187); thus, too, in that year (see plate) he signs
himself "Ro. Calfe Jn[r]"; thus in 1710 "Robert Calfe, Jr.," appears on the
rolls of the Artillery Company (N. E. Hist. and Gen. Register, XXXVIII. 341);
and it is after his father's death that (see plate) in 1719 to a receipted account,
in 1721 to his will, in 1722 to the release of a mortgage, he signed "Rob‑
Calfe", "Ro ꞉ Calfe", "Robert Calfe" (see the last two in Drake's Witchcraft
Delusion, II. xxii, xxiv).

[1] From the author of More Wonders we have two unquestionable autographs: (1) his marginalia of 1695 on Cotton Mather's paper (see below, p. 306,
note 1) and (2) a letter of 1700 presenting a copy of his book to the Earl of
Bellomont, then governor of Massachusetts and New York. A page of the
former is to be photographed in the Massachusetts Historical Society's Proceedings for 1913–1914; and the latter (now in the New York Public Library) is reproduced in full in the Memorial History of Boston (II. 168). Specimens of both
are given in our own plate; and to these are added (1) the signature "Robert
Calef" from the report of two appraisers, October 30, 1693; (2) the signature
"Robt. Calef" from the verdict of a Boston coroner's jury, January 15, 1696; (3)
the same signature, with a line or two of text in the same hand, from the decision
of two arbitrators (Boston, July 29, 1697); and (4) the last lines and the signature of a paper drawn by "Robt. Calef" as a selectman of Roxbury in March,
1717 (?). That all six specimens are in the same hand, and in a hand different from the younger Calef's, will hardly be questioned. Is not the older
Robert, too, more likely than the younger to have been an appraiser in 1693, a
coroner's juror in 1696, and an arbiter in 1697? And (though Calef and Calfe
were undoubtedly pronounced alike or nearly so) is it not less probable that the
author of More Wonders changed the habitual spelling of his signature than that
a younger Robert, if not the author, should thus have distinguished his identity
from his father's? What arguments led the genealogist Stickney to ascribe the
book to the father cannot now be learned: the "full statement of the reasons"

AUTOGRAPHS OF ROBERT CALEF AND OF HIS SON ROBERT
From various originals

well as a seller of cloths.[1] Of his eight children the eldest was, in 1692, a physician in Ipswich. What led to the writing of *More Wonders* he has himself told us in his book. It remains only to testify to the care and exactness which all comparison of his work with the records seems to show, and to remark that to a student of the literature of witchcraft it is evident that his reading is larger than he cares to parade. Though he clearly belonged to the popular party, this is as likely to be a result as a cause—it is probably neither—of his feeling on the subject of the witch superstition; and that he had else any grievance against the Mathers or their colleagues there is no reason to think.

His book, though completed in 1697, was not printed till 1700, and then in London. In June, 1698, Cotton Mather records in his diary that "a sort of a Sadducee in this town" "hath written a Volumn of invented and notorious lies"; "this Volumn," he adds, "hee is, as I understand, sending to England, that it may bee printed there." Why it found no printer in New England can be guessed; the storm it raised when it appeared in print is well known. President Increase Mather "ordered the wicked book to be burnt in the college yard," [2] and his son's diary is eloquent with vexation.

"Some Years ago," runs his entry of November 15, 1700, "a very wicked sort of a Sadducee in this Town, raking together a crue of Libels, which he had written at several Times,

promised by him to the *N. E. Hist. and Gen. Register* (see XXX. 461) was, like his genealogy, never published. But, from an article on "Robert Calef" by Mr. W. S. Harris in the *Granite Monthly* for 1907 (XXXIX. 157–163), and from correspondence with its author, it is learned that another student of the Calef pedigree (Mr. W. W. Lunt, of Hingham, Mass.) has reached that result by a comparison of handwritings. Mr. Harris, it should be added, quotes the Rev. John Kelly as saying in a funeral sermon (1808) for Judge John Calfe (b. 1740) of Hampstead, N. H., that the latter's ancestor (who was the elder Calef, not the younger) was the author of the book.

[1] In 1701 Cotton Mather calls him "the Weaver (though he presumes to call himself Merchant)" (*Some Few Remarks*, p. 35).

[2] Eliot, *Biographical Dictionary* (1809), *s. v.* "Calef."

(especially relating to the *Wonders of the Invisible World,* which have been among us) wherein I am the cheef Butt of his Malice, (tho' many other better Servants of the Lord are also most maliciously abused by him:) he sent this vile Volume to London to be published.   Now, tho' I had often and often cried unto the Lord, that the Cup of this Man's abominable Bundle of Lies, written on purpose, with a Quil under a special Energy and Management of Satan, to damnify my precious Opportunities of Glorifying my Lord Jesus Christ, might pass from me; Yett, in this point, the Lord has denied my Request: the Book is printed, and the Impression is this week arrived here."

It was even felt necessary to print a reply; but the two Mathers held it beneath them to plead in their own vindication. It fell to their parishioners.   "My pious neighbours are so provoked," writes Cotton Mather (December 4), "at the diabolical Wickedness of the Man who has published a Volume of Libels against my Father and myself, that they sett apart whole Dayes of Prayer, to complain unto God against him." The outcome of their communings together was a pamphlet called *Some Few Remarks upon a Scandalous Book against the Gospel and Ministry of New England, written by one Robert Calef.*   It was signed by seven, one of them John Goodwin; but the materials were furnished by their pastors.   It aimed however at their personal exculpation, and has small interest for the public story.[1]

The doughty merchant survived the storm.   In 1702–1704 he served his townsmen as an overseer of the poor, in 1707

[1] Let any who would know the contents of the excessively rare little booklet turn to the works of Upham and Poole mentioned on p. 91; and in his *Diary* (I. 383–384) Mather narrates how the book was compiled.   The *More Wonders* it describes as "a Libellous Book lately come into this Countrey . . . which is writ (with what help we know not) by one Robert Calef, who presumes to call himself Merchant of Boston."   "It was highly rejoicing to us," add the writers, "when we heard that our Booksellers were so well acquainted with the Integrity of our Pastors, as that not one of them could admit of any of those Libels to be vended in their shops."   Pp. 34–50 of its seventy-one pages are taken up by a letter of Cotton Mather to the authors.   It was perhaps a passage in Mather's

was chosen an assessor, in 1710 a tithingman. It was perhaps about this time that he retired to Roxbury, where in 1707 he had bought a place and where he was a selectman of the town when, in 1719, death found him. There, in the old burial ground just opposite his home, a stone still testifies that "Here lyes buried the body of Mr. Robert Calef, aged seventy-one years, died April the Thirteenth, 1719." [1]

Calef's book has been five times reprinted: in 1796, at Salem, by William Carlton (12°, pp. 318); again at Salem, in 1823, a mere reimpression, with the addition, from the court files, of Giles Corey's examination (12°, pp. 312); in Boston, 1828 (24°, pp. 333), again a reimpression; at Salem, 1861, edited by Mr. S. P. Fowler, with Cotton Mather's *Wonders*, in his volume *Salem Witchcraft* (see p. 207); and, more faithfully, in 1866 at Roxbury, as nos. VI., VII., of Woodward's *Historical Series*, under the editorship of S. G. Drake (see pp. 207–208). The present text follows the original edition (1700), but corrects it by the list of *Errata* to be found in the copy (once Cotton Mather's) possessed by the Massachusetts Historical Society. [2]

letter that led " E. P." to think Robert Calef a " young man "; for those words, in italics and with capital initials, stare from a sentence so obscure that to a hasty glance Calef, instead of Mather himself, might easily seem to be meant.

[1] For these and other personal details see Drake's memoir, in his ed. of Calef, and his *History and Antiquities of Boston*, pp. 529, 531; *Boston Record Commissioners' Reports*, I. 156, 160, VII. 210, 218, 225, 229, VIII. 24, 26, 31, 33, 41, 43, 75, IX. 179, 195, XI. 145; *Memorial History of Boston*, IV. 652; F. S. Drake, *The Town of Roxbury* (Boston, 1905), pp. 102, 140–149; *N. E. Hist. and Gen. Register*, XIV. 52; and the above-cited article of W. S. Harris, which has a photograph of the gravestone. From these mentions will be learned also the name of his wife, Mary, and of the two of his eight children who were born (1688, 1691) after his coming to Boston. It will be learned, too, that in 1692 he was a constable, in 1694 hayward and fenceviewer, in 1697 a surveyor of highways, in 1698 a clerk of the market. At least it is to "Robert Calef," not to "Robert Calef, Jr.," that the records award these offices. And it is perhaps to be noticed that while the name of "Robert Calef" is often preceded by "Mr.", that title does not appear before that of "Robert Calef, Jr."

[2] See Drake's ed., III. 223.

MORE WONDERS OF THE INVISIBLE WORLD

*More Wonders of the Invisible World: Or, The Wonders of the
Invisible World, Display'd in Five Parts.*
*Part I.   An Account of the Sufferings of Margaret Rule, Written
by the Reverend Mr. C. M.*
*P. II.   Several Letters to the Author, etc. And his Reply relat-
ing to Witchcraft.*
*P. III.   The Differences between the Inhabitants of Salem Vil-
lage, and Mr. Parris their Minister, in New-England.*
*P. IV.   Letters of a Gentleman uninterested, Endeavouring to
prove the received Opinions about Witchcraft to be Orthodox.
With short Essays to their Answers.*
*P. V.   A short Historical Accou[n]t of Matters of Fact in that
Affair.*
*To which is added, A Postscript relating to a Book intitled, The
Life of Sir William Phips.*
*Collected by Robert Calef, Merchant, of Boston in New-England.
Licensed and Entred according to Order.*
*London: Printed for Nath. Hillar, at the Princes-Arms, in
Leaden-Hall-street, over against St. Mary-Ax, and Joseph
Collyer, at the Golden-Bible, on London-Bridge.   1700.[1]*

*The Epistle to the Reader, And more especially to the Noble
Bereans[2] of this Age, wherever Residing.*

Gentlemen,
    You that are freed from the Slavery of a corrupt Education;
and that in spite of human Precepts, Examples and Presidents,[3]
can hearken to the Dictates of Scripture and Reason:

----

[1] Title-page of original.

[2] *I. e.,* to those with open minds: the Bereans are commended (Acts xvii. 11)
as "more noble" because "they received the word with all readiness of mind,
and searched the Scriptures daily, whether these things were so."

[3] Precedents: this odd spelling was then the current one.

For your sakes I am content, that these Collections of mine, as also my Sentiments should be exposed to publick view; In hopes that having well considered, and compared them with Scripture, you will see reason, as I do, to question a belief so prevalent (as that here treated of) as also the practice flowing from thence; they standing as nearly connext as cause and effect; it being found wholly impracticable, to extirpate the latter without first curing the former.

And if the Buffoon or Satyrical will be exercising their Talents, or if the Biggots wilfully and blindly reject the Testimonies of their own Reason, and more sure word, it is no more than what I expected from them.

But you Gentlemen, I doubt not, are willing to Distinguish between Truth and Error, and if this may be any furtherance to you herein, I shall not miss my Aim.

But if you find the contrary, and that my belief herein is any way Heterodox, I shall be thankful for the Information to any Learned or Reverend Person, or others, that shall take that pains to inform me better by Scripture, or sound Reason, which is what I have been long seeking for in this Country in vain.

In a time when not only England in particular, but almost all Europe had been labouring against the Usurpations of Tyranny and Slavery, The English America has not been behind in a share in the Common calamities; more especially New-England has met not only with such calamities as are common to the rest, but with several aggravations enhansing such Afflictions, by the Devastations and Cruelties of the Barbarous Indians in their Eastern borders, etc.

But this is not all, they have been harrast (on many accounts) by a more dreadful Enemy, as will herein appear to the considerate.

P. 66.[1] Were it as we are told in *Wonders of the Invisible World*, that the Devils were walking about our Streets with

---

[1] This page-number and those which follow refer to the pages of Mather's *Wonders* (original edition), from which the substance of these paragraphs is quoted. The passages quoted will be found in Mather's book at pp. 48, 41, 50, of the first London edition, at pp. 95, 80–82, 100, of that of 1862, at pp. 121–122, 102–104, 128, of the American edition of 1866. They do not belong to the pages reprinted in the present volume.

lengthned Chains making a dreadful noise in our Ears, and
Brimstone, even without a Metaphor, was making a horrid
and a hellish stench in our Nostrils,

P. 49. And that the Devil exhibiting himself ordinarily
as a black-Man,[1] had decoy'd a fearful knot of Proud, Froward, Ignorant, Envious and Malitious Creatures, to list themselves in his horrid Service, by entring their Names in a Book
tendered unto them; and that they have had their Meetings
and Sacraments, and associated themselves to destroy the
Kingdom of our Lord Jesus Christ, in these parts of the World;
having each of them their Spectres, or Devils Commissionated
by them, and representing of them, to be the Engines of their
Malice, by these wicked Spectres siezing poor People about
the Country with various and bloody Torments. And of
those evidently preternatural Torments some to[o] have died.
And that they have bewitched some even so far, as to make
them self destroyers, and others in many Towns here and there
languish'd under their evil hands. The People thus afflicted
miserably scratch'd and bitten; and that the same Invisible
Furies did stick Pins in them, and scald them, distort and dis-
joint them, with a Thousand other Plagues; and sometimes
drag them out of their Chambers, and carry them over Trees
and Hills Miles together, many of them being tempted to sign
the Devils Laws.

P. 7[0]. Those furies whereof several have killed more
People perhaps than would serve to make a Village.[2]

If this be the true state of the Afflictions of this Country,
it is very deplorable, and beyond all other outward Calamities
miserable. But if on the other side, the Matter be as others
do understand it, That the Devil has been too hard for us by
his Temptations, signs, and lying Wonders, with the help of
pernicious notions, formerly imbibed and professed; together
with the Accusations of a parcel of possessed, distracted, or
lying Wenches, accusing their Innocent Neighbours, pretending they see their Spectres (*i. e.*) Devils in their likeness Afflicting of them, and that God in righteous Judgment (after Men

---

[1] How Mather conceived this "black man" to look appears from the description he ascribes to Mercy Short (p. 261, above).

[2] In the original there is here no paragraph, the paragraph beginning after
the next sentence with "But if," etc.

had ascribed his Power to Witches, of Commissionating Devils
to do these things) may have given them over to strong delusions to believe lyes, etc. And to let loose the Devils of
Envy, Hatred, Pride, Cruelty, and Malice against each other;
yet still disguised under the Mask of Zeal for God, and left
them to the branding one another with the odious Name of
Witch; and upon the Accusation of those above mentioned,
Brother to Accuse and Prosecute Brother, Children their
Parents, Pastors and Teachers their immediate Flock unto
death; Shepherds becoming Wolves, Wise Men Infatuated;
People hauled to Prisons, with a bloody noise pursuing to,
and insulting over, the (true) Sufferers at Execution, while
some are fleeing from that call'd Justice, Justice it self fleeing
before such Accusations, when once it did but begin to refrain
further proceedings, and to question such Practises, some
making their Escape out of Prisons, rather than by an obstinate
Defence of their Innocency, to run so apparent hazard of their
Lives; Estates seized, Families of Children and others left to
the Mercy of the Wilderness (not to mention here the Numbers
prescribed,[1] dead in Prisons, or Executed, etc.)

All which Tragedies, tho begun in one Town, or rather by
one Parish, has Plague-like spread more than through that
Country. And by its Eccho giving a brand of Infamy to this
whole Country, throughout the World,

If this were the Miserable case of this Country in the time
thereof, and that the Devil had so far prevailed upon us in our
Sentiments and Actions, as to draw us from so much as look-
ing into the Scriptures for our guidance in these pretended
Intricacies, leading us to a trusting in blind guides, such as the
corrupt practices of some other Countries, or the bloody Ex-
periments of Bodin, and such other Authors—Then tho our
Case be most miserable, yet it must be said of New-England,
Thou hast destroyed thy self, and brought this greatest of
Miseries upon thee.

And now whether the Witches (such as have made a compact by Explicit Covenant with the Devil, having thereby
obtained a power to Commissionate him) have been the cause
of our miseries,

Or whether a Zeal governed by blindness and passion, and

---

[1] "Prescribed," as then often, for "proscribed," *i. e.*, condemned to death.

led by president, has not herein precipitated us into far greater wickedness (if not Witchcrafts) than any have been yet proved against those that suffered,

To be able to distinguish aright in this matter, to which of these two to refer our Miseries is the present Work. As to the former, I know of no sober Man, much less Reverend Christian, that being ask'd dares affirm and abide by it, that Witches have that power; *viz.* to Commissionate Devils to kill and destroy. And as to the latter, it were well if there were not too much of truth in it, which remains to be demonstrated.

But here it will be said, what need of Raking in the Coals that lay buried in oblivion. We cannot recall those to Life again that have suffered, supposing it were unjustly; it tends but to the exposing the Actors, as if they had proceeded irregularly.

Truly I take this to be just as the Devil would have it, so much to fear disobliging men, as not to endeavour to detect his Wiles, that so he may the sooner, and with the greater Advantages set the same on foot again (either here or else where) so dragging us through the Pond twice by the same Cat.[1] And if Reports do not (herein) deceive us, much the same has been acting this present year in Scotland.[2] And what Kingdom or Country is it, that has not had their bloody fits and turns at it. And if this is such a catching disease, and so universal, I presume I need make no Apology for my Endeavours to prevent, as far as in my power, any more such bloody Victims or Sacrifices; tho indeed I had rather any other would

[1] For a description of the joke, played on boobies, of "dragging through a pond with a cat," see the Oxford Dictionary, *s. v.* Cat, III. 14, or Grose, *Dictionary of Vulgar Terms*, *s. v.* "Cat-whipping." "We hope, sir," said in 1682 the *London Gazette*, "that this Nation will be too wise, to be drawn twice through the same Water by the very same Cat."

[2] As Calef is writing in August, 1697, he doubtless has in mind the cases in Renfrewshire, where on June 10 several witches were hanged, then burned, on the Gallow Green of Paisley; a "Relation" then printed recounts "the Diabolical Practices of above Twenty." Neither the relation nor the tidings of the burning could well have reached America by August 11; but the trials had been notorious for months. In Scotland, however, such things had been constant, as may be seen by the records of the Privy Council. Those of this period are chronicled by Robert Chambers in his *Domestic Annals of Scotland.*

have undertaken so offensive, tho necessary a task; yet all things weighed, I had rather thus Expose my self to Censure, than that it should be wholly omitted. Were the notions in question innocent and harmless, respecting the Glory of God, and well being of Men, I should not have engaged in them, but finding them in my esteem so intollerably destructive of both, This together with my being by Warrant called before the Justices, in my own Just Vindication, I took it to be a call from God, to my Power,[1] to Vindicate his Truths, against the Pagan and Popish Assertions, which are so prevalent; for tho Christians in general do own the Scriptures to be their only Rule of Faith and Doctrine, yet these Notions will tell us, that the Scriptures have not sufficiently, nor at all described the crime of Witchcraft, whereby the culpable might be detected, tho it be positive in the Command to punish it by Death; hence the World has been from time to time perplext in the prosecution of the several Diabolical mediums of Heathenish and Popish Invention, to detect an Imaginary Crime (not but that there are Witches, such as the Law of God describes) which has produced a deluge of Blood; hereby rendering the Commands of God not only void but dangerous.

So also they own Gods Providence and Government of the World, and that Tempests and Storms, Afflictions and Diseases, are of his sending; yet these Notions tell us, that the Devil has the power of all these, and can perform them when commission'd by a Witch thereto, and that he has a power at the Witches call to act and do, without and against the course of Nature, and all natural causes, in afflicting and killing of Innocents; and this is that so many have died for.

Also it is generally believed, that if any Man has strength, it is from God the Almighty Being: But these notions will tell us, that the Devil can make one Man as strong as many, which was one of the best proofs, as it was counted, against Mr. Burroughs the Minister;[2] tho his contemporaries in the Schools during his Minority could have testified, that his strength was then as much superiour to theirs as ever (setting aside incredible Romances) it was discovered to be since. Thus rendring the power of God, and his providence of none Effect.

---

[1] *I. e.*, to the utmost of my power.　　　[2] See pp. 219–220, above.

These are some of the destructive notions of this Age, and however the asserters of them seem sometimes to value themselves much upon sheltring their Neighbours from Spectral Accusations, They may deserve as much thanks as that Tyrant, that having industriously obtained an unintelligible charge against his Subjects, in matters wherein it was impossible they should be Guilty, having thereby their lives in his power, yet suffers them of his meer Grace to live, and will be call'd gracious Lord.

It were too Icarian[1] a task for one unfurnish'd with necessary learning, and Library, to give any Just account, from whence so great delusions have sprung, and so long continued. Yet as an Essay from those scraps of reading that I have had opportunity of, it will be no great venture to say, that Signs and Lying Wonders have been one principal cause.[2]

It is written of Justin Martyr, who lived in the second Century, that he was before his conversion a great Philosopher; first in the way of the Stoicks, and after of the Peripateticks, after that of the Pythagorean, and after that of the Platonists sects; and after all proved of Eminent use in the Church of Christ; Yet a certain Author speaking of one Apollonius Tyaneus[3] has these words, "That the most Orthodox themselves began to deem him vested with power sufficient for a Deity; which occasioned that so strange a doubt from Justin Martyr, as cited by the learned Gregory, Fol. 37. Εἰ Θεός ἐστι,[4] etc. If God be the Creator and Lord of the World, how comes it to pass that Apollonius his Telisms,[5] have so much over-ruled the course of things! for we see that they also have stilled the Waves of the Sea, and the raging of the Winds, and prevailed against the Noisome Flies, and Incursions of wild Beasts," etc. If so Eminent and Early a Christian were by these false shews in such doubt, it is the less wonder in our

---

[1] *I. e.*, presumptuous, like the venture of Icarus, who flew so high that the sun melted off his wings.

[2] He is thinking, of course, of such "Remarkables" as those told by the Mathers.

[3] Apollonius of Tyana, the first-century Pythagorean philosopher and wonder-worker, like Justin Martyr, the second-century apologist of Christianity, is perhaps too well known to need a footnote.

[4] Justin Martyr, *Quaestiones et Responsiones ad Orthodoxos*, qu. 24.

[5] *Telesmata*, talismans, magical devices.

depraved times, to meet with what is Equivalent thereto: Besides this a certain Author informs me, that "Julian (afterwards called the Apostate) being instructed in the Philosophy and Disciplines of the Heathen, by Libarius[1] his Tutor, by this means he came to love Philosophy better than the Gospel, and so by degrees turn'd from Christianity to Heathenism."

This same Julian did, when Apostate, forbid that Christians should be instructed in the Discipline of the Gentiles, which (it seems) Socrates a Writer of the Ecclesiastical History, does acknowledge to be by the singular Providence of God; Christians having then begun to degenerate from the Gospel, and to betake themselves to Heathenish learning. And in the *Mercury* for the Month of February, 1695, there is this Account, "That the Christian Doctors conversing much with the writings of the Heathen, for the gaining of Eloquence, A Counsel[2] was held at Carthage, which forbad the reading of the Books of the Gentiles."

From all which it may be easily perceived, that in the Primitive times of Christianity, when not only many Heathen of the Vulgar, but also many learn'd Men and Philosophers had imbraced the Christian Faith, they still retained a love to their Heathen-learning, which as one observes being transplanted into a Christian soile, soon proved productive of pernicious weeds, which over-ran the face of the Church, hence it was so deformed as the Reformation found it.

Among other pernicious Weeds arising from this Root, the Doctrine of the power of Devils and Witchcraft as it is now, and long has been understood, is not the least; the Fables of Homer, Virgil, Horace and Ovid, etc., being for the Elegancy of their Language retained then (and so are to this day) in the schools, have not only introduced, but established such Doctrines to the poisoning the Christian World. A certain Author Expresses it thus, "that as the Christian Schools at first brought Men from Heathenism to the Gospel, so these Schools carry Men from the Gospel to Heathenism, as to their great perfection," and Mr. I. M.[3] in his *Remarkable Providences*, gives an account that (as he calls it) an Old Counsel[4] did

---

[1] Libanius.   [2] Council: the Fourth Council of Carthage, 398 A. D.

[3] Increase Mather.

[4] Council: the Spanish Council of Bracara, 561 A. D.

Anathematize all those that believed such power of the Devils, accounting it a Damnable Doctrine. But as other Evils did afterwards increase in the Church (partly by such Education) so this insensibly grew up with them, tho not to that degree, as that any Counsel[1] I have ever heard or Read of has to this day taken off those Anathema's; yet after this the Church so far declined, that Witchcraft became a Principal Ecclesiastical Engine (as also that of Heresie was) to root up all that stood in their way; and besides the ways of Tryal that we have still in practice, they invented some, which were peculiar to themselves; which when ever they were minded to improve against any Orthodox believer, they could easily make Effectual: That Deluge of Blood which that Scarlet Whore[2] has to answer for, shed under this notion, how amazing is it.

The first in England that I have read of, of any note since the Reformation, that asserts this Doctrine, is the famous Mr. Perkins,[3] he (as also Mr. Gaul,[4] and Mr. Bernard,[5] etc. seems all of them to have undertaken one Task, they) taking notice of the Multiplicity of irregular ways to try them by, invented by Heathen and Papists, made it their business and main work herein to oppose such as they saw to be pernicious. And if they did not look more narrowly into it, but followed the first, viz. Mr. Perkins whose Education (as theirs also) had

---

[1] Council.

[2] He means the Roman church. Revelation, xvii.

[3] William Perkins (1558–1602), the eminent Cambridge divine—"our Perkins," as Increase Mather calls him—whose *Discourse of the Damned Art of Witchcraft* (London, 1608, 1610, and in the many editions of his *Works*) was the highest authority to Puritans.

[4] John Gaule. See p. 216, note 1.

[5] Richard Bernard (1567–1641), long minister of Batcombe in Somersetshire. His *Guide to Grand-Jurymen . . . in cases of Witchcraft* (1627, 1629) was, though credulous and cruel enough, the most mild and cautious of the Puritan monographs. The tiny volume, now very rare, had perhaps never a great circulation (in 1692 Increase Mather declares it, like Gaule's book, "rare to be had"); but its rules for the detection of witches gained much vogue from their adoption by Michael Dalton into his *The Countrey Justice*, the standard manual for the procedure of the lower courts. It is clearly, however, from Bernard's book itself that Cotton Mather has abridged these rules in his *Wonders*; and the book, as well as this extract, was doubtless in the hands of the Salem judges. Increase Mather quotes it often, and by page, and tells us that it "is a solid and a wise treatise." (*Cases of Conscience*, 1693, p. 18.)

forestall'd him into such belief, whom they readily followed, it cannot be wondered at: And that they were men liable to Err, and so not to be trusted to as perfect guides, will manifestly appear to him that shall see their several receits laid down to detect them by their Presumptive and Positive ones. And consider how few of either have any foundation in Scripture or Reason; and how vastly they differ from each other in both, each having his Art by himself, which Forty or an Hundred more may as well imitate, and give theirs, *ad infinitum*, being without all manner of proof.

But tho this be their main design to take off People from those Evil and bloody ways of trial which they speak so much against, Yet this does not hinder to this day, but the same evil ways or as bad are still used to detect them by, and that even among Protestants; and is so far Justified, that a Reverend Person has said lately here, how else shall we detect Witches? And another being urged to prove by Scripture such a sort of Witch as has power to send Devils to kill men, replied, that he did as firmly believe it as any article of his Faith. And that he (the Inquirer) did not go to the Scripture, to learn the Mysteries of his trade or Art. What can be said more to Establish there Heathenish notions and to villifie the Scriptures, our only Rule; and that after we have seen such dire effects thereof, as has threatned the utter Extirpation of this whole Country.

And as to most of the Actors in these Tragedies, tho they are so far from defending their Actions that they will Readily own, that undue steps have been taken, etc., Yet it seems they choose that the same should be Acted over again inforced by their Example, rather than that it should Remain as a Warning to Posterity, wherein they have mist it. So far are they from giving Glory to God, and taking the due shame to themselves.

And now to sum up all in a few words, we have seen a Biggotted Zeal, stirring up a Blind and most Bloody rage, not against Enemies, or Irreligious Proffligate Persons, But (in Judgment of Charity, and to view) against as Vertuous and Religious as any they have left behind them in this Country, which have suffered as Evil doers with the utmost extent of rigour (not that so high a Charactor is due to all that Suffered) and this by the Testimony of Vile Varlets as not only were known before, but have been further apparent since by their Manifest Lives, Whordoms, Incest, etc. The Accusations of these, from their Spectral Sight, being the chief Evidence against those that Suffered. In which Accusations they were upheld by both Magistrates and Ministers, so long as they Apprehended themselves in no Danger.

And then tho they could defend neither the Doctrine, nor the Practice, yet none of them have in such a publick manner as the case Requires, testified against either; tho at the same time they could not but be sensible what a Stain and lasting Infamy they have brought upon the whole Country, to the Indangering the future welfair not only of this but of other places, induced by their Example; if not, to an intailing the Guilt of all the Righteous Blood that has been by the same means Shed, by Heathen or Papists, etc., upon themselves, whose deeds they have so far justified, occasioning the great Dishonour and Blasphemy of the Name of God, Scandalizing the Heathen, hardning of Enemies; and as a Natural effect thereof, to the great Increase of Atheism.

I shall conclude only with acquainting the Reader, that of these Collections, the first, containing more Wonders of the Invisible World, I received of a Gentleman,[1] who had it of the Author and communicated it to me,[2] with his express consent, of which this is a true Copy.[3] As to the Letters, they

---

[1] It has been conjectured that this gentleman may have been one of the two Brattles. In a letter of March 1, 1695 (*More Wonders*, p. 30—not here reprinted), to a "Mr. B." (Brattle?) Calef mentions other papers received from Mather through his hands—but to be returned speedily and not copied. He, however, he says, made notes in the margin where he thought it needful. These papers, as it will rejoice all students to learn, have just been identified by Mr. Worthington C. Ford (to whose courtesy the editor owes his knowledge of them) among those in the keeping of the Massachusetts Historical Society, and they will be published in full—both Mather's text and Calef's marginalia (with a facsimile plate) in that society's *Proceedings* for 1913–1914. See also below, p. 388, at end.

[2] The original has "use"; but this is corrected to "me" in the *Errata* (see p. 295, above).

[3] A copy, not of the "express consent," but of the "More Wonders of the Invisible World"—the Margaret Rule story as a whole—to which the letter of Mather introducing it was perhaps attached as a sort of open "letter to the reader." Between this preface and that letter there intervenes a table of contents, not here reprinted.

are for Substance the same I sent, tho with some small Variation or Addition. Touching the two Letters from a Gentleman, at his request I have forborn naming him. It is great Pity the matters of Fact, and indeed the whole, had not been done by some abler hand better Accomplished and Advantaged with both natural and acquired Judgments, but others not Appearing, I have inforc'd my self to do what is done, my other occasions Will not admit any further Scrutiny therein.

R. C.

BOSTON in New-England, Aug. 11, 1697.

Sir,

I now lay before you a very Entertaining Story, a Story which relates yet more Wonders of the Invisible World,[1] a Story which tells the Remarkable Afflictions and Deliverance of one that had been Prodigiously handled by the Evil Angels. I was my self a daily Eye Witness to a large part of these Occurrences, and there may be produced Scores of Substantial Witnesses to the most of them; yea, I know not of any one Passage of the Story, but what may be sufficiently Attested. I do not Write it with a design of throwing it presently into the Press, but only to preserve the Memory of such Memorable things, the forgetting whereof would neither be pleasing to God, nor useful to Men; as also to give you, with some others of peculiar and obliging Friends, a sight of some Curiosities, and I hope this Apologie will serve to Excuse me, if I mention, as perhaps I may, when I come to a tenth Paragraph in my Writing,[2] some things which I would have omitted in a farther Publication.

COTTON MATHER.[3]

[1] It is, in other words, a supplement to his book thus entitled, as its other name, "Another Brand pluckt out of the Burning," makes it a supplement to his Mercy Short narrative.

[2] See his "Sect. 10" (pp. 316–318, below).

[3] As to this letter see p. 306, note 3. The Margaret Rule MS. is still preserved in the library of the Massachusetts Historical Society; and Poole, who used it for his chapter on witchcraft in the *Memorial History of Boston*, has in a footnote (II. 152) printed a facsimile of the "To bee Return'd unto C. Mather" written on it by its author.

ANOTHER BRAND PLUCKT OUT OF THE BURNING, OR, MORE WONDERS OF THE INVISIBLE WORLD

PART I.

Section I.

The Afflictions of Margaret Rule.

WITHIN these few years there died in the Southern Parts a Christian Indian, who notwithstanding some of his Indian Weakness, had something of a better Character of vertue and Goodness, than many of our People can allow to most of their Countrey-men, that profess the Christian Religion. He had been a Zealous Preacher of the Gospel to his Neighbour-hood, and a sort of Overseer, or Officer, to whose Conduct was owing very much of what good order was maintained among those Proselited Savages: This Man returning home from the Funeral of his Son, was Complemented by an English-Man, expressing Sorrow for his Loss; now, tho' the Indians use, upon the Death of Relations, to be the most Passionate and Outragious Creatures in the World, yet this Converted Indian Handsomely and Chearfully repli'd, "Truly I am sorry, and I am not sorry; I am sorry that I have Buried a dear Son; but I am not sorry that the will of God is done. I know that without the will of God my Son could not have Died, and I know that the will of God is allways just and good, and so I am satisfied." Immediately upon this, even within a few hours, he fell himself Sick of a Disease that quickly kill'd him; in the time of which Disease he called his Folks about him, earnestly perswading them to be Sincere in their Praying unto God, and beware of the Drunkenness, the Idleness, the Lying, whereby so many of that Nation disgrac'd their Profession of Christianity; adding, that he was ashamed when he thought how little Service he had hitherto done for God; and that if God would prolong his Life he would Labour to do better Service, but that he was fully sure he was now going to the Lord Jesus Christ, who had bought him with his own Precious Blood; and for his part he long'd to Die that he might be with his Glorious Lord; and in the mid'st of such passages he gave up

the Ghost, but in such repute, that the English People of good
Fashion did not think much of Travelling a great way to his
Interment.   Lest my Reader do now wonder why I have related this piece of a Story, I will now hasten to abate that
Wonder, by telling that whereto this was intended, but for
an Introduction: Know then that this remarkable Indian
being a little before he Died at work in the Wood making of
Tarr, there appeared unto him a Black-Man, of a Terrible
aspect, and more than humane Dimensions, threatning bitterly
to kill him if he would not promise to leave off Preaching as
he did to his Countrey-Men, and promise particularly, that if
he Preached any more, he would say nothing of Jesus Christ
unto them.   The Indian amaz'd, yet had the courage to answer,
I will in spite of you go on to Preach Christ more than ever I
did, and the God whom I serve will keep me that you shall
never hurt me.   Hereupon the Apparition abating somewhat
of his fierceness, offered to the Indian a Book of a considerable
thickness and a Pen and Ink, and said, that if he would now set
his hand unto that Book, he would require nothing further of
him; but the Man refused the motion with indignation, and
fell down upon his knees into a Fervent and Pious Prayer unto
God for help against the Tempter, whereupon the Dæmon
Vanish't.

This is a Story which I would never have tendered unto
my Reader, if I had not Receiv'd it from an honest and useful
English Man, who is at this time a Preacher of the Gospel to
the Indians,[1] nor would the probable[2] Truth of it have encouraged me to have tendered it, if this also had not been a
fit introduction unto yet a further Narrative.

Sect. 2.   'Twas not much above a year or two, after this
Accident (of which no manner of Noise has been made) that
there was a Prodigious descent of Devils upon divers places
near the Center of this Province, wherein some scores of Mis-

---

[1] Very probably his uncle, the Rev. John Cotton (1640–1699), who had
formerly preached in Martha's Vineyard (1664–1667) and had there learned the
Indian tongue, and who now, at Plymouth, continued to preach to Indians as well
as whites.   In his life of Eliot and in bk. VI. of his *Magnalia* Mather relates
much more of the Christian Indians of Martha's Vineyard and of the witchcrafts
there.

[2] Provable, demonstrable.

erable People were Troubled by horrible appearances of a
Black-Man, accompanied with Spectres, wearing these and
those Humane Shapes, who offer'd them a Book to be by them
sign'd, in token of their being Listed for the Service of the Devil,
and upon their denying to do it, they were Dragoon'd[1] with
a thousand Preternatural Torments, which gave no little terror
to the beholders of these unhappy Energuments.[2]   There was
one in the North part of Boston seized by the Evil-Angels many
Months after the General Storm of the late Inchantments was
over, and when the Countrey had long lain pretty quiet, both
as to Molestations and Accusations from the *Invisible World*,
her Name was Margaret Rule, a Young Woman. She was
born of sober and honest Parents, yet Living, but what her
own Character was before her Visitation, I can speak with the
less confidence of exactness, because I observe that wherever
the Devils have been let loose to worry any Poor Creature
amongst us, a great part of the Neighbourhood presently set
themselves to inquire and relate all the little Vanities of their
Childhood, with such unequal exaggerations, as to make them
appear greater Sinners than any whom the Pilate of Hell has
not yet Preyed upon: But it is affirm'd, that for about half
a year before her Visitation, she was observably improved in
the hopeful symptoms of a new Creature; She was become
seriously concern'd for the everlasting Salvation of her Soul,
and careful to avoid the snares of Evil Company. This Young
Woman had never seen the affliction of Mercy Short, whereof
a Narrative has been already given,[3] and yet about half a
year after the glorious and signal deliverance of that poor
Damsel, this Margaret fell into an affliction, marvellous, resembling hers in almost all the circumstances of it, indeed the
Afflictions were so much alike, that the relation I have given
of the one, would almost serve as the full History of the other,
this was to that, little more than the second part to the same
Tune, indeed Margarets case was in several points less remarkable than Mercies, and in some other things the Entertainment
did a little vary.

Sect. 3. 'Twas upon the Lords Day the 10th of September,
in the Year 1693, that Margaret Rule, after some hours of
previous disturbance in the Publick Assembly, fell into odd

[1] See p. 189, note 2.   [2] Energumens: *i. e.*, demoniacs.   [3] See pp. 255 ff., above.

Fits, which caused her Friends to carry her home, where her
Fits in a few hours grew into a Figure that satisfied the Spectators of their being preternatural; some of the Neighbours
were forward enough to suspect the rise of this Mischief in an
House hard-by, where lived a Miserable Woman, who had
been formerly Imprisoned on the suspicion of Witchcraft, and
who had frequently Cured very painfull Hurts by muttering
over them certain Charms, which I shall not indanger the
Poysoning of my Reader by repeating. This Woman had the
Evening before Margaret fell into her Calamities, very bitterly
treated her, and threatn'd her; but the hazard of hurting a
poor Woman that might be innocent, notwithstanding Sur-
mizes that might have been more strongly grounded than
those, caus'd the pious People in the Vicinity to try rather
whether incessant Supplication to God alone, might not procure a quicker and safer Ease to the Afflicted, than hasty Prosecution of any suppos'd Criminal, and accordingly that unexceptionable course was all that was ever followed; yea, which
I look't on as a token for good, the Afflicted Family was as
averse as any of us all to entertain thoughts of any other course.

   Sect. 4. The Young Woman was assaulted by Eight cruel
Spectres, whereof she imagin'd that she knew three or four,
but the rest came still with their Faces cover'd, so that she
could never have a distinguishing view of the countenance of
those whom she thought she knew; she was very careful of
my reitterated charges to forbear blazing the Names, lest any
good Person should come to suffer any blast of Reputation
thro' the cunning Malice of the great Accuser; nevertheless
having since privately named them to my self, I will venture
to say this of them, that they are a sort of Wretches who for
these many years have gone under as Violent Presumptions of
Witchcraft, as perhaps any creatures yet living upon Earth;
altho' I am farr from thinking that the Visions of this Young
Woman were Evidence enough to prove them so. These
cursed Spectres now brought unto her a Book about a Cubet
long, a Book Red and thick, but not very broad, and they
demanded of her that she would set her Hand to that Book,
or touch it at least with her Hand, as a Sign of her becoming
a Servant of the Devil; upon her peremptory refusal to do
what they asked, they did not after renew the profers of the

Book unto her, but instead thereof, they fell to Tormenting of her in a manner too Hellish to be sufficiently described, in those Torments confining her to her Bed, for just Six weeks together.

Sect. 5.   Sometimes, but not always, together with the Spectres there look't in upon the Young Woman (according to her account) a short and a Black Man, whom they call'd their Master, a Wight exactly of the same Dimensions and Complexion and voice, with the Divel that has exhibited himself unto other infested People, not only in other parts of this Country but also in other Countrys, even of the European World, as the relation of the Enchantments there inform us, they all profest themselves Vassals of this Devil, and in obedience unto him they address themselves unto various ways of Torturing her; accordingly she was cruelly pinch't with Invisible hands very often in a Day, and the black and blew marks of the pinches became immediately visible unto the standers by.   Besides this, when her attendants had left her without so much as one pin about her, that so they might prevent some fear'd inconveniencies; yet she would ever now and then be miserably hurt with Pins which were found stuck into her Neck, Back and Arms, however, the Wounds made by the Pins would in a few minutes ordinarily be cured; she would also be strangely distorted in her Joynts, and thrown into such exorbitant Convulsions as were astonishing unto the Spectators in General; They that could behold the doleful condition of the poor Family without sensible compassions, might have Intrals indeed, but I am sure they could have no true Bowels in them.

Sect. 6.   It were a most Unchristian and uncivil, yea a most unreasonable thing to imagine that the Fitt's of the Young Woman were but meer Impostures: And I believe scarce any, but People of a particular Dirtiness, will harbour such an Uncharitable Censure; however, because I know not how far the Devil may drive the Imagination of poor Creatures when he has possession of them, that at another time when they are themselves would scorn to Dissemble any thing, I shall now confine my Narrative unto passages, wherein there could be no room left for any Dissimulation.   Of these the first that I'll mention shall be this; From the time that Margaret Rule first found herself to be formally besieged by the Spectres untill the Ninth Day following, namely from the Tenth of September to the Eighteenth, she kept an entire Fast, and yet she was unto all appearance as Fresh, as Lively, as Hearty, at the Nine Days End, as before they began; in all this time, tho' she had a very eager Hunger upon her Stomach, yet if any refreshment were brought unto her, her Teeth would be set, and she would be thrown into many Miseries, Indeed once or twice or so in all this time, her Tormentors permitted her to swallow a Mouthful of somewhat that might encrease her Miseries, whereof a Spoonful of Rum was the most considerable; but otherwise, as I said, her Fast unto the Ninth day was very extream and rigid: However, afterwards there scarce passed a day wherein she had not liberty to take something or other for her Sustentation, And I must add this further, that this business of her Fast was carried so, that it was impossible to be dissembled without a Combination of Multitudes of People unacquainted with one another to support the Juggle, but he that can imagine such a thing of a Neighbourhood so fill'd with Vertuous People is a base man, I cannot call him any other.

Sect. 7. But if the Sufferings of this Young Woman were not Imposture, yet might they not be pure Distemper? I will not here inquire of our Saducees, what sort of Distemper 'tis shall stick the Body full of Pins, without any Hand that could be seen to stick them; or whether all the Pin-makers in the World would be willing to be Evaporated into certain ill habits of Body producing a Distemper, but of the Distemper my Reader shall be Judge when I have told him something further of those unusual Sufferings. I do believe that the Evil Angels do often take Advantage from Natural Distempers in the Children of Men to annoy them with such further Mischiefs as we call preternatural. The Malignant Vapours and Humours of our Diseased Bodies may be used by Devils thereinto insinuating as engine of the Execution of their Malice upon those Bodies; and perhaps for this reason one Sex may suffer more Troubles of some kinds from the Invisible World than the other, as well as for that reason for which the Old Serpent made where he did his first Address. But I Pray what will you say to this, Margaret Rule would sometimes have her Jaws forcibly pulled open, whereupon something Invisible would be poured down her Throat; we all saw her swallow, and yet we saw her try all she could by Spitting, Coughing and Shriking,[1] that she might not swalow, but one time the standers by plainly saw something of that odd Liquor it self on the outside of her Neck; She cried out of it as of Scalding Brimstone poured into her, and the whole House would Immediately scent so hot of Brimstone that we were scarce able to endure it, whereof there are scores of Witnesses; but the Young Woman her self would be so monstrously Inflam'd that it would have broke a Heart of Stone to have seen her Agonies. This was a thing that several times happen'd and several times when her Mouth was thus pull'd open, the standers by clapping their Hands close thereupon the distresses that otherwise followed would be diverted. Moreover there was a whitish powder to us Invisible somtimes cast upon the Eyes of this Young Woman, whereby her Eyes would be extreamly incommoded, but one time some of this Powder was fallen actually Visible upon her Cheek, from whence the People in the Room wiped it with their Handkerchiefs, and somtimes the Young Woman would also be so bitterly scorched with the unseen Sulphur thrown upon her, that very sensible Blisters would be raised upon her Skin, whereto her Friends found it necessary to apply the Oyl's proper for common Burning, but the most of these Hurts would be cured in two or three days at farthest: I think I may without Vanity pretend to have read not a few of the best System's of Physick that have been yet seen in these American Regions, but I must confess that I have never yet learned the Name of the Natural Distemper, whereto these odd symptoms do belong: However I might suggest perhaps many a Natural Medicine, which would be of singular use against many of them.

Sect. 8.   But there fell out some other matters far beyond the reach of Natural Distemper: This Margaret Rule once in the middle of the Night Lamented sadly that the Spectres threatned the Drowning of a Young Man in the Neighbourhood, whom she named unto the Company: well it was afterwards found that at that very time this Young Man, having been prest on Board a Man of War then in the Harbour, was

---

[1] Hawking? The word is unknown to the dictionaries.

out of some dissatisfaction attempting to swim ashoar, and he had been Drowned in the attempt, if a Boat had not seasonably taken him up; it was by computation a minute or two after the Young Womans discourse of the Drowning, that the Young Man took the Water. At another time she told us that the Spectres bragg'd and laughed in her hearing about an exploit they had lately done, by stealing from a Gentleman his Will soon after he had written it; and within a few hours after she had spoken this there came to me a Gentleman with a private complaint, that having written his Will it was unaccountably gone out of the way, how or where he could not Imagine; and besides all this, there were wonderful Noises every now and then made about the Room, which our People could Ascribe to no other Authors but the Spectres, yea, the Watchers affirm that they heard those fiends clapping of their hands together with an Audibleness, wherein they could not be Imposed upon: And once her Tormentors pull'd her up to the Cieling of the Chamber, and held her there before a very Numerous Company of Spectators, who found it as much as they could all do to pull her down again. There was also another very surprising circumstance about her, agreeable to what we have not only Read in several Histories concerning the Imps that have been Imployed in Witchcraft; but also known in some of our own afflicted: We once thought we perceived something stir upon her Pillow at a little distance from her, whereupon one present laying his hand there, he to his horror apprehended that he felt, tho' none could see it, a living Creature, not altogether unlike a Rat, which nimbly escap'd from him: and there were diverse other Persons who were thrown into a great consternation by feeling, as they Judg'd, at other times the same Invisible Animal.

Sect. 9. As it has been with a Thousand other Inchanted People, so it was with Margaret Rule in this particular, that there were several words which her Tormentors would not let her hear, especially the words Pray or Prayer, and yet she could so hear the letters of those words distinctly mentioned as to know what they ment. The standers by were forced sometimes thus in discourse to spell a word to her, but because there were some so ridiculous as to count it a sort of Spell or a Charm for any thus to accommodate themselves to the capacity of the Sufferer, little of this kind was done. But that which was more singular in this matter, was that she could not use these words in those penetrating discourses, wherewith she would sometimes address the Spectres that were about her. She would sometimes for a long while together apply herself to the Spectres, whom she supposed the Witches, with such Exhortations to Repentance as would have melted an Heart of Adamant to have heard them; her strains of Expression and Argument were truly Extraordinary; A person perhaps of the best Education and Experience and of Attainments much beyond hers could not have exceeded them: nevertheless when she came to these Words God, Lord, Christ, Good, Repent, and some other such, her Mouth could not utter them, whereupon she would somtimes in an Angry Parenthesis complain of their Wickedness in stopping that Word, but she would then go on with some other Terms that would serve to tell what she ment. And I believe that if the most suspicious Person in the world had beheld all the Circumstances of this matter, he would have said it could not have been dissembled.

Sect. 10. Not only in the Swedish, but also in the Salem Witchcraft the Inchanted People have talked much of a White Spirit from whence they received marvellous Assistances in their Miseries; what lately befel Mercy Short from the Communications of such a Spirit, hath been the just Wonder of us all, but by such a Spirit was Margaret Rule now also visited. She says that she could never see his Face; but that she had a frequent view of his bright, Shining and Glorious Garments; he stood by her Bed-side continually heartning and comforting of her and counselling her to maintain her Faith and hope in God, and never comply with the temptations of her Adversaries; she says he told her, that God had permitted her Afflictions to befall her for the everlasting and unspeakable good of her own Soul, and for the good of many others, and for his own Immortal Glory, and that she should therefore be of good Chear and be assured of a speedy deliverance; And the wonderful resolution of mind wherewith she encountered her Afflictions were but agreeable to such expectations. Moreover a Minister[1] having one Day with some Importunity Prayed for the deliverance of this Young Woman, and pleaded

---

[1] Mather himself, of course.

that she belong'd to his Flock and charge; he had so far a
right unto her as that he was to do the part of a Minister of
our Lord for the bringing of her home unto God; only now the
Devil hindred him in doing that which he had a right thus to
do, and whereas He had a better Title unto her to bring her
home to God than the Divel could have unto her to carry her
away from the Lord, he therefore humbly applied himself
unto God, who alone could right this matter, with a suit that
she might be rescued out of Satans Hands; Immediatly upon
this, tho' she heard nothing of this transaction she began to
call that Minister her Father, and that was the Name whereby
she every day before all sorts of People distinguished him:
the occasion of it she says was this, the white Spirit presently
upon this transaction did after this manner speak to her,
"Margaret, you now are to take notice that" (such a Man)
"is your Father, God has given you to him, do you from this
time look upon him as your Father, obey him, regard him as
your Father, follow his Counsels and you shall do well"; And
tho' there was one passage more, which I do as little know
what to make of as any of the Rest, I am now going to relate
it; more than three times have I seen it fulfilled in the Deliverance of Inchanted and Possest Persons, whom the Providence
of God has cast into my way, that their Deliverance could not
be obtained before the third Fast kept for them, and the third
day still obtain'd the Deliverance, altho' I have thought of
beseeching of the Lord thrice, when buffeted by Satan, yet I
must earnestly Intreat all my Readers to beware of any superstitious conceits upon the Number Three; if our God will
hear us upon once Praying and Fasting before him 'tis well,
and if he will not vouchsafe his Mercy upon our thrice doing
so, yet we must not be so discouraged as to throw by our
Devotion but if the Soveraign Grace of our God will in any
particular Instances count our Patience enough tryed when we
have Solemnly waited upon him for any determinate Number
of times, who shall say to him, what doest thou, and if there
shall be any Number of Instances, wherein this Grace of our
God has exactly holden the same course, it may have a room in
our humble Observations, I hope, without any Superstition;
I say then that after Margaret Rule had been more than five
weeks in her Miseries, this White Spirit said unto her, "Well

this day such a Man" (whom he named [1]) "has kept a third
day for your deliverance, now be of good cheer you shall
speedily be delivered." I inquired whether what had been
said of that Man were true, and I gained exact and certain
Information that it was precisely so, but I doubt lest in relating this Passage that I have used more openness than a Friend
should be treated with, and for that cause I have concealed
several of the most memorable things that have occurred not
only in this but in some former Histories, altho indeed I am
not so well satisfied about the true nature of this white Spirit,
as to count that I can do a Friend much Honour by reporting
what notice this white Spirit may have thus taken of him.

Sect. 11.   On the last day of the Week her Tormentors as
she thought and said, approaching towards her, would be forced
still to recoil and retire as unaccountably unable to meddle
with her, and they would retire to the Fire side with their
Poppets; but going to stick Pins into those Poppets, they
could not (according to their visions) make the Pins to enter,
she insulted over them with a very Proper derision, daring
them now to do their worst, whilst she had the satisfaction to
see their Black Master strike them and kick them, like an
Overseer of so many Negro's, to make them to do their work,
and renew the marks of his vengeance on them, when they
failed of doing of it.   At last being as it were tired with their
ineffectual Attempts to mortifie her they furiously said, "Well
you shant be the last." And after a pause they added, "Go, and
the Devil go with you, we can do no more"; whereupon they
flew out of the Room and she returning perfectly to her self
most affectionately gave thanks to God for her deliverance;
her Tormentors left her extream weak and faint, and over-
whelmed with Vapours, which would not only cause her sometimes to Swoon away, but also now and then for a little while
discompose the reasonableness of her Thoughts; Nevertheless her former troubles returned not, but we are now waiting
to see the good effects of those troubles upon the Souls of all
concern'd.   And now I suppose that some of our Learned witlings of the Coffee-House, for fear lest these proofs of an Invisible-world should spoil some of their sport, will endeavour
to turn them all into sport, for which Buffoonary their only

---

[1] Again there can be little doubt that the writer means himself.

pretence will be, they cant understand how such things as
these could be done, whereas indeed he that is but Philosopher
enough to have read but one Little Treatise, Published in the
Year 1656 by no other Man than the Chyrurgion of an Army,[1]
or but one Chap. of Helmont,[2] which I will not quote at this
time too particularly, may give a far more intelligible account
of these Appearances than most of these Blades can give why
and how their Tobacco makes 'em Spit; or which way the flame
of their Candle becomes illuminating. As for that cavil, the
world would be undone if the Devils could have such power as
they seem to have in several of our stories, it may be Answered
that as to many things the Lying Devils have only known them
to be done, and then pretended unto the doing of those things,
but the true and best Answer is, that by these things we only
see what the Devils could have powers to do, if the great God
should give them those powers, whereas now our Histories
affords a Glorious Evidence for the being of a God, the World
would indeed be undone, and horribly undone, if these Devils,
who now and then get liberty to play some very mischievous
pranks, were not under a daily restraint of some Almighty
Superior from doing more of such Mischiefs.   Wherefore instead of all Apish flouts and jeers at Histories, which have such
undoubted confirmation, as that no Man that has breeding
enough to regard the Common Laws of Humane Society, will
offer to doubt of 'em, it becomes us rather to adore the Goodness of God, who does not permit such things every day to
befall us all, as he sometimes did permit to befall some few of
our miserable Neighbours.
    Sect. 12.   And what, after all my unwearied Cares and

----

[1] Who this "Chyrurgion" was and what his treatise, is a puzzle—as it was
perhaps meant to be.   Balthasar Timäus von Guldenklee (1600–1667), physician
to the Elector of Brandenburg, had earned his nobility by healing the Swedish
army of the pest in 1637, and in his *Casus Medicinales* has a passage on diseases
ascribed to witchcraft; but it does not appear that this work was published before 1662.   Antonius Deusing (1612–1666), physician to the Stadholder of Fries-
land, published in 1656 a treatise on this subject; but it does not appear that he
was ever an army surgeon.

[2] Doubtless the elder, Jan Baptista van Helmont (1577–1644), the eminent
but visionary Flemish physician; and the "one Chap." that on "Recepta injecta"
in his *Tractatus de Morbis*—though he goes into the subject as fully in paragraphs
87–152 of his *De Magnetica Vulnerum Curatione*.

Pains, to rescue the Miserable from the Lions and Bears of Hell, which had siezed them, and after all my Studies to disappoint the Devils in their designs to confound my Neighbourhood, must I be driven to the necessity of an Apologie?   Truly the hard representations wherewith some Ill Men have reviled my conduct, and the Countenance which other Men have given to these representations, oblige me to give Mankind some account of my Behaviour; No Christian can, I say none but evil workers can criminate my visiting such of my poor flock as have at any time fallen under the terrible and sensible molestations of Evil-Angels; let their Afflictions have been what they will, I could not have answered it unto my Glorious Lord, if I had withheld my just Counsels and Comforts from them; and if I have also with some exactness observ'd the methods of the Invisible-World, when they have thus become observable, I have been but a Servant of Mankind in doing so; yea no less a Person than the Venerable Baxter has more than once or twice in the most Publick manner invited Mankind to thank me for that Service.[1]   I have not been insensible of a greater danger attending me in this fulfilment of my Ministry, than if I had been to take Ten Thousand steps over a Rocky Mountain fill'd with Rattle-Snakes, but I have consider'd, he that is wise will observe things, and the Surprizing Explication and confirmation of the biggest part of the Bible, which I have seen given in these things, has abundantly paid me for observing them.   Now in my visiting of the Miserable, I was always of this opinion that we were Ignorant of what Powers the Devils might have to do their mischiefs in the shapes of some that had never been explicitly engaged in Diabolical Confederacies, and that therefore tho' many Witchcrafts had been fairly detected on Enquiries provoked and begun by Specteral Exhibitions, yet we could not easily be too jealous[2] of the Snares laid for us in the devices of Satan; the World knows how many Pages I have Composed and Published, and particular Gentlemen in the Government know how many Letters I have written to prevent the excessive Credit of

[1] Notably in his own book on *The Certainty of the Worlds of Spirits* (London, 1691) and in the preface which he wrote for the London edition of Mather's *Memorable Providences*, published in that year.

[2] Suspicious.

Specteral Accusations, wherefore I have still charged the Afflicted that they should Cry out of no body for Afflicting of 'em. But that if this might be any Advantage they might privately tell their minds to some one Person of discretion enough to make no ill use of their communications, accordingly there has been this effect of it, that the Name of No one good Person in the World ever came under any blemish by means of any Afflicted Person that fell under my particular cognisance, yea no one Man, Woman or Child ever came into any trouble for the sake of any that were Afflicted after I had once begun to look after 'em; how often have I had this thrown into my dish, that many years ago I had an opportunity to have brought forth such People as have in the late storm of Witchcraft been complain'd of, but that I smother'd all, and after that storm was rais'd at Salem, I did myself offer to provide Meat, Drink and Lodging for no less than Six of the Afflicted, that so an Experiment might be made, whether Prayer with Fasting upon the removal of the distressed might not put a Period to the trouble then rising, without giving the Civil Authority the trouble of prosecuting those things which nothing but a Conscientious regard unto the cries of Miserable Families, could have overcome the Reluctancies of the Honourable Judges to meddle with; In short I do humbly but freely affirm it, there is not that Man living in this World who has been more desirous than the poor Man I to shelter my Neighbours from the Inconveniencies of Specteral Outcries, yea I am very jealous I have done so much that way as to Sin in what I have done, such have been the Cowardize and Fearfulness whereunto my regard unto the dissatisfactions of other People has precipitated me. I know a Man in the World, who has thought he has been able to Convict some such Witches as ought to Dye, but his respect unto the Publick Peace has caused him rather to try whether He could not renew them by Repentance: And as I have been Studious to defeat the Devils of their expectations to set people together by the Ears, thus, I have also checked and quell'd those forbidden curiosities, which would have given the Devil an invitation to have tarried amongst us, when I have seen wonderful Snares laid for Curious People, by the secret and future things discovered from the Mouths of Damsels possest with a

Spirit of divination; Indeed I can recollect but one thing
wherein there could be given so much as a Shadow of Reason
for Exceptions, and that is my allowing of so many to come
and see those that were Afflicted, now for that I have this to
say, that I have almost a Thousand times intreated the Friends
of the Miserable, that they would not permit the Intrusion of
any Company, but such as by Prayers or other ways might
be helpful to them; Nevertheless I have not absolutely forbid all Company from coming to your Haunted Chambers,
partly because the Calamities of the Families were such as
required the Assistance of many Friends; partly because I
have been willing that there should be disinterested Witnesses
of all sorts, to confute the Calumnies of such as would say all
was but Imposture; and partly because I saw God had Sanctified the Spectacle of the Miseries on the Afflicted unto the
Souls of many that were Spectators, and it is a very Glorious
thing that I have now to mention—The Devils have with
most horrendous operations broke in upon our Neighbourhood,
and God has at such a rate over-ruled all the Fury and Malice
of those Devils, that all the Afflicted have not only been Delivered, but I hope also savingly brought home unto God,
and the Reputation of no one good Person in the World has
been damaged, but instead thereof the Souls of many, especially
of the rising Generation, have been thereby awaken'd unto
some acquaintance with Religion; our young People who belonged unto the Praying Meetings, of both Sexes, a part would
ordinarily spend whole Nights by the whole Weeks together in
Prayers and Psalms upon these occasions, in which Devotions
the Devils could get nothing but like Fools a Scourge for their
own Backs, and some scores of other young People, who were
strangers to real Piety, were now struck with the lively demonstrations of Hell evidently set forth before their Eyes,
when they saw Persons cruelly Frighted, wounded and Starved
by Devils and Scalded with burning Brimstone, and yet so
preserved in this tortured estate as that at the end of one
Months wretchedness they were as able still to undergo another, so that of these also it might now be said, Behold they
Pray in the whole—The Devil got just nothing; but God got
praises, Christ got Subjects, the Holy Spirit got Temples, the
Church got Addition, and the Souls of Men got everlasting

Benefits; I am not so vain as to say that any Wisdome or
Vertue of mine did contribute unto this good order of things:
But I am so just, as to say I did not hinder this Good. When
therefore there have been those that pickt up little incoherent
scraps and bits of my Discourses in this faithful discharge of
my Ministry, and so traversted[1] 'em in their abusive Pam-
phlets,[2] as to perswade the Town that I was their common
Enemy in those very points, wherein, if in any one thing
whatsoever, I have sensibly approved my self as true a Servant unto 'em as possibly I could, tho my Life and Soul had
been at Stake for it, Yea to do like Satan himself, by sly,
base, unpretending Insinuations, as if I wore not the Modesty
and Gravity which became a Minister of the Gospel, I could
not but think my self unkindly dealt withal, and the neglects
of others to do me justice in this affair has caused me to conclude this Narrative with complaints in another hearing of
such Monstrous Injuries.[3]

[1] Travestied.   [2] See p. 332, below.
[3] The story of Margaret Rule is told again in Mather's *Diary* (I. 171 ff.)
and in a way that throws fresh light on his relation to the case.

"About a Week after the Beginning of September, being sollicitous to do some
further Service, for the Name of God, I took a Journey to Salem. There, I not
only sought a further Supply of my Furniture for my Church-History, but also
endeavoured, that the complete History of the late Witchcrafts and Possessions
might not bee lost. I judg'd that the Preservacion of that History might in a
while bee a singular Benefit unto the Church, and unto the World, which made mee
sollicitous about it. Moreover, I was willing to preach the Word of God unto
the numerous Congregation at Salem; which I did, on both Parts of the Sabbath,
not only with a most glorious Assistence of Heaven, but also with some Assurance of Good thereby to bee done among the People. But I had one singular
Unhappiness, which befel mee, in this Journey. I had largely written three Discourses, which I designed both to preach at Salem, and hereafter to print. These
Notes were before the Sabbath stolen from mee, with such Circumstances, that
I am somewhat satisfied, The Spectres, or Agents in the invisible World, were the
Robbers. This Disaster had like to have disturbed my Designs for the Sabbath;
but God helped mee to remember a great part of what I had written, and to
deliver also many other Things, which else I had not now made use of. So that
the Divel gott nothing!

"Among other things which entertained mee at Salem, one was, a Discourse
with one Mrs. Carver, who had been strangely visited with some shining Spirits,
which were good Angels, in her opinion of them.

"She intimated several things unto mee whereof some were to be kept secret.
Shee also told mee, That a new Storm of Witchcraft would fall upon the Countrey, to chastise the Iniquity that was used in the wilful Smothering and Covering

PART II.

A Letter to Mr. C. M.

BOSTON, Jan. 11th, 1693.[1]

Mr. Cotton Mather,

Reverend Sir, I finding it needful on many accounts, I here present you with the Copy of that Paper, which has been so much Misrepresented, to the End that what shall be found defective or not fairly Represented, if any such shall appear, they may be set right, which Runs thus.

September the 13th, 1693.

In the Evening when the Sun was withdrawn, giving place to Darkness to succeed, I with some others were drawn by curiosity to see Margaret Rule, and so much the rather because it was reported Mr. M——[2] would be there that Night: Being come to her Fathers House into the Chamber wherein she was in Bed, found her of a

of the Last; and that many fierce Opposites to the Discovery of that Witchcraft would bee thereby convinced.

"Unto my Surprise, when I came home, I found one of my Neighbours horribly arrested by evil Spirits. I then beg'd of God, that Hee would help mee wisely to discharge my Duty upon this occasion, and avoid gratifying of the evil Angels in any of their Expectacions. I did then concern myself to use and gett as much Prayer as I could for the afflicted young Woman; and at the same time, to forbid, either her from accusing any of her Neighbours, or others from enquiring any thing of her. Nevertheless, a wicked Man wrote a most lying Libel to revile my Conduct in these matters; which drove mee to the Blessed God, with my Supplications that Hee would wonderfully protect mee, as well from unreasonable Men acted by the Divels, as from the Divels themselves. I did at first, it may bee, too much resent the Injuries of that Libel; but God brought good out of it; it occasioned the Multiplication of my Prayers before Him; it very much promoted the Works of Humiliation and Mortification in my Soul. Indeed, the Divel made that Libel an Occasion of those Paroxysms in the Town, that would have exceedingly gratify'd him, if God had not helped mee to forgive and forgett the Injuries done unto mee, and to bee deaf unto the Sollicitations of those that would have had mee so to have resented the Injuries of some few Persons, as to have deserted the Lecture at the Old Meeting house.

"When the afflicted young woman had undergone six Weeks of præternatural Calamities and when God had helped mee to keep just three Dayes of Prayer on her behalf, I had the Pleasure of seeing the same Success, which I used to have, on my third Fast, for such possessed People, as have been cast into my

---

[1] 1694 of our present calendar.   [2] Mather.

healthy countenance of about seventeen Years Old, lying very still, and speaking very little, what she did say seem'd as if she were Light-headed. Then Mr. M——, Father and Son, came up and others with them, in the whole were about 30 or 40 Persons; they being sat, the Father on a Stool, and the Son upon the Bedside by her, the Son began to question her, Margaret Rule, how do you do? then a pause without any answer. *Question.* What, do there a great many Witches sit upon you? *Answer.* Yes. *Q.* Do you not know that there is a hard Master? Then she was in a Fit; He laid his hand upon her Face and Nose, but, as he said, without perceiving Breath; then he brush'd her on the Face with his Glove, and rubb'd her Stomach (her breast not covered with the Bed-cloaths) and bid others do so too, and said it eased her, then she revived. *Q.* Don't you know there is a hard Master? *A.* Yes. *Reply*; Don't serve that hard Master, you know who. *Q.* Do you believe? Then again she was in a Fit, and he again rub'd her Breast, etc. (about this time Margaret Perd an attendant assisted him in rubbing of her. The Afflicted spake angerely to her saying don't you meddle with me, and hastily put away her hand) he wrought his Fingers before her Eyes and asked her if she saw the Witches? *A.* No. *Q.* Do you

cares. God gave her a glorious Deliverance; The remarkable Circumstances whereof, I have more fully related, in an History of the whole Business.

"As for my missing Notes, the possessed young Woman, of her own Accord, enquir'd whether I missed them not? Shee told mee, the Spectres brag'd in her hearing, that they had rob't mee of them; shee added, Bee n't concern'd; for they confess, they can't keep them alwayes from you; you shall have them all brought you again. (They were Notes on Ps. 119. 19 and Ps. 90. 12 and Hag. 1. 7, 9. I was tender of them and often pray'd unto God, that they might bee return'd.) On the fifth of October following, every Leaf of my Notes again came into my Hands, tho' they were in eighteen separate Quarters of Sheets. They were found drop't here and there, about the Streets of Lyn; but how they came to bee so drop't I cannot imagine; and I as much wonder at the Exactness of their Præservation."

And under October 10th he adds: "On this Day, I also visited a possessed young Woman in the Neighbourhood, whose Distresses were not the least occasion of my being thus before the Lord. I wrestled with God for her: and among other things, I pleaded, that God had made it my Office and Business to engage my Neighbours in the Service of the Lord Jesus Christ; and that this young Woman had expressed her Compliance with my Invitations unto that Service; only that the evil Spirits now hindred her from doing what shee had vowd: and therefore that I had a sort of Right to demand her Deliverance from these invading Divels, and to demand such a Liberty for her as might make her capable of glorifying my Glorious Lord; which I did accordingly. In the close of this Day, a wonderful Spirit, in White and bright Raiment, with a Face unseen, appeared unto this young woman, and bid her count mee her Father, and re-

believe? *A.* Yes. *Q.* Do you believe in you know who? *A.* Yes.
Q. Would you have other people do so too, to believe in you know
who? *A.* Yes. *Q.* Who is it that Afflicts you? *A.* I know not,
there is a great many of them (about this time the Father question'd
if she knew the Spectres? An attendant said, if she did she would
not tell; The Son proceeded) *Q.* You have seen the Black-man,
hant[1] you? *A.* No. *Reply*; I hope you never shall. *Q.* You have
had a Book offered you, hant you? *A.* No. *Q.* The brushing of
you gives you ease, don't it? *A.* Yes. She turn'd her selfe and a
little Groan'd. *Q.* Now the Witches Scratch you and Pinch you,
and Bite you, don't they? *A.* Yes. Then he put his hand upon
her Breast and Belly, *viz.* on the Cloaths over her, and felt a Living
thing, as he said, which moved the Father also to feel, and some
others; *Q.* Don't you feel the Live thing in the Bed? *A.* No.
Reply, that is only Fancie. *Q.* the great company of People increase
your Torment, don't they? *A.* Yes. The People about were desired to withdraw. One Woman said, I am sure I am no Witch, I
will not go; so others, so none withdrew. *Q.* Shall we go to Prayers?
Then she lay in a Fit as before. But this time to revive her, they
waved a Hat and brushed her Head and Pillow therewith. *Q.* Shall
we go to *Pray*, etc. Spelling the Word. *A.* Yes. The Father went

gard mee and obey mee, as her Father; for hee said, the Lord had given her to mee;
and she should now within a few Dayes bee delivered. It proved, accordingly."

And again in December (p. 178): "And one memorable Providence, I must
not forgett. A young Woman being arrested, possessed, afflicted by evil Angels,
her Tormentors made my Image or Picture to appear before her, and then made
themselves Masters of her Tongue so far, that she began in her Fits to complain
that I threatened her and molested her, tho' when shee came out of them, shee
own'd, that they could not so much as make my dead Shape do her any Harm,
and that they putt a Force upon her Tongue in her Exclamations. Her greatest
Out-cries when shee was herself, were, for my poor Prayers to be concerned on
her behalf.

"Being hereupon extremely sensible, how much a malicious Town and Land
would insult over mee, if such a lying Piece of a Story should fly abroad, that
the Divels in my Shape tormented the Neighbourhood, I was putt upon some
Agonies, and singular Salleys and Efforts of Soul, in the Resignation of my
Name unto the Lord; content that if Hee had no further service for my Name,
it should bee torn to pieces with all the Reproches in the world. But I cried
unto the Lord as for the Deliverance of my Name, from the Malice of Hell, so
for the Deliverance of the young Woman, whom the Powers of Hell had now
seized upon. And behold! Without any further Noise, the possessed Person,
upon my praying by her, was delivered from her Captivity, on the very same
Day that shee fell into it; and the whole Plott of the Divel, to reproach a poor
Servant of the Lord Jesus Christ, was defeated."

[1] Haven't, hain't.

to Prayer for perhaps half an Hour, chiefly against the Power of the
Devil and Witchcraft, and that God would bring out the Afflicters:
during Prayer-time, the Son stood by, and when they thought she
was in a Fit, rub'd her and brush'd her as before, and beckned to
others to do the like; after Prayer he proceeded; *Q.* You did not
hear when we were at Prayer, did you? *A.* Yes. *Q.* You dont hear
always, you dont hear sometimes past a Word or two, do you?
A. No. Then turning him about said, this is just another Mercy
Short: Margaret Perd reply'd, she was not like her in her Fits.
Q. What does she eat or drink? *A.* Not eat at all; but drink Rum.
Then he admonished the young People to take warning, etc. Saying
it was a sad thing to be so Tormented by the Devil and his Instruments: A Young-man present in the habit of a Seaman, reply'd
this is the Devil all over. Than[1] the Ministers withdrew. Soon after
they were gon the Afflicted desired the Women to be gone, saying,
that the Company of the Men was not offensive to her, and having
hold of the hand of a Young-man, said to have been her Sweet-heart
formerly, who was withdrawing; She pull'd him again into his Seat,
saying he should not go to Night.

September the 19th, 1693.

This Night I renew'd my Visit, and found her rather of a fresher
Countenance than before, about eight Persons present with her, she
was in a Fit Screeming and making a Noise: Three or four Persons
rub'd and brush'd her with their hands, they said that the brushing
did put them away, if they brush'd or rub'd in the right place; therefore they brush'd and rub'd in several places, and said that when they
did it in the right place she could fetch her Breath, and by that they
knew. She being come to her self was soon in a merry talking Fit.
A Young-man came in and ask'd her how she did? She answered
very bad, but at present a little better; he soon told her he must be
gon and bid her good Night, at which she seem'd troubled, saying,
that she liked his Company, and said she would not have him go till
she was well; adding, for I shall Die when you are gon. Then she
complained they did not put her on a clean Cap, but let her ly so
like a Beast, saying, she should lose her Fellows. She said she wondered any People should be so Wicked as to think she was not Afflicted,
but to think she Dissembled. A Young-woman answered Yes, if
they were to see you in this merry Fit, they would say you Dissembled indeed; She reply'd, Mr. M—— said this was her laughing time,
she must laugh now: She said Mr. M—— had been there this
Evening, and she enquired, how long he had been gon? She said,

[1] Then.

he stay'd alone with her in the room half an Hour, and said that he told her there were some that came for Spies, and to report about Town that she was not Afflicted.   That during the said time she had no Fit, that he asked her if she knew how many times he had Prayed for her to Day?   And that she answered that she could not tell; and that he replyed he had Prayed for her Nine times to Day; the Attendants said that she was sometimes in a Fit that none could open her Joynts, and that there came an Old Iron-jaw'd Woman and try'd, but could not do it; they likewise said, that her Head could not be moved from the Pillow; I try'd to move her head, and found no more difficulty than another Bodies (and so did others) but was not willing to offend by lifting it up, one being reproved for endeavouring it, they saying angrily you will break her Neck; The Attendants said Mr. M—— would not go to Prayer with her when People were in the Room, as they did one Night, that Night he felt the Live Creature.   Margaret Perd and another said they smelt Brimstone; I and others said we did not smell any; then they said they did not know what it was: This Margaret said, she wish'd she had been here when Mr. M—— was here, another Attendant said, if you had been here you might not have been permitted in, for her own Mother was not suffered to be present.

Sir, after the sorest Affliction and greatest blemish to Religion that ever befel this Countrey, and after most Men began to Fear that some undue steps had been taken, and after His Excellency (with their Majesties Approbation[1] as is said) had put a stop to Executions, and Men began to hope there would never be a return of the like; finding these Accounts to contain in them something extraordinary, I writ them down the same Nights in order to attain the certainty of them, and soon found them so confirmed that I have (besides other Demonstrations) the whole, under the Hands of two Persons are ready to attest the Truth of it; but not satisfied herewith, I shewed them to some of your particular Friends,

---

[1] The answer to Governor Phips's letter of October 12 (see pp. 196–198, above) was indeed a royal order of January 26 "approving his action in stopping the proceedings against the witches in New England, and directing that in all future proceedings against persons accused of witchcraft or of possession by the devil, all circumspection be used so far as may be without impediment to the ordinary course of justice"—what Frederick the Great would have called "a vague answer—in the Austrian style—that should mean nothing."   It of course did not reach America till after the despatch of Sir William's letter of February 21 (pp. 198–202, above).

that so I might have the greater certainty: But was much
surprized with the Message you sent me, that I should be
Arrested for Slander, and at your calling me one of the worst
of Lyars, making it Pulpit news with the Name of Pernicious
Libels, etc. This occasion'd my first Letter.

September the 29th, 1693.
Reverend Sir,
   I having written from the Mouths of several Persons, who affirm
they were present with Margaret Rule, the 13th Instant, her Answers
and Behaviours, etc. And having shewed it to several of my Friends,
as also yours, and understanding you are offended at it; This is to
acquaint you, that if you and any one particular Friend, will please
to meet me and some other Indifferent Person with me, at Mr. Wilkins, or at Ben. Harris's,[1] you intimating the time, I shall be ready
there to read it to you, as also a further Account of proceedings the
19th Instant, which may be needful to prevent Groundless prejudices,
and let deserved blame be cast where it ought; From,
   Sir, yours in what I may,
R. C.

   The effects of which, Sir, (not to mention that long Letter
only once read to me) was, you sent me word you would meet
me at Mr. Wilkins, but before that Answer, at yours and your
Fathers complaint, I was brought before their Majesties Justice, by Warrant, as for Scandalous Libels against your self,
and was bound over to Answer at Sessions; I do not remember
you then objected against the Truth of what I had wrote, but
asserted it was wronged by omissions, which if it were so was
past any Power of mine to remedy, having given a faithful
account of all that came to my knowledge; And Sir, that you
might not be without some Cognisance of the reasons why I
took so much pains in it, as also for my own Information, if
it might have been, I wrote to you my second Letter to this
effect.

November the 24th, 1693.
Reverend Sir,
   Having expected some Weeks, your meeting me at Mr. Wilkins ac-
cording to what you intimated to Mr. J. M.——[2] and the time draw-

---

[1] The two Boston booksellers'.

[2] It is perhaps idle to guess at the identity of this gentleman; but his initials
suggest the Rev. Joshua Moodey, whose kindlier attitude toward witches and

ing near for our meeting elsewhere, I thought it not amiss to give you a Summary of my thoughts in the great concern, which as you say has been agitated with so much heat. That there are Witches is not the doubt, the Scriptures else were in vain, which assign their Punishment to be by Death; But what this Witchcraft is, or wherein it does consist, seems to be the whole difficulty: And as it may be easily demonstrated, that all that bear that Name cannot be justly so accounted, so that some things and Actions not so esteemed by the most, yet upon due examination will be found to merit no better Character.

In your late Book you lay down a brief Synopsis of what has been written on that Subject, by a Triumvirate of as Eminent Men as ever handled it (as you are pleas'd to call them) *Viz*. Mr. Perkins,[1] Gaule,[2] and Bernard[3] consisting of about 30 Tokens to know them by, many of them distinct from, if not thwarting each other: Among all of which I can find but one decisive, *Viz*. That of Mr. Gaule, Head IV. and runs thus; Among the most unhappy Circumstances to convict a Witch, one is a maligning and oppugning the Word, Work, or Worship of God, and by any extraordinary Sign seeking to seduce any from it, see Deu. 13. 1, 2.   Mat. 24. 24.   Acts. 13. 8, 10.   2 Tim. 3. 8.   Do but mark well the places, and for this very property of thus opposing and perverting, they are all there concluded Arrant and absolute Witches.[4]

This Head as here laid down and inserted by you, either is a Truth or not; if not, why is it here inserted from one of the Triumvirate, if it be a Truth, as the Scriptures quoted will abundantly testifie, whence is it that it is so little regarded, tho it be the only Head well proved by Scripture, or that the rest of the Triumvirate should so far forget their Work as not to mention it. It were to be unjust to the Memory of those otherwise Wise Men, to suppose them to have any Sinister design; But perhaps the force of a prevailing opinion, together with an Education thereto Suited, might over-

their defenders may be inferred from his course in the case of Philip English (see pp. 187–188, note), and who, though early in 1693 he returned to Portsmouth, was still often in Boston. Nor may it be forgotten that the initials of the Rev. Increase Mather are by the printer constantly made "J. M."

[1] See above, p. 304, note 3.

[2] See above, p. 216, note 1, and p. 219.

[3] See above, p. 304, note 5.

[4] To the end of the paragraph the words are Gaule's. Calef is quoting them, not from Gaule's book, but from Mather's *Wonders*; for Gaule numbers this rule, not IV., but X., and the introductory words ("Among the most unhappy Circumstances to convict a witch, one is") are not his, but Mather's— and there are other slight departures from Gaule's wording.

shadow their Judgments, as being wont to be but too prevalent in
many other cases. But if the above be Truth, then the Scripture is
full and plain, What is Witchcraft? And if so, what need of his next
Head of Hanging of People without as full and clear Evidence as in
other Cases? Or what need of the rest of the Receipts of the Triumvirate? what need of Praying that the Afflicted may be able to discover who tis that Afflicts them? or what need of Searching for Tet's
for the Devil to Suck in his Old Age, or the Experiment of saying the
Lords Prayer, etc. Which[1] a multitude more practised in some
places Superstitiously inclin'd. Other Actions have been practised
for easing the Afflicted, less justifiable, if not strongly savouring of
Witchcraft it self, viz. Fondly Imagining by the Hand, etc., to drive
off Spectres, or to knock off Invisible Chains, or by striking in the
Air to Wound either the Afflicted or others, etc. I write not this to
accuse any, but that all may beware believing, That the Devil's
bounds are set, which he cannot pass, That the Devils are so full of
Malice, That it cant be added to by Mankind, That where he hath
Power, he neither can nor will omit Executing it, That 'tis only the
Almighty that sets bounds to his rage, and that only can Commissionate him to hurt or destroy any.

These last, Sir, are such Foundations of Truth, in my esteem,
that I cannot but own it to be my duty to ascert them, when call'd
tho' with the hazard of my All: And consequently to detect such as
these, That a Witch can Commissionate Devils to Afflict Mortals,
That he can at his or the Witches pleasure Assume any Shape, That
Hanging or Chaining of Witches can lessen his Power of Afflicting,
or restore those that were at a distance Tormented, with many others
depending on these; all tending, in my esteem, highly to the Dishonour of God, and the Indangering the well-being of a People, and
do further add, that as the Scriptures are full that there is Witchcraft, (ut sup.) so 'tis as plain that there are Possessions, and that
the Bodies of the Possest have hence been not only Afflicted, but
strangely agitated, if not their Tongues improved to foretell futuri-
ties, etc. and why not to accuse the Innocent, as bewitching them;
having pretence to Divination to gain credence. This being reasonable to be expected, from him who is the Father of Lies, to the end
he may thereby involve a Countrey in Blood, Mallice, and Evil, sur-
mising which he greedily seeks after, and so finally lead them from
their fear and dependence upon God to fear him, and a supposed
Witch thereby attaining his end upon Mankind; and not only so,
but Natural Distemper, as has been frequently observed by the
Judicious, have so operated as to deceive, more than the Vulgar, as

---

[1] With.

is testified by many Famous Physicians, and others. And as for that proof of Multitudes of Confessions, this Countrey may be by this time thought Competent Judges, what credence we ought to give them, having had such numerous Instances, as also how obtain'd.

And now Sir, if herein be any thing in your esteem valuable, let me intreat you, not to account it the worse for coming from so mean a hand; which however you may have receiv'd Prejudices, etc., Am ready to serve you to my Power; but if you Judge otherwise hereof, you may take your own Methods for my better Information. Who am, Sir, yours to command, in what I may,   R. C.[1]

In Answer to this last, Sir, you replyed to the Gentleman that presented it, that you had nothing to Prosecute against me; and said as to your Sentiments in your Books, you did not bind any to believe them, and then again renew'd your promise of meeting me, as before, tho' not yet performed. Accordingly, tho' I waited at Sessions, there was none to object ought against me, upon which I was dismissed. This gave me some reason to believe that you intended all should have been forgotten; But instead of that, I find the Coals are fresh blown up, I being supposed to be represented, in a late Manuscript, *More Wonders of the*, etc., as Traversing[2] your Discourse in your Faithful discharge of your Duty, etc. And such as see not with the Authors Eyes, rendred Sadducees and Witlins,[3] etc., and the Arguments that square not with the Sentiments therein contain'd, Buffoonary; rarely no doubt, agreeing with the Spirit of Christ, and his dealings with an unbelieving Thomas, yet whose infidelity was without compare less excusable, but the Author having resolved long since, to have no more than one single Grain of Patience, with them that deny,[4] etc., the Wonder is the less. It must needs be that offences come, but wo to him by whom they come. To vindicate my self therefore from such false Imputations, of Satanlike insinuations, and misrepresenting your Actions, etc., and to vindicate your self, Sir, as much as is in my Power from those Suggestions, said to be Insinuated, as if you wore not the Modesty and Gravity, that becomes a Minister of the Gospel; which it seems, some that never saw the said Narra-

---

[1] By a misprint the original has "P. C."

[2] Travestying. See p. 323, above.

[3] See p. 318, above.   [4] See p. 123, above.

tives, report them to contain; I say, Sir, for these reasons, I here present you with the first Coppy that ever was taken, etc. And purpose for a Weeks time to be ready, if you shall intimate your pleasure, to wait upon you, either at the place formerly appointed, or any other that is indifferent to the End; that if there shall appear any defects in that Narrative, they may be amended.

Thus, Sir, I have given you a genuine account of my Sentiments and Actions in this Affair; and do request and pray, that if I err, I may be shewed it from Scripture, or sound Reason, and not by quotations out of Virgil, nor Spanish Rhetorick. For I find the Witlings mentioned, are so far from answering your profound questions, that they cannot so much as pretend to shew a distinction between Witchcraft in the Common notion of it, and Possession; Nor so much as to demonstrate that ever the Jews or primitive Christians did believe, that a Witch could send a Devil to Afflict her Neighbours; but to all these, Sir, (ye being the Salt of the Earth, etc.) I have reason to hope for a Satisfactory Answer to him, who is one that reverences your Person and Office; And am, Sir, yours to Command in what I may,

R. C.

BOSTON, January the 15th, 169¾.

Mr. R. C.

Whereas you intimate your desires, that what's not fairly, (I take it for granted you mean truly also,) represented in a Paper you lately sent me, containing a pretended Narrative of a Visit by my Father and self to an Afflicted Young woman, whom we apprehended to be under a Diabolical Possession, might be rectified: I have this to say, as I have often already said, that I do scarcely find any one thing in the whole Paper, whether respecting my Father or self, either fairly or truly represented. Nor can I think that any that know my Parents Circumstances, but must think him deserving a better Character by far, than this Narrative can be thought to give him. When the main design we managed in Visiting the poor Afflicted Creature, was to prevent the Accusations of the Neighbourhood, can it be fairly represented that our design was to draw out such Accusations, which is the representation of the Paper?   We have Testimonies of the best Witnesses and in Number not a few, That when we asked Rule whether she thought she knew who Tormented her? the Question was but an Introduction to the Solemn charges which we then largely gave, that she should rather Dye than tell the Names of any whom she might Imagine that she knew.   Your Informers have reported the Question, and report nothing of what follows, as essential to the giving of that Question: And can this be termed a piece of fairness?   Fair it cannot be, that when Ministers Faithfully and Carefully discharge their Duty to the Miserable in their Flock, little bits, scraps and shreds of their Discourses should be tackt together to make them contemtible, when there shall be no notice of all the Necessary, Seasonable, and Profitable things that occur'd, in those Discourses; And without which, the occasion of the lesser Passages cannot be understood; And yet I am furnished with abundant Evidences, ready to be Sworn, that will possitively prove this part of unfairness, by the above mention'd Narrative, to be done both to my Father and self.   Again, it seems not fair or reasonable that I should be expos'd, for which your self (not to say some others) might have expos'd me for, if I had not done, *Viz.* for discouraging so much Company from flocking about the Possest Maid, and yet, as I perswade my self, you cannot but think it to be good advice, to keep much Company from such haunted Chambers; besides the unfairness doth more appear, in that I find nothing repeated of what I said about the advantage, which the Devil takes from too much Observation and Curiosity.

In that several of the Questions in the Paper are so Worded, as to carry in them a presuppoal of the things inquired after, to say the best of it is very unfair: But this is not all, the Narrative contains a number of Mistakes and Falshoods; which were they willful and design'd, might justly be termed gross Lies.   The representations are far from true, when 'tis affirm'd my Father and self being come into the Room, I began the Discourse; I hope I understand breeding a little better than so: For proof of this, did occasion serve, sundry can depose the contrary.

'Tis no less untrue, that either my Father or self put the Question, how many Witches sit upon you?   We always cautiously avoided that expression; It being contrary to our inward belief: All the standers by will (I believe) Swear they did not hear us use it (your Witnesses excepted) and I tremble to think how hardy those woful Creatures must be, to call the Almighty by an Oath, to so false a thing. As false a representation 'tis, that I rub'd Rule's Stomach, her Breast not being covered. The Oath of the nearest Spectators, giving a true account of that matter will prove this to be little less than a gross (if not a doubled) Lie; and to be somewhat plainer, it carries the Face of a Lie contrived on purpose (by them at least, to whom you are beholden for the Narrative) Wickedly and Basely to expose me. For you cannot but know how much this Representation hath contributed, to make People believe a Smutty thing of me; I am far from thinking, but that in your own Conscience you believe, that no indecent Action of that Nature could then be done by me before such observers, had I been so Wicked as to have been inclin'd to what is Base. It looks next to impossible that a reparation shoud be made me for the wrong done to, I hope, as to any Scandal, an unblemish'd, tho' weak and small Servant of the Church of God. Nor is what follows a less untruth, that 'twas an Attendant and not my self who said, if Rule knows who Afflicts her, yet she wont tell. I therefore spoke it that I might incourage her to continue in that concealment of all Names whatsoever; to this I am able to furnish my self with the Attestation of Sufficient Oaths. 'Tis as far from true, that my apprehension of the Imp, about Rule, was on her Belly, for the Oaths of the Spectators, and even of those that thought they felt it, can testify that 'twas upon the Pillow, at a distance from her Body. As untrue a Representation is that which follows, *Viz.* That it was said unto her, that her not Apprehending of that odd palpable, tho' not visible, Mover was from her Fancy, for I endeavoured to perswade her that it might be but Fancy in others, that there was any such thing at all. Witnesses every way sufficient can be produced for this also. 'Tis falsely represented that my Father felt on the Young-woman after the appearance mentioned, for his hand was never near her; Oath can sufficiently vindicate him. 'Tis very untrue that my Father Prayed for perhaps half an Hour, against the power of the Devil and Witchcraft, and that God would bring out the

Afflictors. Witnesses of the best Credit, can depose, that his Prayer was not a quarter of an Hour, and that there was no more than about one clause towards the close of the Prayer, which was of this import; And this clause also was guarded with a singular wariness and modesty, *Viz.* If there were any evil Instruments in this matter God would please to discover them: And that there was more than common reason for that Petition I can satisfie any one that will please to Inquire of me. And strange it is, that a Gentleman that from 18 to 54 hath been an Exemplary Minister of the Gospel; and that besides a station in the Church of God, as considerable as any that his own Country can afford, hath for divers years come off with Honour, in his Application to three Crown'd Heads, and the chiefest Nobility of three Kingdoms, Knows not yet how to make one short Prayer of a quarter of an hour, but in New-England he must be Libell'd for it. There are divers other down-right mistakes, which you have permitted your self, I would hope not knowingly, and with a Malicious design, to be receiver or Compiler of, which I shall now forbear to Animadvert upon. As for the Appendix of the Narrative I do find myself therein Injuriously treated, for the utmost of your proof for what you say of me, amounts to little more than, *viz.* Some People told you, that others told them, that such and such things did pass, but you may assure yourself, that I am not unfurnish'd with Witnesses, that can convict the same. Whereas you would give me to believe the bottom of these your Methods, to be some dissatisfaction about the commonly receiv'd Power of Devils and Witches; I do not only with all freedom offer you the use of any part of my Library, which you may see cause to peruse on that Subject, but also if you and any else, whom you please, will visit me at my Study, yea, or meet me at any other place, less inconvenient than those by you propos'd; I will with all the fairness and calmness in the World dispute the point. I beg of God that he would bestow as many Blessings on you, as ever on myself, and out of a sincere wish, that you may be made yet more capable of these Blessings, I take this occasion to lay before you the faults (not few nor small ones neither) which the Paper contained, you lately sent me in order to be Examined by me. In case you want a true and full Narrative of my

Visit, whereof such an indecent Traversty (to say the best) hath been made, I am not unwilling to communicate it, in mean time must take liberty to say, 'Tis scarcely consistent with Common Civility, much less Christian Charity, to offer the Narrative, now with you, for a true one, till you have a truer, or for a full one, till you have a fuller. Your Sincere (tho Injur'd) Friend and Servant,

C. MATHER.

The Copy of a Paper Receiv'd with the above Letter.

I do Testifie that I have seen Margaret Rule in her Afflictions from the Invisible World, lifted up from her Bed, wholly by an Invisible force, a great way towards the top of the Room where she lay; in her being so lifted, she had no Assistance from any use of her own Arms or Hands, or any other part of her Body, not so much as her Heels touching her Bed, or resting on any support whatsoever. And I have seen her thus lifted, when not only a strong Person hath thrown his whole weight a cross her to pull her down; but several other Persons have endeavoured, with all their might, to hinder her from being so raised up, which I suppose that several others will testifie as well as my self, when call'd unto it. Witness my Hand,

SAMUEL AVES.

We can also Testifie to the substance of what is above Written, and have several times seen Margaret Rule so lifted up from her Bed, as that she had no use of her own Lims to help her up, but it was the declared apprehension of us, as well as others that saw it, impossible for any hands, but some of the Invisible World to lift her.

ROBERT EARLE.
Copia.   JOHN WILKINS.
DAN. WILLIAMS.

We whose Names are under-writted do testifie, That one Evening when we were in the Chamber where Margaret Rule then lay, in her late Affliction, we observed her to be, by an

Invisible Force, lifted up from the Bed whereon she lay, so as to touch the Garret Floor, while yet neither her Feet, nor any other part of her Body rested either on the Bed, or any other support, but were also by the same force, lifted up from all that was under her, and all this for a considerable while, we judg'd it several Minutes; and it was as much as several of us could do, with all our strength to pull her down. All which happened when there was not only we two in the Chamber, but we suppose ten or a dozen more, whose Names we have forgotten,

Copia.   THOMAS THORNTON.

William Hudson Testifies to the substance of Thorntons Testimony, to which he also hath set his Hand.

BOSTON, Jan. 18, 1693.[1]

Mr. Cotton Mather,
       Reverend Sir,
       Yours of the 15th Instant, I receiv'd yesterday; and soon found I had promised my self too much by it, *Viz*, Either concurrence with, or a denial of those Fundamentals mentioned in mine, of Novem. the 24th, finding this waved by an Invitation to your Library, etc. I thank God I have the Bible, and do Judge that sufficient to demonstrate that cited Head of Mr. Gaule to be a Truth, as also those other Heads mentioned, as the Foundations of Religion. And in my apprehension, if it be asked any Christian, whether God governs the World, and whether it be he only can Commissionate Devils, and such other Fundamentals, He ought to be as ready as in the Question, who made him? (a little Writing certainly might be of more use, to clear up the controverted points, than either looking over many Books in a well furnish'd Library, or than a dispute, if I were qualified for it; the Inconveniencies of Passion being this way best avoided) And am not without hopes that you will yet oblige me so far, as to consider that Letter, and if I Err, to let me see it by Scripture, etc.
       Yours, almost the whole of it, is concerning the Narrative I sent to you, and you seem to intimate as if I were giving

_____
[1] 1694 of new style.

Characters, Reflections, and Libell's, etc. concerning your self
and Relations; all which were as far from my thoughts, as
ever they were in writing after either your self, or any other
Minister.   In the front you declare your apprehension to be,
that the Afflicted was under a Diabolical Possession, and if so,
I see not how it should be occasion'd by any Witchcraft (unless
we ascribe that Power to a Witch, which is only the Prerogative of the Almighty, of Sending or Commissionating the Devils
to Afflict her.)   But to your particular Objections against the
Narrative; and to the first my intelligence not giving me any
further, I could not insert that I knew not.   And it seems improbable that a Question should be put, whether she knew (or
rather who they were) and at the same time to charge her,
and that upon her Life, not to tell, and if you had done so, I
see but little good you could promise your self or others by it,
she being Possest, as also having it inculcated so much to her
of Witchcraft.   And as to the next Objection about company
flocking, etc., I do profess my Ignorance, not knowing what
you mean by it.   And Sir, that most of the Questions did carry
with them a presupposing the things inquired after, is evident,
if there were such as those relating to the Black-man and a
Book, and about her hearing the Prayer, etc. (related in the
said Narrative, which I find no Objection against.)   As to
that which is said of mentioning your self first discoursing and
your hopes that your breeding was better (I doubt it not) nor
do I doubt your Father might first apply himself to others;
but my intelligence is, that you first spake to the Afflicted or
Possessed, for which you had the advantage of a nearer approach.   The next two Objections are founded upon mistakes:
I find not in the Narrative any such Question, as how many
Witches sit upon you? and that her Breast was not covered, in
which those material words "with the Bed-Cloaths" are wholly
omitted; I am not willing to retort here your own Language
upon you; but can tell you, that your own discourse of it
publickly, at Sir W. P.'s[1] Table, has much more contributed
to, etc.   As to the Reply, if she could she would not tell,
whether either or both spake it it matters not much.   Neither
does the Narrative say you felt the live thing on her Belly;
tho I omit now to say what further demonstrations there are

---

[1] Sir William Phips's.

of it. As to that Reply, that is only her fancy, I find the word "her" added. And as to your Fathers feeling for the live Creature after you had felt it, if it were on the Bed it was not so very far from her. And for the length of his Prayer, possibly your Witnesses might keep a more exact account of the time than those others, and I stand not for a few Minutes. For the rest of the Objections I suppose them of less moment, if less can be (however shall be ready to receive them, those matters of greatest concern I find no Objections against). These being all that yet appear, it may be thought that if the Narrative be not fully exact, it was as near as Memory could bear away; but should be glad to see one more perfect (which yet is not to be expected, seeing none writ at the time). You mention the appendix, by which I understand the Second Visit, and if you be by the possessed belyed (as being half an hour with her alone, excluding her own Mother, and as telling her you had Prayed for her Nine times that day, and that now was her Laughing time, she must Laugh now) I can see no Wonder in it; what can be expected less from the Father of Lies, by whom, you Judge, she was possest.

And besides the above Letter, you were pleased to send me another Paper containing several Testimonies of the Possessed being lifted up, and held a space of several Minutes to the Garret floor, etc., but they omit giving the account, whether after she was down they bound her down: or kept holding her: And relate not how many were to pull her down, which hinders the knowledge what number they must be to be stronger than an Invisible Force. Upon the whole, I suppose you expect I should believe it; and if so, the only advantage gain'd, is that which has been so long controverted between Protestants and Papists, whether Miracles are ceast, will hereby seem to be decided for the latter; it being, for ought I can see, if so, as true a Miracle as for Iron to swim, and that the Devil can work such Miracles.

But Sir, leaving these little disputable things, I do again pray that you would let me have the happiness of your approbation or confutation of that Letter before referred to.

And now, Sir, that the God of all Grace may enable us Zealously to own his Truths, and to follow those things that tend to Peace, and that yourself may be as an useful Instru-

ment in his hand, effectually to ruin the remainders of Heathenish and Popish Superstitions, is the earnest desire and prayer
of yours to command, in what I may.

R. C.[1]

.   .   .   .

PART V.

An Impartial Account of the most Memorable Matters of Fact,
touching the supposed Witchcraft in New England.[2]

Mr. Parris had been some years a Minister in Salem-Village,[3] when this sad Calamity (as a deluge) overflowed them,
spreading it self far and near: He was a Gentleman of Liberal
Education, and not meeting with any great Encouragement,
or Advantage in Merchandizing, to which for some time he
apply'd himself, betook himself to the work of the Ministry;
this Village being then vacant, he met with so much Encouragement, as to settle in that Capacity among them.

After he had been there about two years, he obtained a
Grant from a part of the Town, that the House and Land he
Occupied, and which had been Alotted by the whole People
to the Ministry, should be and remain to him, etc. as his own
Estate in Fee Simple. This occasioned great Divisions both
between the Inhabitants themselves, and between a considerable part of them and their said Minister, which Divisions were
but as a beginning or Præludium to what immediately followed.

It was the latter end of February 1691,[4] when divers
young Persons belonging to Mr. Parris's Family, and one or

---

[1] Between this letter and the pages of Calef's book which here follow there
intervene (1) further letters from him to Mather and to other Boston ministers,
on whom he urges his views, (2) a body of documents relating to the controversy
between the Rev. Mr. Parris and his disaffected parishioners at Salem Village
between the period of the witch-trials and his removal, (3) an epistolary discussion as to the theory of witchcraft between Calef and a Scotsman named Stuart.

[2] *I. e.*, the witchcraft at Salem in 1692.

[3] As to Parris and Salem Village, and in general as to the Salem witchcraft,
which is the subject of the rest of Calef's narrative, see the introduction and notes
to Lawson's *Brief Account* (pp. 147–164, above). That account (as also the
parallel narrative of Hale, at pp. 413 ff., below) should be constantly compared
with the present one.

[4] 1692 of our calendar.

more of the Neighbourhood, began to Act, after a strange
and unusual manner, *viz.* as by getting into Holes, and creeping under Chairs and Stools, and to use sundry odd Postures
and Antick Gestures, uttering foolish, ridiculous Speeches,
which neither they themselves nor any others could make
sense of; the Physicians that were called could assign no
reason for this; but it seems one of them,[1] having recourse to
the old shift, told them he was afraid they were Bewitched;
upon such suggestions, they that were concerned applied
themselves to Fasting and Prayer, which was attended not
only in their own private Families, but with calling in the
help of others.

March the 11*th.*   Mr. Parris invited several Neighbouring
Ministers to join with him in keeping a Solemn day of Prayer
at his own House; the time of the exercise those Persons were
for the most part silent, but after any one Prayer was ended,
they would Act and Speak strangely and Ridiculously, yet
were such as had been well Educated and of good Behaviour,
the one, a Girl of 11 or 12 years old,[2] would sometimes seem
to be in a Convulsion Fit, her Limbs being twisted several
ways, and very stiff, but presently her Fit would be over.

A few days before this Solemn day of Prayer, Mr. Parris's
Indian Man and Woman[3] made a Cake of Rye Meal, with
the Childrens Water, and Baked it in the Ashes, and as is
said, gave it to the Dog; this was done as a means to Discover Witchcraft;[4] soon after which those ill affected or afflicted
Persons named several that they said they saw, when in their
Fits, afflicting of them.

[1] Doubtless **Dr. William Griggs**, of Salem Village, whose wife's niece, a
maid in his household, was one of the "afflicted."

[2] Abigail Williams, Parris's niece.

[3] West-Indian slaves, brought back with him from Barbadoes.

[4] It was suggested by the wife of a neighbor. When, a fortnight later, she
was disciplined by the village church for this dabbling in superstition, Parris
himself wrote in the church-record book: "It is well known that when these
Calamities first began, which was in my own Family, the Affliction was several
weeks before such hellish Operations as Witchcraft was suspected; Nay, it never
broke forth to any considerable Light, until diabolical Means was used, by the
making of a cake by my Indian Man, who had his Directions from this our Sister
Mary Sibly; since which Apparitions have been plenty, and exceeding much
Mischief hath followed." (Upham, *Salem Witchcraft*, II. 95; Hanson, *Danvers*,
p. 289, quoted by Drake.)

The first complain'd of, was the said Indian Woman, named Tituba. She confessed that the Devil urged her to sign a Book, which he presented to her, and also to work Mischief to the Children, etc. She was afterwards Committed to Prison, and lay there till Sold for her Fees.[1] The account she since gives of it is, that her Master did beat her and otherways abuse her, to make her confess and accuse (such as he call'd) her Sister-Witches, and that whatsoever she said by way of confessing or accusing others, was the effect of such usage; her Master refused to pay her Fees, unless she would stand to what she had said.[2]

The Children complained likewise of two other Women, to be the Authors of their Hurt, *Viz.* Sarah Good, who had long been counted a Melancholy or Distracted Woman, and one Osburn, an Old Bed-rid Woman; which two were Persons so ill thought of, that the accusation was the more readily believed; and after Examination before two Salem Magistrates,[3] were committed:

March the 19*th*, Mr. Lawson (who had been formerly a Preacher at the said Village) came thither, and hath since set fourth in Print an account of what then passed, about which time, as he saith, they complained of Goodwife Cory, and Goodwife Nurse, Members of the Churches at the Village and at Salem, many others being by that time Accused.

March the 21*st*, Goodwife Cory was examined before the Magistrates of Salem, at the Meeting House in the Village, a throng of Spectators being present to see the Novelty. Mr. Noyes, one of the Ministers of Salem, began with Prayer, after which the Prisoner being call'd, in order to answer to what should be Alledged against her, she desired that she might go to Prayer, and was answered by the Magistrates, that they did not come to hear her pray, but to examine her.

The number of the Afflicted were at that time about Ten,

---

[1] *I. e.*, to meet her prison expenses. She lay there for a year and a month.

[2] Besides the documents of Tituba's case printed in the *Records of Salem Witchcraft* (I. 41–50), a much fuller report of her examination (March 1–2, 1692) strangely differing from that already printed, is appended to Drake's edition of Mather and Calef (*The Witchcraft Delusion in New England*, III. 185–195).

[3] On March 1, before John Hathorne and Jonathan Corwin. From this point to his entry of April 3 Calef's narrative rests wholly on that of Lawson.

Viz. Mrs. Pope, Mrs. Putman, Goodwife Bibber, and Goodwife Goodall, Mary Wolcott, Mercy Lewes (at Thomas Putmans) and Dr. Griggs Maid, and three Girls, *Viz.* Elizabeth Parris, Daughter to the Minister, Abigail Williams his Neice, and Ann Putman, which last three were not only the beginners, but were also the chief in these Accusations. These Ten were most of them present at the Examination, and did vehemently accuse her of Afflicting them, by Biting, Pinching, Strangling, etc. And they said, they did in their Fits see her likeness coming to them, and bringing a Book for them to Sign; Mr. Hathorn, a Magistrate of Salem, asked her, why she Afflicted those Children? she said, she did not Afflict them; he asked her, who did then? she said, "I do not know, how should I know?" she said, they were Poor Distracted Creatures, and no heed to be given to what they said; Mr. Hathorn and Mr. Noyes replied that it was the Judgment of all that were there present, that they were bewitched, and only she (the Accused) said they were Distracted: She was Accused by them, that the Black Man Whispered to her in her Ear now (while she was upon Examination) and that she had a Yellow Bird, that did use to Suck between her Fingers, and that the said Bird did Suck now in the Assembly; order being given to look in that place to see if there were any sign, the Girl that pretended to see it said, that it was too late now, for she had removed a Pin, and put it on her Head, it was upon search found, that a Pin was there sticking upright. When the Accused had any motion of their Body, Hands or Mouth, the Accusers would cry out, as when she bit her Lip, they would cry out of being bitten, if she grasped one hand with the other, they would cry out of being Pinched by her, and would produce marks, so of the other motions of her Body, as complaining of being Prest, when she lean'd to the seat next her, if she stirred her Feet, they would stamp and cry out of Pain there. After the hearing the said Cory was committed to Salem Prison, and then their crying out of her abated.

March the 24th, Goodwife Nurse was brought before Mr. Hathorn and Mr. Curwin (Magistrates) in the Meeting House. Mr. Hale, Minister of Beverly, began with Prayer, after which she being Accus'd of much the same Crimes made the like answers, asserting her own Innocence with earnestness. The Accusers were mostly the same, Tho. Putmans Wife, etc. complaining much. The dreadful Shreiking from her and others, was very amazing, which was heard at a great distance; she was also Committed to Prison.

A Child of Sarah Goods was likewise apprehended, being between 4 and 5 years Old. The Accusers said this Child bit them, and would shew such like marks, as those of a small Sett of Teeth upon their Arms; as many of the Afflicted as the Child cast its Eye upon, would complain they were in Torment; which Child they also Committed.

Concerning these that had been hitherto Examined and Committed, it is among other things observed by Mr. Lawson (in Print[1]) that they were by the Accusers charged to belong to a Company that did muster in Arms, and were reported by them to keep Days of Fast, Thanksgiving and Sacraments; and that those Afflicted (or Accusers) did in the Assembly Cure each others, even with a touch of their Hand, when strangled and otherways tortured, and would endeavour to get to the Afflicted to relieve them thereby (for hitherto they had not used the Experiment of bringing the Accused to touch the Afflicted, in order to their Cure) and could foretel one anothers Fits to be coming, and would say, look to such a one, she will have a Fit presently and so it happened, and that at the same time when the Accused person was present, the Afflicted said they saw her Spectre or likeness in other places of the Meeting House Suckling[2] of their Familiars.

The said Mr. Lawson being to Preach at the Village, after the Psalm was Sung, Abigail Williams said, "Now stand up and name your Text"; after it was read, she said, "It is a long Text." Mrs. Pope in the beginning of Sermon said to him, "Now there is enough of that." In Sermon, he referring to his Doctrine, Abigail Williams said to him, "I know no Doctrine you had, if you did name one I have forgot it." Ann Putman, an afflicted Girl, said, There was a Yellow Bird sate on his Hat as it hung on the Pin in the Pulpit.

March 31, 1692. Was set apart as a day of Solemn Humiliation at Salem, upon the Account of this Business, on which day Abigail Williams said, That she saw a great number

---

[1] See above, pp. 162–164.   [2] "Sucking" in original; corrected in *Errata*.

of Persons in the Village at the Administration of a Mock Sacrament, where they had Bread as read as raw Flesh, and red Drink.

April 1.   Mercy Lewis affirmed, That she saw a man in white, with whom she went into a Glorious Place, *viz.* In her fits, where was no Light of the Sun, much less of Candles, yet was full of Light and Brightness, with a great Multitude in White Glittering Robes, who Sang the Song in 5. Rev. 9. and the 110 and 149 Psalms; And was grieved that she might tarry no longer in this place.   This White Man is said to have appeared several times to others of them, and to have given them notice how long it should be before they should have another Fit.

April the 3*d.*   Being Sacrament Day at the Village, Sarah Cloys, Sister to Goodwife Nurse, a Member to one of the Churches, was (tho' it seems with difficulty prevail'd with to be) present; but being entred the place, and Mr. Parris naming his Text, 6 John, 70. *Have not I chosen you Twelve, and one of you is a Devil* (for what cause may rest as a doubt whether upon the account of her Sisters being Committed, or because of the choice of that Text) she rose up and went out, the wind shutting the Door forcibly, gave occasion to some to suppose she went out in Anger, and might occasion a suspicion of her; however she was soon after complain'd of, examin'd and Committed.

April the 11*th.*   By this time the number of the Accused and Accusers being much encreased, was a Publick Examination at Salem, Six of the Magistrates with several Ministers being present;[1] there appeared several who complain'd against others with hidious clamors and Screechings.   Goodwife Proctor was brought thither, being Accused or cryed out against; her Husband coming to attend and assist her, as there might

---

[1] Among them was Samuel Sewall, who wrote in his diary for that day: "Went to Salem, where, in the Meeting-house, the persons accused of Witchcraft were examined; was a very great Assembly; 'twas awfull to see how the afflicted persons were agitated. Mr. Noyes pray'd at the beginning, and Mr. Higginson concluded." In the margin he has later added: "*Vae, Vae, Vae,* Witchcraft"—*i. e.,* "woe, woe, woe!" So many (seven) of the magistrates were present that the court took the form of a "council" (the highest of colonial tribunals), under the presidency of Deputy-governor Danforth (*Records of Salem Witchcraft,* I. 101; Hutchinson, *Massachusetts,* second ed., II. 27–30).

be need, the Accusers cryed out of him also, and that with
so much earnestness, that he was Committed with his Wife.
About this time besides the Experiment of the Afflicted falling at the sight, etc., they put the Accused upon saying the
Lords Prayer, which one among them performed, except in
that petition, *Deliver us from Evil,* she exprest it thus, *Deliver
us from all Evil.* This was lookt upon as if she Prayed against
what she was now justly under, and being put upon it again,
and repeating those words, *Hallowed be thy name,* she exprest
it, *Hollowed be thy Name,* this was counted a depraving the
words, as signifying to make void, and so a Curse rather then[1]
a Prayer, upon the whole it was concluded that she also could
not say it, etc. Proceeding in this work of examination and
Commitment, many were sent to Prison. As an Instance, see
the following Mittimus:

To their Majesties Goal-keeper[2] in Salem.

You are in Their Majesties Names hereby required to take into
your care, and safe custody, the Bodies of William Hobs, and Deborah[3] his Wife, Mary Easty, the Wife of Isaac Easty, and Sarah
Wild, the Wife of John Wild, all of Topsfield; and Edward Bishop
of Salem-Village, Husbandman, and Sarah his Wife, and Mary Black,
a Negro of Lieutenant Nathaniel Putmans of Salem-Village; also
Mary English the Wife of Philip English, Merchant in Salem;[4] who
stand charged with High Suspicion of Sundry Acts of Witchcraft,
done or committed by them lately upon the Bodies of Ann Putman,
Mercy Lewis[5] and Abigail Williams, of Salem-Village, whereby great
Hurt and Damage hath been done to the Bodies of the said Persons,
[as] according to the complaint of Thomas Putman and John Buxton
of Salem-Village, Exhibited Salem, Apr 21, 1692, appears, whom you
are to secure in order to their further Examination. Fail not.

JOHN HATHORN,
JONA. CURWIN, } *Assistants.*

Dated SALEM, April 22, 1692.

[1] *I. e.,* than. This spelling was then usual. [2] Jail-keeper. [3] Deliverance.

[4] Mary Esty, aged 56, was a sister of Rebecca Nurse and Sarah Cloyse.
We shall meet her again. As to these Topsfield cases, see above, p. 237, note 1.
Edward Bishop, aged 44, was probably a step-son of Bridget Bishop (see above,
pp. 223–229, and below, p. 356), and his wife was a daughter of John Wilds. On
Mary Black, see Chandler, *American Criminal Trials,* I. 427, and Upham, *Salem
Witchcraft,* II. 136–137. As for Mary English, see below, p. 371.

[5] "Mary" in original; corrected in *Errata.*

To Marshal George Herrick of Salem Essex.

You are in their Majesties Names hereby required to convey the above-named to the Goal at Salem. Fail not.

JOHN HATHORN, ⎱ *Assistants.*
JONA. CURWIN, ⎰

Dated SALEM, Apr 22, 1692.

The occasion of Bishops being cry'd out of[1] was, he being at an Examination in Salem, when at the Inn an afflicted Indian[2] was very unruly, whom he undertook, and so managed him, that he was very orderly, after which in riding home, in company of him and other Accusers, the Indian fell into a fit, and clapping hold with his Teeth on the back of the Man that rode before him, thereby held himself upon the Horse, but said Bishop striking him with his stick, the Indian soon recovered, and promised he would do so no more; to which Bishop replied, that he doubted not, but he could cure them all, with more to the same effect; immediately after he was parted from them, he was cried out of, etc.

May 14, 1692. Sir William Phips arrived with Commission from Their Majesties to be Governour, pursuant to the New-Charter; which he now brought with him; the Ancient Charter having been vacated by King Charles, and King James (by which they had a power not only to make their own Laws; but also to chuse their own Governour and Officers;) and the Countrey for some years was put under an absolute Commission-Government, till the Revolution,[3] at which time tho more than two thirds of the People were for reassuming their ancient Government, (to which they had encouragement by His then Royal Highness's Proclamation) yet some that might have been better imployed (in another Station)[4] made it their business (by printing, as well as speaking) to their

---

[1] *I. e.*, cried out against, accused.

[2] *The* afflicted Indian, *i. e.*, Parris's John: it is clearly a misprint.

[3] *I. e.*, the English Revolution and the overthrow in New England of the Andros government (1689).

[4] He doubtless means especially Cotton Mather. So, at least, Mather assumes in his reply (his letter in *Some Few Remarks*, etc., pp. 46–47) and vigorously denies that he opposed the reassumption.

utmost to divert them from such a settlement; and so far prevailed, that for about seven Weeks after the Revolution, here was not so much as a face of any Government; but some few Men upon their own Nomination would be called a Committee of Safety; but at length the Assembly prevailed with those that had been of the Government, to promise that they would reassume; and accordingly a Proclamation was drawn, but before publishing it, it was underwritten, that they would not have it understood that they did reassume Charter-Government; so that between Government and no Government, this Countrey remained till Sir William arrived; Agents being in this time impowered in England, which no doubt did not all of them act according to the Minds or Interests of those that impowered them, which is manifest by their not acting jointly in what was done; so that this place is perhaps a single Instance (even in the best of Reigns) of a Charter not restored after so happy a Revolution.

This settlement by Sir William Phips his being come Governour put an end to all disputes of these things, and being arrived, and having read his Commission, the first thing he exerted his Power in, was said to be his giving Orders that Irons should be put upon those in Prison; for tho for some time after these were Committed, the Accusers ceased to cry out of them;[1] yet now the cry against them was renewed, which occasioned such Order; and tho there was partiality in the executing it (some having taken them off [2] almost as soon as put on) yet the cry of these Accusers against such ceased after this Order.[3]

May 24. Mrs. Cary of Charlestown, was Examined and Committed. Her Husband Mr. Nathaniel Cary[4] has given account thereof, as also of her Escape, to this Effect,

[1] See p. 348, note 1.

[2] Doubtless a misprint for "having them taken off."

[3] The reason for the irons was the assertion of the "afflicted" that their sufferings did not cease till the accused were thus in fetters. An account of the prison-keeper (Hanson, *Danvers*, p. 290) has such items as: "May 9th, To Chains for Sarah Good and Sarah Osborn, 14s. May 23d, To Shackles for 10 Prisoners. May 29th, to 1 pr. Irons." See also *Records of Salem Witchcraft*, II. 212, 213. Even little Dorcas Good was put into chains.

[4] Captain Nathaniel Cary was a shipmaster, a man of ability and prominence, later a member of the General Court and a justice.

I having heard some days, that my Wife was accused of Witch-craft, being much disturbed at it, by advice, we went to Salem-Village, to see if the afflicted did know her; we arrived there, 24 May, it happened to be a day appointed for Examination; accordingly soon after our arrival, Mr. Hathorn and Mr. Curwin, etc., went to the Meeting-house, which was the place appointed for that Work, the Minister began with Prayer, and having taken care to get a convenient place, I observed, that the afflicted were two Girls of about Ten Years old,[1] and about two or three other, of about eighteen, one of the Girls talked most, and could discern more than the rest. The Prisoners were called in one by one, and as they came in were cried out of, etc. The Prisoner was placed about 7 or 8 foot from the Justices, and the Accusers between the Justices and them; the Prisoner was ordered to stand right before the Justices, with an Officer appointed to hold each hand, least they should therewith afflict them, and the Prisoners Eyes must be constantly on the Justices; for if they look'd on the afflicted, they would either fall into their Fits, or cry out of being hurt by them; after Examination of the Prisoners, who it was afflicted these Girls, etc., they were put upon saying the Lords Prayer, as a tryal of their guilt; after the afflicted seem'd to be out of their Fits, they would look steadfastly on some one person, and frequently not speak; and then the Justices said they were struck dumb, and after a little time would speak again; then the Justices said to the Accusers, "which of you will go and touch the Prisoner at the Bar?" then the most couragious would adventure, but before they had made three steps would ordinarily fall down as in a Fit; the Justices ordered that they should be taken up and carried to the Prisoner, that she might touch them; and as soon as they were touched by the accused, the Justices would say, they are well, before I could discern any alteration; by which I observed that the Justices understood the manner of it. Thus far I was only as a Spectator, my Wife also was there part of the time, but no notice taken of her by the afflicted, except once or twice they came to her and asked her name.

But I having an opportunity to Discourse[2] Mr. Hale[3] (with whom I had formerly acquaintance) I took his advice, what I had best to do, and desired of him that I might have an opportunity to speak with her that accused my Wife; which he promised should be, I acquainting him that I reposed my trust in him.

Accordingly he came to me after the Examination was over, and told me I had now an opportunity to speak with the said Accuser,

[1] Abigail Williams and Ann Putnam.   [2] Talk with.
[3] The Rev. John Hale, of Beverly. As to his part in the trials see below, p. 369.

viz. Abigail Williams, a Girl of 11 or 12 Years old; but that we could
not be in private at Mr. Parris's House, as he had promised me; we
went therefore into the Alehouse, where an Indian Man attended us,
who it seems was one of the afflicted: to him we gave some Cyder,
he shewed several Scars, that seemed as if they had been long there,
and shewed them as done by Witchcraft, and acquainted us that his
Wife, who also was a Slave, was imprison'd for Witchcraft.[1] And
now instead of one Accuser, they all came in, who began to tumble
down like Swine, and then three Women were called in to attend
them. We in the Room were all at a stand, to see who they would
cry out of; but in a short time they cried out, Cary; and immediately
after a Warrant was sent from the Justices to bring my Wife before
them, who were sitting in a Chamber near by, waiting for this.

Being brought before the Justices, her chief accusers were two
Girls; my Wife declared to the Justices, that she never had any
knowledge of them before that day; she was forced to stand with her
Arms stretched out. I did request that I might hold one of her
hands, but it was denied me; then she desired me to wipe the Tears
from her Eyes, and the Sweat from her Face, which I did; then she
desired she might lean her self on me, saying, she should faint.

Justice Hathorn replied, she had strength enough to torment
those persons, and she should have strength enough to stand. I
speaking something against their cruel proceedings, they commanded
me to be silent, or else I should be turned out of the Room. The
Indian before mentioned, was also brought in, to be one of her
Accusers: being come in, he now (when before the Justices) fell down
and tumbled about like a Hog, but said nothing. The Justices asked
the Girls, who afflicted the Indian? they answered she (meaning my
Wife) and now lay upon him; the Justices ordered her to touch him,
in order to his cure, but her head must be turned another way, least
instead of curing, she should make him worse, by her looking on
him, her hand being guided to take hold of his; but the Indian took
hold on her hand, and pulled her down on the Floor, in a barbarous
manner; then his hand was taken off, and her hand put on his, and
the cure was quickly wrought. I being extreamly troubled at their
Inhumane dealings, uttered a hasty Speech (That God would take
vengeance on them, and desired that God would deliver us out of the
hands of unmerciful men.) Then her Mittimus was writ. I did
with difficulty and charge obtain the liberty of a Room, but no Beds
in it; if there had, could have taken but little rest that Night. She
was committed to Boston Prison; but I obtained a Habeas Corpus
to remove her to Cambridge Prison, which is in our County of Mid-

---

[1] Cary is speaking, of course, of "John Indian" and Tituba.

dlesex. Having been there one Night, next Morning the Jaylor put Irons on her legs (having received such a command) the weight of them was about eight pounds; these Irons and her other Afflictions, soon brought her into Convulsion Fits, so that I thought she would have died that Night. I sent to intreat that the Irons might be taken off, but all intreaties were in vain, if it would have saved her Life, so that in this condition she must continue. The Tryals at Salem coming on, I went thither, to see how things were there managed; and finding that the Spectre-Evidence was there received, together with Idle, if not malicious Stories, against Peoples Lives, I did easily perceive which way the rest would go; for the same Evidence that served for one, would serve for all the rest. I acquainted her with her danger; and that if she were carried to Salem to be tried, I feared she would never return. I did my utmost that she might have her Tryal in our own County, I with several others Petitioning the Judge for it, and were put in hopes of it; but I soon saw so much, that I understood thereby it was not intended, which put me upon consulting the means of her escape; which thro the goodness of God was effected, and she got to Road Island,[1] but soon found her self not safe when there, by reason of the pursuit after her; from thence she went to New-York, along with some others that had escaped their cruel hands; where we found his Excellency Benjamin Fletcher, Esq; Governour, who was very courteous to us. After this some of my Goods were seized in a Friends hands, with whom I had left them, and my self imprisoned by the Sheriff, and kept in Custody half a day, and then dismist; but to speak of their usage of the Prisoners, and their Inhumanity shewn to them, at the time of their Execution, no sober Christian could bear; they had also tryals of cruel mockings; which is the more, considering what a People for Religion, I mean the profession of it, we have been; those that suffered being many of them Church-Members, and most of them unspotted in their Conversation, till their Adversary the Devil took up this Method for accusing them.

Per NATHANIEL[2] CARY.

May 31. Captain John Aldin[3] was Examined at Salem, and Committed to Boston Prison. The Prison-Keeper seeing

---

[1] Rhode Island. "July 30, 1692. Mrs. Cary makes her escape out of Cambridge-Prison, who was Committed for Witchcraft." (Sewall, *Diary*, I. 362.)

[2] "Jonathan" in original: corrected to "Nathaniel" in *Errata*.

[3] See above, pp. 170, note 2, and 178, note 6. Captain Alden, Indian fighter, naval commander, now at seventy a man of wealth, was one of the leading figures of New England.

such a Man Committed, of whom he had a good esteem, was after this the more Compassionate to those that were in Prison on the like account; and did refrain from such hard things to the Prisoners, as before he had used. Mr. Aldin himself has given account of his Examination, in these Words.

An Account how John Aldin, Senior, was dealt with at Salem-Village.

John Aldin Senior, of Boston, in the County of Suffolk, Marriner, on the 28th Day of May, 1692, was sent for by the Magistrates of Salem, in the County of Essex, upon the Accusation of a company of poor distracted, or possessed Creatures or Witches; and being sent by Mr. Stoughton,[1] arrived there the 31st of May, and appeared at Salem-Village, before Mr. Gidney,[2] Mr. Hathorn, and Mr. Curwin.

Those Wenches being present, who plaid their jugling tricks, falling down, crying out, and staring in Peoples Faces; the Magistrates demanded of them several times, who it was of all the People in the Room that hurt them? one of these Accusers pointed several times at one Captain Hill, there present, but spake nothing; the same Accuser had a Man standing at her back to hold her up; he stooped down to her Ear, then she cried out, Aldin, Aldin afflicted her; one of the Magistrates asked her if she had ever seen Aldin, she answered no, he asked her how she knew it was Aldin? She said, the Man told her so.

Then all were ordered to go down into the Street, where a Ring was made; and the same Accuser cried out, "there stands Aldin, a bold fellow with his Hat on before the Judges, he sells Powder and Shot to the Indians and French, and lies with the Indian Squaes, and has Indian Papooses." Then was Aldin committed to the Marshal's Custody, and his Sword taken from him; for they said he afflicted them with his Sword. After some hours Aldin was sent for to the Meeting-house in the Village before the Magistrates; who required Aldin to stand upon a Chair, to the open view of all the People.

The Accusers cried out that Aldin did pinch them, then, when he stood upon the Chair, in the sight of all the People, a good way distant from them, one of the Magistrates bid the Marshal to hold open Aldin's hands, that he might not pinch those Creatures. Aldin asked

---

[1] The lieutenant-governor—soon to be head of the special court for the trial of the witches. See above, p. 183, note 2, and p. 199.

[2] Bartholomew Gedney, of Salem, the third magistrate, was, like his colleagues, an assistant of the province.

them why they should think, that he should come to that Village to
afflict those persons that he never knew or saw before? Mr. Gidney
bid Aldin confess, and give glory to God; Aldin said he hoped he
should give glory to God, and hoped he should never gratifie the Devil;
but appealed to all that ever knew him, if they ever suspected him
to be such a person, and challenged any one, that could bring in any
thing upon their own knowledge, that might give suspicion of his
being such an one. Mr. Gidney said he had known Aldin many
Years, and had been at Sea with him, and always look'd upon him
to be an honest Man, but now he did see cause to alter his judgment:
Aldin answered, he was sorry for that, but he hoped God would
clear up his Innocency, that he would recall that judgment again,
and added that he hoped that he should with Job maintain his Integrity till he died. They bid Aldin look upon the Accusers, which
he did, and then they fell down. Aldin asked Mr. Gidney, what
Reason there could be given, why Aldin's looking upon *him* did not
strike *him* down as well; but no reason was given that I heard. But
the Accusers were brought to Aldin to touch them, and this touch
they said made them well. Aldin began to speak of the Providence
of God in suffering these Creatures to accuse Innocent persons. Mr.
Noyes asked Aldin why he would offer to speak of the Providence of
God. God by his Providence (said Mr. Noyes) governs the World,
and keeps it in peace; and so went on with Discourse, and stopt
Aldin's mouth, as to that. Aldin told Mr. Gidney, that he could
assure him that there was a lying Spirit in them, for I can assure you
that there is not a word of truth in all these say of me. But Aldin
was again committed to the Marshal, and his Mittimus written,
which was as follows.

*To Mr. John Arnold, Keeper of the Prison in Boston, in the County
of Suffolk.*

Whereas Captain John Aldin of Boston, Marriner, and Sarah
Rice, Wife of Nicholas Rice of Reding, Husbandman, have been
this day brought before us, John Hathorn and Jonathan Curwin,
Esquires; being accused and suspected of perpetrating divers acts
of Witchcraft, contrary to the form of the Statute, in that Case made
and provided: These are therefore in Their Majesties, King William
and Queen Marys Names, to Will and require you, to take into your
Custody, the bodies of the said John Aldin, and Sarah Rice, and
them safely keep, until they shall thence be delivered by due course
of Law; as you will answer the contrary at your peril; and this shall
be your sufficient Warrant. Given under our hands at Salem
Village, the 31st of May, in the Fourth Year of the Reign of our

Sovereign Lord and Lady, William and Mary, now King and Queen over England, etc., Anno Dom. 1692.

JOHN HATHORN, ⎫
JONATHAN CURWIN, ⎬ *Assistants.*

To Boston Aldin was carried by a Constable, no Bail would be taken for him; but was delivered to the Prison-keeper, where he remained Fifteen Weeks;[1] and then observing the manner of Tryals, and Evidence then taken, was at length prevailed with to make his Escape, and being returned, was bound over to Answer at the Superior Court at Boston, the last Tuesday in April, Anno 1693. And was there cleared by Proclamation, none appearing against him.

Per JOHN ALDIN.

At Examination, and at other times, 'twas usual for the Accusers to tell of the black Man, or of a Spectre, as being then on the Table, etc. The People about would strike with Swords, or sticks at those places. One Justice broke his Cane at this Exercise, and sometimes the Accusers would say, they struck the Spectre, and it is reported several of the accused were hurt and wounded thereby, though at home at the same time.

The Justices proceeding in these works of Examination, and Commitment, to the end of May, there was by that time about a Hundred persons Imprisoned upon that Account.

June 2. A special Commission of Oyer and Terminer having been Issued out, to Mr. Stoughton, the New Lieutenant Governour, Major Saltonstall, Major Richards, Major Gidny, Mr. Wait Winthrop, Captain Sewall, and Mr. Sergeant;[2] These (a Quorum of them) sat at Salem this day; where the

---

[1] Captain Alden's case seems to have made a great stir. On July 20 there was held a special "Fast at the house of Capt. Alden, upon his account." Judge Sewall read a sermon, and Willard, Allen, and Cotton Mather prayed, then Captain Hill and Captain Scottow; "concluded about 5. aclock." (Sewall, *Diary*, I. 361–362.) A year later, on June 12, 1693, Sewall records: "I visit Capt. Alden and his wife, and tell them I was sorry for their Sorrow and Temptations by reason of his Imprisonment, and that [I] was glad of his Restauration."

[2] See above, pp. 183–185, 196–198. These gentlemen were all members of the new Council of the province. Saltonstall, out of dissatisfaction with the proceedings, early withdrew (see above, p. 184), and was later himself accused (Sewall's *Diary*, I. 373). Jonathan Corwin took his place. A quorum was five. All the judges had had experience in the colony's Court of Assistants; but none had had a legal training.

most that was done this Week, was the Tryal of one Bishop, *alias* Oliver, of Salem; who having long undergone the repute of a Witch, occasioned by the Accusations of one Samuel Gray: he about 20 Years since, having charged her with such Crimes, and though upon his Death-bed he testified his sorrow and repentance for such Accusations, as being wholly groundless; yet the report taken up by his means continued, and she being accused by those afflicted, and upon search a Tet, as they call it, being found, she was brought in guilty by the Jury; she received her Sentence of Death, and was Executed, June 10, but made not the least Confession of any thing relating to Witchcraft.[1]

June 15.   Several Ministers in and near Boston, having been to that end consulted by his Excellency,[2] exprest their minds to this effect, *viz.*

That they were affected with the deplorable state of the afflicted; That they were thankful for the diligent care of the Rulers, to detect the abominable Witchcrafts, which have been committed in the Country, praying for a perfect discovery thereof.   But advised to a cautious proceeding, least many Evils ensue, etc.   And that tenderness be used towards those accused, relating to matters presumptive and convictive, and also to privacy in Examinations, and to consult Mr. Perkins and Mr. Bernard,[3] what tests to make use of in the Scrutiny: That Presumptions and Convictions ought to have better grounds, than the Accusers affirming that they see such persons Spectres afflicting them: And that the Devil may afflict in the shape of good Men; and that falling at the sight, and rising at the touch of the Accused, is no infallible proof of guilt; That seeing the Devils strength consists in such Accusations, our disbelieving them may be a means to put a period to the dreadful Calamities; Nevertheless they humbly recommend to the Government, the speedy and vigorous prosecu-

---

[1] As to the trial of Bridget Bishop see above, pp. 223–229.   Before her last marriage she had been a widow Oliver.   The testimony against her includes the deposition of a Samuel Gray (*Records of Salem Witchcraft*, I. 152–153) as to her bewitching to death his child some fourteen years before.   Of his repentance at his death, which must have been recent when Calef wrote, the writer doubtless speaks from personal knowledge.

[2] See above, p. 194.   [3] See above, p. 304, notes 3, 5.

tion of such as have rendered themselves obnoxious, according to the direction given in the Laws of God, and the wholesome Statutes of the English Nation, for the Detection of Witchcraft.

This is briefly the substance of what may be seen more at large in *Cases of Conscience, (ult.)*[1] And one of them[2] since taking occasion to repeat some part of this advice, *Wonders of the Invisible World*, p. 83, declares, (notwithstanding the Dissatisfaction of others) that if his said Book may conduce to promote thankfulness to God for such Executions, he shall rejoyce, etc.

The 30*th of June*, the Court according to Adjournment again sat; five more were tried, *viz.* Sarah Good and Rebecca Nurse, of Salem-Village; Susanna Martin of Amsbury; Elizabeth How of Ipswich; and Sarah Wildes of Topsfield; these were all condemned that Sessions, and were all Executed on the 19th of July.[3]

At the Tryal of Sarah Good, one of the afflicted fell in a Fit, and after coming out of it, she cried out of the Prisoner, for stabing her in the breast with a Knife, and that she had broken the Knife in stabbing of her, accordingly a piece of the blade of a Knife was found about her. Immediately information being given to the Court, a young Man was called, who produced a Haft and part of the Blade, which the Court having viewed and compared, saw it to be the same. And upon inquiry the young Man affirmed, that yesterday he happened to break that Knife, and that he cast away the upper part, this afflicted person being then present. The young Man was

---

[1] The full text of the document, that is, may be found at the end of Increase Mather's *Cases of Conscience* (London, 1693). With that book, or from it, it has been often reprinted. In his life of Phips (and in its reprint in his *Magnalia*) Cotton Mather tells us that it was drawn up by himself; but it doubtless embodied a compromise. Increase Mather calls it "the humble Advice which twelve Ministers concurringly presented before his Excellency and Council," and it entitles itself "The Return of several Ministers consulted by his Excellency, and the Honourable Council, upon the present Witchcrafts in Salem Village."

[2] Cotton Mather, of course.

[3] As to the trials of Susanna Martin and Elizabeth How see above, pp. 229–240, and records there cited. The documents for those of Sarah Good, Rebecca Nurse, Sarah Wildes, may be found in *Records of Salem Witchcraft* (I. 11–34, 76–99, 180–189), but for the two last more fully in the *Historical Collections* of the Topsfield Historical Society (XIII. 80–92).

dismist, and she was bidden by the Court not to tell lyes; and was improved (after as she had been before) to give Evidence against the Prisoners.

At Execution, Mr. Noyes urged Sarah Good to Confess, and told her she was a Witch, and she knew she was a Witch, to which she replied, "you are a lyer; I am no more a Witch than you are a Wizard, and if you take away my Life, God will give you Blood to drink."

At the Tryal of Rebecka Nurse, this was remarkable that the Jury brought in their Verdict not Guilty, immediately all the accusers in the Court, and suddenly after all the afflicted out of Court, made an hideous out-cry, to the amazement, not only of the Spectators, but the Court also seemed strangely surprized; one of the Judges exprest himself not satisfied, another of them as he was going off the Bench, said they would have her Indicted anew.   The chief Judge said he would not Impose upon the Jury; but intimated, as if they had not well considered one Expression of the Prisoners, when she was upon Tryal, *viz.* That when one Hobbs, who had confessed her self to be a Witch, was brought into the Court to witness against her, the Prisoner turning her head to her, said, "What, do you bring her? she is one of us," or to that effect; this together with the Clamours of the Accusers, induced the Jury to go out again, after their Verdict, not Guilty.   But not agreeing, they came into the Court, and she being then at the Bar, her words were repeated to her, in order to have had her explanation of them, and she making no Reply to them, they found the Bill, and brought her in Guilty; these words being the Inducement to it, as the Foreman has signified in writing, as follows.

July 4, 1692.   I Thomas Fisk, the Subscriber hereof, being one of them that were of the Jury the last week at Salem-Court, upon the Tryal of Rebecka Nurse, etc., being desired by some of the Relations to give a Reason why the Jury brought her in Guilty, after her Verdict not Guilty; I do hereby give my Reasons to be as follows, *viz.*

When the Verdict not Guilty was, the honoured Court was pleased to object against it, saying to them, that they think they let slip the words, which the Prisoner at the Bar spake against her self, which were spoken in reply to Goodwife Hobbs and her Daughter, who had been faulty in setting their hands to the Devils Book, as they have confessed formerly; the words were "What, do these per-

sons give in Evidence against me now, they used to come among us."
After the honoured Court had manifested their dissatisfaction of the
Verdict, several of the Jury declared themselves desirous to go out
again, and thereupon the honoured Court gave leave; but when we
came to consider of the Case, I could not tell how to take her words,
as an Evidence against her, till she had a further opportunity to put
her Sense upon them, if she would take it; and then going into Court,
I mentioned the words aforesaid, which by one of the Court were
affirmed to have been spoken by her, she being then at the Bar, but
made no reply, nor interpretation of them; whereupon these words
were to me a principal Evidence against her.

THOMAS FISK.

When Goodwife Nurse was informed what use was made
of these words, she put in this following Declaration into the
Court.

These presents do humbly shew, to the honoured Court and
Jury, that I being informed, that the Jury brought me in Guilty,
upon my saying that Goodwife Hobbs and her Daughter were of our
Company; but I intended no otherways, then as[1] they were Prisoners
with us, and therefore did then, and yet do judge them not legal
Evidence against their fellow Prisoners. And I being something
hard of hearing, and full of grief, none informing me how the Court
took up my words, and therefore had not opportunity to declare
what I intended, when I said they were of our Company.

REBECKA NURSE.

After her Condemnation she was by one of the Ministers
of Salem excommunicated;[2] yet the Governour saw cause to
grant a Reprieve, which when known (and some say immediately upon granting) the Accusers renewed their dismal out-
cries against her, insomuch that the Governour was by some
Salem Gentleman prevailed with to recall the Reprieve, and
she was Executed with the rest.

[1] *I. e.*, than that.

[2] By Mr. Noyes, of whose church in Salem Town she was a member. Says
the church record: "1692, July 3.—After sacrament, the elders propounded to
the church,—and it was, by an unanimous vote, consented to,—that our sister
Nurse, being a convicted witch by the Court, and condemned to die, should be
excommunicated; which was accordingly done in the afternoon, she being
present." (Upham, *Salem Witchcraft*, II. 290.) Upham, himself long pastor
of this church, has drawn a powerful picture of the probable scene.

The Testimonials of her Christian behaviour, both in the course of her Life, and at her Death, and her extraordinary care in educating her Children, and setting them good Examples, etc., under the hands of so many, are so numerous, that for brevity they are here omitted.[1]

It was at the Tryal of these that one of the Accusers cried out publickly of Mr. Willard Minister in Boston,[2] as afflicting of her; she was sent out of the Court, and it was told about she was mistaken in the person.

August 5. The Court again sitting, six more were tried on the same Account, *viz.* Mr. George Burroughs, sometime minister of Wells, John Procter, and Elizabeth Procter his Wife, with John Willard of Salem-Village, George Jacobs Senior, of Salem, and Martha Carryer of Andover;[3] these were all brought in Guilty and Condemned; and were all Executed Aug. 19, except Procter's Wife, who pleaded Pregnancy.[4]

Mr. Burroughs was carried in a Cart with the others, through the streets of Salem to Execution; when he was upon the Ladder, he made a Speech for the clearing of his Innocency, with such Solemn and Serious Expressions, as were to the Admiration of all present; his Prayer (which he concluded by repeating the Lord's Prayer,) was so well worded, and uttered with such composedness, and such (at least seeming) fervency of Spirit, as was very affecting, and drew Tears from many (so that it seemed to some, that the Spectators would hinder

---

[1] Two of these testimonials, one of them signed by thirty-eight of her neighbors, are printed by Upham (*Salem Witchcraft*, II. 271–272), and more exactly, from the still extant MSS., in the *Historical Collections* of the Topsfield Historical Society (XIII. 57–58)—and with them the touching evidence of the neighbors who first bore her the news of her accusation.

[2] See above, pp. 22, 184, and 186, note 3.

[3] As to the trials of Burroughs and Goodwife Carrier see above, pp. 215–222, 241–244, and records there cited. Those relating to Procter and his wife, to Willard, and to Jacobs may be found in *Records of Salem Witchcraft* (I. 60–74, 99–117, 266–279, 253–265). The testimonials on behalf of the Procters are reprinted (with corrections) by Upham (*Salem Witchcraft*, II. 305–307). As to Willard other papers will be found in Dr. S. A. Green's *Groton in the Witchcraft Times* (Groton, 1883), pp. 23–29. The documents relating to Jacobs are to be found also in the *Collections* of the Essex Institute (II. 49–57), where (and in I. 52–56) are further details as to him and his household.

[4] For Brattle's account of their execution see above, p. 177.

the Execution). The accusers said the black Man stood and dictated to him; as soon as he was turned off, Mr. Cotton Mather, being mounted upon a Horse, addressed himself to the People, partly to declare, that he was no ordained Minister, and partly to possess the People of his guilt; saying, That the Devil has often been transformed into an Angel of Light; and this did somewhat appease the People, and the Executions went on; when he was cut down, he was dragged by the Halter to a Hole, or Grave, between the Rocks, about two foot deep, his Shirt and Breeches being pulled off, and an old pair of Trousers of one Executed, put on his lower parts, he was so put in, together with Willard and Carryer, one of his Hands and his Chin, and a Foot of one [of] them being left uncovered.[1]

John Willard had been imployed to fetch in several that were accused; but taking dissatisfaction from his being sent, to fetch up some that he had better thoughts of, he declined the Service, and presently after he himself was accused of the same Crime, and that with such vehemency, that they sent after him to apprehend him; he had made his Escape as far as Nashawag,[2] about 40 Miles from Salem; yet 'tis said those Accusers did then presently tell the exact time, saying, now Willard is taken.

John Procter and his Wife being in Prison, the Sheriff came to his House and seized all the Goods, Provisions, and Cattle that he could come at, and sold some of the Cattle at half price, and killed others, and put them up for the West-Indies; threw out the Beer out of a Barrel, and carried away the Barrel; emptied a Pot of Broath, and took away the Pot, and left nothing in the House for the support of the Children: No part of the said Goods are known to be returned. Procter earnestly requested Mr. Noyes to pray with and for him, but

---

[1] "This day," writes Judge Sewall in his diary, "George Burrough, John Willard, Jno. Procter, Martha Carrier and George Jacobs were executed at Salem, a very great number of Spectators being present. Mr. Cotton Mather was there, Mr. Sims, Hale, Noyes, Chiever, etc. All of them said they were innocent, Carrier and all. Mr. Mather says they all died by a Righteous Sentence. Mr. Burrough by his Speech, Prayer, protestation of his Innocence, did much move unthinking persons, which occasions their speaking hardly concerning his being executed." In the margin he later added "Dolefull Witchcraft!"

[2] Nashaway, an old name of Lancaster.

it was wholly denied, because he would not own himself to be a Witch.

During his Imprisonment he sent the following Letter, in behalf of himself and others.

SALEM-PRISON, July 23, 1692.

Mr. Mather, Mr. Allen,
Mr. Moody, Mr. Willard, and
Mr. Bailey.[1]

Reverend Gentlemen.

The innocency of our Case with the Enmity of our Accusers and our Judges, and Jury, whom nothing but our Innocent Blood will serve their turn, having Condemned us already before our Tryals, being so much incensed and engaged against us by the Devil, makes us bold to Beg and Implore your Favourable Assistance of this our Humble Petition to his Excellency, That if it be possible our Innocent Blood may be spared, which undoubtedly otherwise will be shed, if the Lord doth not mercifully step in. The Magistrates, Ministers, Jewries,[2] and all the People in general, being so much inraged and incensed against us by the Delusion of the Devil, which we can term no other, by reason we know in our own Consciences, we are all Innocent Persons. Here are five Persons who have lately

---

[1] By "Mr. Mather" is unquestionably meant Increase Mather. He alone, as the senior in age and in dignity, could with propriety be thus given the first place; and his son, if named at all, would have been identified as "Mr. Cotton Mather." That he is not named at all needs no explanation to those who have read his own words as to accusers and accused and his complaints as to the blame heaped upon himself. Of Moody, Willard, Bailey, we have perhaps seen enough in earlier pages to guess why such an appeal might with hope be addressed to them. The Boston Tory Joshua Broadbent, writing on June 21 from New York, reported that "Mrs. Moody, Parson Moody's wife, is said to be one" of the witches. (*Calendar of State Papers, Colonial,* 1689–1692, p. 653.) Of Allen, the well-to-do minister of the First Church, who seems to have been a man of much caution, it may be well to remember that prior to 1678 he had owned the estate at Salem Village since occupied, but not yet in full ownership, by the Nurses, Procter's near neighbors, and that he was doubtless personally known to the petitioner. Bailey, who had come to America in 1683, had at first assisted Willard at the South Church, and, after a pastorate at Watertown, was now Allen's assistant at the First.

[2] Juries. It should not be overlooked that in these trials of 1692 the jurors were chosen from among church-members only, not, as later, from all who had the property to make them voters under the new charter. The act establishing this qualification for the jurors was not passed till November 25. (See Goodell in Mass. Hist. Soc., *Proceedings,* second series, I. 67–68.)

confessed themselves to be Witches, and do accuse some of us, of being along with them at a Sacrament, since we were committed into close Prison, which we know to be Lies. Two of the 5 are (Carriers Sons[1]) Young-men, who would not confess any thing till they tyed them Neck and Heels[2] till the Blood was ready to come out of their Noses, and 'tis credibly believed and reported this was the occasion of making them confess that[3] they never did, by reason they said one had been a Witch a Month, and another five Weeks, and that their Mother had made them so, who has been confined here this nine Weeks. My son William Procter, when he was examin'd, because he would not confess that he was Guilty, when he was Innocent, they tyed him Neck and Heels till the Blood gushed out at his Nose, and would have kept him so 24 Hours, if one more Merciful than the rest, had not taken pity on him, and caused him to be unbound. These actions are very like the Popish Cruelties. They have already undone us in our Estates, and that will not serve their turns, without our Innocent Bloods. If it cannot be granted that we can have our

---

[1] Richard and Andrew, sons of Martha Carrier, of Andover. (See above, pp. 241–244.) Richard was 18.

[2] As to this form of torture see above, p. 102 and note 1. For some of the evidence extorted by it in this case see *Records of Salem Witchcraft*, p. 198. The use of torture in cases of witchcraft had been recommended by Perkins, the Puritan oracle, and yet more warmly by King James; and despite protesting jurists it came into use. Even Coke, who maintains that "there is no Law to warrant tortures in this land, nor can they be justified by any prescription," has to add "being so lately brought in" (*Institutes*, III., cap. 2). As to its actual use in English witch-trials see Notestein, *Witchcraft in England*, index, *s. v.* "Torture." But Massachusetts law, from 1641 on, had straitly forbidden it except, after conviction, to extort the names of accomplices; and even then forbade "such tortures as be barbarous and inhumane" (see *Body of Liberties*, par. 45; ed. of 1660, p. 67; ed. of 1672, p. 129). If in 1648 the highest court of the colony, learning with admiration of the achievements of Matthew Hopkins in England, was "desirous that the same course which hath been taken in England for the discovery of witches, by watchinge, may also be taken here," and ordered, in the case of a witch, that "a strict watch be set about her every night, and that her husband be confined to a private room, and watched also" (*Records of Massachusetts*, III. 126), their phrasing betrays how little they understood the rigor of the English method. In 1692 even Cotton Mather declared himself "farr from urging the un-English method of torture" (*Mather Papers*, p. 394), though he urged on the judges "whatever hath a tendency to put the witches into confusion," such as "Crosse and Swift Questions." But the procedure of that day, like our own, drew a line between what might be used in the courts and what might be permitted to extra-judicial inquiry, and we shall see yet more of methods used at Salem to extort confession.

[3] That which.

Trials at Boston, we humbly beg that you would endeavour to have these Magistrates changed, and others in their rooms, begging also and beseeching you would be pleased to be here, if not all, some of you at our Trials, hoping thereby you may be the means of saving the shedding our Innocent Bloods, desiring your Prayers to the Lord in our behalf, we rest your Poor Afflicted Servants,

JOHN PROCTER, etc.

He pleaded very hard at Execution, for a little respite of time, saying that he was not fit to Die; but it was not granted.

Old Jacobs being Condemned, the Sheriff and Officers came and seized all he had, his Wife had her Wedding Ring taken from her, but with great difficulty obtained it again. She was forced to buy Provisions of the Sheriff, such as he had taken, towards her own support, which not being sufficient, the Neighbours of Charity relieved her.[1]

Margaret Jacobs being one that had confessed her own Guilt, and testified against her Grand-Father Jacobs, Mr. Burroughs, and John Willard, She the day before Executions, came to Mr. Burroughs, acknowledging that she had belyed them,[2] and begged Mr. Burroughs Forgiveness, who not only

---

[1] *I. e.*, out of charity the neighbors relieved her.

[2] How she was brought to confess she herself told in a brave paper:

"The humble declaration of Margaret Jacobs unto the honoured court now sitting at Salem, sheweth

"That whereas your poor and humble declarant being closely confined here in Salem jail for the crime of witchcraft, which crime, thanks be to the Lord, I am altogether ignorant of, as will appear at the great day of judgment. May it please the honoured court, I was cried out upon by some of the possessed persons, as afflicting of them; whereupon I was brought to my examination, which persons at the sight of me fell down, which did very much startle and affright me. The Lord above knows I knew nothing, in the least measure, how or who afflicted them; they told me, without doubt I did, or else they would not fall down at me; they told me if I would not confess, I should be put down into the dungeon and would be hanged, but if I would confess I should have my life; the which did so affright me, with my own vile wicked heart, to save my life made me make the confession I did, which confession, may it please the honoured court, is altogether false and untrue. The very first night after I had made my confession, I was in such horror of conscience that I could not sleep, for fear the Devil should carry me away for telling such horrid lies. I was, may it please the honoured court, sworn to my confession, as I understand since, but then, at that time, was ignorant of it, not knowing what an oath did mean. The Lord, I hope, in whom I trust, out of the abundance of his mercy, will forgive me my false for-

forgave her, but also Prayed with and for her.   She wrote the following Letter to her Father.

From the Dungeon in Salem-Prison, August 20, 92.

Honoured Father,

After my Humble Duty Remembred to you, hoping in the Lord of your good Health, as Blessed be God I enjoy, tho in abundance of Affliction, being close confined here in a loathsome Dungeon, the Lord look down in mercy upon me, not knowing how soon I shall be put to Death, by means of the Afflicted Persons; my Grand-Father having Suffered already, and all his Estate Seized for the King.   The reason of my Confinement is this, I having, through the Magistrates Threatnings, and my own Vile and Wretched Heart, confessed several things contrary to my Conscience and Knowledg, tho to the Wounding of my own Soul, the Lord pardon me for it; but Oh! the terrors of a wounded Conscience who can bear.   But blessed be the Lord, he would not let me go on in my Sins, but in mercy I hope so my Soul would not suffer me to keep it in any longer, but I was forced to confess the truth of all before the Magistrates, who would not believe me, but tis their pleasure to put me in here, and God knows how soon I shall be put to death.   Dear Father, let me beg your Prayers to the Lord on my behalf, and send us a Joyful and Happy meeting in Heaven.   My Mother poor Woman is very Crazey, and

swearing myself. What I said was altogether false, against my grandfather, and Mr. Burroughs, which I did to save my life and to have my liberty; but the Lord, charging it to my conscience, made me in so much horror, that I could not contain myself before I had denied my confession, which I did, though I saw nothing but death before me, choosing rather death with a quiet conscience, than to live in such horror, which I could not suffer.   Whereupon my denying my confession, I was committed to close prison, where I have enjoyed more felicity in spirit a thousand times than I did before in my enlargement.

"And now, may it please your honours, your poor and humble declarant having, in part, given your honours a description of my condition, do leave it to your honours pious and judicious discretions to take pity and compassion on my young and tender years; to act and do with me as the Lord above and your honours shall see good, having no friend but the Lord to plead my cause for me; not being guilty in the least measure of the crime of witchcraft, nor any other sin that deserves death from man; and your poor and humble declarant shall forever pray, as she is bound in duty, for your honours' happiness in this life, and eternal felicity in the world to come.   So prays your honours declarant.

"MARGARET JACOBS."

The document is preserved by Hutchinson, and may be found in the first chapter of his second volume (or in Poole's reprint of an earlier draft, *N. E. Hist. and Gen. Register*, XXIV. 402–403).

remembers her kind Love to you, and to Uncle, *viz.* D. A.[1] So leaving you to the protection of the Lord, I rest your Dutiful Daughter,

MARGARET JACOBS.

At the time appointed for her Tryal, she had an Imposthume in her head, which was her Escape.[2]

September 9. Six more were tried, and received Sentance of Death, *viz.* Martha Cory of Salem-Village, Mary Easty of Topsfield, Alice Parker and Ann Pudeater of Salem, Dorcas Hoar of Beverly, and Mary Bradberry of Salisbury.[3] *September* 16, Giles Cory was prest to Death.

September 17. Nine more received Sentance of Death, *viz.* Margaret Scot of Rowly, Goodwife Redd of Marblehead, Samuel Wardwell, and Mary Parker of Andover, also Abigail Falkner of Andover, who pleaded Pregnancy, Rebecka Eames of Boxford, Mary Lacy, and Ann Foster of Andover, and Abigail Hobbs of Topsfield.[4] Of these Eight were Executed,

---

[1] Daniel Andrew, the kinsman and neighbor who had fled with her father. He had been a leading man, a teacher, a deputy to the General Court, and apparently a staunch opponent of the panic. As to the crazed mother, see p. 371, below, and the grandmother's petition in Mass. Hist. Soc., *Collections*, V. 79 (or in Chandler's *American Criminal Trials*, I. 431–432).

[2] For a little more of her story see below, p. 371. She was acquitted in January, but had to remain in jail, even after the governor by proclamation had freed the prisoners (May, 1693), for want of means to pay her prison fees. A stranger, touched with compassion on hearing of her case, advanced the money —and was in time repaid. (Upham, *Salem Witchcraft*, II. 353–354.)

[3] The papers relating to Ann Pudeater (*Records of Salem Witchcraft*, II. 12–22) have been embodied in a study of her case by G. F. Chever in the *Collections* of the Essex Institute (II. 37–42, 49–54). The widow Dorcas Hoar seems to have earned some suspicion by an interest in fortune-telling (*Records of Salem Witchcraft*, I. 235–253), and, though she confessed, she was condemned; but she had potent friends. "A petition is sent to Town," says Sewall in his *Diary* on September 21, "in behalf of Dorcas Hoar, who now confesses. Accordingly an order is sent to the Sheriff to forbear her Execution." "This is," he adds, "the first condemned person who has confess'd." The aged Mrs. Bradbury, daughter of John Perkins of Ipswich and wife of Captain Thomas Bradbury of Salisbury, was not only one of the most socially eminent but one of the most venerated women of her region, and her arrest enlisted in her defence the public sentiment of all the district (see *Records of Salem Witchcraft*, II. 160–174). She was aided to escape from prison, and so from death.

[4] For the Andover and Topsfield cases reference may again be made to Mrs. Bailey's *Historical Sketches of Andover* and to vol. XIII. of the *Collections* of the Topsfield Historical Society as well as to the *Records of Salem Witchcraft*. The

September 22, *viz.* Martha Cory, Mary Easty, Alice Parker, Ann Pudeater, Margaret Scot, Willmet Redd, Samuel Wardwell, and Mary Parker.

Giles Cory pleaded not Guilty to his Indictment, but would not put himself upon Tryal by the Jury (they having cleared none upon Tryal) and knowing there would be the same Witnesses against him, rather chose to undergo what Death they would put him to. In pressing his Tongue being prest out of his Mouth, the Sheriff with his Cane forced it in again, when he was dying. He was the first in New-England, that was ever prest to Death.[1]

The Cart going up the Hill with these Eight to Execution, was for some time at a sett; the afflicted and others said, that the Devil hindred it, etc.

Martha Cory, Wife to Giles Cory, protesting her Innocency, concluded her Life with an Eminent Prayer upon the Ladder.

Wardwell having formerly confessed himself Guilty, and after denied it, was soon brought upon his Tryal; his former Confession and Spectre Testimony was all that appeared against him. At Execution while he was speaking to the People, protesting his Innocency, the Executioner being at the same time smoaking Tobacco, the smoak coming in his Face, interrupted his Discourse, those Accusers said, the Devil hindred him with smoak.

Mary Easty, Sister also to Rebecka Nurse, when she took

papers as to Wilmot Redd, or Reed, are in the *Records* (II. 97–106); Margaret Scott's seem lost. The examinations of Mary Lacy and Ann Foster should be studied in Hutchinson's chapter as well as in the *Records* (II. 135–142), and see also p. 244, above, and pp. 418–419, below.

[1] This was, of course, the old English "peine forte et dure" for those who, in cases of petty treason or of felony, will not "put themselves upon the country," or, as Coke has it, "when the offender standeth mute, and refuseth to be tryed by the common law of the land." (See Pollock and Maitland, *History of English Law*, second ed., II. 650–652.) Whether in Giles Corey's case this was mere proud protest or had some ulterior end is not yet clear. The theory that he hoped thereby to save himself from attainder and preserve his right to bequeath his property has been learnedly contested by G. H. Moore (see especially his *Final Notes on Witchcraft in Massachusetts*, New York, 1885, pp. 40–59). As to Giles Corey see also p. 250, above, and *Records of Salem Witchcraft*, II. 175–180. The missing report of his examination is printed at the end of Calef's book in the editions of 1823, 1861, and 1866.

her last farewell of her Husband, Children and Friends, was, as is reported by them present, as Serious, Religious, Distinct, and Affectionate as could well be exprest, drawing Tears from the Eyes of almost all present. It seems besides the Testimony of the Accusers and Confessors, another proof, as it was counted, appeared against her, it having been usual to search the Accused for Tets; upon some parts of her Body, not here to be named, was found an Excrescence, which they called a Tet. Before her Death she put up the following Petition:

To the Honorable Judge and Bench now sitting in Judicature in Salem and the Reverend Ministers, humbly sheweth, That whereas your humble poor Petitioner being Condemned to die, doth humbly beg of you, to take it into your Judicious and Pious Consideration, that your poor and humble Petitioner knowing my own Innocency (blessed be the Lord for it) and seeing plainly the Wiles and Subtilty of my Accusers, by my self, cannot but judge charitably of others, that are going the same way with my self, if the Lord step not mightily in. I was confined a whole Month on the same account that I am now condemned for, and then cleared by the Afflicted persons, as some of your Honours know, and in two days time I was cried out upon by them, and have been confined, and now am condemned to die. The Lord above knows my Innocency then, and likewise doth now, as at the great day will be known to Men and Angels. I Petition to your Honours not for my own Life, for I know I must die, and my appointed time is set; but the Lord he knows it is, if it be possible, that no more Innocent Blood be shed, which undoubtedly cannot be avoided in the way and course you go in. I question not, but your Honours do to the utmost of your powers, in the discovery and detecting of Witchcraft and Witches, and would not be guilty of Innocent Blood for the World; but by my own Innocency I know you are in the wrong way. The Lord in his infinite Mercy direct you in this great work, if it be his blessed will, that Innocent Blood be not shed; I would humbly beg of you, that your Honours would be pleased to Examine some of those confessing Witches, I being confident there are several of them have belyed themselves and others, as will appear, if not in this World, I am sure in the World to come, whither I am going; and I question not, but your selves will see an alteration in these things: They say, my self and others have made a league with the Devil, we cannot confess. I know and the Lord he knows (as will shortly appear) they belye me, and so I question not but they do others; the Lord alone, who is the searcher of all hearts, knows that as I shall answer it at the

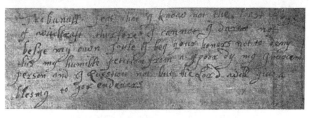

PETITION OF MARY ESTY

From the original at the Essex County Court House, Salem.
(The lower part of the plate shows the conclusion of the
petition, on the reverse of the page)

Tribunal Seat, that I know not the least thing of Witchcraft, there-fore I cannot, I durst not belye my own Soul. I beg your Honours not to deny this my humble Petition, from a poor dying Innocent person, and I question not but the Lord will give a blessing to your Endeavours.   MARY ESTY.

After Execution Mr. Noyes turning him to the Bodies, said, what a sad thing it is to see Eight Firebrands of Hell hanging there.

In *October* 1692, One of Wenham[1] complained of Mrs. Hale, whose Husband, the Minister of Beverly, had been very forward in these Prosecutions, but being fully satisfied of his Wives sincere Christianity, caused him to alter his Judgment; for it was come to a stated Controversie, among the New-England Divines, whether the Devil could Afflict in a good Man's shape; it seems nothing else could convince him: yet when it came so near to himself, he was soon convinc'd that the Devil might so Afflict.[2] Which same reason did after-

[1] Mary Herrick. At least the following remarkable tale of hers (first published in the *N. E. Hist. and Gen. Register*, XXVII. 55) must have had to do with Mr. Hale's change of view:

"An Account Received from the mouth of Mary Herrick aged about 17 yeares having been Afflicted [by] the Devill or some of his instruments, about 2 month. She saith she had oft been Afflicted and that the shape of Mrs. Hayle had been represented to her, One amongst others, but she knew not what hand Afflicted her then, but on the 5th of the 9th [*i. e.*, November] She Appeared again with the Ghost of Gooddee Easty, and that then Mrs. Hayle did sorely Afflict her by pinching, pricking and Choaking her. On the 12th of the 9th she Came again and Gooddee Easty with her and then Mrs. Hayle did Afflict her as formerly. Sd Easty made as if she would speake but did not, but on the same night they Came again and Mrs. Hayle did sorely Afflict her, and asked her if she thought she was a Witch. The Girl answered no, You be the Devill. Then said Easty sd and speake, She Came to tell her She had been put to Death wrongfully and was Innocent of Witchcraft, and she Came to Vindicate her Cause and she Cryed Vengeance, Vengeance, and bid her reveal this to Mr. Hayle and Gerish, and then she would rise no more, nor should Mrs. Hayle Afflict her any more. Memorand: that Just before sd Easty was Executed, She Appeared to sd Girl, and said I am going upon the Ladder to be hanged for a Witch, but I am innocent, and before a 12 Month be past you shall believe it. Sd Girl sd she speake not of this before because she believed she was Guilty, Till Mrs. Hayle appeared to her and Afflicted her, but now she believeth it is all a Delusion of the Devil.

"This before Mr. Hayle and Gerish 14th of the 9th 1692."

"Gerish" means the Rev. Joseph Gerrish, of Wenham, who is doubtless here the scribe.

[2] But see (at pp. 404, 405, below) Hale's own account of this change of view.

wards prevail with many others; and much influenced to the succeeding change at Tryals.[1]

October 7. (Edward Bishop and his Wife having made their Escape out of Prison) this day Mr. Corwin the Sheriff, came and Seiz'd his Goods, and Cattle, and had it not been for his second Son (who borrowed Ten Pound and gave it him) they had been wholly lost, the Receipt follows; but it seems they must be content with such a Receipt as he would give them.

Received this 7th day of October 1692, of Samuel Bishop of the Town of Salem, of the County of Essex, in New-England, Cordwainer, in full satisfaction, a valuable Summ of Money, for the Goods and Chattels of Edward Bishop, Senior, of the Town and County aforesaid, Husbandman; which Goods and Chattels being seized, for that the said Edward Bishop, and Sarah his Wife, having been committed for Witchcraft and Felony, have made their Escape; and their Goods and Chattles were forfeited unto their Majesties, and now being in Possession of the said Samuel Bishop; and in behalf of Their Majesties, I do hereby discharge the said Goods and Chattels, the day and year above written, as witness my hand,

GEORGE CORWIN, *Sheriff*.

But before this the said Bishops Eldest Son, having Married into that Family of the Putmans,[2] who were chief Prosecutors in this business; he holding a Cow to be branded lest it should be seiz'd, and having a Push or Boyl upon his Thigh, with his straining it broke; this is that that was pretended to be burnt with the said Brand; and is one of the bones thrown to the Dogmatical to pick, in *Wonders of the Invisible World*, P. 143.[3] the other, of a Corner of a Sheet, pretended to be taken from a Spectre, it is known that it was provided the day before, by that Afflicted person, and the third bone of a Spindle is almost as easily provided, as the piece of the Knife; so that Apollo needs not herein be consulted,[4] etc.

[1] Hale's whole book (see below, pp. 397–432) is a commentary on this passage.

[2] His wife was a daughter of John Putnam, brother of Nathaniel and uncle of Deacon Edward and of the Thomas whose wife and daughter were of the "afflicted." As to the Bishops see (besides Upham) Essex Institute *Collections*, XLII. 146 ff.

[3] At pp. 247–248, above.

[4] *I. e.*, it needs no oracle to explain the matter; see p. 248, note 1.

Mr. Philip English and his Wife having made their Escape out of Prison, Mr. Corwin the Sheriff seiz'd his Estate, to the value of about Fifteen Hundred Pound, which was wholly lost to him, except about Three Hundred Pound value, (which was afterward restored.)[1]

After Goodwife Hoar was Condemned, her Estate was seiz'd, and was also bought again for Eight Pound.

George Jacobs, Son to old Jacobs,[2] being accused, he fled, then the Officers came to his House, his Wife was a Woman Crazy in her Senses and had been so several Years. She it seems had been also accused; there were in the House with her only four small Children, and one of them suck'd, her Eldest Daughter[3] being in Prison; the Officer perswaded her out of the House, to go along with him, telling her she should speedily return, the Children ran a great way after her crying.

When she came where the Afflicted were, being asked, they said they did not know her, at length one said, don't you know Jacobs the old Witch, and then they cry'd out of her, and fell down in their Fits; she was sent to Prison, and lay there Ten Months, the Neighbours of pitty took care of the Children to preserve them from perishing.

About this time a New Scene was begun, one Joseph Ballard of Andover, whose Wife was ill (and after died of a Fever) sent to Salem for some of those Accusers, to tell him who

---

[1] Philip English was the foremost ship-owner of Salem, a man of large wealth and exceptional prominence. He had come in early life from the island of Jersey and at Salem had married, in 1675, the daughter and heiress of the merchant William Hollingworth. His wife, now thirty-nine, a lady of education and refinement, was arrested on April 22 (see p. 347, above) and on April 30 a warrant was issued for himself, but he could not be found. Detected, however, in his Boston hiding-place, he was on May 31 committed, but was allowed to give bail, and with his wife was kept in loose custody at Boston. As to their escape thence, see above, pp. 178, 186, note 3; and for their story in general the articles by G. F. Chever in the Essex Institute's *Collections*, I., II., *Salem Witchcraft Records*, I. 189–193, the evidence of William Beale appended by Drake to his ed. of Mather and Calef (III. 177–185), the documents printed in the *Publications* of the Colonial Society of Massachusetts, X. 17–20, a letter of Dr. Bentley in Mass. Hist. Soc., *Collections*, first ser., X. 64–66, and a passage from his diary quoted by R. D. Paine in *The Ships and Sailors of Old Salem* (New York, 1909), pp. 26–28.

[2] See above, pp. 360, 364.　　　[3] Margaret. See pp. 364–366.

afflicted his Wife; others did the like: Horse and Man were sent from several places to fetch those Accusers who had the Spectral sight, that they might thereby tell who afflicted those that were any ways ill.

When these came into any place where such were, usually they fell into a Fit; after which being asked who it was that afflicted the person, they would, for the most part, name one whom they said sat on the head, and another that sat on the lower parts of the afflicted. Soon after Ballard's sending (as above) more than Fifty of the People of Andover were complained of, for afflicting their Neighbours. Here it was that many accused themselves, of Riding upon Poles through the Air; Many Parents believing their Children to be Witches, and many Husbands their Wives, etc. When these Accusers came to the House of any upon such account, it was ordinary for other young People to be taken in Fits, and to have the same Spectral sight.

Mr. Dudley Bradstreet,[1] a Justice of Peace in Andover, having granted out Warrants against, and Committed Thirty or Forty to Prisons, for the supposed Witchcrafts, at length saw cause to forbear granting out any more Warrants. Soon after which he and his Wife were cried out of, himself was (by them) said to have killed Nine persons by Witchcraft, and found it his safest course to make his Escape.

A Dog being afflicted at Salem-Village, those that had the Spectral sight being sent for, they accused Mr. John Bradstreet (Brother to the Justice) that he afflicted the said Dog, and now rid upon him: He made his Escape into Pescattequa-Government,[2] and the Dog was put to death, and was all of the Afflicted that suffered death.

At Andover, the Afflicted complained of a Dog, as afflicting of them, and would fall into their Fits at the Dogs looking upon them; the Dog was put to death.

A worthy Gentleman of Boston, being about this time accused by those at Andover, he sent by some particular Friends a Writ to Arrest those Accusers in a Thousand Pound Action for Defamation, with instructions to them, to inform themselves of the certainty of the proof, in doing which their business was

---

[1] A son of the venerable Governor Bradstreet and himself a man of station.
[2] *I. e.*, New Hampshire.

perceived, and from thence forward the Accusations at Andover generally ceased.[1]

In October some of these Accusers were sent for to Glocester, and occasioned four Women to be sent to Prison, but Salem Prison being so full it could receive no more, two were sent to Ipswich Prison. In November they were sent for again by Lieutenant Stephens, who was told that a Sister of his was bewitched; in their way passing over Ipswich-bridge, they met with an old Woman, and instantly fell into their Fits: But by this time the validity of such Accusations being much questioned, they found not that Encouragement they. had done elsewhere, and soon withdrew.

These Accusers swore that they saw three persons sitting upon Lieutenant Stephens's Sister till she died; yet Bond was accepted for those Three.

And now Nineteen persons having been hang'd, and one prest to death, and Eight more condemned, in all Twenty and Eight, of which above a third part were Members of some of the Churches in N. England, and more than half of them of a good Conversation in general, and not one clear'd; About Fifty having confest themselves to be Witches, of which not one Executed; above an Hundred and Fifty in Prison, and above Two Hundred more accused; The Special Commission of Oyer and Terminer comes to a period,[2] which has no other foundation than the Governours Commission,[3] and had proceeded in the manner of swearing Witnesses, *viz.* By holding up the hand, (and by receiving Evidences in writing) according to the Ancient Usage of this Countrey; as also having their Indictments in English. In the Tryals, when any were Indicted for Afflicting, Pining, and wasting the Bodies of particular persons by Witchcraft; it was usual to hear Evidence of matter foreign, and of perhaps Twenty or Thirty years standing, about over-setting Carts, the death of Cattle, un-

[1] On this Andover episode see also pp. 180–181, 241–244, above.

[2] Its last session was on September 22, though the court was not definitely dropped till the end of October. See above, p. 200 and note 1.

[3] The implication perhaps is that the governor exceeded his powers. That question has been much and hotly debated—most learnedly by Mr. A. C. Goodell in his *Further Notes on the History of Witchcraft in Massachusetts* (Cambridge, 1884), pp. 20 ff., and Dr. G. H. Moore in his *Final Notes on Witchcraft in Massachusetts* (New York, 1885), pp. 71–84.

kindness to Relations, or unexpected Accidents befalling after some quarrel. Whether this was admitted by the Law of England, or by what other Law, wants to be determined; the Executions seemed mixt, in pressing to death for not pleading, which most agrees with the Laws of England, and Sentencing Women to be hanged for Witchcraft, according to the former practice of this Country, and not by burning, as is said to have been the Law of England.[1] And though the confessing Witches were many; yet not one of them that confessed their own guilt, and abode by their Confession were put to Death.[2]

Here followeth what account some of those miserable Creatures give of their Confession under their own hands.

We whose Names are under written, Inhabitants of Andover, when as that horrible and tremendous Judgment beginning at Salem-Village, in the Year 1692, (by some) call'd Witchcraft, first breaking forth at Mr. Parris's House, several Young persons being seemingly afflicted, did accuse several persons for afflicting them, and many there believing it so to be; we being informed that if a person were sick, that the afflicted persons could tell, what or who was the cause of that sickness. Joseph Ballard of Andover (his Wife being sick at the same time) he either from himself, or by the advice of others, fetch'd two of the persons call'd the afflicted persons, from Salem-Village to Andover. Which was the beginning of that dreadful Calamity that befel us in Andover. And the Authority in Andover, believing the said Accusations to be true, sent for the said persons to come together, to the Meeting-house in Andover (the afflicted per-

---

[1] This is an error. In England, too, witches were hanged—unless convicted of bewitching to death their husbands, when for husband-murder, "petty treason," they were burned (see Coke, *Institutes*, pt. III., cap. 2, 6, 101, and the records of the courts). Sir Matthew Hale indeed makes witchcraft "at Common Law" still "punished with death, as Heresie, by Writ *De Hæretico Comburendo*" (*Pleas of the Crown*, p. 6). But this, of course, was after trial by an ecclesiastical court; and since the Reformation ecclesiastical courts had not had cognizance of such cases.

[2] This, the most striking feature of the Salem trials, is perhaps partially explained by the closing suggestion of Cotton Mather's advice to the judges (*Mather Papers*, p. 396): "What if some of the lesser Criminalls be onely scourged with lesser punishments, and also put upon some solemn, open, Publike and Explicitt renunciation of the Divil? . . . Or what if the death of some of the offenders were either diverted or inflicted, according to the successe of such their renunciation?" If it was unique that those who confessed escaped death, it was nothing unique that they should be reckoned "lesser Criminalls."

sons being there.) After Mr. Bernard[1] had been at Prayer, we were blindfolded, and our hands were laid upon the afflicted persons, they being in their Fits, and falling into their Fits at our coming into their presence (as they said) and some led us and laid our hands upon them, and then they said they were well, and that we were guilty of afflicting of them; whereupon we were all seized as Prisoners, by a Warrant from the Justice of the Peace, and forthwith carried to Salem. And by reason of that suddain surprizal, we knowing our selves altogether Innocent of that Crime, we were all exceedingly astonished and amazed, and consternated and affrighted even out of our Reason; and our nearest and dearest Relations, seeing us in that dreadful condition, and knowing our great danger, apprehending that there was no other way to save our lives, as the case was then circumstantiated, but by our confessing our selves to be such and such persons, as the afflicted represented us to be, they out of tender love and pitty perswaded us to confess what we did confess. And indeed that Confession, that is said we made, was no other than what was suggested to us by some Gentlemen; they telling us, that we were Witches, and they knew it, and we knew it, and they knew that we knew it, which made us think that it was so; and our understanding, our reason, and our faculties almost gone, we were not capable of judging our condition; as also the hard measures they used with us, rendred us uncapable of making our Defence; but said any thing and every thing which they desired, and most of what we said, was but in effect a consenting to what they said. Sometime after when we were better composed, they telling of us what we had confessed, we did profess that we were Innocent, and Ignorant of such things. And we hearing that Samuel Wardwell had renounced his Confession, and quickly after Condemned and Executed, some of us were told that we were going after Wardwell.

MARY OSGOOD, MARY TILER, DELIV. DANE, ABIGAIL BARKER, SARAH WILSON, HANNAH TILER.[2]

It may here be further added concerning those that did Confess, that besides that powerful Argument, of Life (and

[1] The Rev. Thomas Barnard, associate minister at Andover. Dane, his senior, seems to have been averse to the proceedings.

[2] This is doubtless what Brattle calls (p. 189, above) "a petition lately offered to the chief Judge." The examination and confession of Mary Osgood may be found in Hutchinson's *Massachusetts*, II. ch. I. (or in Poole's reprint, *N. E. Hist. and Gen. Register*, XXIV. 398). She, the two Tylers, and Abigail Barker were tried and acquitted in January at the first session of the new Superior Court (see in vol. X. of the *Publications* of the Colonial Society of Massachusetts the brief but valuable paper of John Noble, pp. 12–26).

freedom from hardships and Irons not only promised, but also performed to all that owned their guilt), There are numerous Instances, too many to be here inserted, of the tedious Examinations before private persons, many hours together; they all that time urging them to Confess (and taking turns to perswade them) till the accused were wearied out by being forced to stand so long, or for want of Sleep, etc. and so brought to give an Assent to what they said; they then asking them, Were you at such a Witch-meeting, or have you signed the Devil's Book, etc. upon their replying, yes, the whole was drawn into form as their Confession.

But that which did mightily further such Confessions, was their nearest and dearest Relations urging them to it. These seeing no other way of escape for them, thought it the best advice that could be given; hence it was that the Husbands of some, by counsel often urging, and utmost earnestness, and Children upon their Knees intreating, have at length prevailed with them, to say they were guilty.[1]

As to the manner of Tryals, and the Evidence taken for Convictions at Salem, it is already set forth in Print, by the

---

[1] The best commentary on these words is a remarkable paper which more than a century ago came into the hands of the Massachusetts Historical Society and was published in its *Collections* (second series, III. 221–225). As Dr. Belknap, who prepared it for publication, labelled it "Remainder of the account of the Salem Witchcraft" and seems to have meant it to be printed with Brattle's letter (see pp. 169–190, above), it is not improbable that, with that document, it had come from the family of Brattle and that it was originally his. In that case it is by no means impossible that in his hands Calef may have seen it and that from him he may have received the recantation printed just above. The added paper runs:

"*Salem, Oct.* 19, '92. The Rev. Mr. I. Mather went to Salem [to visit] the confessours (so called): He conferred with several of them, and they spake as follows:"

[Then are narrated the explanations given by eleven of the women, the most suggestive being this:] "Goodwife Tyler did say, that when she was first apprehended, she had no fears upon her, and did think that nothing could have made her confesse against herself; but since, she had found to her great grief, that she had wronged the truth, and falsely accused herself: she said, that when she was brought to Salem, her brother Bridges rode with her, and that all along the way from Andover to Salem, her brother kept telling her that she must needs be a witch, since the afflicted accused her, and at her touch were raised out of their fitts, and urging her to confess herself a witch; she as constantly told him,

Reverend Mr. Cotton Mather, in his *Wonders of the Invisible World*, at the Command of his Excellency, Sir William Phips; with not only the Recommendation, but thanks of the Lieutenant Governour;[1] and with the Approbation of the Reverend Mr. J. M.[2] in his Postscript to his *Cases of Conscience*;

that she was no witch, that she knew nothing of witchcraft, and begg'd of him not to urge her to confesse; however when she came to Salem, she was carried to a room, where her brother on one side and Mr. John Emerson on the other side did tell her that she was certainly a witch, and that she saw the devill before her eyes at that time (and accordingly the said Emerson would attempt with his hand to beat him away from her eyes) and they so urged her to confesse, that she wished herself in any dungeon, rather than be so treated: Mr. Emerson told her once and again, Well! I see you will not confesse! Well! I will now leave you, and then you are undone, body and soul forever: Her brother urged her to confesse, and told her that in so doing she could not lye; to which she answered, Good brother, do not say so, for I shall lye if I confesse, and then who shall answer unto God for my lye? He still asserted it, and said that God would not suffer so many good men to be in such an errour about it, and that she would be hang'd, if she did not confesse, and continued so long and so violently to urge and presse her to confesse, that she thought verily her life would have gone from her, and became so terrifyed in her mind, that she own'd at length almost any thing that they propounded to her; but she had wronged her conscience in so doing, she was guilty of a great sin in belying of herself, and desired to mourn for it as long as she lived: This she said and a great deal more of the like nature, and all of it with such affection, sorrow, relenting, grief, and mourning as that it exceeds any pen for to describe and expresse the same."

The "Mr. John Emerson" of this episode was that clerical schoolmaster whom we have already met in New Hampshire (see p. 37, note 3), but who was now a teacher at Charlestown. (Sibley, *Harvard Graduates*, II. 471–474.) If so personal an activity of President Mather surprise, let it be remembered how widely the persecution was now striking. His parishioner Lady Phips was among the accused, and the Quaker John Whiting has a yet more startling suggestion: commenting in 1702 on the account just printed in Cotton Mather's *Magnalia*, he mentions the "two Hundred more accused, some of which of great Estates in Boston," and in the margin adds, "Query, Was not the Governour's Wife, and C. M.'s Mother, some of them?" (*Truth and Innocency Defended*, p. 140.)

Yet not all dared to retract. "More than one or two of those now in Prison," writes Increase Mather (*Cases of Conscience*, Postscript), "have freely and credibly acknowledged their Communion and Familiarity with the Spirits of Darkness; and have also declared unto me the Time and Occasion, with the particular Circumstances of their Hellish Obligations and Abominations."

[1] For Cotton Mather's *Wonders*, with its *imprimatur* by Phips and its preface by Stoughton, see above, pp. 205 ff.

[2] Increase Mather: the printer seems unable to distinguish Calef's *I* from his *J*.

which last Book was set forth by the consent of the Ministers in and near Boston.[1]

Two of the Judges have also given their Sentiments in these words, p. 147.

The Reverend and worthy Author, having at the direction of his Excellency the Governour, so far obliged the Publick, as to give some account of the sufferings, brought upon the Countrey by Witchcrafts, and of the Tryals which have passed upon several executed for the same.

Upon perusal thereof, We find the matters of Fact and Evidence truly reported, and a prospect given of the Methods of Conviction, used in the proceedings of the Court at Salem.

BOSTON, October 11,   WILLIAM STOUGHTON,
    1692.   SAMUEL SEWALL.

And considering that this may fall into the hands of such as never saw those Wonders, it may be needful to transcribe the whole account he has given thereof, without any variation (but with one of the Indictments annext to the Tryal of each).[2]

.   .   .   .

Thus far the Account given in *Wonders of the Invisible World*; in which setting aside such words as these, in the Tryal of G. B. *viz.*, "They (*i. e.* the Witnesses) were enough to fix the character of a Witch upon him."[3]

In the Tryal of Bishop, these words, "but there was no need of them," *i. e.* of further Testimony.[4]

In the Tryal of How, where it is said, "and there came in Testimony of preternatural Mischiefs, presently befalling some that had been instrumental to debar her from the Communion, whereupon she was intruding."[5]   Martin is call'd "one of

---

[1] The book, with all its credulity, is in the main a vigorous and learned argument against improper methods for detecting witches, and chiefly against reliance on the testimony of the bewitched. Commended by the ministers, fourteen of whom sign the preface "to the Christian reader," it may have done something to allay the panic. But, though it is dated by the author "October 3," the title-page date of 1693 suggests that, like his son's *Wonders* (see p. 207, note 1), it was long in the press or withheld from the public.

[2] As the pages of Mather's *Wonders* containing these trials are reprinted in full above (pp. 215–244), it is needless here to repeat them. They occupy pp. 113–139 of Calef's book.   Then comes what here follows.

[3] See p. 216.   [4] See p. 229.   [5] See p. 237.

the most impudent, scurrilous, wicked Creatures in the World."
In his Account of Martha Carryer, he is pleased to call her "a
Rampant Hag," [1] etc.

These Expressions, as they manifest that he wrote more
like an Advocate than an Historian,[2] so also that those that
were his Imployers[3] were not mistaken in their choice of him
for that work, however he may have mist it in other things.

As in his owning (in the Tryal of G. B.) That the Testimony of the bewitched and confessors was not enough against
the Accused, for it is known that not only in New-England,
such Evidence has been taken for sufficient, but also in England, as himself there owns, and will also hold true of Scotland,
etc., they having proceeded upon such Evidence, to the taking
away of the Lives of many, to assert that this is not enough is
to tell the World that such Executions were but so many
Bloody Murders; which surely was not his intent to say.

His telling that the Court began to think that Burroughs
stept aside to put on invisibility, is a rendring them so mean
Philosophers, and such weak Christians, as to be fit to be imposed upon by any silly pretender.

His calling the Evidence against How trivial, and others
against Burroughs, he accounts no part of his Conviction; and
that of lifting a Gun with one Finger, its being not made use
of as Evidence, renders the whole but the more perplext.
(Not to mention the many mistakes therein contain'd.)[4]

Yet all this (and more that might have been hinted at)
does not hinder, but that his Account of the manner of Trials
of those for Witchcraft is as faithfully related as any Tryals
of that kind, that was ever yet made publick;[5] and it may also

---

[1] See p. 244.

[2] The author had himself said, "I report matters not as an Advocate, but
as an Historian."

[3] Phips, Stoughton, and the latter's fellow-judges.

[4] As to the insertion in Mather's account of evidence not given at the trial,
and as to his errors of statement, see the careful analysis of Upham in his "Salem
Witchcraft and Cotton Mather," pp. 46–48 (*Historical Magazine*, n. s., VI.
175–177).

[5] To those who know the wretched chap-books which have had to serve as
records of the English witch-trials—and these alone Calef was likely to know—
this will not seem high praise. The modern student can, however, compare for
himself Mather's accounts with the court records—and, where mere transcription
is concerned, will find them faithful.

be reasonably thought that there was as careful a Scrutiny, and as unquestion'd Evidences improved, as had been formerly used in the Tryals of others, for such crimes in other places. Tho indeed a second part might be very useful, to set forth which was the Evidence Convictive in these Tryals, for it is not supposed, that Romantick or Ridiculous stories should have any influence, such as biting a Spectres Finger, so that the Blood flowed out, or such as Shattock's Story of 12 Years standing, which yet was presently 18 Years or more, and yet a Man of that excellent Memory, as to be able to recall a small difference his Wife had with another Woman, when Eighteen Years were past.[1]

As it is not to be supposed that such as these could Influence any Judge or Jury, so not unkindness to relations, or God's having given to one Man more strength than to some others, the over-setting of Carts, or the death of Cattle, nor yet Excrescencies (call'd Tets) nor little bits of Rags tied together (call'd Poppets.) Much less any persons illness, or having their Cloaths rent when a Spectre has been well banged, much less the burning the Mares Fart, mentioned in the Tryal of How.[2]

None of these being in the least capable of proving the Indictment; The supposed Criminals were Indicted for Afflicting, etc., such and such particular persons by Witchcraft, to which none of these Evidences have one word to say, and the Afflicted and Confessors being declared not enough, the matter needs yet further explaining.[3]

[1] See pp. 225–227. Shattuck, testifying in 1692, placed in 1680 his child's bewitchment, but "about 17 or 18 years after" the exposure of the witch.

[2] See pp. 239–240.

[3] The offense charged, in the indictments printed by Calef, was that the accused "wickedly and feloniously hath used certain detestable arts, called witch-crafts and sorceries, by which said wicked arts" the said bewitched "was and is tortured, afflicted, pined, consumed, wasted and tormented against the peace of our sovereign lord and lady, the King and Queen, and against the form of the statute in that case made and provided." This was the usual form; but four of the indictments extant (against Rebecca Eames, Samuel Wardwell, Rebecca Jacobs, *Records of Salem Witchcraft*, II. 24, 143, 147–148, and William Barker's, preserved by Chandler, *American Criminal Trials*, I. 429) charge instead that the accused "wickedly and feloniously a covenant with the Evil Spirit the Devil did make," and in two of these "the statute of King James the First" is expressly named as contravened. That statute, indeed, punished alike with death those

But to proceed, the General Court having sat and enacted Laws, particularly one against Witchcraft, assigning the Penalty of Death to any that shall feed, reward or employ, etc., Evil Spirits, though it has not yet been explained what is intended thereby, or what it is to feed, reward or imploy Devils, etc., yet some of the Legislators have given this instead of an Explanation, that they had therein but Copied the Law of another Country.[1]

who should "consult, covenant with, entertain, employ, feed, or reward any evil or wicked spirit," and the laws of Massachusetts made it death "if any man or woman be a witch (that is, hath or consulteth with a familiar spirit)"—without a mention of harm to man or beast as element of the crime. That the indictments specify such harm was perhaps only because the public attorney—Thomas Newton (succeeded on July 26 by Anthony Checkley)—was fresh from English practice; but, as Calef implies, the proof should meet the indictment. Newton (1660–1721) had come to Boston in 1688. Mr. Goodell, who studied the originals, says the quoted indictments mentioning the English statute "appear to have been drawn in blank by him, and afterwards filled in by Checkley" (*Further Notes*, p. 37). As to Newton see the study of Moore (*Final Notes*, pp. 94–103). Edward Randolph says of him (V. 143) that he was "a person well known in the practice in the Courts in England and New England," while Checkley he calls "a man ignorant in the Laws of England." In 1691 Newton had been attorney general at New York.

[1] The laws of the colony had never ceased to be operative; and the first act passed (June 15, 1692) by the General Court under the new charter was for the continuance of these laws, "being not repugnant to the laws of England nor inconsistent with the present constitution," in full force till November 10. On October 29 the Court passed a general "act for the punishing of capital offenders," in which the old Massachusetts law as to witchcraft—"If any man or woman be a witch, that is, hath or consulteth with a familiar spirit, they shall be put to death"—retains its old place and wording. And on December 14, "for more particular direction in the execution of the law against witchcraft," the same General Court enacted the long English statute of 1604 (1 James I., cap. 12)—omitting only the penalty of loss of "the privilege and benefit of clergy and sanctuary" and the clauses saving dower and inheritance to widow and heir of the convicted and providing that peers shall be tried by peers, substituting as the place of pillorying "some shire town" for "some market town upon the market day or at such time as any fair shall be kept there," and adding to the penalty (for the lighter degrees of sorcery) of imprisonment, pillory, and public confession of the offence, the clause: "which said offense shall be written in capital letters, and placed upon the breast of said offender." The commission creating the Court of Oyer and Terminer (May 27, 1692) antedated, however, all these laws, and instructed that body "to enquire of, hear and determine for this time, according to the law and custom of England and of this their Majesties' province, all and all manner of crimes." (For a learned study of witchcraft laws in England and New England see Moore's *Notes on Witchcraft*, pp. 3–11.)

January 3. By vertue of an Act of the General Court, the first Superior Court was held at Salem, for the County of Essex, the Judges appointed were Mr. William Stoughton (the Lieutenant Governour) Thomas Danforth, John Richards, Wait Winthorp,[1] and Samuel Sewall, Esquires, Where Ignoramus[2] was found upon the several Bills of Indictment against Thirty, and *Billa Vera*[3] against Twenty six more; of all these Three only were found Guilty by the Jewry upon Trial, two of which were (as appears by their Behaviour) the most senseless and Ignorant Creatures that could be found;[4] besides which it does not appear what came in against those more than against the rest that were acquitted.[5]

The Third was the Wife of Wardwell, who was one of the Twenty Executed, and it seems they had both confessed themselves Guilty; but he retracting his said Confession, was tried and Executed;[6] it is supposed that this Woman fearing her Husbands fate, was not so stiff in her denyals of her former Confession, such as it was. These Three received Sentence of Death.

At these Tryals some of the Jewry made Inquiry of the Court, what Account they ought to make of the Spectre Evidence? and received for Answer "as much as of Chips in Wort."[7]

January 31, 169⅔. The Superior Court began at Charlestown, for the County of Middlesex, Mr. Stoughton, Mr. Danforth, Mr. Winthorp, and Mr. Sewall Judges, where several had Ignoramus returned upon their Bills of Indictment, and *Billa Vera* upon others.

In the time the Court sat, word was brought in, that a Reprieve was sent to Salem,[8] and had prevented the Execution of Seven of those that were there Condemned, which so moved the chief Judge,[9] that he said to this effect, "We were in a way to have cleared the Land of these, etc.; who it is ob-

---

[1] Winthrop.   [2] "We do not know"—*i. e.*, no basis for prosecution.
[3] "A true bill."

[4] Elizabeth Johnson and Mary Post. Elizabeth Johnson (as to whom see also p. 420) was reprieved, and after six months' imprisonment was freed. Her grandfather, the Rev. Francis Dane, said of her "she is but simplish at the best." Mary Post and Sarah Wardwell likewise escaped death.

[5] And so the public attorney told the governor (see p. 201).

[6] See pp. 366–367.   [7] *I. e.*, as of less than no worth.

[8] By Governor Phips (see p. 201).   [9] Stoughton.

structs the course of Justice I know not; the Lord be merciful
to the Countrey," and so went off the Bench, and came no
more that Court: The most remarkable of the Tryals, was
of Sarah Daston, she was a Woman of about 70 or 80 Years
of Age. To usher in her Tryal, a report went before, that if
there were a Witch in the World she was one, as having been
so accounted of, for 20 or 30 Years; which drew many People
from Boston, etc., to hear her Tryal. There were a multitude
of Witnesses produced against her; but what Testimony they
gave in seemed wholly forreign, as of accidents, illness, etc.,
befalling them, or theirs after some Quarrel; what these testified was much of it of Actions said to be done 20 Years before
that time. The Spectre-Evidence was not made use of in
these Tryals, so that the Jewry soon brought her in not Guilty;
her Daughter and Grand-daughter, and the rest that were
then tried, were also acquitted. After she was cleared Judge
Danforth Admonished her in these words, "Woman, Woman,
repent, there are shrewd things come in against you"; she was
remanded to Prison for her Fees, and there in a short time
expired. One of Boston that had been at the Tryal of Daston,
being the same Evening in company with one of the Judges
in a publick place, acquainted him that some that had been
both at the Tryals at Salem and at this at Charlestown, had
asserted that there was more Evidence against the said Daston than against any at Salem, to which the said Judge con-
ceeded, saying, That it was so. It was replied by that person, that he dare give it under his hand, that there was not
enough come in against her to bear a just reproof.[1]

   April 25, 1693. The first Superiour Court was held at
Boston, for the County of Suffolk, the Judges were the Lieu-
tenant Governour, Mr. Danforth, Mr. Richards and Mr.
Sewall, Esquires.

   Where (besides the acquitting Mr. John Aldin by Proclamation) the most remarkable was, what related to Mary Watkins, who had been a Servant, and lived about Seven Miles
from Boston, having formerly Accused her Mistress of Witch-

---

[1] On Sarah Daston's case see documents printed in the *Publications* (X.
12–16) of the Colonial Society of Massachusetts and the brief account of her
trial by an eye-witness in the letter prefixed to the London edition of Increase
Mather's *Cases of Conscience*.

craft, and was supposed to be distracted, she was threatned
if she persisted in such Accusations to be punished; this with
the necessary care to recover her Health, had that good effect,
that she not only had her Health restored, but also wholly
acquitted her Mistress of any such Crimes, and continued in
Health till the return of the Year, and then again falling into
Melancholly humours she was found strangling her self; her
Life being hereby prolonged, she immediately accused her
self of being a Witch; was carried before a Magistrate and
committed. At this Court a Bill of Indictment was brought
to the Grand Jury against her, and her confession upon her
Examination given in as Evidence, but these not wholly satisfied herewith, sent for her, who gave such account of her self,
that they (after they had returned into the Court to ask some
Questions) Twelve of them agreed to find Ignoramus, but the
Court was pleased to send them out again, who again at coming in returned it as before.

She was continued for some time in Prison, etc., and at
length was sold to Virginia.[1] About this time the Prisoners
in all the Prisons were released.[2]

To omit here the mentioning of several Wenches in Boston,
etc., who pretended to be Afflicted, and accused several, the
Ministers often visiting them, and praying with them, concerning whose Affliction Narratives are in being in Manuscript.[3]
Not only these, but the generality of those Accusers may have
since convinc'd the Ministers by their vicious courses that
they might err in extending too much Charity to them.

The conclusion of the whole in the Massachusetts Colony
was, Sir William Phips, Governour, being call'd home, before
he went he pardon'd such as had been condemned, for which
they gave about 30 Shillings each to the Kings Attorney.[4]

---

[1] As to Mary Watkins see an article in the *N. E. Hist. and Gen. Register*
(XLIV. 168 ff.). She lived at Milton, was white, and on August 11 was still in
prison, but was asking the jail-keeper to provide a master to carry her "out of
this country into Virginia."

[2] *I. e.*, on payment of fees. See pp. 343, 366.

[3] He means, of course, Mercy Short (see above, pp. 255 ff.) and Margaret
Rule (see pp. 308–323). From this sentence it seems clear that this account of
the Salem episode was written before the earlier pages of his book, which begins
with the narrative of Margaret Rule and takes its title from it.

[4] Phips left for England November 17, 1694. (Sewall's *Diary*, I. 393.)

In *August* 1697. The Superiour Court sat at Hartford, in the Colony of Connecticut, where one Mistress Benom was tried for Witchcraft, she had been accused by some Children that pretended to the Spectral sight; they searched her several times for Tets; they tried the Experiment of casting her into the Water,[1] and after this she was Excommunicated by the Minister of Wallinsford.[2] Upon her Tryal nothing material appearing against her, save Spectre Evidence, she was acquitted, as also her Daughter, a Girl of Twelve or Thirteen Years old, who had been likewise Accused; but upon renewed Complaints against them, they both fled into New-York Government.[3]

Before this the Government Issued forth the following Proclamation.[4]

By the Honourable the Lieutenant Governour, Council and Assembly of his Majesties Province of the Massachusetts Bay, in General Court Assembled.

Whereas the Anger of God is not yet turned away, but his Hand is still stretched out against his People in manifold Judgments, particularly in drawing out to such a length the troubles of Europe, by a perplexing War; and more especially, respecting ourselves in this Province, in that God is pleased still to go on in diminishing our Substance, cutting short our Harvest, blasting our most promising undertakings more ways than one, unsetling of us,[5] and by his more

---

[1] See above, p. 21.   [2] Wallingford.

[3] Of Winifred Benham, mother and daughter, Mr. Taylor (*The Witchcraft Delusion in Colonial Connecticut*, p. 155) learns only—from "Records Court of Assistants (1 : 74, 77) "—that they were in August, 1697, tried and acquitted at Hartford, and in October indicted on new complaints, the jury returning "Ignoramus." They were doubtless the widow and daughter of that "Joseph Benham of New Haven," who in 1656/7 was married at Boston to Winifred King (*N. E. Hist. and Gen. Register*, XI. 203) and later became one of the first settlers of Wallingford. (See also Davis, *History of Wallingford and Meriden*, p. 412, cited by Levermore, in the *New Englander*, XLIV. 815.)

[4] For the interesting story of this proclamation see the *Diary* (I. 439–441) of Judge Sewall, who drafted its final form, and that of Cotton Mather (I. 211), who drew a rejected one. The draft itself, with a careful study of these proceedings, see in Moore's *Notes on Witchcraft* (pp. 14–19).

[5] The punctuation of the copy in the Massachusetts archives, as printed in a note to Sewall's *Diary* (I. 440), joins "more ways than one" to "unsettling of us."

Immediate hand, snatching away many out of our Embraces, by sudden and violent Deaths, even at this time when the Sword is devouring so many both at home and abroad, and that after many days of publick and Solemn addressing of him, And altho considering the many Sins prevailing in the midst of us, we cannot but wonder at the Patience and Mercy moderating these Rebukes; yet we cannot but also fear that there is something still wanting to accompany our Supplications. And doubtless there are some particular Sins, which God is Angry with our Israel for, that have not been duly seen and resented by us, about which God expects to be sought, if ever he turn again our Captivity.

Wherefore it is Commanded and Appointed, that Thursday the Fourteenth of January next be observed as a Day of Prayer, with Fasting throughout this Province, strictly forbidding all Servile labour thereon; that so all Gods People may offer up fervent Supplications unto him, for the Preservation, and Prosperity of his Majesty's Royal Person and Government, and Success to attend his Affairs both at home and abroad; that all iniquity may be put away which hath stirred God's Holy jealousie against this Land; that he would shew us what we know not, and help us wherein we have done amiss to do so no more; and especially that whatever mistakes on either hand have been fallen into, either by the body of this People, or any orders of men, referring to the late Tragedy, raised among us by Satan and his Instruments, thro the awful Judgment of God, he would humble us therefore[1] and pardon all the Errors of his Servants and People, that desire to love his Name and be attoned to his Land; that he would remove the Rod of the wicked from off the Lot of the Righteous; that he would bring the American Heathen, and cause them to hear and obey his Voice.

Given at Boston, Decemb. 17, 1696, in the 8th Year of his Majesties Reign.

ISAAC ADDINGTON, *Secretary.*

Upon the Day of the Fast in the full Assembly, at the South Meeting-House in Boston, one of the Honourable Judges, who had sat in Judicature in Salem, delivered in a Paper,[2] and while it was in reading stood up, But the Copy being not to be obtained at present, It can only be reported by Memory to this effect, *viz.* It was to desire the Prayers

---

[1] *I. e.*, therefor.

[2] Samuel Sewall. The exact wording of his paper he gives in his *Diary* (I. 445):

"Copy of the Bill I put up on the Fast day; giving it to Mr. Willard as he

of God's People for him and his, and that God having visited
his Family, etc., he was apprehensive that he might have
fallen into some Errors in the Matters at Salem, and pray that
the Guilt of such Miscarriages may not be imputed either to
the Country in general, or to him or his family in particular.

*Some that had been of several Jewries, have given forth a Paper, Sign'd
with their own hands in these words.*

We whose names are under written, being in the Year 1692
called to serve as Jurors, in Court at Salem, on Tryal of many, who
were by some suspected Guilty of doing Acts of Witchcraft upon
the Bodies of sundry Persons:

We confess that we our selves were not capable to understand,
nor able to withstand the mysterious delusions of the Powers of
Darkness, and Prince of the Air; but were for want of Knowledge in
our selves, and better Information from others, prevailed with to take
up with such Evidence against the Accused, as on further consideration, and better Information, we justly fear was insufficient for the
touching the Lives of any, Deut. 17. 6, whereby we fear we have
been instrumental with others, tho Ignorantly and unwittingly, to
bring upon our selves, and this People of the Lord, the Guilt of Innocent Blood; which Sin the Lord saith in Scripture, he would not
pardon, 2 Kings 24. 4, that is we suppose in regard of his temporal
Judgments. We do therefore hereby signifie to all in general (and
to the surviving Sufferers in especial) our deep sense of, and sorrow
for our Errors, in acting on such Evidence to the condemning of any
person.

And do hereby declare that we justly fear that we were sadly
deluded and mistaken, for which we are much disquieted and dis-

pass'd by, and standing up at the reading of it, and bowing when finished; in the
Afternoon.

"Samuel Sewall, sensible of the reiterated strokes of God upon himself and
family; and being sensible, that as to the Guilt contracted upon the opening of
the late Commission of Oyer and Terminer at Salem (to which the order for this
Day relates) he is, upon many accounts, more concerned than any that he knows
of, Desires to take the Blame and shame of it, Asking pardon of men, And especially desiring prayers that God, who has an Unlimited Authority, would pardon that sin and all other his sins, personal and Relative: And according to
his infinite Benignity, and Sovereignty, Not Visit the sin of him, or of any other,
upon himself or any of his, nor upon the Land: But that He would powerfully
defend him against all Temptations to Sin, for the future; and vouchsafe him
the efficacious, saving Conduct of his Word and Spirit."

tressed in our minds; and do therefore humbly beg forgiveness, first of God for Christ's sake for this our Error; And pray that God would not impute the guilt of it to our selves, nor others; and we also pray that we may be considered candidly, and aright by the living Sufferers as being then under the power of a strong and general Delusion, utterly unacquainted with, and not experienced in matters of that Nature.

We do heartily ask forgiveness of you all, whom we have justly offended, and do declare according to our present minds, we would none of us do such things again on such grounds for the whole World; praying you to accept of this in way of Satisfaction for our Offence; and that you would bless the Inheritance of the Lord, that he may be intreated for the Land.

Foreman, THOMAS FISK,	THOMAS PERLY, *Senior*
WILLIAM FISK,	JOHN PEBODY,
JOHN BATCHELER,	THOMAS PERKINS,
THOMAS FISK, *Junior*	SAMUEL SAYER,
JOHN DANE,	ANDREW ELLIOTT,
JOSEPH EVELITH,	HENRY HERRICK, *Senior.*[1]

.   .   .   .

Mr. C. M. having been very forward to write Books of Witchcraft, has not been so forward either to explain or defend the Doctrinal part thereof, and his belief (which he had a Years time to compose) he durst not venture so as to be copied.[2]

---

[1] This ends the book, as first written; but the author adds a "Postscript," called out by the publication, in 1697, of Cotton Mather's life of Sir William Phips, who had died in London early in 1695. Not the achievements of Sir William, thinks Calef, but Increase Mather's negotiation in England and his procuring of the new charter, "are the things principally driven at in the book," and "another principal thing is to set forth the supposed witchcrafts in New-England, and how well Mr. Mather the Younger therein acquitted himself." Wherefore, after freeing his mind as to the matter of the charter, he takes up Mather's allegations as to the Salem episode, and, pointing out that, "tho this Book pretends to raise a Statue in Honour of Sir William, yet it appears it was the least part of the design of the Author to Honour him, but rather to Honour himself, and the Ministers," since by so printing the advice of the ministers (see above, p. 356) "as to give a full Account of the cautions given him, but design-edly hiding from the Reader the Incouragements and Exhortations to proceed," it really throws the blame upon Phips, he devotes the remaining pages, here re-printed, to Cotton Mather's real views and their influence. The *Life of Phips,* now a rare book, is reprinted in Mather's *Magnalia.*

[2] In a part of his book not here reprinted (pp. 85 ff.) Calef speaks more fully of this paper, lent him early in 1695, but on condition of its return within a fort-

Yet in this of the Life of Sir William he sufficiently testifies his retaining that Heterodox belief, seeking by frightfull stories of the sufferings of some, and the refined sight of others, etc., P. 69 to obtrude upon the World, and confirm it in such a belief, as hitherto he either cannot or will not defend, as if the Blood already shed thereby were not sufficient.

Mr. I. Mather, in his *Cases of Conscience*, P. 25, tells of a Bewitched Eye, and that such can see more than others. They were certainly bewitched Eyes that could see as well shut as open, and that could see what never was, that could see the Prisoners upon the Afflicted, harming of them, when those whose Eyes were not bewitched could have sworn that they did not stir from the Bar. The Accusers are said to have suffered much by biting, P. 73. And the prints of just such a set of Teeth, as those they Accused, had, but such as had not such bewitch'd Eyes have seen the Accusers bite themselves, and then complain of the Accused. It has also been seen when the Accused, instead of having just such a set of Teeth, has not had one in his head. They were such bewitched Eyes that could see the Poisonous Powder (brought by Spectres P. 70.) And that could see in the Ashes the print of the Brand, there invisibly heated to torment the pretended Sufferers with, etc.

These with the rest of such Legends have this direct tendency, *viz.* To tell the World that the Devil is more ready to serve his Votaries, by his doing for them things above or against the course of Nature, shewing himself to them, and making explicit contract with them, etc., than the Divine Being is to his faithful Servants, and that as he is willing, so also able to perform their desires. The way whereby these People are believed to arrive at a power to Afflict their Neighbours, is by a compact with the Devil, and that they have a power to Commissionate him to those Evils, P. 72. However Irrational, or Inscriptural such Assertions are, yet they seem

night and uncopied. It was perhaps the MS. described by Poole (*Memorial History*, II. 152, note) as now in the possession of the Massachusetts Historical Society, and called "Cotton Mather's belief and practice in those thorny difficulties which have distracted us in the day of temptation"—having "marginal reflections in another hand." [Since the foregoing words were written, this conjecture has been proved true. See above, p. 306, note 1.]

a necessary part of the Faith of such as maintain the belief of such a sort of Witches.

As the Scriptures know nothing of a covenanting or commissioning Witch, so Reason cannot conceive how Mortals should by their Wickedness arrive at a power to Commissionate Angels, Fallen Angels, against their Innocent Neighbours. But the Scriptures are full in it, and the Instances numerous, that the Almighty, Divine Being has this prerogative to make use of what Instrument he pleaseth, in Afflicting any, and consequently to commissionate Devils: And tho this word commissioning, in the Authors former Books, might be thought to be by inadvertency; yet now after he hath been caution'd of it, still to persist in it seems highly Criminal. And therefore in the name of God, I here charge such belief as guilty of Sacriledge in the highest Nature, and so much worse than stealing Church Plate, etc., As it is a higher Offence to steal any of the glorious Attributes of the Almighty, to bestow them upon Mortals, than it is to steal the Utensils appropriated to his Service. And whether to ascribe such power of commissioning Devils to the worst of Men, be not direct Blasphemy, I leave to others better able to determine. When the Pharisees were so wicked as to ascribe to Beelzebub, the mighty works of Christ (whereby he did manifestly shew forth his Power and Godhead) then it was that our Saviour declar'd the Sin against the Holy Ghost to be unpardonable.

When the Righteous God is contending with Apostate Sinners, for their departures from him, by his Judgments, as Plagues, Earthquakes, Storms and Tempests, Sicknesses and Diseases, Wars, loss of Cattle, etc. Then not only to ascribe this to the Devil, but to charge one another with sending or commissionating those Devils to these things, is so abominable and so wicked, that it requires a better Judgment than mine to give it its just denomination.

But that Christians so called should not only charge their fellow Christians therewith, but proceed to Tryals and Executions; crediting that Enemy to all Goodness, and Accuser of the Brethren, rather than believe their Neighbours in their own Defence; This is so Diabolical a Wickedness as cannot proceed, but from a Doctrine of Devils; how far damnable it is let others discuss. Tho such things were acting in this

Country in Sir Williams time, yet p. 65. there is a Discourse of a Guardian Angel, as then over-seeing it, which notion, however it may suit the Faith of Ethnicks,[1] or the fancies of Trithemius;[2] it is certain that the Omnipresent Being stands not in need as Earthly Potentates do, of governing the World by Vicegerents. And if Sir William had such an Invisible pattern to imitate, no wonder tho some of his Actions were unaccountable, especially those relating to Witchcraft: For if there was in those Actions an Angel super-intending, there is little reason to think it was Gabriel or the Spirit of Mercury, nor Hanael the Angel or Spirit of Venus, nor yet Samuel the Angel or Spirit of Mars; Names feigned by the said Trithemius, etc. It may rather be thought to be Apollyon, or Abaddon.

Obj.[3] But here it will be said, "What, are there no Witches? Do's not the Law of God command that they should be extirpated? Is the Command vain and Unintelligible?" *Sol.*[4] For any to say that a Witch is one that makes a compact with, and Commissions Devils, etc., is indeed to render the Law of God vain and Unintelligible, as having provided no way whereby they might be detected, and proved to be such; And how the Jews waded thro this difficulty for so many Ages, without the Supplement of Mr. Perkins and Bernard thereto, would be very mysterious. But to him that can read the Scriptures without prejudice from Education, etc., it will manifestly appear that the Scripture is full and Intelligible, both as to the Crime and means to detect the culpable. He that shall hereafter see any person, who to confirm People in a false belief, about the power of Witches and Devils, pretending to a sign to confirm it, such as knocking off of invisible Chains with the hand, driving away Devils by brushing, striking with a Sword or Stick, to wound a person at a great distance, etc., may (according to that head of Mr. Gauls, quoted by Mr. C. M. and so often herein before recited, and so well proved by Scripture) conclude that he has seen Witchcraft performed.

---

[1] Pagans.

[2] A German abbot and scholar who in the early sixteenth century wrote most credulously about witches and angels.

[3] *Objection.*　　　　　　　　　　　　　　　[4] *Solution.*

If Baalam became a Sorcerer by Sacrifizing and Praying to the true God against his visible people; Then he that shall pray that the afflicted (by their Spectral Sight) may accuse some other Person (whereby their reputations and lives may be indangered) such will justly deserve the Name of a Sorcerer. If any Person pretends to know more then[1] can be known by humane means, and professeth at the same time that they have it from the Black-Man, i. e. the Devil, and shall from hence give Testimony against the Lives of others, they are manifestly such as have a familiar Spirit; and if any, knowing them to have their Information from the Black-Man, shall be inquisitive of them for their Testimony against others, they therein are dealing with such as have a Familiar-Spirit.

And if these shall pretend to see the dead by their Spectral Sight, and others shall be inquisitive of them, and receive their Answers what it is the dead say, and who it is they accuse, both the one and the other are by Scripture Guilty of Necromancy.

These are all of them crimes as easily proved as any whatsoever, and that by such proof as the Law of God requires, so that it is no Unintelligible Law.

But if the Iniquity of the times be such, that these Criminals not only Escape Indemnified,[2] but are Incouraged in their Wickedness, and made use of to take away the Lives of others, this is worse than a making the Law of God Vain, it being a rendring of it dangerous, against the Lives of Innocents, and without all hopes of better, so long as these Bloody Principles remain.

As long as Christians do Esteem the Law of God to be Imperfect, as not describing that crime that it requires to be Punish'd by Death;

As long as men suffer themselves to be Poison'd in their Education, and be grounded in a False Belief by the Books of the Heathen;

As long as the Devil shall be believed to have a Natural Power, to Act above and against a course of Nature;

As long as the Witches shall be believed to have a Power to Commission him;

As long as the Devils Testimony, by the pretended afflicted,

---

[1] I. e., than.   [2] Unpunished.

shall be received as more valid to Condemn, than their Plea of Not Guilty to acquit;

As long as the Accused shall have their Lives and Liberties confirmed and restored to them, upon their Confessing themselves Guilty;

As long as the Accused shall be forc't to undergo Hardships and Torments for their not Confessing;

As long as Tets for the Devil to Suck are searched for upon the Bodies of the accused, as a token of guilt;

As long as the Lords Prayer shall be profaned, by being made a Test, who are culpable;

As long as Witchcraft, Sorcery, Familiar Spirits, and Necromancy, shall be improved to discover who are Witches, etc.,

So long it may be expected that Innocents will suffer as Witches.

So long God will be Daily dishonoured, And so long his Judgments must be expected to be continued.

Finis.

A MODEST INQUIRY INTO THE NATURE OF
WITCHCRAFT, BY JOHN HALE, 1702

INTRODUCTION

THE Rev. John Hale (1636–1700), a native of the colony and a graduate of Harvard in its class of 1657, had since 1665 been pastor at Beverly, the parish lying north of Salem, from which it was severed by a narrow arm of the sea, and at the west adjoining yet more closely Salem Village, through which lay the land route connecting Beverly with Salem and with Boston. Many of those connected with the beginnings of the witch panic had, prior to the erection of the Village parish, been in attendance at the Beverly church. Some were still so; and the spreading suspicion soon invaded this parish itself. It was not strange, then, that from the first, as we have seen already, Hale's interest in the proceedings was close and attentive.[1] There can be no question that, as Calef says, "he had been very forward in these Prosecutions," and, like his neighbor pastors Parris and Noyes, had held the most credulous views as to the worth of the testimony of the "afflicted." How those views changed after the accusation of his loved and honored wife we have also seen;[2] and of all this he himself tells us with a touching sincerity in the pages now to follow. His little book is no apology, but a manly attempt to make amends for what he now felt to be error by setting forth to others what he had learned. Judge Sewall, who likewise had repented of his error and likewise frankly owned it, records in

[1] See above, pp. 158, 184, 342, 344, 350, 369. More than once (as against Bridget Bishop and Dorcas Hoar) he himself became a witness as to the reputation or career of the accused. That already then there was thought of his writing upon the subject may perhaps be inferred from Cotton Mather's letter quoted on p. 206; and see also p. 214.

[2] See p. 369, and note 1.

his diary on November 19, 1697, when he was on a visit to Salem: "Mr. Hale and I lodg'd together: He discours'd me about writing a History of the Witchcraft; I fear lest he go into the other extream."

The Rev. John Higginson (1616–1708), the aged senior pastor of Salem, who writes for Hale the introduction, is also no stranger to us;[1] and we have seen what reason there is to think him hesitant all along as to the proceedings. Yet how far he had been from incredulity as to human dealings with the Devil appears not only from his own words here, but from the materials he furnished Increase Mather for his *Providences*.[2] Perhaps he, too, consulted Judge Sewall as to his part in the little book; for before the words just cited the latter writes: "Mr. Higginson comes as far as Brother's to see me; which I wonder'd at."

Though completed early in 1698—since Higginson had read it before signing his introduction on March 23—the book, as may be seen from its imprint, was not published till 1702, after Hale's death. Perhaps that was its author's wish: so, Judge Sewall tells us,[3] Higginson withheld his treatise on periwigs. The *Modest Enquiry* is now one of the rarest books in the literature of witchcraft. Its single reimpression (Boston, 1771) is said to be yet rarer than the original. Happily, that part of the book which narrates the story of the Salem episode was taken up by Cotton Mather into his *Magnalia* (at the end of his Book VI.); and from that work, though it gives Hale due credit, it is often quoted as if Mather's own.[4]

---

[1] See above, pp. 245, 248, note 2.   [2] *Mather Papers*, pp. 282–287.

[3] *Diary*, I. 463–464.

[4] As to Hale's career see a memoir in Mass. Hist. Soc., *Collections*, third series, VII. 255–269; also Sibley, *Harvard Graduates*, I. 509–520, and authorities there cited.

HALE'S A MODEST INQUIRY

A Modest Enquiry Into the Nature of Witchcraft, and How Persons Guilty of that Crime may be Convicted: And the means used for their Discovery Discussed, both Negatively and Affirmatively, according to Scripture and Experience.
By John Hale, Pastor of the Church of Christ in Beverley, Anno Domini 1697.
When they say unto you, seek unto them that have Familiar Spirits and unto Wizzards, that peep, etc., To the Law and to the Testimony; if they speak not according to this word, it is because there is no light in them. Isaiah VIII. 19. 20.
That which I see not teach thou me, Job 34. 32.
Boston in N. E. Printed by B. Green and J. Allen, for Benjamin Eliot under the Town House. 1702.[1]

Any general Custom against the Law of God is void. St. Germans, *Abridgment of Common Law.* Lib. 1. C. 6.

Omnium legum est inanis censura nisi Divinæ legis imaginem gerat.[2] Finch, *Common Law.* Lib. 4. C. 3.

Where a Law is grounded upon a Presumption, if the Presumption fail the Law is not to be holden in Conscience. *Abridgment of C. Law.* Lib. 1. C. 19.[3]

An Epistle to the Reader.

IT hath been said of Old, That Time is the Mother of Truth, and Truth is the Daughter of Time. It is the Prerogative of the God of Truth, to know all the truth in all things at once and together: It is also his Glory to conceal a matter, Prov. 25. 2, And to bring the truth to light in that manner and measure, and the times appointed, as it pleaseth him; it is

---

[1] Title-page of original.
[2] "No law hath any validity unless it bear the image of divine law."
[3] Reverse of title-page.

our duty in all humility, and with fear and trembling, to search after truth, knowing that secret things belong to God, and only things revealed belong to us, and so far as they are revealed; for in many things it may be said, what God is doing we know not now; but we, or others that succeed us, shall know hereafter. Omitting other Examples, I shall Instance only in the matter of Witchcraft, which on the Humane side, is one of the most hidden Works of Darkness, managed by the Rulers of the darkness of this World, to the doing of great spoil amongst the Children of men: And on the Divine side, it is one of the most awful and tremendous Judgments of God which can be inflicted on the Societies of men, especially when the Lord shall please for his own Holy Ends to Enlarge Satans Commission in more than an ordinary way.

It is known to all men, that it pleased God some few years ago, to suffer Satan to raise much trouble amongst us in that respect, the beginning of which was very small, and looked on at first as an ordinary case which had fallen out before at several times in other places, and would be quickly over. Only one or two persons belonging to Salem Village about five miles from the Town being suspected were Examined, etc. But in the progress of the matter, a multitude of other persons both in this and other Neighbour Towns, were Accused, Examined, Imprisoned, and came to their Trials, at Salem, the County Town, where about Twenty of them Suffered as Witches; and many others in danger of the same Tragical End: and still the number of the Accused increased unto many Scores; amongst whom were many Persons of unquestionable Credit, never under any grounds of suspicion of that or any other Scandalous Evil. This brought a general Consternation upon all sorts of People, doubting what would be the issue of such a dreadful Judgment of God upon the Country; but the Lord was pleased suddenly to put a stop to those proceedings, that there was no further trouble, as hath been related by others. But it left in the minds of men a sad remembrance of that sorrowful time; and a Doubt whether some Innocent Persons might not Suffer, and some guilty Persons Escape. There is no doubt but the Judges and Juries proceeded in their Integrity, with a zeal of God against Sin, according to their best light, and according to Law and Evidence; but there is a Question yet unresolved, Whether some of the Laws, Customs and Principles used by the Judges and Juries in the Trials of Witches in England (which were followed as Patterns here) were not insufficient and unsafe.

As for my Self, being under the Infirmities of a decrepit Old Age, I stirred little abroad, and was much disenabled (both in body and mind) from Knowing and judging of Occurrents and Transactions of that time: But my Reverend Brother Mr. Hale, having for above Thirty Years been Pastor of the Church at Beverly (but Two Miles from Salem, where the Tryals were) was frequently present, and was a diligent Observer of all that passed, and being one of a Singular Prudence and Sagacity, in searching into the narrows of things: He hath (after much deliberation) in this Treatise, related the Substance of the Case as it was, and given Reasons from Scripture against some of the Principles and Practises then used in the Tryals of Witchcraft; and said something also in a Positive way, and shewing the right Application that is to be made of the whole, and all this in such a pious and modest Manner, as cannot be offensive to any, but may be generally acceptable to all the lovers of Truth and Peace.

I am the more willing to accompany him to the Press, because I am perswaded such a Treatise as this is needful and useful, upon divers accounts. As,

1. That the Works of God may be known; and that God may be more acknowledged and adored, in his Justice, and in his Mercy: in his Justice, by letting loose Evil Angels, to make so great a spoyl amongst us as they did, for the Punishment of a declining People: And in his Mercy, by Countermanding of Satans Commission, and keeping of him in Chains of restraint, that he should proceed no further. Psal. 83, last.

2. That the Truth of things may be more fully known, so far as God shall please to reveal the same in the use of lawful means; for the Judgments of God are a great deep, and he is wont to make known truth by degrees; and Experience teacheth us, there is need of more to be said than hath been yet, for the clearing up of difficulties about the matter of Witchcraft. We ought to be fellow helpers to the truth. 3 Epistle of John, 8. v.

3. That whatever Errors or Mistakes we fell into, in the

dark hour of Temptation that was upon us, may be (upon more light) so discovered, acknowledged and disowned by us, as that it may be a matter of Warning and Caution to those that come after us, that they may not fall into the like.   1 Cor. 10. 11.   *Fœlix quem faciunt aliena pericula cautum.*[1]

4. And that it may Occasion the most Learned and Pious men to make a further and fuller Enquiry into the matter of Witchcraft, especially into the positive part, How Witches may be so discovered, that innocent persons may be preserved, and none but the guilty may suffer.   Prov. 17. 15.

Verily whosoever shall by the Grace of God be enabled to Contribute further light in this matter, will do good Service to God and Men in his Generation.

I would also propound and leave it as an Object of Consideration to our Honoured Magistrates and Reverend Ministers, Whether the Æquity of that Law in Leviticus, Chap. 4, for a Sin offering for the Rulers and for the Congregation, in the case of Sins of Ignorance, when they come to be known, be not Obliging, and for direction to us in a Gospel way.

Now the Father of Lights and Mercies grant unto us, that Mercy and Truth may meet together, that righteousness and peace may kiss each other, that the Glory of God may dwell in our Land; and that it may be said of New England, The Lord Bless thee, O Habitation of Justice and Mountain of Holiness,

Finally, That the Blessing of Heaven may go along with this little Treatise to attain the good Ends thereof, is, and shall be the Prayer of him who is daily waiting for his Change, and looking for the Mercy of the Lord Jesus Christ unto Eternal Life.

JOHN HIGGINSON,

March 23d,   *Pastor of the Church, of Salem.*
1697, 8.   *Ætatis* 82.[2]

The Preface to the Christian Reader.

THE Holy Scriptures inform us that the Doctrine of Godliness is a great Mystery, containing the Mysteries of the

[1] "Happy the man whom the perils of others make cautious."

[2] "In the 82d year of his age." As to the aged senior pastor of Salem see p. 398.

Kingdom of Heaven: Mysteries which require great search
for the finding out: And as the Lord hath his Mysteries to
bring us to Eternal Glory; so Satan hath his Mysteries to
bring us to Eternal Ruine: Mysteries not easily understood, whereby the depths of Satan are managed in hidden
wayes. So the Whore of Babylon makes the Inhabitants of
the Earth drunk with the Wine of her Fornication, by the
Mystery of her abominations, Rev. 17. 2. And the man of
Sin hath his Mystery of iniquity whereby he deceiveth men
through the working of Satan in signes and lying wonders,
2 Thes. 2. 3, 7, 9.

And among Satans Mysteries of iniquity, this of Witchcraft is one of the most difficult to be searched out by the Sons
of men; as appeareth by the great endeavours of Learned and
Holy men to search it out, and the great differences that are
found among them, in the rules laid down for the bringing to
light these hidden works of darkness. So that it may seem
presumption in me to undertake so difficult a Theam, and to
lay down such rules as are different from the Sentiments of
many Eminent writers, and from the Presidents and practices
of able Lawyers; yea and from the Common Law it self.

But my Apology for this undertaking is;

1. That there hath been such a dark dispensation by the
Lord, letting loose upon us the Devil, *Anno.* 1691 and 1692,[1]
as we never experienced before: And thereupon apprehending
and condemning persons for Witchcraft; and nextly acquitting others no less liable to such a charge; which evidently
shew we were in the dark, and knew not what to do; but have
gone too far on the one or other side, if not on both. Hereupon
I esteemed it necessary for some person to Collect a Summary
of that affair, with some animadversions upon it, which might
at least give some light to them which come after, to shun
those Rocks by which we were bruised, and narrowly escaped
Shipwrack upon. And I have waited five years for some
other person to undertake it, who might doe it better than I
can, but find none; and judge it better to do what I can, than
that such a work should be left undone. Better sincerely
though weakly done, then not at all, or with such a byas of
prejudice as will put false glosses upon that which was man-

---

[1] "1691" because the troubles began before March 25.

aged with uprightness of heart, though there was not so great a spirit of discerning, as were to be wished in so weighty a Concernment.

2. I have been present at several Examinations and Tryals, and knew sundry of those that Suffered upon that account in former years, and in this last affair, and so have more advantages than a stranger, to give account of these Proceedings.

3. I have been from my Youth trained up in the knowledge and belief of most of those principles I here question as unsafe to be used. The first person that suffered on this account in New-England, about Fifty years since, was my Neighbour, and I heard much of what was charged upon her, and others in those times; and the reverence I bore to aged, learned and judicious persons, caused me to drink in their principles in these things, with a kind of Implicit Faith. *Quo semel est imbuta recens servabit odorem, Testa diu.*[1] A Child will not easily forsake the principles he hath been trained up in from his Cradle.

But observing the Events of that sad Catastrophe, *Anno* 1692, I was brought to a more strict scanning of the principles I had imbibed, and by scanning, to question, and by questioning at length to reject many of them, upon the reasons shewed in the ensuing Discourse. It is an approved saying *Nihil certius, quam quod ex dubio fit certum;*[2] No truth more certain to a man, than that which he hath formerly doubted or denied, and is recovered from his error, by the convincing evidence of Scripture and reason. Yet I know and am sensible, that while we know but in part, man is apt in flying from a discovered error, to run into the contrary extream.

Incidit in Scyllam qui vult vitare Charybdim.[3]

The middle way is commonly the way of truth. And if any can shew me a better middle way than I have here laid down, I shall be ready to embrace it: But the conviction must not be by vinegar or drollery, but by strength of argument.

4. I have had a deep sence of the sad consequence of mis-

---

[1] Literally, "the fresh-made pot will long retain the odor in which once 'tis steeped." The line is from Horace.

[2] Literally, "nothing is surer than what out of doubt is made sure."

[3] "Into Scylla falls he who tries to keep clear of Charybdis."

takes in matters Capital; and their impossibility of recovering when compleated. And what grief of heart it brings to a tender conscience, to have been unwittingly encouraging of the Sufferings of the innocent. And I hope a zeal to prevent for the future such sufferings is pardonable, although there should be much weakness, and some errors in the pursuit thereof.

5. I observe the failings that have been on the one hand, have driven some into that which is indeed an extream on the other hand, and of dangerous consequences, *viz.* To deny any such persons to be under the New Testament, who by the Devils aid discover Secrets, or do work wonders. Therefore in the latter part of this discourse, I have taken pains to prove the Affirmative, yet with brevity, because it hath been done already by Perkins of *Witchcraft.*[1] Glanvil his *Saducismus Triumphatus,*[2] Pt. 1. p. 1 to 90 and Pt. 2. p. 1 to 80. Yet I would not be understood to justify all his notions in those discourses, but acknowledge he hath strongly proved the being of Witches.

6. I have special reasons moving me to bear my testimony about these matters, before I go hence and be no more; the which I have here done, and I hope with some assistance of his Spirit, to whom I commit my self and this my labour, even that God whose I am and whom I serve: Desiring his Mercy in Jesus Christ to Pardon all the Errors of his People in the day of darkness; and to enable us to fight with Satan by Spiritual Weapons, putting on the whole Armour of God.

And tho' Satan by his Messengers may buffet Gods Children, yet there's a promise upon right *Resisting, he shall flee from them,* Jam. 4. 7. *And that all things shall work together for the good of those that Love the Lord,* Rom. 8. 28. So that I believe Gods Children shall be gainers by the assaults of Satan, which occasion'd this Discourse; which that they may, is the Prayer of, Thine in the Service of the Gospel.

JOHN HALE.

BEVERLY, Decemb.
    15th, 1697.

---

[1] See above, p. 304, note 3.

[2] *Saducismus Triumphatus* was the name given Glanvill's book in the enlarged edition (1681) brought out after the author's death by Henry More. In later impressions the word becomes *Sadducismus.* As to Glanvill, see above, p. 5.

A MODEST ENQUIRY, INTO THE NATURE OF WITCHCRAFT

Chapter I.

Sect. 1. The Angels who kept not their First Estate, by Sin against God, lost their primitive purity, and glorious Excellency, as to their moral qualifications, and became unclean, wicked, envious, lyars, and full of all wickedness, which as Spirits they are capable of. Yet I do not find in Scripture that they lost their natural abilities of understanding or power of Operation.

1. As for their Understanding, they are called *Daimon* (which we Translate Devil) because they are full of wisdom, cunning, skill, subtilty and knowledge. He hath also the name of Serpent from his subtilty, 2 Cor. 11. 3. And his knowledge in the Scriptures, and wittiness to pervert them, appears by his quoting Scripture to our Saviour when he tempted him. Mat. 4.

And as there be many Devils, and these active, quick, swift and piercing Spirits, so they going to and fro in the earth, and walking up and down in it, have advantages to know all the actions of the Children of men, both open and secret, their discourses, consultations, and much of the inward affections of men thereby; though still its Gods prerogative immediately to know the heart. Jer. 17. 10.

2. As to their natural power as Spirits, its very great, if not equal to that of the Holy Angels: For,

1. They are called *Principalities and Powers*. Rom. 8. 38. Eph. 6. 12. Col. 2. 14, 15, compared with Heb. 2. 14, 15. Now these are names given to the Holy Angels. Eph. 1. 21, and 3. 10.

2. They are called, *Rulers of the darkness of this world, the Prince of the power of the Air*. Eph. 6. 12 and 2. 2.

3. Such was their power that they contended with Michael and the Angels about the Body of Moses. 2 Pet. 2. 11. Jude 9. That is, as I conceive, about preventing the Burial of the Body of Moses: For it's said, Deut. 34. 6, The Lord buried him, and no man knoweth of his Sepulcher to this day.

That is, he did it by the Ministry of Angels (for the Lord gave the Law, Exod. 20. 1, and that it was by the Ministry of Angels, see Gal. 3. 19. so probably was the burial of Moses's Body) and the Devils endeavour if possible, to discover Moses's Body, or place of its burial, that they might draw Israel to commit Idolatry in worshipping at his Tomb (as our Popish Fore-fathers did at Thomas Beckets in Kent) from the Veneration they had to him as their Law giver.

4. The Devils actings against Job, Chap. 1 and 2, and what he did to the Gadarene Swine, etc., Shew his great power. So that we may conclude, had the Devils liberty to reveal all that they know of the affairs of mankind, or to do all that is in their power to perform, they would bring dreadful confusions and desolations upon the World.

Sect. 2. The way God governs Devils is by Chains. 2 Pet. 2. 4. Jude 6 ver. Rev. 20. 1, 2, 7, 8, whereby they are kept Prisoners. Men are governed by Laws, by convictions of Conscience. Rom. 2. 12, 13, 14, 15. By Scripture Rules, Humane Laws, and also by Gods Spirit. 1 John 2. 20. But Devils have no such Laws, or tenderness of Conscience to bridle or restrain them. But the Lord hath his Chains, which are called Everlasting, and are always lasting; so that they are never wholly without a Chain. This Chain is sometimes greater and shorter, other times lesser and longer, as the Lord pleaseth, for his own Glory, Rev. 20. 1, 2, 7, 8. For as the *wrath of man praiseth the Lord, and the remainder of wrath he doth restrain*, Psal. 76. 10, So may we say of the Devils wrath.

Sect. 3. The Devil is full of malice against man, and frames his designs against him, chiefly to destroy his Soul, as, 1 Pet. 5. 8, 2 Cor. 11. 3, and other Scriptures abundantly testify. Hence probably at sometimes he doth not all the hurt to mans Body that he could, lest thereby he should awaken man to repentance and prayer; he seeks to keep men in a false peace. Luk. 11. 21. Yet at other times he disturbs and afflicts men in Body and Estate; as Scripture and experience shew. Among the Devices Satan useth to ruine man, one is to allure him into such a familiarity with him, that by Sorceries, Inchantments, Divinations, and such like, he may lead them Captive at his pleasure. This snare of his we are warned against, Deut. 18. 10, 11, and in other Scriptures. This Sin of men hearkening after Satan in these ways, is called Witchcraft; of which it is my purpose to treat: But first I shall speak something Historically what hath been done in New England, in prosecution of persons suspected of this Crime.

Sect. 4. Several persons have been Charged with and suffered for the Crime of Witchcraft in the Governments of the Massachusetts, New Haven, or Stratford[1] and Connecticut, from the year 1646 to the year 1692.

Sect. 5. The first was a Woman of Charlestown, *Anno* 1647 or 48.[2] She was suspected partly because that after some angry words passing between her and her Neighbours, some mischief befel such Neighbours in their Creatures, or the like: partly because some things supposed to be bewitched, or have a Charm upon them, being burned, she came to the fire and seemed concerned.

The day of her Execution, I went in company of some Neighbours,[3] who took great pains to bring her to confession and repentance. But she constantly professed her self innocent of that crime: Then one prayed her to consider if God did not bring this punishment upon her for some other crime, and asked, if she had not been guilty of Stealing many years ago; she answered, she had stolen something, but it was long since, and she had repented of it, and there was Grace enough in Christ to pardon that long agoe; but as for Witchcraft she was wholly free from it, and so she said unto her Death.

Sect. 6. Another that suffered on that account some time after, was a Dorchester Woman.[4] And upon the day of her

---

[1] *I. e.*, "New Haven (or Stratford)": Hale was not sure (see p. 410) whether the case in mind was at New Haven or at Stratford. Stratford, though so near New Haven, was under the Connecticut government. Under that of New Haven there were, so far as is known, no witch-executions.

[2] Margaret Jones, executed at Boston on June 15, 1648. See Winthrop, *Journal*, II. 344–345 (of the edition in this series, II. 397 of ed. of 1853), and Poole in *Memorial History of Boston*, II. 135–137; also, above, p. 363, note 2—for it was doubtless to Margaret Jones that the resolution as to "watchinge" referred, and it suggests that her accusation too may have been the outcome of the witch-hunt which had just been raging in the Puritan counties of England. She was not, as thinks Hale, the first New England victim; in Connecticut Alse Young was hanged, May 26, 1647.

[3] The writer was then a boy of twelve.

[4] Doubtless that "H. Lake's wife, of Dorchester, whom," as Nathaniel Mather in 1684 wrote to his brother Increase of having heard, "the devill drew in

Execution Mr. Thompson Minister at Brantry,[1] and J. P.[2] her former Master took pains with her to bring her to repentance, And she utterly denyed her guilt of Witchcraft: yet justifyed God for bringing her to that punishment: for she had when a single woman played the harlot, and being with Child used means to destroy the fruit of her body to conceal her sin and shame, and although she did not effect it, yet she was a Murderer in the sight of God for her endeavours, and shewed great penitency for that sin; but owned nothing of the crime laid to her charge.

Sect. 7. Another suffering in this kind was a Woman of Cambridge, against whom a principal evidence was a Watertown Nurse, who testifyed, that the said Kendal (so was the accused called) did bewitch to Death a Child of Goodman Genings of Watertown; for the said Kendal did make much of the Child, and then the Child was well, but quickly changed its colour and dyed in a few hours after. The Court took this evidence among others, the said Genings not knowing of it. But after Kendal was Executed (who also denyed her guilt to the Death,) Mr. Rich. Brown knowing and hoping better things of Kendal, asked said Genings if they suspected her to bewitch their Child, they answered No. But they judged the true cause of the Childs Death to be thus, *viz.* The Nurse had the night before carryed out the Child and kept it abroad in the Cold a long time, when the red gum was come out upon it, and the Cold had struck in the red gum, and this they judged the cause of the Childs death. And that said Kendal did come in that day and make much of the Child, but they apprehended no wrong to come to the Child by her. After this the said Nurse was put into Prison for Adultery, and there delivered of her base Child, and Mr. Brown went to her and told her, It was just with God to leave her to this wickedness

by appearing to her in the likenes, and acting the part of a child of hers then lately dead, on whom her heart was much set." (See *Mather Papers*, p. 58, and Poole in *N. E. Hist. and Gen. Register*, XXIV. 3, note.) Mather had lived in Dorchester prior to his migration to England, about 1650; but, as he had been in constant communication with friends in America, it is not at all sure that his knowledge of this case antedates his leaving. In Hale's account there seems some confusion with the case of Mary Parsons (p. 410).

[1] Braintree.

[2] Probably John Phillips of Dorchester—the conjecture is Farmer's.

as a Punishment for her Murdering goody Kendal by her false witness bearing. But the Nurse dyed in Prison, and so the matter was not farther inquired into.

There was another Executed, of Boston *Anno* 1656. for that crime.[1] And two or three of Springfield, one of which confessed; and said the occasion of her familiarity with Satan was this: She had lost a Child and was exceedingly discontented at it and longed; Oh that she might see her Child again! And at last the Devil in likeness of her Child came to her bed side and talked with her, and asked to come into the bed to her, and she received it into the bed to her that night and several nights after, and so entred into covenant with Satan and became a Witch.[2] This was the only confessor in these times in that Government.

Sect. 8. Another at Hartford, *viz.* Mary Johnson, mentioned in *Remarkable Providences*, p. 62, 63,[3] Confessed her self a Witch. Who upon discontent and slouthfulness agreed with the Devil to do her work for her, and fetch up the Swine. And upon her immoderate laughter at the running of the Swine, as the Devil drove them, as she her self said, was suspected and upon examination confessed. I have also heard of a Girl at New Haven or Stratford, that confessed her guilt.[4] But all others denyed it unto the death unless one Greensmith, at Hartford.[5]

Sect. 9. But it is not my purpose to give a full relation of all that have suffered for that Sin, or of all the particulars

[1] Mrs. Ann Hibbins, widow of one of the foremost men in Boston and said to have been a sister of Governor Bellingham. (See *Records of Massachusetts*, IV., pt. 1, p. 269; Hutchinson, *Massachusetts*, second ed., I. 187–188; *Memorial History of Boston*, II. 138–141.)

[2] This was the case of Mary Parsons and her husband Hugh, whom she accused (1651). (See Drake, *Annals of Witchcraft*, pp. 64–72, and especially the appended papers of Hugh Parsons's case, pp. 219–258. The originals of these papers are now in the New York Public Library. Others, from the Suffolk court files, are printed in the *N. E. Hist. and Gen. Register*, XXXV. 152–153.)

[3] Not in the *Remarkable Providences* of Increase Mather, but in the *Memorable Providences* of Cotton Mather at the pages named (see above, pp. 135–136).

[4] Probably that "Goody Bassett" who was on trial at Stratford in 1651 (*Connecticut Records*, I. 220), and of whom we know from testimony given at New Haven in 1654 (*New Haven Records*, II. 83) that she was condemned and that she confessed.

[5] See above, pp. 19–20.

charged upon them, which probably is now impossible, many witnessing *Viva voce*, those particulars which were not fully recorded. But that I chiefly intend is to shew the principles formerly acted upon in Convicting of that Crime; which were such as these.

1. The first great principle laid down by a person Eminent for Wisdom, Piety and Learning[1] was; That the Devil could not assume the shape of an innocent person in doing mischief unto mankind: for if the Lord should suffer him in this he would subvert the course of humane Justice, by bringing men to suffer for what he did in their Shapes.

2. Witchcraft being an habitual Crime, one single witness to one Act of Witchcraft, and another single witness to another such fact, made two witnesses against the Crime and the party suspected.

3. There was searching of the bodies of the suspected for such like teats, or spots (which writers speak of) called the Devils marks; and if found, these were accounted a presumption at least of guilt in those that had them.

4. I observed that people laid great weight upon this; when things supposed to be bewitched were burnt, and the suspected person came to the fire in the time of it.[2] Although that Eminent person above said[3] condemned this way of tryal, as going to the Devil to find the Devil.

5. If after anger between Neighbours mischief followed, this oft bred suspicion of Witchcraft in the matter. In fine, the presumptions and convictions used in former times were for substance the same which we may read of in Keeble of the

---

[1] When in 1669 the Connecticut court asked the ministers their opinion as to this point, they answered in almost these words (see Taylor, *The Witchcraft Delusion in Colonial Connecticut*, p. 58). This opinion is said to be in the handwriting of the Rev. Gershom Bulkeley, the author of *Will and Doom*. But it does not follow that he was its author, much less that he was the originator of this dictum. Whatever its source, it is to be suspected that it had originally nothing to do with "spectral evidence," but was only a protest against such pleas as that of the bishop who, caught under the bed of a nun, maintained later that the culprit was only the Devil impersonating him. On Bulkeley and his rational attitude toward later charges of witchcraft, see his *Will and Doom* (Conn. Hist. Soc., *Collections*, III.), introduction and pp. 233–235.

[2] See above, p. 239, note 1.

[3] See above, in paragraph 1.

Common Law,[1] and in Bernard,[2] and other Authors of that subject.

Sect. 10. About 16 or 17 years since was accused a Woman of Newbury,[3] and upon her tryal the Jury brought her in Guilty. Yet the Governour Simon Bradstreet Esq. and some of the Magistrates repreived her, being unsatisfyed in the Verdict upon these grounds.

1. They were not satisfyed that a Specter doing mischief in her likeness, should be imputed to her person, as a ground of guilt.

2. They did not esteem one single witness to one fact, and another single witness to another fact, for two witnesses, against the person in a matter Capital. She being reprived, was carried to her own home, and her Husband (who was esteemed a Sincere and understanding Christian by those that knew him) desired some Neighbour Ministers, of whom I was one, to meet together and discourse his Wife; the which we did: and her discourse was very Christian among us, and still pleaded her innocence as to that which was laid to her charge. We did not esteem it prudence for us to pass any definitive Sentance upon one under her circumstances, yet we inclined to the more charitable side.

In her last Sickness she was in much darkness and trouble of Spirit, which occasioned a Judicious friend to examine her strictly, Whether she had been guilty of Witchcraft, but she said No: But the ground of her trouble was some impatient and passionate Speeches and Actions of hers while in Prison, upon the account of her suffering wrongfully; whereby she had provoked the Lord, by putting some contempt upon his word. And in fine, she sought her pardon and comfort from God in Christ, and dyed so far as I understood, praying to and resting upon God in Christ for Salvation.

Sect. 11. The next that Suffered was an Irish Woman of Boston,[4] suspected to bewitch John Goodwins Children, who upon her Tryal did in Irish (as was testified by the Interpreters) confess her self guilty, and was condemned out of her own

---

[1] What is meant, as is clear from Hale's later quotations, is Keble's *Assistance to Justices.* See above, p. 163, note 2.

[2] See above, p. 304, note 5.   [3] Mrs. Morse. See above, pp. 23–31.

[4] Goody Glover. See above, pp. 100 ff.

mouth; (as Christ saith, Luk. 19. 22. *Out of thine own mouth will I Judge thee.*) The History of which is published by Mr. Cotton Mather, (and attested by the other Ministers of Boston and Charlstown.) in his Book, Entituled, *Memorable Providences*, Printed *Anno* 1689.[1] Thus far of the History of Witches before the year, 1692.

Chapter II.

I. In the latter end of the year 1691,[2] Mr. Samuel Paris, Pastor of the Church in Salem-Village, had a Daughter of Nine, and a Neice of about Eleven years of Age, sadly Afflicted of they knew not what Distempers; and he made his application to Physitians, yet still they grew worse: And at length one Physitian gave his opinion, that they were under an Evil Hand. This the Neighbours quickly took up, and concluded they were bewitched. He had also an Indian Man servant, and his Wife who afterwards confessed, that without the knowledge of their Master or Mistress, they had taken some of the Afflicted persons Urine, and mixing it with meal had made a Cake, and baked it, to find out the Witch, as they said. After this, the Afflicted persons cryed out of the Indian Woman, named Tituba, that she did pinch, prick, and grievously torment them, and that they saw her here and there, where no body else could. Yea they could tell where she was, and what she did, when out of their humane sight. These Children were bitten and pinched by invisible agents; their arms, necks, and backs turned this way and that way, and returned back again, so as it was impossible for them to do of themselves, and beyond the power of any Epileptick Fits, or natural Disease to effect. Sometimes they were taken dumb, their mouths stopped, their throats choaked, their limbs wracked and tormented so as might move an heart of stone, to sympathize with them, with bowels of compassion for them. I will not enlarge in the description of their cruel Sufferings, because they were in all things afflicted as bad as John Goodwins Children at Boston, in the year 1689. So that he that

---

[1] See above, pp. 91 ff.

[2] *I. e.*, in February and March of the year we call 1692. As to all this story see above the parallel narratives of Lawson (pp. 147 ff.) and Calef (pp. 341 ff.).

will read Mr. Mathers Book of *Memorable Providences*, page 3, etc., may Read part of what these Children, and afterwards sundry grown persons suffered by the hand of Satan, at Salem Village, and parts adjacent, *Anno* 1691, 2. Yet there was more in these Sufferings, than in those at Boston, by pins invisibly stuck into their flesh, pricking with Irons, (As in part published in a Book Printed 1693, *viz. The Wonders of the Invisible World*).[1] Mr. Paris seeing the distressed condition of his Family, desired the presence of some Worthy Gentlemen of Salem, and some Neighbour Ministers to consult together at his House; who when they came, and had enquired diligently into the Sufferings of the Afflicted, concluded they were preternatural, and feared the hand of Satan was in them.

II. The advice given to Mr. Paris by them was, that he should sit still and wait upon the Providence of God to see what time might discover; and to be much in prayer for the discovery of what was yet secret. They also Examined Tituba, who confessed the making a Cake, as is above mentioned, and said her Mistress in her own Country was a Witch, and had taught her some means to be used for the discovery of a Witch and for the prevention of being bewitched, etc. But said that she her self was not a Witch.

III. Soon after this, there were two or three private Fasts at the Ministers House, one of which was kept by sundry Neighbour Ministers, and after this, another in Publick at the Village, and several days afterwards of publick Humiliation, during these molestations, not only there, but in other Congregations for them. And one General Fast by Order of the General Court, observed throughout the Colony to seek the Lord that he would rebuke Satan, and be a light unto his people in this day of darkness.[2]

But I return to the History of these troubles. In a short time after other persons who were of age to be witnesses, were molested by Satan, and in their fits cryed out upon Tituba and Goody O. and S. G.[3] that they or Specters in their Shapes did grievously torment them; hereupon some of their Village

---

[1] See above, pp. 205 ff.

[2] This fast, enacted on May 6, was celebrated on May 26, 1692 (Massachusetts *Acts and Resolves*, VII. 459).

[3] Sarah Osborn and Sarah Good.

Neighbours complained to the Magistrates at Salem, desiring they would come and examine the afflicted and accused together; the which they did: the effect of which examination was, that Tituba confessed she was a Witch, and that she with the two others accused did torment and bewitch the complainers, and that these with two others whose names she knew not, had their Witch-meeting together; relating the times when and places where they met, with many other circumstances to be seen at large. Upon this the said Tituba and O. and S. G. were committed to Prison upon suspicion of acting Witchcraft. After this the said Tituba was again examined in Prison, and owned her first confession in all points, and then was her self afflicted and complained of her fellow Witches tormenting of her, for her confession, and accusing them, and being searched by a Woman, she was found to have upon her body the marks of the Devils wounding of her.

IV.   Here were these things rendred her confession credible. (1.) That at this examination she answered every question just as she did at the first. And it was thought that if she had feigned her confession, she could not have remembred her answers so exactly. A lyar we say, had need of a good memory, but truth being always consistent with it self is the same to day as it was yesterday. (2.) She seemed very penitent for her Sin in covenanting with the Devil. (3.) She became a sufferer her self and as she said for her confession. (4.) Her confession agreed exactly (which was afterwards verified in the other confessors) with the accusations of the afflicted. Soon after these afflicted persons complained of other persons afflicting of them in their fits, and the number of the afflicted and accused began to increase. And the success of Tituba's confession encouraged those in Authority to examine others that were suspected, and the event was, that more confessed themselves guilty of the Crimes they were suspected for. And thus was this matter driven on.

V.   I observed in the prosecution of these affairs, that there was in the Justices, Judges and others concerned, a conscientious endeavour to do the thing that was right. And to that end they consulted the Presidents[1] of former times and precepts laid down by Learned Writers about Witchcraft.

[1] Precedents.

As Keeble on the *Common Law*, Chapt. Conjuration, (an Author approved by the Twelve Judges of our Nation.)[1]   Also Sir Mathew Hales *Tryal of Witches*, Printed *Anno* 1682.[2]   Glanvils *Collection of sundry tryals in England and Ireland*, in the years 1658, 61, 63, 64, and 81.[3]   Bernards *Guide to Jurymen*,[4] Baxter and R. Burton, their Histories about Witches and their discoveries.[5]   Cotton Mather's *Memorable Providences relating to Witchcrafts*, Printed *Anno* 1689.

VI.   But that which chiefly carried on this matter to such an height, was the increasing of confessors till they amounted to near about Fifty: and four or six of them upon their tryals owned their guilt of this crime, and were condemned for the same, but not Executed.   And many of the confessors confirmed their confessions with very strong circumstances: As their exact agreement with the accusations of the afflicted; their punctual agreement with their fellow confessors; their relating the times when they covenanted with Satan, and the reasons that moved them thereunto; their Witch meetings, and that they had their mock Sacraments of Baptism and the Supper, in some of them; their signing the Devils book: and some shewed the Scars of the wounds which they said were made to fetch blood with, to sign the Devils book; and some

[1] See above, p. 163, note 2.   "Conjuration" is the heading given by Keble to his section on witchcraft (pp. 217–220).

[2] The account is not Sir Matthew's own, nor yet an official record, but one taken down "for his own satisfaction" "by a Person then Attending the Court," and so did not till 1682 find its way into print.   As we have seen (p. 215, note 1) it was embodied by Cotton Mather in his *Wonders*.

[3] See above, pp. 5–6.

[4] See above, p. 304, note 5.

[5] Baxter's *Certainty of the Worlds of Spirits* (1691), really a collection of witch stories, has been earlier described (p. 98, note 2).   The name of "R. Burton," or "R. B.," the pseudonym under which the prolific London publisher Nathaniel Crouch concealed his identity, is attached to a multitude of chapbooks; but that here in question was undoubtedly his *The Kingdom of Darkness* (London, 1688), a pictorial "history of dæmons, specters, witches, apparitions, possessions, disturbances, and other wonderful and supernatural delusions, mischievous feats, and malicious impostures of the Devil," "together with a preface obviating the common objections and allegations of the Sadduces and Atheists of the age."   It is, in other words, a credulous hodge-podge of all the older witch and devil tales that could be packed into its duodecimo pages; tales made vivid by its startling frontispiece and the crude but awful woodcuts that adorn its text.

said they had Imps to suck them, and shewed Sores raw where they said they were sucked by them.

VII. I shall give the Reader a tast of these things in a few Instances. The Afflicted complained that the Spectres which vexed them, urged them to set their Hands to a Book represented to them (as to them it seemed) with threatnings of great torments, if they signed not, and promises of ease if they obeyed.

Among these D. H.[1] did as she said (which sundry others confessed afterwards) being overcome by the extremity of her pains, sign the Book presented, and had the promised ease; and immediately upon it a Spectre in her Shape afflicted another person, and said, I have signed the Book and have ease, now do you sign, and so shall you have ease. And one day this afflicted person pointed at a certain place in the room, and said, there is D. H., upon which a man with his Rapier struck at the place, though he saw no Shape; and the Afflicted called out, saying, you have wounded her side, and soon after the afflicted person pointed at another place, saying, there she is; whereupon a man struck at the place, and the afflicted said, you have given her a small prick about the eye. Soon after this, the said D. H. confessed her self to be made a Witch by signing the Devils Book as above said; and declared that she had afflicted the Maid that complained of her, and in doing of it had received two wounds by a Sword or Rapier, a small one about the eye, which she shewed to the Magistrates, and a bigger on the side of which she was searched by a discreet woman, who reported, that D. H. had on her side the sign of a wound newly healed.

This D. H. confessed that she was at a Witch Meeting at Salem Village, where were many persons that she named, some of whom were in Prison then or soon after upon suspicion of Witchcraft: And the said G. B.[2] preached to them, and such a Woman was their Deacon, and there they had a Sacrament.

VIII. Several others after this confessed the same things

---

[1] Deliverance Hobbs—called by error "Deborah" on p. 347. The court record of her examination may be found in *Records of Salem Witchcraft*, II. 186–192.

[2] George Burroughs.

with D. H. In particular Goody F.[1] said (*Inter alia*[2]) that she with two others (one of whom acknowledged the same) Rode from Andover to the same Village Witch meeting upon a stick above ground, and that in the way the stick brake, and gave the said F. a fall: whereupon, said she, I got a fall and hurt of which I am still sore. I happened to be present in Prison when this F. owned again her former confession to the Magistrates. And then I moved she might be further questioned about some particulars: It was answered, the Magistrates had not time to stay longer; but I should have liberty to Examine her farther by my self; The which thing I did; and I asked her if she rode to the Meeting on a Stick; she said, yea. I enquired what she did for Victuals; she answered that she carried Bread and Cheese in her pocket, and that she and the Andover Company came to the Village before the Meeting began, and sat down together under a tree and eat their food, and that she drank water out of a Brook to quench her thirst. And that the Meeting was upon a plain grassy place, by which was a Cart path, and sandy ground in the path, in which were the tracks of Horses feet. And she also told me how long they were going and returning. And some time after told me, she had some trouble upon her spirit, and when I enquired what? she said, she was in fear that G. B. and M. C.[3] would kill her; for they appeared unto her (in Spectre, for their persons were kept in other Rooms in the Prison) and brought a sharp pointed iron like a spindle, but four square, and threatned to stab her to death with it; because she had confessed her Witchcraft, and told of them, that they were with her, and that M. C. above named was the person that made her a Witch. About a month after the said F. took occasion to tell me the same Story of her fears that G. B. and E. C.[4] would kill her, and that the thing was much upon her Spirits.

IX. It was not long before M. L.[5] Daughter of said F. confessed that she rode with her Mother to the said Witch

---

[1] Ann Foster. See above, pp. 244, 366. As her son later alleged, she "suffered imprisonment twenty-one weeks and upon her Tryall was condemned for supposed witchcraft . . . and died in prison."

[2] "Among other things."

[3] Martha Carrier. See above, pp. 241–244.

[4] Doubtless a printer's error for M. C. (Martha Carrier).

[5] Mary Lacy. See pp. 244, 366. Though condemned, she escaped death.

Meeting, and confirmed the substance of her Mothers Confession. At another time, M. L. junior the Grand Daughter, aged about seventeen years, confesseth the substance of what her Grand mother and Mother had related, and declareth, that when they with E. C.[1] rode on a stick or pole in the Air, She the said Grand-Daughter with R. C.[2] Rode upon another; (and she said R. C. acknowledged the same) and that they sat their hands to the Devils Book. And (*inter alia*) said, " O Mother, why did you give me to the Devil?" twice or thrice over. The Mother said, she was sorry at the heart for it, it was through that wicked one. Her Daughter bid her repent and call upon God. And said, " Oh Mother, your wishes are now come to pass! for how often have you wished that the Devil would fetch me away alive?" And then said, "Oh! my heart will break within me"; Then she wept bitterly, crying out, "O Lord comfort me, and bring out all the Witches." And she said to her Grandmother, "O Grandmother, why did you give me to the Devil? Why did you perswade me, O Grandmother do not deny it." Then the Grandmother gave account of several things about their confederates and acts of Witchcrafts too long to rehearse.

Chapter III.

Nextly I will insert the Confession of a man about Forty years of Age, W. B.,[3] which he wrote himself in Prison, and sent to the Magistrates, to confirm his former Confession to them, *viz*.

God having called me to Confess my sin and Apostasy in that fall in giving the Devil advantage over me appearing to me like a Black, in the evening to set my hand to his Book, as I have owned to my shame. He told me that I should not want so doing. At Salem Village, there being a little off the Meeting-House, about an hundred five Blades,[4] some with Rapiers by their side, which was called and might be more for ought I know by B and Bu.[5] and the

---

[1] Again a misprint for M. C. (see Mary Lacy's testimony in *Records of Salem Witchcraft*, II. 140: "her mother Foster, Goody Carrier and herself rid upon a pole to Salem Village meeting").

[2] Richard Carrier, son of Martha.   [3] William Barker, of Andover.
[4] Bravoes.   [5] Bishop and Burroughs?

Trumpet sounded, and Bread and Wine which they called the Sacrament, but I had none; being carried over all on a Stick, never being at any other Meeting. I being at Cart a Saturday last, all the day, of Hay and English Corn, the Devil brought my Shape to Salem, and did afflict M. S.[1] and R. F.[2] by clitching my Hand; and a Sabbath day my Shape afflicted A. M.[3] and at night afflicted M. S. and A. M. E. I.[4] and A. F.[5] have been my Enticers to this great abomination, as one have owned and charged her to her Sister with the same. And the design was to Destroy Salem Village, and to begin at the Ministers House, and to destroy the Church of God, and to set up Satans Kingdom, and then all will be well. And now I hope God in some measure has made me something sensible of my sin and apostasy, begging pardon of God, and of the Honourable Magistrates and all Gods people, hoping and promising by the help of God, to set to my heart and hand to do what in me lyeth to destroy such wicked worship, humbly begging the prayers of all Gods People for me, I may walk humbly under this great affliction and that I may procure to my self, the sure mercies of David, and the blessing of Abraham.

Concerning this Confession.   (1) Note it was his own free act in Prison.   (2) He saith the Devil like a Black.   This he had before explained to be like a Black man.   (3) That on a certain day was heard in the Air the sound of a Trumpet at Salem Village nigh the Meeting-House, and upon all enquiry it could not be found that any mortal man did sound it.   (4) The three persons he saith the Devil in his Shape afflicted, had been as to the times and manner afflicted as he confesseth.   (5) That E. I. confessed as much as W. B. chargeth her with.   (6) Many others confessed a Witch Meeting, or Witch meetings at the Village as well as he.

Note also that these Confessors did not only witness against themselves, but against one another; and against many if not all those that Suffered for that Crime.   As for example, when

---

[1] Martha Sprague.   [2] Rose Foster.   [3] Abigail Martin.

[4] Elizabeth Johnson. Her daughter, of the same name, was also accused and confessed (see p. 382, note 4, above).

[5] Abigail Falkner. She and her sister Elizabeth Johnson were daughters of the Rev. Francis Dane (or Deane), senior pastor at Andover, who seems from the first to have stood against the panic and who was largely instrumental in ending it. All those here accused were Andover folk, neighbors of Barker. See as to them Mrs. Bailey's chapter on "Witchcraft at Andover" (in her *Historical Sketches of Andover*).

G. B.[1] was Tryed, seven or eight of these Confessors severally called, said, they knew the said B. and saw him at a Witch-Meeting at the Village, and heard him exhort the Company to pull down the Kingdom of God, and set up the Kingdom of the Devil. He denied all, yet said he justified the Judges and Jury in Condemning of him; because there were so many positive witnesses against him: But said he dyed by false Witnesses. I seriously spake to one that witnessed (of his Exhorting at the Witch Meeting at the Village) saying to her; You are one that bring this man to Death, if you have charged any thing upon him that is not true, recal it before it be too late, while he is alive. She answered me, she had nothing to charge her self with, upon that account.

M. C.[2] had to witness against her, two or three of her own Children, and several of her Neighbours that said they were in confederacy with her in their Witchcraft.

A. F.[3] Had three of her Children, and some of the Neighbours, her own Sister, and a Servant, who confessed themselves Witches, and said, she was in confederacy with them: But alas, I am weary with relating particulars; those that would see more of this kind, let them have recourse to the Records.

By these things you see how this matter was carried on, *viz.* chiefly by the complaints and accusations of the Afflicted, Bewitched ones, as it was supposed, and then by the Confessions of the Accused, condemning themselves, and others. Yet experience shewed that the more there were apprehended, the more were still Afflicted by Satan, and the number of Confessors increasing, did but increase the number of the Accused, and the Executing some, made way for the apprehending of others; for still the Afflicted complained of being tormented by new objects as the former were removed. So that those that were concerned, grew amazed at the numbers and quality of the persons accused and feared that Satan by his wiles had inwrapped innocent persons under the imputation of that Crime.

---

[1] George Burroughs.   [2] Martha Carrier.
[3] Abigail Falkner (see pp. 366, 420). "She was urged," says the record, "to confes the truth for the creddit of hir Town," but "she refused to do it, saying God would not require her to confess that that she was not guilty of" (*Records of Salem Witchcraft*, II. 128–135, where may also be found the evidence against her). She was condemned, but not executed.

And at last it was evidently seen that there must be a stop put, or the Generation of the Children of God would fall under that condemnation.

Henceforth therefore the Juries generally acquitted such as were Tried, fearing they had gone too far before.   And Sir William Phips, Governour, Reprieved all that were Condemned, even the Confessors, as well as others.   And the Confessors generally fell off from their Confessions; some saying, they remembred nothing of what they said; others said they had belied themselves and others.   Some brake Prison and ran away, and were not strictly searched after, some acquitted, some dismissed and one way or other all that had been accused were set or left at liberty.

And although had the times been calm, the condition of the Confessors might have called for a *melius inquirendum*;[1] yet considering the combustion[2] and confusion this matter had brought us unto; it was thought safer to under do than over do, especially in matters Capital, where what is once compleated cannot be retrieved: but what is left at one time, may be corrected at another, upon a review and clearer discovery of the state of the Case.   Thus this matter issued somewhat abruptly.

Chapter IV.

Here was generally acknowledged to be an error (at least on the one hand) but the Querie is, Wherein?

[*A.*] 1. I have heard it said, That the Presidents[3] in England were not so exactly followed, because in those there had been previous quarrels and threatnings of the Afflicted by those that were Condemned for Witchcraft; but here, say they, not so.   To which I answer.

1. In many of these cases there had been antecedent personal quarrels, and so occasions of revenge; for some of those Condemned, had been suspected by their Neighbours several years, because after quarrelling with their Neighbours, evils had befallen those Neighbours.   As may be seen in the Printed Tryals of S. M. and B. B.[4] and others: See *Wonders of the In-*

---

[1] "Better investigation"—*i. e.*, a writ for a fresh inquiry.
[2] Excitement.   [3] Precedents.
[4] Susannah Martin and Bridget Bishop.

visible World, Page 105 to 137.[1]   And there were other like Cases not Printed.

2. Several confessors acknowledged they engaged in the quarrels of other their confederates to afflict persons.   As one Timothy Swan suffered great things by Witchcrafts, as he supposed and testifyed.   And several of the confessors said they did so torment him for the sake of one of their partners who had some offence offer'd her by the said Swan.   And others owned they did the like in the behalf of some of their confederates.[2]

3. There were others that confessed their fellowship in these works of darkness, was to destroy the Church of God (as is above in part rehearsed) which is a greater piece of revenge then[3] to be avenged upon one particular person.

[*A.*] 2. It may be queried then, How doth it appear that there was a going too far in this affair.

1. By the numbers of the persons accused which at length increased to about an hundred and it cannot be imagined that in a place of so much knowledge, so many in so small a compass of Land should so abominably leap into the Devils lap at once.

2. The quality of several of the accused was such as did bespeak better things, and things that accompany salvation. Persons whose blameless and holy lives before did testify for them.   Persons that had taken great pains to bring up their Children in the nurture and admonition of the Lord: Such as we had Charity for, as for our own Souls: and Charity is a Christian duty commended to us.   1 Cor. 13 Chapt., Col. 3. 14, and in many other Scriptures.

3. The number of the afflicted by Satan dayly increased, till about Fifty persons were thus vexed by the Devil.   This gave just ground to suspect some mistake, which gave advantage to the accuser of the Brethren[4] to make a breach upon us.

4. It was considerable[5] that Nineteen were Executed, and all denyed the Crime to the Death, and some of them were

---

[1] At pp. 223–236, above.

[2] Timothy Swan, aged thirty, died early in February, 1692/3 (*N. E. Hist. and Gen. Reg.*, II. 380; Mrs. Bailey, *Historical Sketches of Andover*, p. 237).

[3] Than.   [4] *I. e.*, Satan (see Rev. xii. 10).

[5] Deserving of consideration.

knowing persons, and had before this been accounted blameless livers.   And it is not to be imagined, but that if all had been guilty, some would have had so much tenderness as to seek Mercy for their Souls in the way of Confession and sorrow for such a Sin.   And as for the condemned confessors at the Bar (they being reprieved) we had no experience whether they would stand to their Self-condemning confessions, when they came to dye.

5. When this prosecution ceased, the Lord so chained up Satan, that the afflicted grew presently well.   The accused are generally quiet, and for five years since, we have no such molestations by them.

6. It sways much with me that I have since heard and read of the like mistakes in other places.   As in Suffolk in England about the year 1645 was such a prosecution, until they saw that unless they put a stop it would bring all into blood and confusion.[1]   The like hath been in France, till 900 were put to Death,[2] And in some other places the like; So that N. England is not the only place circumvented by the wiles of the wicked and wisely Serpent in this kind.

Wierus *de Prœstigiis Demonum*, p. 678,[3] Relates, That an Inquisitor in the Subalpine Valleys, enquired after Women Witches, and consumed above an hundred in the Flames, and daily made new offerings to Vulcan of those that needed Helebore more than Fire,[4] Until the Country people rose and by force of Arms hindred him, and refer the matter to the Bishop. Their Husbands, men of good Faith, affirmed that in that very time they said of them, that they played and danced under a tree, they were in bed with them.

---

[1] The famous witch-hunt in which Matthew Hopkins was the leading spirit (1645–1646).

[2] What is in thought is doubtless the boast of Nicolas Remy (Remigius), on the title-page of his *Dœmonolatreia* (1595), that his book rests on the trials of nine hundred, put to death for witchcraft within fifteen years; but this was in Lorraine, not yet a part of France, though in close relations with it.

[3] Lib. VI., cap. 20, of this notable book by which the eminent Rhenish physician Wierus (Johann Weyer, 1515–1588) gave to the zeal of the witch-haters its first effective check.   This passage, however, he borrows bodily from the *Parergon Juris* (VIII. 22) of an earlier opponent of witch persecution, the Italian jurist Andrea Alciati.

[4] *I. e.*, those crazed more than criminal: hellebore was counted a cure for insanity.

R. Burton of Witches, etc. p. 158,[1] Saith, That in Chelms-
ford in Essex, *Anno* 1645, were Thirty tryed at once before
Judge Coniers, and Fourteen of them hanged, and an hundred
more contained in several Prisons in Suffolk and Essex.

If there were an Error in the proceedings in other places,
and in N. England, it must be in the principles proceeded upon
in prosecuting the suspected, or in the misapplication of the
principles made use of. Now as to the case at Salem, I conceive it proceeded from some mistaken principles made use
of; for the evincing whereof, I shall instance some principles
made use of here, and in other Countrys also, which I find
defended by learned Authors writing upon that Subject.[2]

·   ·   ·   ·   ·   ·   ·   ·

Chapter XVIII.

I shall conclude this Discourse with some Application of
the whole.

1. We may hence see ground to fear, that there hath been
a great deal of innocent blood shed in the Christian World,
by proceeding upon unsafe principles, in condemning persons
for Malefick Witchcraft.[3]

2. That there have been great sinful neglects in sparing
others, who by their divinings about things future, or discovering things secret, as stollen Goods, etc., or by their informing
of persons and things absent at a great distance, have implored
the assistance of a familiar spirit, yet coloured over with
specious pretences, and have drawn people to enquire of them:
A sin frequently forbidden in Scripture, as Lev. 19. 31 and
20. 6, Isa. 8. 19, 20. and yet let alone, and in many parts of

---

[1] See p. 416, note 5. "Burton" has merely inserted into his *Kingdom of
Darkness* (pp. 148–159) the contents of the contemporary *True and Exact Relation* (1645) which narrates this Essex persecution.

[2] The following chapters (V.–XVII.) are devoted to the nature of witchcraft and the proper means for its detection.

[3] "Black Witches, or Malefick Witches," explains Hale a little earlier, are
those "who by their enchantments do call in the Devils aid, for revenge, to do
hurt to the bodies and health of their neighbours, or to their cattle, goods, and the
like. These are the persons commonly called Witches, and against whom the
spirits of men and the laws of men are most bent, for their prosecution and
punishment."

the World, have been countenanced in their diabolical skill and profession; because they serve the interest of those that have a vain curiosity, to pry into things God hath forbidden, and concealed from discovery by lawful means. And of others that by their inchantments, have raised mists, strange sights, and the like, to beget admiration, and please Spectators, etc., When as[1] these divinations and operations are the Witchcraft more condemned in Scripture than the other.

3. But to come nigher home, we have cause to be humbled for the mistakes and errors which have been in these Colonies, in their Proceedings against persons for this crime, above fourty years ago and downwards, upon insufficient presumptions and presidents[2] of our Nation, whence they came. I do not say, that all those were innocent, that suffered in those times upon this account. But that such grounds were then laid down to proceed upon, which were too slender to evidence the crime they were brought to prove; and thereby a foundation laid to lead into error those that came after. May we not say in this matter, as it is, Psal. 106. 6. *We have sinned with our fathers?* And as, Lam. 5. 7. *Our fathers have sinned and are not, and we have born their iniquities?* And whether this be not one of the sins the Lord hath been many years contending with us for, is worthy our serious enquiry. If the Lord punished Israel with famine three years for a sin of misguided zeal fourty years before that, committed by the breach of a Covenant made four hundred years before that: 2 Sam. 21. 1, 2, Why may not the Lord visit upon us the misguided zeal of our Predecessors about Witchcraft above fourty years ago, even when that Generation is gathered to their Fathers.

4. But I would come yet nearer to our own times, and bewail the errors and mistakes that have been in the year 1692. In the apprehending too many we may believe were innocent, and executing of some, I fear, not to have been condemned; by following such traditions of our fathers, maxims of the Common Law, and Presidents[2] and Principles, which now we may see weighed in the balance of the Sanctuary, are found too light. I heartily concur with that direction for our publick prayers, emitted December 17, 1696, by our General Assembly, in an order for a general Fast, *viz.* "That God

---

[1] *I. e.*, "whenas": whereas.   [2] Precedents.

would shew us what we know not, and help us wherein we have done amiss, to do so no more: And especially that whatever mistakes on either hand, have been fallen into, either by the body of this people, or any order of men, referring to the late tragedy raised among us by Satan and his Instruments, through the awful Judgment of God: He would humble us therefore, and pardon all the errors of his Servants and People, that desire to love his Name, and be attoned to his land." I am abundantly satisfyed that those who were most concerned to act and judge in those matters, did not willingly depart from the rules of righteousness. But such was the darkness of that day, the tortures and lamentations of the afflicted, and the power of former presidents, that we walked in the clouds, and could not see our way. And we have most cause to be humbled for error on that hand, which cannot be retrieved. So that we must beseech the Lord, that if any innocent blood hath been shed, in the hour of temptation, the Lord will not lay it to our charge, but be merciful to his people whom he hath redeemed, Deut. 21. 8, And that in the day when he shall visit, he will not visit this sin upon our land, but blot it out, and wash it away with the blood of Jesus Christ.

5. I would humbly propose whether it be not expedient, that some what more should be publickly done then[1] yet hath, for clearing the good name and reputation of some that have suffered upon this account, against whom the evidence of their guilt was more slender, and the grounds for charity for them more convincing. And this (in order to our obtaining from the Lord farther reconciliation to our land,) and that none of their surviving relations, may suffer reproach upon that account. I have both read and heard of several in England, that have been executed for Capital crimes, and afterwards upon sence of an error in the process against them, have been restored in blood and honour by some publick act. My Lord Cook[2] relates a story. A man going to correct a Girle his Neice, for some offence, in an upper room, the Girle strove to save her self, till her nose bled, and wiping it with a cloath, threw the bloody cloath out at the window, and cryed Murder; and then ran down staires, got away and hid her self. Her Uncle was prosecuted by her friends upon suspicion of

---

[1] Than.   [2] Sir Edward Coke.

Murdering her, because she could not be found. He declared that she made her escape, as above said. Then time was allowed him to bring her forth, but he could not hear of her within the time, and fearing he should dy if she could not be found, procures another Girle very like her, to appear in Court, and declare she was his Neice that had been missing: But her relations examine this counterfeit, until they find her out, and she confesseth she was suborned and counterfeited the true Neice. Upon these presumptions the man was found guilty of Murdering his Neice, and thereupon executed. And after his execution his true Neice comes abroad and shews her self alive and well. Then all that saw it were convinced of the Uncles innocency, and vanity of such presumptions. The Printing and Publishing of this relation Vindicates the good name of the Uncle, from the imputation of the crime of Murder. And this is one end of this present discourse, to take off (so far as a discourse of this nature can) infamy from the names and memory of such sufferers in this kind, as do not deserve the same.

6. Here it may be suitable for us to enquire, What the Lord speaks to us by such a stupendeous providence, in his letting loose Satan upon us in this unusual way? *Ans.* 1. We may say of this, as our Saviour said of his washing his disciples feet, Joh. 13. *What I do thou knowest not now, but thou shalt know hereafter. The Judgments of the Lord are a great deep,* Psal. 36. 6. *How unsearchable are his judgments, and his ways past finding out.* 2. Yet somewhat of his counsel at present for our instruction may be known, by comparing the Word and works of God together.

1. As when Joshua the high Priest though an holy chosen man of God, stood before the Angel, Satan stood at his right hand to resist him, or to be his adversary: And the advantage Satan had was by the filthy garments Joshua was clothed with before the Angels: That is, some iniquity which yet was not passed away, Zech. 3. 1, 3, 4. So we may say here were among Gods own Children filthy garments. The sins of Lukewarmness, loss of our first love, unprofitableness under the Gospel, slumbering and sleeping in the wise, as well as foolish Virgins, worldliness, pride, carnal security, and many other sins. By these and such like sins the accuser of the Breth-

ren got advantage to stand at our right hand (the place of
an Accuser in Courts of Justice) and there accuse us and
resist us.

2. When the Egyptians refused to let Israel go to sacrifice
and keep a feast to the Lord in the Wilderness: The Lord cast
upon [them] the fierceness of his wrath, by sending Evil Angels
among them, Psal. 78. 49. Egypts sins were (1.) Coveteousness;
they would not let Israel go, because they gained by their
labours. (2.) Contempt of God and his Instituted Worship,
and Ordinances. They did not count them of such concernment, that Israel should go into the Wilderness to observe them.
Both these sins have too much increased in our Land. (1.)
Coveteousness, an inordinate love of the World gave Satan
advantage upon us. (2.) Contempt of Gods Worship and Instituted Ordinances. The Errand of our Fathers into this
Wilderness, was to Sacrifice to the Lord; that is, to worship
God in purity of heart and life, and to wait upon the Lord,
walking in the faith and order of the Gospel in Church fellowship; that they might enjoy Christ in all his Ordinances. But
these things have been greatly neglected and despised by many
born, or bred up in the Land. We have much forgotten what
our Fathers came into the Wilderness to see. The sealing
Ordinances of the Covenant of Grace in Church-Communion
have been much slighted and neglected;, and the fury of this
Storm raised by Satan hath fallen very heavily upon many
that lived under these neglects. The Lord sends Evil Angels
to awaken and punish our negligence: And to my knowledge
some have been hereby excited to enter into the Chamber of
Gods Ordinances, to hide themselves, until the indignation be
over past.

3. David when he removed the Ark from Kirjathjearim,
had the Ark put into a new Cart, which should have been carried by the Kohathites. Numb. 3. 31. And David thought
this was right, until the Lord slew Uzza for touching the Ark:
But then he looked more exactly into the will of God; and
confesseth that the Lord made a breach upon them, because
they sought him not after the due order, 1 Chron. 13. 5, 7, 9,
10, and 15. 11, 12, 13. Had not the Lord made that breach
upon them, they had persisted securely in their error. So I
may say in this case. In the prosecution of Witchcraft, we

sought not the Lord after the due order; but have proceeded after the methods used in former times and other places, until the Lord in this tremendous way made a breach upon us. And hereby we are made sensible that the methods formerly used are not sufficient to prove the guilt of such a crime. And this I conceive was one end of the Lords letting Satan loose to torment and accuse so many; that hereby we may search out the truth more exactly. For had it not been for this dreadful dispensation, many would have lived and dyed in that error, which they are now convinced of.

4. The Lord delivered into the hand of Satan the Estate, Children, and Body of Job, for the tryal of Jobs faith and patience, and proof of his perfection and uprightness. So the Lord hath delivered into Satans hand mens Children and Bodies, yea names and estates into Satans hand for the tryal of their faith and patience, and farther manifestation of the sincerity of their professions.

7.[1] From that part of the discourse which shews the power of Satan to torment the bodies, and disturb the minds of those, he is let loose upon, Chap. 6, I would infer, that Satan may be suffered so to darken the minds of some pious Souls, as to cause them to destroy themselves by drowning, hanging, or the like. And when he hath so far prevailed upon some, that formerly lived a Christian life, but were under the prevalency of a distracting Melancholy at their latter end, We may have Charity that their Souls are Saved, notwithstanding the sad conclusion of their lives. I speak not to excuse any that having the free use of their reason willingly destroy themselves, out of pride, discontent, impatience, etc. Achitophel who out of height of Spirit because his Counsel was not followed, and to prevent Davids executing of him, for his rebellion and treason, destroyed himself, hath left his name to stink unto all generations.[2] And Judas who for his unparalelled treachery in betraying his Master, and the Lord of life, was justly left to hange himself; and the rope breaking or slipping he fell down head long, or with his face down ward, so that he burst asunder in the midst, and all his bowels gushed out, Math. 27. 5. with Act. 1. 13, left by his sin and punishment in the last act of

---

[1] Such is the numbering of the original.

[2] The story of Ahithophel is to be found in II Samuel xv.–xvii.

his life the black character of a Son of perdition. But those that being out of their right minds, and hurried by an evil Spirit, as persons under a force to be their own executioners, are not always to be ranked with these.

8. Seeing we have been too fierce against supposed Malefick Witchcraft, let us take heed we do not on the contrary become too favourable to divining Witchcraft: And become like Saul who was too zealous against the Gibeonites, and at last turned to seek after one that had a familiar Spirit, to his own destruction. Let us not, if we can help it, suffer Satan to set up an ensuring office for stolen Goods. That after he hath brought the curse of God into the house of the thief, by tempting him to steal, he may not bring about the curse into the houses of them from whom the goods were stolen, by alluring them to go to the god of Ekron to enquire. That men may not give their Souls to the Devil in exchange, for his restoring to them their goods again, in such a way of divination. The Lord grant it may be said of New England, as is prophecyed of Judah, Mic. 5. 12. *I will cut off Witchcrafts out of thine hand, and thou shalt have no more soothsayers.*

9. Another extream we must beware of, is, *viz.* Because our fathers in the beginning times of this Land, did not see so far into these mysteries of iniquity, as hath been since discovered, Let us not undervalue the good foundations they laid for God and his people, and for us in Church and Civil Government. For Paul that eminent Apostle knew but in part; no wonder then, if our Fathers were imperfect men. In the purest times in Israel, there were some Clouds of ignorance over-shadowing of them. Abraham, David, and the best Patriarchs were generally ignorant of the sin of Polygamy. And although Solomon far exceeded Nehemiah in wisdom; yet Nehemiah saw farther into the evil of Marrying Outlandish Women, than that wisest of Kings, and meer fallen men. Neh. 13. 26. Josiah kept the Passeover more exactly, than David, and all the Reforming Kings of Judah, 2 Chron. 35. 18.

All the godly Judges and Kings of Judah were unacquainted with, and so negligent of the right observation of the feast of Tabernacles, until it came to Nehemiahs time: And he understood and revived an ordinance of God, that lay buried in oblivion, near about a thousand years. Now he that shall reject all the good in doctrine and practice, which was maintained, professed and practiced by so many Godly leaders, because of some few errors found among them, will be found to fight against God. A dwarf upon a giants shoulders, can see farther than the giant.

It was a glorious enterprize of the beginners of these Colonies, to leave their native Country to propagate the Gospel: And a very high pitch of faith, zeal, and courage that carryed them forth, to follow the Lord into this wilderness, into a land that was not sown. Then was New England holiness to the Lord, and all that did devour them, or attempted so to do, did offend, and evil did come upon them. And the Lord did graciously remember this kindness of their Youth, and love of their Espousals; In granting them many eminent tokens of his favour; by his presence with them in his Ordinances, for the Conversion of Souls, and edifying and comforting the hearts of his Servants: By signal answering their prayers in times of difficulty: By protecting them from their Enemies; By guiding of, and providing for them in a Desart. And the Lord will still remember this their kindness unto their Posterity, unless that by their Apostasy from the Lord, they vex his Holy Spirit, to turn to be their Enemy: And thereby cut off the Entail of his Covenant Mercies; which God forbid. *Oh that the Lord may be with us, as he was with our Fathers; and that he may not leave us, nor forsake us!*

Finis.

THE VIRGINIA CASE OF GRACE SHERWOOD, 1706

INTRODUCTION

To those who know what elements made up the earliest population of Virginia it is needless to point out why there we find no such abiding fear of the Devil and his minions as among the religious exiles of New England. There no Mosaic law was enacted into statute; and the well-known Cavalier sympathies of the colony suggest why the mid-century witch-panic of England's Presbyterian counties found there no echo. Fear of witches, indeed, Virginia did not wholly escape; but her witch-terrors found their source in folk-lore more than in theology, and, though her courts could not keep altogether clear of the matter, their influence seems to have been almost wholly a restraining one. The testimony of their records has, in part at least, been diligently ferreted out,[1] and the historian of the social and economic life of the colony has summarized it in a lucid chapter[2] which is the best introduction to the single episode here to be narrated. By the middle of the century the bandying of the abusive name of "witch" was calling forth actions for slander and vigorous rulings by the courts; and in 1656 a clergyman from Scotland brought against one William Harding the only legal process which is known to have ended in conviction and a penalty—ten stripes and banishment from the county. Suits enough from that time on there were; but they were brought by the accused for damages, or failed to convince the jury. Especially that southeastern region known

[1] Notably by Mr. Edward W. James, who published his gleanings first in the *William and Mary College Historical Quarterly* (I.–IV.—1892–1896), then in the *Lower Norfolk County Virginia Antiquary* (I.–III.).

[2] Philip Alexander Bruce, *Institutional History of Virginia in the Seventeenth Century*, I. 276–289.

as "Lower Norfolk County," and, above all, its eastern strip, along the Atlantic, which in 1691 became Princess Anne County, seems to have been disturbed by these suspicions. There in 1675 and 1679 juries of women had been impanelled to search Jane Jenkins and Alice Cartwright, "according to the 118th chapter of Dalton," for the Devil's marks;[1] and there in 1698 Anne Byrd appealed in vain to a court against wild charges of "riding" her neighbors as a witch. In that same year Grace Sherwood, wife of James Sherwood, planter, a woman in middle life whose father, John White, had long dwelt there as carpenter and planter, was accused by one John Gisburne of bewitching his hogs and cotton. She with her husband brought an action for slander, but lost it, and was as unsuccessful against Anthony Barnes, who charged her with riding his wife and then escaping through the keyhole in the shape of a black cat. It was this Grace Sherwood against whom in 1706 was brought that culminating action for witchcraft to which belong the following papers. Her story has been often told—and often with a generous use of the imagination. More than once the records have been printed, as by President Cushing of Hampden-Sidney in the *Collections* (I. 67–68) of the Virginia Historical and Philosophical Society and by Henry Howe in his *Historical Collections of Virginia* (Charleston, 1845), pp. 436–438; but most fully and carefully by Edward W. James, whose pages in the *William and Mary College Quarterly* (III. 190–192, 242–245; IV. 18–20) have furnished our text. It has, however, been collated afresh with the record at Princess Anne by the editor of the present volume—and not without correction. It will be noticed that the

---

[1] What is meant is of course that paragraph of Michael Dalton's many-editioned handbook of procedure, *The Countrey Justice*, which, prescribing tests for the detection of witches, avers that the witch's imp, or familiar, "hath some big or little teat upon their body, and in some secret place, where he sucketh them." "And besides their sucking, the Devil leaveth other marks upon their body," which "being pricked will not bleed, and be often in their secretest parts, and therefore require diligent and careful search."

court clerk uses a sort of short-hand, abbreviating sometimes by a lavish use of "superiors" (as "som^d" for "summoned," "Ex^{ly}" for "Excellency"), sometimes by mere omission of letters. The peculiarities of the text are such that in this instance we have preserved forms which it is now more usual to expand into shapes more easily legible; but the obscurer signs (as "y" for "th," or "ff" for "F," or the stroke above a final "con" to make it "cion") have not been reproduced.[1]

---

[1] Though the old record book through which these entries are scattered is still in good condition, the passages relating to this interesting case are beginning to suffer from wear, and from the first four lines of the entry for July 5, which come at the bottom of a page, a few words have crumbled away, and are preserved only by the transcripts. In the margin of the entry for May 2 are the words "Ag^t Grace Sherwood for witchcraft," and in that of the entry for June 6 the words "Bousch Att^r for Queen vs. Sherwood"

THE CASE OF GRACE SHERWOOD

Princess Ann ss.   At a Court held the 3ᵈ of Janʳʸ 170⅝.

Whereas Luke Hill and uxor[1] Somᵈ Grace Sherwood to this Court[2] in Suspetion of witchcraft and she fayling to apear it is therefore ordʳ that attachmᵗ to the Sherʳ[3] do Issue to Attach her body to ansʳ the sᵈ Som next Court.

[Under February 6, 1705/6.]

Suite for Suspition of witchcraft brought by Luke Hill agᵗ Grace Sherwood is ordʳ to be referr till to morrᵒ.

[Under February 7, 1705/6.]

Whereas a Complᵗ was brought agᵗ Grace Sherrwood on Suspition of witchcraft by Luke Hill, etc.: and the matter being after a long time debated and ordʳ that the sᵈ Hill pay all fees of this Complᵗ and that the sᵈ Grace be here next Court to be Searched according to the Complᵗ by a Jury of women to decide the sᵈ Differr: and the Sherr is Likewise ordʳ to Som an able Jury accordingly.

[Under March 7, 1705/6.]

Present: Colᵒ Edward Moseley, Lieuᵗ [Colᵒ] Adam Thorrowgood, Majʳ Henry Sprat, Capᵗⁿ Horatio Woodhouse, Mʳ Jnᵒ Cornick, Capᵗⁿ Henry Chapman, Mʳ Wᵐ Smith, Mʳ Jnᵒ Richason, Capᵗⁿ Geo: Handcock, Justices.

---

[1] Luke Hill and wife. Against them in December, 1705, Grace Sherwood had brought action for assault and battery, claiming £50 of damages and receiving twenty shillings. What this affray may have had to do with the charge of witchcraft does not appear.

[2] The court was the county court, its members a group of "gentlemen of the county, called justices of the peace." Their names appear just below, in the entry for March 7. Such a panel of the court heads the record of each of the sessions named, but its repetition has seemed unnecessary. Grace Sherwood's case was only one of many dealt with at each session. Usually only four or five justices were present.   [3] Sheriff.

Whereas a Complaint have been [made] to this Court by
Luke Hill and his wife that one grace Sherrwood of this County
was and Have been a Long time Suspected of witchcraft and
have been as Such Represented wherefore the Sherr at the last
Court was ord^d to Som a Jury of women to this Court to Serch
her on the s^d Suspicion, She assenting to the Same.   And after
the Jury was impannelld and Sworn and Sent out to make
Due inquirery and Inspection into all Cercumstances, After a
Mature Consideracion They bring in this verditt: wee of the
Jury have Serch^{tt} Grace Sherwood and have found Two things
like titts wth Severall other Spotts: Eliz^h Barnes, forewoman,
Sarah Norris, Marg^{rtt} Watkins, Hannah Dinnis, Sarah Good-
acre, Mary Burgess, Sarah Sergeant, winifred Davis, Ursula
Henly, Ann Bridg^s, Ezable waples, Mary Cotle.[1]

[Under May 2, 1706.]

Whereas a former Compl^t was brought ag^t Grace Sherwood
for Suspicion of Witchcraft, wch by the Atturny Gen^{rll} Report
to his Ex^{cly} in Councill was to[2] Generall and not Charging her
with any perticular Act, therefore represented to them that
Princess Ann Court might if they thought fitt have her ex-

---

[1] At this point the court reached the limit of its powers, and Luke Hill,
doubtless at its instance, petitioned the highest tribunal of the colony, the General
Court, *i. e.*, the Governor and Council, informing them that "one Grace Sherwood of Princess Anne County being suspected of witchcraft upon his complaint
to that county court that she had bewitched the petitioner's wife, the court
ordered a jury of women to search the said Grace Sherwood who upon search
brought in a verdict against the said Grace, but the court not knowing how to
proceed to judgment thereon, the petitioner prays that the Attorney Generall
may be directed to prosecute the said Grace for the same."   But the attorney
general, to whom on March 28 the matter was referred, reported on April 16
that he found the charge too general and that the county court ought to have
made a fuller examination of the matters of fact, and that "pursuant to the
directions and powers to County Courts given by a late act of Assembly" they
ought, if they thought there was sufficient cause, to have committed the accused
to the general prison of the colony, "whereby it would have come regularly before
the Generall Court."   Wherefore he suggested "that the said County Court do
make a further Enquiry into the matter," and, if they find cause for action, to
follow the said law; and it was ordered that a copy of his report "be sent to the
court of Princess Anne County for their direction in the premises."   (*Cf.* Palmer's
Calendar of Virginia State Papers, I. 100: at some points this corrects Mr. James's
readings, at others needs correction by them.)

[2] Too.

amined De Novo, and the Court Being of Oppinion that there is great Cause of Suspicion Doe therefore ord^r that the Sherr take the Said Grace into his Safe Costody untill She Shall give bond and Security for her Appearance to the next Court to be examined Denovo and that the Constable of that precinkt go with the Sherr and Serch the Sd graces House and all Suspicious places Carfully for all Images[1] and Such like things as may any way Strengthen The Suspicion, and it is likewise Ordered that the Sherr Som an Able Jury of Women, also all Evidences as Cann give in anything ag^t her in Evidence, in behalf of our Soveraign Lady the Queen, To Attend the next Court Accordingly.

[*Under June* 6, 1706.]

Whereas Grace Sherwood of this County have been Complained of as a person Suspected of Witchcraft, and now being Brought before this Court in ord^r for examinacion, this Court have therefore requested m^r Maxm^{ll} Boush to present Informacion ag^t her as Councill in behalf of our Soveraign Lady the Queen in order to her being brought to a regular Tryall.

.   .   .   .

Whereas an Informacion in Behalf of her Mag^{ty} was presented by Luk Hill, to the Court in pursuance To Mr Gen^{rll} Att^{rys} Tomson report on his Excell^{cy} ord in Councill the 16th Aprill Last About Grace Sherwood being Suspected of Witchcraft, have thereupon Sworn Severall Evidences ag^t her by wch it Doth very likely appear.

[*Under June* 7, 1706.]

Whereas at the Last Court an ord^r was past that the Sherr should Sommons an able Jury of Women to Serch Grace Sherwood on Suspicion of witchcraft, wch although the Same was performed by the Sherr yet they refused And did not appear, it is therefore ord^r that the Same persons be againe Som^d by the

---

[1] Such "images," of course, as witches were believed to make of those they wished to afflict (see above, pp. 104, 163, 219, 228). "They have often," says Dalton, whose book these justices doubtless had open before them, "Pictures of Clay or Wax (like a Man, etc., made of such as they would bewitch) found in their House, or which they roast, or bury in the Earth, that as the Picture consumes, so may the parties bewitched consume."

Sherr for their Contempt To be Dealt wth according to the uttmost Severity of the Law, and that a new Jury of Women be by him Som^d To appear next Court to Serch her on the aforesaid Suspicion, and that he likewise Som all evidences that he Shall Be informed of as materiall in the Complaint, and that She continue in the Sherr Costody unless She give good bond And Security for her Appearance at the next Court, and that She be of the Good behaviour towards her Majestie and all her Leidge people in the mean time.

[*Under July* 5, 1706.]

Present, Mr Jn° Richason, Cap^tn Jn° Moseley, Cap^tn Henry Chapman, Cap^tn Wm Smyth, Justices.

Whereas for this Severall Courts the Business between luke hill and Grace Sherwood on Suspicion of witchcraft have Been for Severall things omitted, perticularly for want of a Jury to Serch her, and the Court being Doubtfull That they Should not get one this Court, and being willing to have all means possible tryed either to acquit her or to Give more Strength to the Suspicion that She might be Dealt wth as Deserved, therefore it was Ord^rd that this Day by her own Consent to be tried in the water by Ducking,[1] but the weather being very Rainy and Bad Soe that possibly it might endanger her health, it is therefore ord^rd that the Sherr request the Justices precisely to appear on wednessday next by tenn of the Clock at the Court house, and that he Secure the body of the Sd Grace till that time to be forth Coming, then to be Dealt wth as afore sd. Jn° Richason, Henry Chapman.[2]

[*Under July* 10, 1706.]

Whereas Grace Sherwood being Suspected of witchcraft have a long time waited for a Fit uppertunity For a Further Examinacion, and by her Consent and Approbacion of this Court, it is ord^r that the Sherr take all Such Convenient assistance of boats and men as Shall be by him thought Fitt, to meet at Jn° Harpers plantacion in ord^r to take the Sd Grace forthwith and put her into above mans Debth and try her how

---

[1] As to this water ordeal for witches see above, p. 21, and note 3.

[2] These gentlemen were doubtless a committee charged with the matter.

She Swims Therein, alwayes having Care of her life to preserve her from Drowning, and as Soon as She Comes Out that he request as many Ansient and Knowing women as possible he Cann to Serch her Carefully For all teats spotts and marks about her body not usuall on Others, and that as they Find the Same to make report on Oath To the truth thereof to the Court, and further it is ord^r that Som women be requested to Shift and Serch her before She goe into the water, that She Carry nothing about her to cause any Further Suspicion.

·   ·   ·   ·   ·   ·   ·   ·

Wheras[1] on complaint of Luke hill in behalf of her Majesty that now is ag^t Grace Sherwood for a person Suspected of witchcraft, and having had Sundry Evidences Sworne ag^t her, proving Many Cercumstances to which She could not make any excuse or Little or nothing to say in her own Behalf, only Seemed to Rely on what the Court should Doe, and thereupon consented to be tryed in the Water and Likewise to be Serched againe, wch experim^{ts} being tryed and She Swiming when therein and bound Contrary To Custom and the Judg^t of all the Spectators, and afterwards being Serched by Five antient weomen who have all Declared on Oath that She is not like them nor noe Other woman that they knew of, having two things like titts on her private parts of a Black Coller, being Blacker than the Rest of her Body, all which Cercumstance the Court weighing in their Consideracion Doe therefore ord^r that the Sherr take the Sd Grace Into his Costody and to Commit her body to the Common Goal of this County there to Secure her by irons, or otherwise there to Remaine till Such time as he Shall be otherwise Directed in ord^r for her coming to the Common Goale of the country[2] to bee brought to a Future Tryall there.[3]   Edward Moseley and M^r. Richason.[4]

[1] This entry is made later on the same day: the court had merely taken a recess for the "ducking."

[2] *I. e.*, at Williamsburg. See p. 439, note 1.

[3] If, at the next session of the General Court, Grace Sherwood came up for trial, the records are missing, and probably perished in the burning of the State Courthouse in 1865. She at least survived the trial; for in 1708 she was confessing judgment for six hundred pounds of tobacco, and in 1733 willing her estate to her three sons. It is not till 1740 that the proving of that will shows her deceased.

[4] Perhaps the committee that drafted this verdict.

INDEX

INDEX

A CATALOG OF SELECTED
DOVER BOOKS
IN ALL FIELDS OF INTEREST

A CATALOG OF SELECTED DOVER
BOOKS IN ALL FIELDS OF INTEREST

CONCERNING THE SPIRITUAL IN ART, Wassily Kandinsky. Pioneering work by father of abstract art. Thoughts on color theory, nature of art. Analysis of earlier masters. 12 illustrations. 80pp. of text. 5⅜ x 8½. 23411-8

ANIMALS: 1,419 Copyright-Free Illustrations of Mammals, Birds, Fish, Insects, etc., Jim Harter (ed.). Clear wood engravings present, in extremely lifelike poses, over 1,000 species of animals. One of the most extensive pictorial sourcebooks of its kind. Captions. Index. 284pp. 9 x 12. 23766-4

CELTIC ART: The Methods of Construction, George Bain. Simple geometric techniques for making Celtic interlacements, spirals, Kells-type initials, animals, humans, etc. Over 500 illustrations. 160pp. 9 x 12. (Available in U.S. only.) 22923-8

AN ATLAS OF ANATOMY FOR ARTISTS, Fritz Schider. Most thorough reference work on art anatomy in the world. Hundreds of illustrations, including selections from works by Vesalius, Leonardo, Goya, Ingres, Michelangelo, others. 593 illustrations. 192pp. 7⅛ x 10¼. 20241-0

CELTIC HAND STROKE-BY-STROKE (Irish Half-Uncial from "The Book of Kells"): An Arthur Baker Calligraphy Manual, Arthur Baker. Complete guide to creating each letter of the alphabet in distinctive Celtic manner. Covers hand position, strokes, pens, inks, paper, more. Illustrated. 48pp. 8¼ x 11. 24336-2

EASY ORIGAMI, John Montroll. Charming collection of 32 projects (hat, cup, pelican, piano, swan, many more) specially designed for the novice origami hobbyist. Clearly illustrated easy-to-follow instructions insure that even beginning papercrafters will achieve successful results. 48pp. 8¼ x 11. 27298-2

THE COMPLETE BOOK OF BIRDHOUSE CONSTRUCTION FOR WOODWORKERS, Scott D. Campbell. Detailed instructions, illustrations, tables. Also data on bird habitat and instinct patterns. Bibliography. 3 tables. 63 illustrations in 15 figures. 48pp. 5¼ x 8½. 24407-5

BLOOMINGDALE'S ILLUSTRATED 1886 CATALOG: Fashions, Dry Goods and Housewares, Bloomingdale Brothers. Famed merchants' extremely rare catalog depicting about 1,700 products: clothing, housewares, firearms, dry goods, jewelry, more. Invaluable for dating, identifying vintage items. Also, copyright-free graphics for artists, designers. Co-published with Henry Ford Museum & Greenfield Village. 160pp. 8¼ x 11. 25780-0

HISTORIC COSTUME IN PICTURES, Braun & Schneider. Over 1,450 costumed figures in clearly detailed engravings–from dawn of civilization to end of 19th century. Captions. Many folk costumes. 256pp. 8⅜ x 11¾. 23150-X

STICKLEY CRAFTSMAN FURNITURE CATALOGS, Gustav Stickley and L. & J. G. Stickley. Beautiful, functional furniture in two authentic catalogs from 1910. 594 illustrations, including 277 photos, show settles, rockers, armchairs, reclining chairs, bookcases, desks, tables. 183pp. 6½ x 9¼. 23838-5

AMERICAN LOCOMOTIVES IN HISTORIC PHOTOGRAPHS: 1858 to 1949, Ron Ziel (ed.). A rare collection of 126 meticulously detailed official photographs, called "builder portraits," of American locomotives that majestically chronicle the rise of steam locomotive power in America. Introduction. Detailed captions. xi+ 129pp. 9 x 12. 27393-8

AMERICA'S LIGHTHOUSES: An Illustrated History, Francis Ross Holland, Jr. Delightfully written, profusely illustrated fact-filled survey of over 200 American lighthouses since 1716. History, anecdotes, technological advances, more. 240pp. 8 x 10¾. 25576-X

TOWARDS A NEW ARCHITECTURE, Le Corbusier. Pioneering manifesto by founder of "International School." Technical and aesthetic theories, views of industry, economics, relation of form to function, "mass-production split" and much more. Profusely illustrated. 320pp. 6⅛ x 9¼. (Available in U.S. only.) 25023-7

HOW THE OTHER HALF LIVES, Jacob Riis. Famous journalistic record, exposing poverty and degradation of New York slums around 1900, by major social reformer. 100 striking and influential photographs. 233pp. 10 x 7⅞. 22012-5

FRUIT KEY AND TWIG KEY TO TREES AND SHRUBS, William M. Harlow. One of the handiest and most widely used identification aids. Fruit key covers 120 deciduous and evergreen species; twig key 160 deciduous species. Easily used. Over 300 photographs. 126pp. 5⅜ x 8½. 20511-8

COMMON BIRD SONGS, Dr. Donald J. Borror. Songs of 60 most common U.S. birds: robins, sparrows, cardinals, bluejays, finches, more–arranged in order of increasing complexity. Up to 9 variations of songs of each species.
Cassette and manual 99911-4

ORCHIDS AS HOUSE PLANTS, Rebecca Tyson Northen. Grow cattleyas and many other kinds of orchids–in a window, in a case, or under artificial light. 63 illustrations. 148pp. 5⅜ x 8½. 23261-1

MONSTER MAZES, Dave Phillips. Masterful mazes at four levels of difficulty. Avoid deadly perils and evil creatures to find magical treasures. Solutions for all 32 exciting illustrated puzzles. 48pp. 8¼ x 11. 26005-4

MOZART'S DON GIOVANNI (DOVER OPERA LIBRETTO SERIES), Wolfgang Amadeus Mozart. Introduced and translated by Ellen H. Bleiler. Standard Italian libretto, with complete English translation. Convenient and thoroughly portable–an ideal companion for reading along with a recording or the performance itself. Introduction. List of characters. Plot summary. 121pp. 5¼ x 8½. 24944-1

TECHNICAL MANUAL AND DICTIONARY OF CLASSICAL BALLET, Gail Grant. Defines, explains, comments on steps, movements, poses and concepts. 15-page pictorial section. Basic book for student, viewer. 127pp. 5⅜ x 8½. 21843-0

THE CLARINET AND CLARINET PLAYING, David Pino. Lively, comprehensive work features suggestions about technique, musicianship, and musical interpretation, as well as guidelines for teaching, making your own reeds, and preparing for public performance. Includes an intriguing look at clarinet history. "A godsend," *The Clarinet,* Journal of the International Clarinet Society. Appendixes. 7 illus. 320pp. 5⅜ x 8½. 40270-3

HOLLYWOOD GLAMOR PORTRAITS, John Kobal (ed.). 145 photos from 1926-49. Harlow, Gable, Bogart, Bacall; 94 stars in all. Full background on photographers, technical aspects. 160pp. 8⅜ x 11¼. 23352-9

THE ANNOTATED CASEY AT THE BAT: A Collection of Ballads about the Mighty Casey/Third, Revised Edition, Martin Gardner (ed.). Amusing sequels and parodies of one of America's best-loved poems: Casey's Revenge, Why Casey Whiffed, Casey's Sister at the Bat, others. 256pp. 5⅜ x 8½. 28598-7

THE RAVEN AND OTHER FAVORITE POEMS, Edgar Allan Poe. Over 40 of the author's most memorable poems: "The Bells," "Ulalume," "Israfel," "To Helen," "The Conqueror Worm," "Eldorado," "Annabel Lee," many more. Alphabetic lists of titles and first lines. 64pp. 5$\frac{3}{16}$ x 8¼. 26685-0

PERSONAL MEMOIRS OF U. S. GRANT, Ulysses Simpson Grant. Intelligent, deeply moving firsthand account of Civil War campaigns, considered by many the finest military memoirs ever written. Includes letters, historic photographs, maps and more. 528pp. 6⅛ x 9¼. 28587-1

ANCIENT EGYPTIAN MATERIALS AND INDUSTRIES, A. Lucas and J. Harris. Fascinating, comprehensive, thoroughly documented text describes this ancient civilization's vast resources and the processes that incorporated them in daily life, including the use of animal products, building materials, cosmetics, perfumes and incense, fibers, glazed ware, glass and its manufacture, materials used in the mummification process, and much more. 544pp. 6⅛ x 9¼. (Available in U.S. only.) 40446-3

RUSSIAN STORIES/RUSSKIE RASSKAZY: A Dual-Language Book, edited by Gleb Struve. Twelve tales by such masters as Chekhov, Tolstoy, Dostoevsky, Pushkin, others. Excellent word-for-word English translations on facing pages, plus teaching and study aids, Russian/English vocabulary, biographical/critical introductions, more. 416pp. 5⅜ x 8½. 26244-8

PHILADELPHIA THEN AND NOW: 60 Sites Photographed in the Past and Present, Kenneth Finkel and Susan Oyama. Rare photographs of City Hall, Logan Square, Independence Hall, Betsy Ross House, other landmarks juxtaposed with contemporary views. Captures changing face of historic city. Introduction. Captions. 128pp. 8¼ x 11. 25790-8

AIA ARCHITECTURAL GUIDE TO NASSAU AND SUFFOLK COUNTIES, LONG ISLAND, The American Institute of Architects, Long Island Chapter, and the Society for the Preservation of Long Island Antiquities. Comprehensive, well-researched and generously illustrated volume brings to life over three centuries of Long Island's great architectural heritage. More than 240 photographs with authoritative, extensively detailed captions. 176pp. 8¼ x 11. 26946-9

NORTH AMERICAN INDIAN LIFE: Customs and Traditions of 23 Tribes, Elsie Clews Parsons (ed.). 27 fictionalized essays by noted anthropologists examine religion, customs, government, additional facets of life among the Winnebago, Crow, Zuni, Eskimo, other tribes. 480pp. 6⅛ x 9¼. 27377-6

FRANK LLOYD WRIGHT'S DANA HOUSE, Donald Hoffmann. Pictorial essay of residential masterpiece with over 160 interior and exterior photos, plans, elevations, sketches and studies. 128pp. 9¼ x 10¾. 29120-0

THE MALE AND FEMALE FIGURE IN MOTION: 60 Classic Photographic Sequences, Eadweard Muybridge. 60 true-action photographs of men and women walking, running, climbing, bending, turning, etc., reproduced from rare 19th-century masterpiece. vi + 121pp. 9 x 12. 24745-7

1001 QUESTIONS ANSWERED ABOUT THE SEASHORE, N. J. Berrill and Jacquelyn Berrill. Queries answered about dolphins, sea snails, sponges, starfish, fishes, shore birds, many others. Covers appearance, breeding, growth, feeding, much more. 305pp. 5¼ x 8¼. 23366-9

ATTRACTING BIRDS TO YOUR YARD, William J. Weber. Easy-to-follow guide offers advice on how to attract the greatest diversity of birds: birdhouses, feeders, water and waterers, much more. 96pp. 5³/₁₆ x 8¼. 28927-3

MEDICINAL AND OTHER USES OF NORTH AMERICAN PLANTS: A Historical Survey with Special Reference to the Eastern Indian Tribes, Charlotte Erichsen-Brown. Chronological historical citations document 500 years of usage of plants, trees, shrubs native to eastern Canada, northeastern U.S. Also complete identifying information. 343 illustrations. 544pp. 6½ x 9¼. 25951-X

STORYBOOK MAZES, Dave Phillips. 23 stories and mazes on two-page spreads: Wizard of Oz, Treasure Island, Robin Hood, etc. Solutions. 64pp. 8¼ x 11. 23628-5

AMERICAN NEGRO SONGS: 230 Folk Songs and Spirituals, Religious and Secular, John W. Work. This authoritative study traces the African influences of songs sung and played by black Americans at work, in church, and as entertainment. The author discusses the lyric significance of such songs as "Swing Low, Sweet Chariot," "John Henry," and others and offers the words and music for 230 songs. Bibliography. Index of Song Titles. 272pp. 6½ x 9¼. 40271-1

MOVIE-STAR PORTRAITS OF THE FORTIES, John Kobal (ed.). 163 glamor, studio photos of 106 stars of the 1940s: Rita Hayworth, Ava Gardner, Marlon Brando, Clark Gable, many more. 176pp. 8⅜ x 11¼. 23546-7

BENCHLEY LOST AND FOUND, Robert Benchley. Finest humor from early 30s, about pet peeves, child psychologists, post office and others. Mostly unavailable elsewhere. 73 illustrations by Peter Arno and others. 183pp. 5⅜ x 8½. 22410-4

YEKL and THE IMPORTED BRIDEGROOM AND OTHER STORIES OF YIDDISH NEW YORK, Abraham Cahan. Film Hester Street based on *Yekl* (1896). Novel, other stories among first about Jewish immigrants on N.Y.'s East Side. 240pp. 5⅜ x 8½. 22427-9

SELECTED POEMS, Walt Whitman. Generous sampling from *Leaves of Grass*. Twenty-four poems include "I Hear America Singing," "Song of the Open Road," "I Sing the Body Electric," "When Lilacs Last in the Dooryard Bloom'd," "O Captain! My Captain!"–all reprinted from an authoritative edition. Lists of titles and first lines. 128pp. 5³/₁₆ x 8¼. 26878-0

THE BEST TALES OF HOFFMANN, E. T. A. Hoffmann. 10 of Hoffmann's most important stories: "Nutcracker and the King of Mice," "The Golden Flowerpot," etc. 458pp. 5⅜ x 8½. 21793-0

FROM FETISH TO GOD IN ANCIENT EGYPT, E. A. Wallis Budge. Rich detailed survey of Egyptian conception of "God" and gods, magic, cult of animals, Osiris, more. Also, superb English translations of hymns and legends. 240 illustrations. 545pp. 5⅜ x 8½. 25803-3

FRENCH STORIES/CONTES FRANÇAIS: A Dual-Language Book, Wallace Fowlie. Ten stories by French masters, Voltaire to Camus: "Micromegas" by Voltaire; "The Atheist's Mass" by Balzac; "Minuet" by de Maupassant; "The Guest" by Camus, six more. Excellent English translations on facing pages. Also French-English vocabulary list, exercises, more. 352pp. 5⅜ x 8½. 26443-2

CHICAGO AT THE TURN OF THE CENTURY IN PHOTOGRAPHS: 122 Historic Views from the Collections of the Chicago Historical Society, Larry A. Viskochil. Rare large-format prints offer detailed views of City Hall, State Street, the Loop, Hull House, Union Station, many other landmarks, circa 1904-1913. Introduction. Captions. Maps. 144pp. 9⅜ x 12¼. 24656-6

OLD BROOKLYN IN EARLY PHOTOGRAPHS, 1865-1929, William Lee Younger. Luna Park, Gravesend race track, construction of Grand Army Plaza, moving of Hotel Brighton, etc. 157 previously unpublished photographs. 165pp. 8⅞ x 11¾. 23587-4

THE MYTHS OF THE NORTH AMERICAN INDIANS, Lewis Spence. Rich anthology of the myths and legends of the Algonquins, Iroquois, Pawnees and Sioux, prefaced by an extensive historical and ethnological commentary. 36 illustrations. 480pp. 5⅜ x 8½. 25967-6

AN ENCYCLOPEDIA OF BATTLES: Accounts of Over 1,560 Battles from 1479 B.C. to the Present, David Eggenberger. Essential details of every major battle in recorded history from the first battle of Megiddo in 1479 B.C. to Grenada in 1984. List of Battle Maps. New Appendix covering the years 1967-1984. Index. 99 illustrations. 544pp. 6½ x 9¼. 24913-1

SAILING ALONE AROUND THE WORLD, Captain Joshua Slocum. First man to sail around the world, alone, in small boat. One of great feats of seamanship told in delightful manner. 67 illustrations. 294pp. 5⅜ x 8½. 20326-3

ANARCHISM AND OTHER ESSAYS, Emma Goldman. Powerful, penetrating, prophetic essays on direct action, role of minorities, prison reform, puritan hypocrisy, violence, etc. 271pp. 5⅜ x 8½. 22484-8

MYTHS OF THE HINDUS AND BUDDHISTS, Ananda K. Coomaraswamy and Sister Nivedita. Great stories of the epics; deeds of Krishna, Shiva, taken from puranas, Vedas, folk tales; etc. 32 illustrations. 400pp. 5⅜ x 8½. 21759-0

THE TRAUMA OF BIRTH, Otto Rank. Rank's controversial thesis that anxiety neurosis is caused by profound psychological trauma which occurs at birth. 256pp. 5⅜ x 8½. 27974-X

A THEOLOGICO-POLITICAL TREATISE, Benedict Spinoza. Also contains unfinished Political Treatise. Great classic on religious liberty, theory of government on common consent. R. Elwes translation. Total of 421pp. 5⅜ x 8½. 20249-6

MY BONDAGE AND MY FREEDOM, Frederick Douglass. Born a slave, Douglass became outspoken force in antislavery movement. The best of Douglass' autobiographies. Graphic description of slave life. 464pp. 5⅜ x 8½. 22457-0

FOLLOWING THE EQUATOR: A Journey Around the World, Mark Twain. Fascinating humorous account of 1897 voyage to Hawaii, Australia, India, New Zealand, etc. Ironic, bemused reports on peoples, customs, climate, flora and fauna, politics, much more. 197 illustrations. 720pp. 5⅜ x 8½. 26113-1

THE PEOPLE CALLED SHAKERS, Edward D. Andrews. Definitive study of Shakers: origins, beliefs, practices, dances, social organization, furniture and crafts, etc. 33 illustrations. 351pp. 5⅜ x 8½. 21081-2

THE MYTHS OF GREECE AND ROME, H. A. Guerber. A classic of mythology, generously illustrated, long prized for its simple, graphic, accurate retelling of the principal myths of Greece and Rome, and for its commentary on their origins and significance. With 64 illustrations by Michelangelo, Raphael, Titian, Rubens, Canova, Bernini and others. 480pp. 5⅜ x 8½. 27584-1

PSYCHOLOGY OF MUSIC, Carl E. Seashore. Classic work discusses music as a medium from psychological viewpoint. Clear treatment of physical acoustics, auditory apparatus, sound perception, development of musical skills, nature of musical feeling, host of other topics. 88 figures. 408pp. 5⅜ x 8½. 21851-1

THE PHILOSOPHY OF HISTORY, Georg W. Hegel. Great classic of Western thought develops concept that history is not chance but rational process, the evolution of freedom. 457pp. 5⅜ x 8½. 20112-0

THE BOOK OF TEA, Kakuzo Okakura. Minor classic of the Orient: entertaining, charming explanation, interpretation of traditional Japanese culture in terms of tea ceremony. 94pp. 5⅜ x 8½. 20070-1

LIFE IN ANCIENT EGYPT, Adolf Erman. Fullest, most thorough, detailed older account with much not in more recent books, domestic life, religion, magic, medicine, commerce, much more. Many illustrations reproduce tomb paintings, carvings, hieroglyphs, etc. 597pp. 5⅜ x 8½. 22632-8

SUNDIALS, Their Theory and Construction, Albert Waugh. Far and away the best, most thorough coverage of ideas, mathematics concerned, types, construction, adjusting anywhere. Simple, nontechnical treatment allows even children to build several of these dials. Over 100 illustrations. 230pp. 5⅜ x 8½. 22947-5

THEORETICAL HYDRODYNAMICS, L. M. Milne-Thomson. Classic exposition of the mathematical theory of fluid motion, applicable to both hydrodynamics and aerodynamics. Over 600 exercises. 768pp. 6⅛ x 9¼. 68970-0

SONGS OF EXPERIENCE: Facsimile Reproduction with 26 Plates in Full Color, William Blake. 26 full-color plates from a rare 1826 edition. Includes "The Tyger," "London," "Holy Thursday," and other poems. Printed text of poems. 48pp. 5¼ x 7. 24636-1

OLD-TIME VIGNETTES IN FULL COLOR, Carol Belanger Grafton (ed.). Over 390 charming, often sentimental illustrations, selected from archives of Victorian graphics—pretty women posing, children playing, food, flowers, kittens and puppies, smiling cherubs, birds and butterflies, much more. All copyright-free. 48pp. 9¼ x 12¼. 27269-9

PERSPECTIVE FOR ARTISTS, Rex Vicat Cole. Depth, perspective of sky and sea, shadows, much more, not usually covered. 391 diagrams, 81 reproductions of drawings and paintings. 279pp. 5⅜ x 8½. 22487-2

DRAWING THE LIVING FIGURE, Joseph Sheppard. Innovative approach to artistic anatomy focuses on specifics of surface anatomy, rather than muscles and bones. Over 170 drawings of live models in front, back and side views, and in widely varying poses. Accompanying diagrams. 177 illustrations. Introduction. Index. 144pp. 8⅜ x11¼. 26723-7

GOTHIC AND OLD ENGLISH ALPHABETS: 100 Complete Fonts, Dan X. Solo. Add power, elegance to posters, signs, other graphics with 100 stunning copyright-free alphabets: Blackstone, Dolbey, Germania, 97 more–including many lower-case, numerals, punctuation marks. 104pp. 8⅛ x 11. 24695-7

HOW TO DO BEADWORK, Mary White. Fundamental book on craft from simple projects to five-bead chains and woven works. 106 illustrations. 142pp. 5⅜ x 8. 20697-1

THE BOOK OF WOOD CARVING, Charles Marshall Sayers. Finest book for beginners discusses fundamentals and offers 34 designs. "Absolutely first rate . . . well thought out and well executed."–E. J. Tangerman. 118pp. 7¾ x 10⅝. 23654-4

ILLUSTRATED CATALOG OF CIVIL WAR MILITARY GOODS: Union Army Weapons, Insignia, Uniform Accessories, and Other Equipment, Schuyler, Hartley, and Graham. Rare, profusely illustrated 1846 catalog includes Union Army uniform and dress regulations, arms and ammunition, coats, insignia, flags, swords, rifles, etc. 226 illustrations. 160pp. 9 x 12. 24939-5

WOMEN'S FASHIONS OF THE EARLY 1900s: An Unabridged Republication of "New York Fashions, 1909," National Cloak & Suit Co. Rare catalog of mail-order fashions documents women's and children's clothing styles shortly after the turn of the century. Captions offer full descriptions, prices. Invaluable resource for fashion, costume historians. Approximately 725 illustrations. 128pp. 8⅜ x 11¼. 27276-1

THE 1912 AND 1915 GUSTAV STICKLEY FURNITURE CATALOGS, Gustav Stickley. With over 200 detailed illustrations and descriptions, these two catalogs are essential reading and reference materials and identification guides for Stickley furniture. Captions cite materials, dimensions and prices. 112pp. 6½ x 9¼. 26676-1

EARLY AMERICAN LOCOMOTIVES, John H. White, Jr. Finest locomotive engravings from early 19th century: historical (1804–74), main-line (after 1870), special, foreign, etc. 147 plates. 142pp. 11⅜ x 8¼. 22772-3

THE TALL SHIPS OF TODAY IN PHOTOGRAPHS, Frank O. Braynard. Lavishly illustrated tribute to nearly 100 majestic contemporary sailing vessels: Amerigo Vespucci, Clearwater, Constitution, Eagle, Mayflower, Sea Cloud, Victory, many more. Authoritative captions provide statistics, background on each ship. 190 black-and-white photographs and illustrations. Introduction. 128pp. 8⅞ x 11¾. 27163-3

LITTLE BOOK OF EARLY AMERICAN CRAFTS AND TRADES, Peter Stockham (ed.). 1807 children's book explains crafts and trades: baker, hatter, cooper, potter, and many others. 23 copperplate illustrations. 140pp. 4⅝ x 6.   23336-7

VICTORIAN FASHIONS AND COSTUMES FROM HARPER'S BAZAR, 1867–1898, Stella Blum (ed.). Day costumes, evening wear, sports clothes, shoes, hats, other accessories in over 1,000 detailed engravings. 320pp. 9⅜ x 12¼. 22990-4

GUSTAV STICKLEY, THE CRAFTSMAN, Mary Ann Smith. Superb study surveys broad scope of Stickley's achievement, especially in architecture. Design philosophy, rise and fall of the Craftsman empire, descriptions and floor plans for many Craftsman houses, more. 86 black-and-white halftones. 31 line illustrations. Introduction 208pp. 6½ x 9¼.   27210-9

THE LONG ISLAND RAIL ROAD IN EARLY PHOTOGRAPHS, Ron Ziel. Over 220 rare photos, informative text document origin (1844) and development of rail service on Long Island. Vintage views of early trains, locomotives, stations, passengers, crews, much more. Captions. 8⅞ x 11¾.   26301-0

VOYAGE OF THE LIBERDADE, Joshua Slocum. Great 19th-century mariner's thrilling, first-hand account of the wreck of his ship off South America, the 35-foot boat he built from the wreckage, and its remarkable voyage home. 128pp. 5⅜ x 8½.
          40022-0

TEN BOOKS ON ARCHITECTURE, Vitruvius. The most important book ever written on architecture. Early Roman aesthetics, technology, classical orders, site selection, all other aspects. Morgan translation. 331pp. 5⅜ x 8½.   20645-9

THE HUMAN FIGURE IN MOTION, Eadweard Muybridge. More than 4,500 stopped-action photos, in action series, showing undraped men, women, children jumping, lying down, throwing, sitting, wrestling, carrying, etc. 390pp. 7⅞ x 10⅝.
          20204-6 Clothbd.

TREES OF THE EASTERN AND CENTRAL UNITED STATES AND CANADA, William M. Harlow. Best one-volume guide to 140 trees. Full descriptions, woodlore, range, etc. Over 600 illustrations. Handy size. 288pp. 4½ x 6⅜.   20395-6

SONGS OF WESTERN BIRDS, Dr. Donald J. Borror. Complete song and call repertoire of 60 western species, including flycatchers, juncoes, cactus wrens, many more–includes fully illustrated booklet.   Cassette and manual 99913-0

GROWING AND USING HERBS AND SPICES, Milo Miloradovich. Versatile handbook provides all the information needed for cultivation and use of all the herbs and spices available in North America. 4 illustrations. Index. Glossary. 236pp. 5⅜ x 8½.
          25058-X

BIG BOOK OF MAZES AND LABYRINTHS, Walter Shepherd. 50 mazes and labyrinths in all–classical, solid, ripple, and more–in one great volume. Perfect inexpensive puzzler for clever youngsters. Full solutions. 112pp. 8⅛ x 11.   22951-3

PIANO TUNING, J. Cree Fischer. Clearest, best book for beginner, amateur. Simple repairs, raising dropped notes, tuning by easy method of flattened fifths. No previous skills needed. 4 illustrations. 201pp. 5⅜ x 8½. 23267-0

HINTS TO SINGERS, Lillian Nordica. Selecting the right teacher, developing confidence, overcoming stage fright, and many other important skills receive thoughtful discussion in this indispensible guide, written by a world-famous diva of four decades' experience. 96pp. 5⅜ x 8½. 40094-8

THE COMPLETE NONSENSE OF EDWARD LEAR, Edward Lear. All nonsense limericks, zany alphabets, Owl and Pussycat, songs, nonsense botany, etc., illustrated by Lear. Total of 320pp. 5⅜ x 8½. (Available in U.S. only.) 20167-8

VICTORIAN PARLOUR POETRY: An Annotated Anthology, Michael R. Turner. 117 gems by Longfellow, Tennyson, Browning, many lesser-known poets. "The Village Blacksmith," "Curfew Must Not Ring Tonight," "Only a Baby Small," dozens more, often difficult to find elsewhere. Index of poets, titles, first lines. xxiii + 325pp. 5⅜ x 8¼. 27044-0

DUBLINERS, James Joyce. Fifteen stories offer vivid, tightly focused observations of the lives of Dublin's poorer classes. At least one, "The Dead," is considered a masterpiece. Reprinted complete and unabridged from standard edition. 160pp. 5³⁄₁₆ x 8¼. 26870-5

GREAT WEIRD TALES: 14 Stories by Lovecraft, Blackwood, Machen and Others, S. T. Joshi (ed.). 14 spellbinding tales, including "The Sin Eater," by Fiona McLeod, "The Eye Above the Mantel," by Frank Belknap Long, as well as renowned works by R. H. Barlow, Lord Dunsany, Arthur Machen, W. C. Morrow and eight other masters of the genre. 256pp. 5⅜ x 8½. (Available in U.S. only.) 40436-6

THE BOOK OF THE SACRED MAGIC OF ABRAMELIN THE MAGE, translated by S. MacGregor Mathers. Medieval manuscript of ceremonial magic. Basic document in Aleister Crowley, Golden Dawn groups. 268pp. 5⅜ x 8½. 23211-5

NEW RUSSIAN-ENGLISH AND ENGLISH-RUSSIAN DICTIONARY, M. A. O'Brien. This is a remarkably handy Russian dictionary, containing a surprising amount of information, including over 70,000 entries. 366pp. 4½ x 6⅛. 20208-9

HISTORIC HOMES OF THE AMERICAN PRESIDENTS, Second, Revised Edition, Irvin Haas. A traveler's guide to American Presidential homes, most open to the public, depicting and describing homes occupied by every American President from George Washington to George Bush. With visiting hours, admission charges, travel routes. 175 photographs. Index. 160pp. 8¼ x 11. 26751-2

NEW YORK IN THE FORTIES, Andreas Feininger. 162 brilliant photographs by the well-known photographer, formerly with *Life* magazine. Commuters, shoppers, Times Square at night, much else from city at its peak. Captions by John von Hartz. 181pp. 9¼ x 10¾. 23585-8

INDIAN SIGN LANGUAGE, William Tomkins. Over 525 signs developed by Sioux and other tribes. Written instructions and diagrams. Also 290 pictographs. 111pp. 6⅛ x 9¼. 22029-X

ANATOMY: A Complete Guide for Artists, Joseph Sheppard. A master of figure drawing shows artists how to render human anatomy convincingly. Over 460 illustrations. 224pp. 8⅜ x 11¼. 27279-6

MEDIEVAL CALLIGRAPHY: Its History and Technique, Marc Drogin. Spirited history, comprehensive instruction manual covers 13 styles (ca. 4th century through 15th). Excellent photographs; directions for duplicating medieval techniques with modern tools. 224pp. 8⅜ x 11¼. 26142-5

DRIED FLOWERS: How to Prepare Them, Sarah Whitlock and Martha Rankin. Complete instructions on how to use silica gel, meal and borax, perlite aggregate, sand and borax, glycerine and water to create attractive permanent flower arrangements. 12 illustrations. 32pp. 5⅜ x 8½. 21802-3

EASY-TO-MAKE BIRD FEEDERS FOR WOODWORKERS, Scott D. Campbell. Detailed, simple-to-use guide for designing, constructing, caring for and using feeders. Text, illustrations for 12 classic and contemporary designs. 96pp. 5⅜ x 8½.

25847-5

SCOTTISH WONDER TALES FROM MYTH AND LEGEND, Donald A. Mackenzie. 16 lively tales tell of giants rumbling down mountainsides, of a magic wand that turns stone pillars into warriors, of gods and goddesses, evil hags, powerful forces and more. 240pp. 5⅜ x 8½. 29677-6

THE HISTORY OF UNDERCLOTHES, C. Willett Cunnington and Phyllis Cunnington. Fascinating, well-documented survey covering six centuries of English undergarments, enhanced with over 100 illustrations: 12th-century laced-up bodice, footed long drawers (1795), 19th-century bustles, 19th-century corsets for men, Victorian "bust improvers," much more. 272pp. 5⅜ x 8¼. 27124-2

ARTS AND CRAFTS FURNITURE: The Complete Brooks Catalog of 1912, Brooks Manufacturing Co. Photos and detailed descriptions of more than 150 now very collectible furniture designs from the Arts and Crafts movement depict davenports, settees, buffets, desks, tables, chairs, bedsteads, dressers and more, all built of solid, quarter-sawed oak. Invaluable for students and enthusiasts of antiques, Americana and the decorative arts. 80pp. 6½ x 9¼. 27471-3

WILBUR AND ORVILLE: A Biography of the Wright Brothers, Fred Howard. Definitive, crisply written study tells the full story of the brothers' lives and work. A vividly written biography, unparalleled in scope and color, that also captures the spirit of an extraordinary era. 560pp. 6⅛ x 9¼. 40297-5

THE ARTS OF THE SAILOR: Knotting, Splicing and Ropework, Hervey Garrett Smith. Indispensable shipboard reference covers tools, basic knots and useful hitches; handsewing and canvas work, more. Over 100 illustrations. Delightful reading for sea lovers. 256pp. 5⅜ x 8½. 26440-8

FRANK LLOYD WRIGHT'S FALLINGWATER: The House and Its History, Second, Revised Edition, Donald Hoffmann. A total revision—both in text and illustrations—of the standard document on Fallingwater, the boldest, most personal architectural statement of Wright's mature years, updated with valuable new material from the recently opened Frank Lloyd Wright Archives. "Fascinating"—*The New York Times*. 116 illustrations. 128pp. 9¼ x 10¾. 27430-6

PHOTOGRAPHIC SKETCHBOOK OF THE CIVIL WAR, Alexander Gardner. 100 photos taken on field during the Civil War. Famous shots of Manassas Harper's Ferry, Lincoln, Richmond, slave pens, etc. 244pp. 10⅞ x 8¼. 22731-6

FIVE ACRES AND INDEPENDENCE, Maurice G. Kains. Great back-to-the-land classic explains basics of self-sufficient farming. The one book to get. 95 illustrations. 397pp. 5⅜ x 8½. 20974-1

SONGS OF EASTERN BIRDS, Dr. Donald J. Borror. Songs and calls of 60 species most common to eastern U.S.: warblers, woodpeckers, flycatchers, thrushes, larks, many more in high-quality recording. Cassette and manual 99912-2

A MODERN HERBAL, Margaret Grieve. Much the fullest, most exact, most useful compilation of herbal material. Gigantic alphabetical encyclopedia, from aconite to zedoary, gives botanical information, medical properties, folklore, economic uses, much else. Indispensable to serious reader. 161 illustrations. 888pp. 6½ x 9¼. 2-vol. set. (Available in U.S. only.) Vol. I: 22798-7
Vol. II: 22799-5

HIDDEN TREASURE MAZE BOOK, Dave Phillips. Solve 34 challenging mazes accompanied by heroic tales of adventure. Evil dragons, people-eating plants, blood-thirsty giants, many more dangerous adversaries lurk at every twist and turn. 34 mazes, stories, solutions. 48pp. 8¼ x 11. 24566-7

LETTERS OF W. A. MOZART, Wolfgang A. Mozart. Remarkable letters show bawdy wit, humor, imagination, musical insights, contemporary musical world; includes some letters from Leopold Mozart. 276pp. 5⅜ x 8½. 22859-2

BASIC PRINCIPLES OF CLASSICAL BALLET, Agrippina Vaganova. Great Russian theoretician, teacher explains methods for teaching classical ballet. 118 illustrations. 175pp. 5⅜ x 8½. 22036-2

THE JUMPING FROG, Mark Twain. Revenge edition. The original story of The Celebrated Jumping Frog of Calaveras County, a hapless French translation, and Twain's hilarious "retranslation" from the French. 12 illustrations. 66pp. 5⅜ x 8½. 22686-7

BEST REMEMBERED POEMS, Martin Gardner (ed.). The 126 poems in this superb collection of 19th- and 20th-century British and American verse range from Shelley's "To a Skylark" to the impassioned "Renascence" of Edna St. Vincent Millay and to Edward Lear's whimsical "The Owl and the Pussycat." 224pp. 5⅜ x 8½. 27165-X

COMPLETE SONNETS, William Shakespeare. Over 150 exquisite poems deal with love, friendship, the tyranny of time, beauty's evanescence, death and other themes in language of remarkable power, precision and beauty. Glossary of archaic terms. 80pp. 5³⁄₁₆ x 8¼. 26686-9

THE BATTLES THAT CHANGED HISTORY, Fletcher Pratt. Eminent historian profiles 16 crucial conflicts, ancient to modern, that changed the course of civilization. 352pp. 5⅜ x 8½. 41129-X

THE WIT AND HUMOR OF OSCAR WILDE, Alvin Redman (ed.). More than 1,000 ripostes, paradoxes, wisecracks: Work is the curse of the drinking classes; I can resist everything except temptation; etc. 258pp. 5⅜ x 8½. 20602-5

SHAKESPEARE LEXICON AND QUOTATION DICTIONARY, Alexander Schmidt. Full definitions, locations, shades of meaning in every word in plays and poems. More than 50,000 exact quotations. 1,485pp. 6½ x 9¼. 2-vol. set.
Vol. 1: 22726-X
Vol. 2: 22727-8

SELECTED POEMS, Emily Dickinson. Over 100 best-known, best-loved poems by one of America's foremost poets, reprinted from authoritative early editions. No comparable edition at this price. Index of first lines. 64pp. 5³⁄₁₆ x 8¼. 26466-1

THE INSIDIOUS DR. FU-MANCHU, Sax Rohmer. The first of the popular mystery series introduces a pair of English detectives to their archnemesis, the diabolical Dr. Fu-Manchu. Flavorful atmosphere, fast-paced action, and colorful characters enliven this classic of the genre. 208pp. 5³⁄₁₆ x 8¼. 29898-1

THE MALLEUS MALEFICARUM OF KRAMER AND SPRENGER, translated by Montague Summers. Full text of most important witchhunter's "bible," used by both Catholics and Protestants. 278pp. 6⅝ x 10. 22802-9

SPANISH STORIES/CUENTOS ESPAÑOLES: A Dual-Language Book, Angel Flores (ed.). Unique format offers 13 great stories in Spanish by Cervantes, Borges, others. Faithful English translations on facing pages. 352pp. 5⅜ x 8½. 25399-6

GARDEN CITY, LONG ISLAND, IN EARLY PHOTOGRAPHS, 1869–1919, Mildred H. Smith. Handsome treasury of 118 vintage pictures, accompanied by carefully researched captions, document the Garden City Hotel fire (1899), the Vanderbilt Cup Race (1908), the first airmail flight departing from the Nassau Boulevard Aerodrome (1911), and much more. 96pp. 8⅞ x 11¾. 40669-5

OLD QUEENS, N.Y., IN EARLY PHOTOGRAPHS, Vincent F. Seyfried and William Asadorian. Over 160 rare photographs of Maspeth, Jamaica, Jackson Heights, and other areas. Vintage views of DeWitt Clinton mansion, 1939 World's Fair and more. Captions. 192pp. 8⅞ x 11. 26358-4

CAPTURED BY THE INDIANS: 15 Firsthand Accounts, 1750-1870, Frederick Drimmer. Astounding true historical accounts of grisly torture, bloody conflicts, relentless pursuits, miraculous escapes and more, by people who lived to tell the tale. 384pp. 5⅜ x 8½. 24901-8

THE WORLD'S GREAT SPEECHES (Fourth Enlarged Edition), Lewis Copeland, Lawrence W. Lamm, and Stephen J. McKenna. Nearly 300 speeches provide public speakers with a wealth of updated quotes and inspiration–from Pericles' funeral oration and William Jennings Bryan's "Cross of Gold Speech" to Malcolm X's powerful words on the Black Revolution and Earl of Spenser's tribute to his sister, Diana, Princess of Wales. 944pp. 5⅜ x 8⅜. 40903-1

THE BOOK OF THE SWORD, Sir Richard F. Burton. Great Victorian scholar/adventurer's eloquent, erudite history of the "queen of weapons"–from prehistory to early Roman Empire. Evolution and development of early swords, variations (sabre, broadsword, cutlass, scimitar, etc.), much more. 336pp. 6⅛ x 9¼. 25434-8

CATALOG OF DOVER BOOKS

AUTOBIOGRAPHY: The Story of My Experiments with Truth, Mohandas K. Gandhi. Boyhood, legal studies, purification, the growth of the Satyagraha (nonviolent protest) movement. Critical, inspiring work of the man responsible for the freedom of India. 480pp. 5⅜ x 8½. (Available in U.S. only.) 24593-4

CELTIC MYTHS AND LEGENDS, T. W. Rolleston. Masterful retelling of Irish and Welsh stories and tales. Cuchulain, King Arthur, Deirdre, the Grail, many more. First paperback edition. 58 full-page illustrations. 512pp. 5⅜ x 8½. 26507-2

THE PRINCIPLES OF PSYCHOLOGY, William James. Famous long course complete, unabridged. Stream of thought, time perception, memory, experimental methods; great work decades ahead of its time. 94 figures. 1,391pp. 5⅜ x 8½. 2-vol. set.
Vol. I: 20381-6 Vol. II: 20382-4

THE WORLD AS WILL AND REPRESENTATION, Arthur Schopenhauer. Definitive English translation of Schopenhauer's life work, correcting more than 1,000 errors, omissions in earlier translations. Translated by E. F. J. Payne. Total of 1,269pp. 5⅜ x 8½. 2-vol. set. Vol. 1: 21761-2 Vol. 2: 21762-0

MAGIC AND MYSTERY IN TIBET, Madame Alexandra David-Neel. Experiences among lamas, magicians, sages, sorcerers, Bonpa wizards. A true psychic discovery. 32 illustrations. 321pp. 5⅜ x 8½. (Available in U.S. only.) 22682-4

THE EGYPTIAN BOOK OF THE DEAD, E. A. Wallis Budge. Complete reproduction of Ani's papyrus, finest ever found. Full hieroglyphic text, interlinear transliteration, word-for-word translation, smooth translation. 533pp. 6½ x 9¼. 21866-X

MATHEMATICS FOR THE NONMATHEMATICIAN, Morris Kline. Detailed, college-level treatment of mathematics in cultural and historical context, with numerous exercises. Recommended Reading Lists. Tables. Numerous figures. 641pp. 5⅜ x 8½. 24823-2

PROBABILISTIC METHODS IN THE THEORY OF STRUCTURES, Isaac Elishakoff. Well-written introduction covers the elements of the theory of probability from two or more random variables, the reliability of such multivariable structures, the theory of random function, Monte Carlo methods of treating problems incapable of exact solution, and more. Examples. 502pp. 5⅜ x 8½. 40691-1

THE RIME OF THE ANCIENT MARINER, Gustave Doré, S. T. Coleridge. Doré's finest work; 34 plates capture moods, subtleties of poem. Flawless full-size reproductions printed on facing pages with authoritative text of poem. "Beautiful. Simply beautiful."–*Publisher's Weekly*. 77pp. 9¼ x 12. 22305-1

NORTH AMERICAN INDIAN DESIGNS FOR ARTISTS AND CRAFTSPEOPLE, Eva Wilson. Over 360 authentic copyright-free designs adapted from Navajo blankets, Hopi pottery, Sioux buffalo hides, more. Geometrics, symbolic figures, plant and animal motifs, etc. 128pp. 8⅜ x 11. (Not for sale in the United Kingdom.) 25341-4

SCULPTURE: Principles and Practice, Louis Slobodkin. Step-by-step approach to clay, plaster, metals, stone; classical and modern. 253 drawings, photos. 255pp. 8⅛ x 11. 22960-2

THE INFLUENCE OF SEA POWER UPON HISTORY, 1660–1783, A. T. Mahan. Influential classic of naval history and tactics still used as text in war colleges. First paperback edition. 4 maps. 24 battle plans. 640pp. 5⅜ x 8½. 25509-3

THE STORY OF THE TITANIC AS TOLD BY ITS SURVIVORS, Jack Winocour (ed.). What it was really like. Panic, despair, shocking inefficiency, and a little heroism. More thrilling than any fictional account. 26 illustrations. 320pp. 5⅜ x 8½.
20610-6

FAIRY AND FOLK TALES OF THE IRISH PEASANTRY, William Butler Yeats (ed.). Treasury of 64 tales from the twilight world of Celtic myth and legend: "The Soul Cages," "The Kildare Pooka," "King O'Toole and his Goose," many more. Introduction and Notes by W. B. Yeats. 352pp. 5⅜ x 8½.
26941-8

BUDDHIST MAHAYANA TEXTS, E. B. Cowell and others (eds.). Superb, accurate translations of basic documents in Mahayana Buddhism, highly important in history of religions. The Buddha-karita of Asvaghosha, Larger Sukhavativyuha, more. 448pp. 5⅜ x 8½.
25552-2

ONE TWO THREE . . . INFINITY: Facts and Speculations of Science, George Gamow. Great physicist's fascinating, readable overview of contemporary science: number theory, relativity, fourth dimension, entropy, genes, atomic structure, much more. 128 illustrations. Index. 352pp. 5⅜ x 8½.
25664-2

EXPERIMENTATION AND MEASUREMENT, W. J. Youden. Introductory manual explains laws of measurement in simple terms and offers tips for achieving accuracy and minimizing errors. Mathematics of measurement, use of instruments, experimenting with machines. 1994 edition. Foreword. Preface. Introduction. Epilogue. Selected Readings. Glossary. Index. Tables and figures. 128pp. 5⅜ x 8½.
40451-X

DALÍ ON MODERN ART: The Cuckolds of Antiquated Modern Art, Salvador Dalí. Influential painter skewers modern art and its practitioners. Outrageous evaluations of Picasso, Cézanne, Turner, more. 15 renderings of paintings discussed. 44 calligraphic decorations by Dalí. 96pp. 5⅜ x 8½. (Available in U.S. only.)
29220-7

ANTIQUE PLAYING CARDS: A Pictorial History, Henry René D'Allemagne. Over 900 elaborate, decorative images from rare playing cards (14th–20th centuries): Bacchus, death, dancing dogs, hunting scenes, royal coats of arms, players cheating, much more. 96pp. 9¼ x 12¼.
29265-7

MAKING FURNITURE MASTERPIECES: 30 Projects with Measured Drawings, Franklin H. Gottshall. Step-by-step instructions, illustrations for constructing handsome, useful pieces, among them a Sheraton desk, Chippendale chair, Spanish desk, Queen Anne table and a William and Mary dressing mirror. 224pp. 8⅛ x 11¼.
29338-6

THE FOSSIL BOOK: A Record of Prehistoric Life, Patricia V. Rich et al. Profusely illustrated definitive guide covers everything from single-celled organisms and dinosaurs to birds and mammals and the interplay between climate and man. Over 1,500 illustrations. 760pp. 7½ x 10⅛.
29371-8